THE
CULTURAL CONTEXT
OF AGING

THE
CULTURAL CONTEXT
OF AGING

WORLDWIDE PERSPECTIVES

Edited by **Jay Sokolovsky**

BERGIN & GARVEY PUBLISHERS

New York • Westport, Connecticut • London

Library of Congress Cataloging-in-Publication Data

The cultural context of aging : worldwide perspectives / edited by Jay
  Sokolovsky.
  p. cm.
 Includes bibliographical references.
 ISBN 0–89789–193–7 (lib. bdg. : alk. paper). — ISBN 0–89789–192–9
(pbk. : alk. paper)
  1. Aged — Cross-cultural studies. 2. Aging — Cross-cultural
studies. I. Sokolovsky, Jay.
HQ1061.C79 1990
305.26 – dc20   89–18370

Library of Congress Catalog Card Number: 89–18370
ISBN: 0–89789–193–7
ISBN (pbk): 0–89789–192–9

First published in 1990

Bergin & Garvey, One Madison Avenue, New York, NY 10010
An imprint of Greenwood Publishing Group, Inc.

Printed in the United States of America

The paper used in this book complies with the
Permanent Paper Standard issued by the National
Information Standards Organization (Z39.48–1984).

10 9 8 7 6 5 4 3 2

Copyright Acknowledgment

Grateful acknowledgment is given for permission to use:

Excerpted selection from "Fieldwork Among the Tiwi, 1928–1929" by C. W. M. Hart in
Being an Anthropologist: Fieldwork in Eleven Cultures, edited by George D.
Spindler, copyright © 1970 by Holt, Rinehart and Winston, Inc., reprinted by
permission of the publisher.

CONTENTS

PREFACE

As the last decade of the twentieth century quickly approaches, maturing adults have in their reach the possibility of becoming the great social pioneers of the next 100 years. They are people who will radically redefine the meaning of old age as a stage of human existence and as a way of constructing a sense of personhood. Some changes are already quite apparent in industrialized societies — in the guise of political groups such as the Gray Panthers, in a multitude of new forms of housing and self-help groups, in Universities of the Third Age, and in changing attitudes about such things as retirement, late-life divorce and sexuality. As the Western world plunges headlong into a new conception of old age it will do well to examine the variations that exist within and without narrow societal boundaries. This is a premise that has strongly shaped the idea for and the organization of this volume. Instructors should note that a guide to using this book for a cross-cultural aging course is found in Francis, Shenk and Sokolovsky (1990).

I would like to express my deeply felt appreciation to the many people who made this book possible. Special thanks to Rhonda Hudson who "in put" large parts of this manuscript and managed the delicate process of keeping all the files straight. Thanks also to Mary Pat Tucker, Sue Hahn, and Pat Richardson who have all contributed to the completion of this book. A special thanks to Professor Derek Gill who has been a constant source of encouragement and support. My editor at Bergin & Garvey, Ann Gross, has played an especially important role in guiding my work through its many stages. Finally, a thanks to the students in my anthropology of aging classes who provided many insightful comments.

To my parents, Shirley and Harry, my daughter Rebecca,
and my dear aunt Minnie

INTRODUCTION

We do not have elders because we have a human gift and modern capacity for keeping the weak alive; instead, we are human because we have elders.

—David Gutmann

A unique aspect of the evolution of the human species, compared to other primates, is that we alone have a distinct, significant postreproductive phase of life. As the words of clinical psychiatrist David Gutmann imply, aging need not be thought of only in the catastrophic terms of abandonment and loss but also in terms of the crucial roles that elders play in their kinship and community groups throughout the range of human societies. This "strong face of aging," as Gutmann terms it, derives from the function of elders in our species' early history, as a vital link in the transmission of our socially learned systems of belief and behavior which imbue children with the essence of humanity.

Although the evolutionary legacy of aging and being old also includes a powerful biological dimension of senescence, or decline in functioning, a global perspective on aging yields a wondrous array of social responses to the physical imperatives of growing old. It will be the purpose of this book to employ such a worldwide view to explore two broad interrelated facets of elderhood: (1) how older adults function as social actors in the context of diverse societies and (2) how the cultural context in which people grow old creates a varied reality of what aging means.

THE CULTURAL CONTEXT OF AGING

These issues will be examined by considering the fabric of values, perceptions, human relationships, and socially engineered behavior which clothe people as they pass through the older adult years. Such varied patterns of created ideology, social organization, and the ways people produce and distribute valued objects constitute the cultural systems into which all humans grow. Each cultural system creates a perceptual lens composed of potent symbols through which a particular version of reality is developed. For example, in the United States J. Scott Francher (1973) suggests that the symbolic themes represented in the glorification of the youthful, competitively self-reliant, and action-oriented "Pepsi Generation" present a set of core values contradictory and harmful to the self-esteem of the old. However, as will be seen, the ethnic mix of the American social landscape greatly complicates such a simple analysis.

Culture only exists in relation to the contextual framework in which human actors find themselves. Such "background" factors can be relevant at various levels of analysis. On the personal level, this might involve looking at how childlessness or poor health affect the chances for aging well. On a societal scale, one could examine how, for example, differential access to wealth and status (class variation) or even the structural differences between communities in the same society alter culturally based premises about how one grows old. In section V, Christine Fry, Jennie Keith and Charlotte Ikels show precisely how intercommunity variation interacts with cultural systems to influence how people define sucessful aging. Such situational factors can be strong enough to completely reverse patterns of respect and support linked to cultural traditions. As Anthony Glascock demonstrates in section I, "death hastening" of the aged can take place in societies that, in general, claim to revere the aged. Yet the decision to quicken the demise of an elderly person is vitally connected to situational conditions, such as very low levels of functioning by an elder or their lack of close kin. Such factors can completely reverse culturally mandated patterns of respect and support. Similarly, in section IV Jay Sokolovsky shows how the clash of ethnic cultures and contextual realities in the United States can dramtically transform the traditional meaning of "filial devotion" toward the elderly in some Asian groups.

In this volume the cultural context of aging is to be understood as the way in which cultural traditions actually function in the situational framework of personal lives and societal functioning. By exploring aging in this fashion, we can discover how social groups construct shared expectations about aging that interweave notions of time, life cycle, intergenerational relations, dependency, and death. It is this cultural context of aging which gives rise to the exciting diversity of experience, perception, and achievement during the last phases of the human life cycle. Such divergence in the nonphysical manifestations of old age is to be seen both within and across the multitude of world societies. Even among very small-scale societal types such as hunters and gatherers (or tribal horticultural peoples), a wide variation exists in how older people are evaluated and dealt with. Some such societies regard their older citizens as revered personages to be carried on one's back as communities move over the landscape, while others see them as excess baggage to be left to the elements when they can no longer keep up. To see this, students can compare the extremely positive situation of the !Kung (Rosenberg, chapter 1) or Mbuti (Turnbull 1965) people of Africa with the much-less-favored position of the Siriono of eastern Bolivia (Holmberg 1969) or the Chipewyan Indians of northern Canada (Sharp 1981).

THE ANTHROPOLOGICAL ENCOUNTER WITH AGING AND THE AGED

Typically, cultural anthropologists have chosen to study human variation by establishing themselves for long-term stays in locales where people carry out their everyday lives. The prolonged, very personal encounter of an anthropologist with persons under study can provide a special insight into how people confront and deal with the cultural context life has dealt them. In this volume, I have asked most of the authors to use the experience of real people to illuminate how aging is actually lived in such places as China, urban Nigeria, a tiny South Seas island, or New York's skid row.

While gerontological research as an anthropological specialty is quite new, studies conducted earlier in this century can provide revealing, yet tantalizingly incomplete, glimpses of the elderly in non-Western cultural settings (see especially Warner 1937; Arensberg and Kimball 1940; Hart and Pilling 1961; Spencer 1965; Turnbull 1965). For example, in 1928 C. W. Hart encountered the cultural context of frail old age among a preliterate people called the Tiwi, who generally accorded the elderly high levels of respect. As seen in this description of his early fieldwork, the severe physical and cognitive decline of a particular Tiwi woman set in motion a dramatic ritual for dealing with this situation.

> After a few weeks on the islands I also became aware that [the Tiwi] were often uneasy with me because I had no kinship linkage to them. This was shown in many ways, among others in their dissatisfaction with the negative reply they always got to their question, "What clan does he belong to?" Around the Mission, to answer it by saying "White men have no clans" was at least a possible answer, but among the pagan bands like the Malauila and Munupula such an answer was incomprehensible — to them everybody must have a clan, just as everybody must have an age. If I had a clan I would be inside the kinship system, everybody would know how to act toward me, I would know how to act toward everybody else, and life would be easier and smoother for all.
>
> How to get myself into the clan and kinship system was quite a problem. Even Mariano [Hart's native guide], while admitting the desirability, saw no way of getting me in. There did not seem much hope and then suddenly

the problem was solved entirely by a lucky accident. I was in a camp where there was an old woman who had been making herself a terrible nuisance. Toothless, almost blind, withered, and stumbling around, she was physically quite revolting and mentally rather senile. She kept hanging round me asking for tobacco, whining, wheedling, snivelling, until I got thoroughly fed up with her. As I had by now learned the Tiwi equivalents of "Go to hell" and "Get lost," I rather enjoyed being rude to her and telling her where she ought to go. Listening to my swearing in Tiwi, the rest of the camp thought it a great joke and no doubt egged her on so that they could listen to my attempts to get rid of her. This had been going on for some time when one day the old hag used a new approach. "Oh, my son," she said, "please give me tobacco." Unthinkingly I replied, "Oh, my mother, go jump in the ocean." Immediately a howl of delight arose from everybody within earshot and they all gathered round me patting me on the shoulder and calling me by a kinship term. She was my mother and I was her son. This gave a handle to everybody else to address me by a kinship term. Her other sons from then on called me brother, her brothers called me "sister's son"; and so on. I was now in the kinship system; my clan was Jabijabui (a bird) because my mother was Jabijabui.

From then on the change in the atmosphere between me and the tribe at large was remarkable. Strangers were now told that I was Jabijabui and that my mother was the old so-and-so and when told this, stern old men would relax, smile and say "then you are my brother" (or my son, or my sister's son, or whatever category was appropriate) and I would struggle to respond properly by addressing them by the proper term.

How seriously they took my presence in their kinship system is something I never will be sure about. However, toward the end of my time on the islands an incident occurred that surprised me because it suggested that some of them had been taking my presence in the kinship system much more seriously than I had thought. I was approached by a group of about eight or nine senior men all of whom I knew. They were all senior members of the Jabijabui clan and they had decided among themselves that the time had come to get rid of the decrepit old woman who had first called me son and whom I now called mother. As I knew, they said, it was Tiwi custom, when an old woman became too feeble to look after herself, to "cover her up." This could only be done by her sons and her brothers and all of them had to agree beforehand, since once it was done they did not want any dissension among the brothers or clansmen, as that might lead to a feud. My "mother" was now completely blind, she was constantly falling over logs or into fires, and they, her senior clansmen, were in agreement that she would be better out of the way. Did I agree? I already knew about "covering up." The Tiwi, like many other hunting and gathering peoples, sometimes got rid of their ancient and decrepit females. The method was to dig a hole in the ground in some lonely place, put the old woman in the hole and fill it in with earth until only her head was showing. Everybody went away for a day or two and then went back to the hole to discover to their surprise, that the old woman was dead, having been too feeble to raise her arms from the earth. Nobody had "killed" her, her death in Tiwi eyes was a natural one. She had been alive when her relatives last saw her. I had never seen it done, though I knew it was the custom, so I asked my brothers if it was necessary for me to attend the "covering up." They said no and they would do it, but only after they had my agreement. Of course I agreed, and a week or two later we heard in our camp that my "mother" was dead, and we all wailed and put on the trimmings of mourning. (Hart 1970:149–54)

AGING AND THE ANTHROPOLOGICAL PARADIGM

This brief encounter with aging among the Tiwi can help introduce students to the way in which an anthropological approach can help us understand the last phase of adulthood in cross-cultural context. Such an anthropological paradigm has a dual lens: an internal focus (called an *emic* perspective) that seeks to comprehend the "native's" view of why certain behaviors are performed or images about the world are held; and an external, comparative focus (called an *etic* perspective) that uses the world's societies as a natural laboratory to separate the universal from the particular. From combining both perspectives to study aging and the aged there has emerged in the last decade an important new specialty variously referred to as "comparative sociocultural gerontology," "ethnogerontology," or "anthropology of aging." Despite the early seminal book by Leo Simmons, *The Role of the Aged in Primitive Society* (1945), and articles by such luminaries as Gregory Bateson (1950), and Margaret Mead (1951, 1967), concern for a worldwide, cross-cultural analysis of aging has developed slowly. It was not until the publication of the volume *Aging and Modernization*, edited by Cowgill and Holmes in 1972, that knowledge from modern ethnographic studies was employed to test gerontological theory. Here detailed studies of fourteen different societies (seven being non-Western) were compared to examine the impact of industrialization, urbanization, and Western-ization on the status of the aged. As will be seen in section III, the theoretical propositions developed by Cowgill and Holmes in *Aging and Modernization* and later works (1974, 1986) have served as a most controversial stimulus to subsequent work on aging done around the world. The maturing of an anthropological specialty in aging has unfolded through gerontologically focused ethnographies and edited books (Myerhoff and Simic 1978; Fry 1980, 1981; Amoss and Harrell 1981; Hendricks 1981; Morgan 1985; Silverman 1987; Sokolovsky 1987; Strange and Teitelbaum 1987), texts (Keith 1982; Holmes 1983: Foner 1984a; Cowgill 1986), and special journal issues (Keith 1978; Beall 1982; Sokolovsky 1982b; Sokolovsky and Sokolovsky 1983a; Nydegger 1984). Importantly, two new works, *New Methods for Old Age Research* (Fry and Keith 1986) and *Age and Anthropological Theory*

(Kertzer and Keith 1984), have finally brought to bear the distinct realm of anthropological methods and theory to questions of aging and the aged.

THE "NATIVE" VIEW OF AGING

The *emic* component of the anthropological paradigm which seeks to see the world through the eyes of the people being studied is grounded in the methods of modern cultural anthropology. Hart's research among the Tiwi was a classic example of the research strategy called ethnography—gathering data by actually living for a prolonged period with the people one is trying to comprehend. The holistic construction of cultural systems is learned through direct observation, participating in daily life, and recording in the native language the meanings of things, persons, and actions. This generalized process of "participant-observation" was exemplified by Hart's experience. The Tiwi, themselves, incorporated Hart into their kinship system and made use of him in a difficult decision, just as he used his designation as "son" and clan member to study their society on an intimate basis.

Participant-observation is critical in developing an emic understanding of old age and even in learning appropriate questions to ask. This applies as much to studying aging in small villages in the South Pacific as it does in an American nursing home, the Afro-American community, or among homeless men in New York City. We will see in section IV that Jane Peterson-LaFargue, in trying to understand Seattle's black aged, entered into the midst of their cultural world by working as a nurse for a church group that provided important services to the elderly. In my own work on skid row, I found that asking seemingly straightforward questions without a clear understanding of the lifestyle of long-term homelessness resulted in almost worthless data and frequent hostility. It was necessary not only to learn the colorful argot of the streets—such as "carrying the banner" (sleeping outdoors)—and travel with men on their daily round but also to work in a soup kitchen which fed many of the aged I studied.

To understand the Tiwi in their own cultural context, we begin by noting that they are a foraging, seminomadic, small-scale society where kin-based groups (clans) named after mythological ancestors control key elements of the life cycle. How one enters adulthood, who one marries, and the consequences of frailty in old age are largely determined by the cluster of elder males who have membership in a given clan. The Tiwi represent one of the few actual cases of gerontocracy—rule by the eldest group of males—and an exaggerated case of what has been called "gerontogamy." This latter term denotes a case in which a society not only practices polygyny (men can have more than one spouse at the same time) but also where the older adult males have greater access than the younger men to the youngest, most desirable women. Typically, men above middle age already have several wives, including very young teenagers, while a man marrying for the first time after age twenty-five might be wed to a forty-five-year-old widow.

While not controlling material wealth, as might be the case in an agrarian tribal society, groups of elder males cautiously dole out to younger persons esoteric knowledge without which persons cannot relate to spiritual forces, or function as culturally competent adults. Regarded with a mixture of fear and reverence, the oldest males sit at the top of a generational pyramid, authoritatively dominating society by the exclusive possession of key cultural knowledge. These elders, as a group, also control the dramatic life-cycle rituals which stimulate the transit from status to status as one goes from birth to death. Unlike the Western linear view of the life cycle which sees death as a discontinuity from life, the Tiwi have a cyclical, mythologically linked notion of time and the passage of life forms through it. From this perspective, ancestors can have a powerful influence on the fate of the living and can be reborn in a future generation. As Judith Barker shows in her article dealing with another Pacific Island people (chapter 16), an emic understanding of belief systems is necessary to comprehend the radical change in societal attitude which can accompany the shift from healthy old age to severe senescence.

While females among the Tiwi had much fewer formal bases of power, one must not assume from the very limited segment of Hart's research that women in old age are a totally repressed lot. Subsequent work among the Tiwi by Jane Goodale (1971) shows the impressive amount of de facto power women could accumulate by middle age, especially through their ability to control conflict in the community. Recent ethnographic studies (see especially Cool and McCabe 1987 and Catherine Coles's chapter in this volume) have demonstrated how even in quite "male chauvinistic" cultural contexts older women can acquire an importance and power far beyond the normative societal constraints placed on females.

THE COMPARATIVE VIEW OF AGING

How are we to apply the second part of the anthropological paradigm? The treatment of the frail and possibly demented older woman in Hart's narrative must not only be examined through an emic understanding of the process of "covering up" but also by applying an etic comparative perspective. One way of doing this is to translate the insider's "folk" view into comparable categories, such as "abandoning" or "forsaking," that can be used to construct theories and test hypotheses. The broadest such research design, called "holocultural analysis," makes use of the major anthropological data bank, the Human Relations Area Files (HRAF), which contains ethnographic data representing over 1,000 societies. The intent of this approach is to statistically measure "the relationship between two or more theoretically defined and operationalized variables in a world sample of human societies" (Rohner et al. 1978:128). In this way it is hoped that we may eventually comprehend what aspects of aging are universal, as opposed to those factors that are largely shaped by the sociocultural system.

As demonstrated by Anthony Glascock in chapter 2, carefully defining types of "death-hastening" behaviors allows us to make powerful use of the holocultural method. Using this approach, Glascock's research demonstrates that, counter to what one might expect, about half of his worldwide sample acts out variants of behavior that lead to the death of older citizens. As the case of Hart's Tiwi "mother" exemplifies, this is seldom a simple matter and usually is predicated on severe physical and cognitive decline and the redefinition of the person from a functional to a nonfunctional individual.

Leo Simmons was the first to apply the holocultural method to the subject of aging. His 1945 study examined the interrelation of 109 sociocultural traits grouped under habitat and economy, political and social organization, and religious beliefs and ritual. Despite some serious methodological flaws, Simmons's book and subsequent summary articles (1946, 1952, 1959, 1960) remained the main font of anthropological knowledge on the elderly for over twenty-five years. One reason was Simmons's attempt to go beyond numbers and treat his data as an elaborate cross-cultural analysis from which hypotheses could be extracted.

Here it is important to distinguish *cross-national* from *cross-cultural* studies in gerontological research (Fry 1988). The first type of study takes as the unit of analysis the nation-state and compares whole countries by measuring, through survey questionnaires, a large array of primarily demographic, interactional, and health-related variables (see Arnoff, Leon and Lorge 1964; Heikkinen, Waters, and Brzezinski 1983; Seefeldt 1984; Andrews et al. 1986; and Altergott 1988).[1] One of the first (and arguably the best) of such efforts was *Old People in Three Industrial Societies*, based on work carried out in the early 1960s in England, Denmark, and the United States (Shanas et al. 1968). A significant contribution of the study lies in its demonstration of the similar impact of industrialization in all these countries where bureaucratic structures of care were created to link retired status to a separate category of person called "old." The authors show that in each country the majority of persons over sixty reject this designation and the concomitant attempt by the social order to keep them "at arms length from the social structure" (p. 425). Yet they show that a large majority (75 percent) of those sixty-five years old or older live in close proximity to at least one child, and of those aged with children fully 80 percent claimed to have seen their offspring during the prior week. What such structural data reveal, however, is merely the potential for social integration. They do not tell us about differential cultural meaning or the reality of how older persons connect with their kinship network. As Sokolovsky shows in chapter 10 when comparing ethnic family interaction, such commonly used variables as "frequency of contact with kin" provide a very poor, and sometimes erroneous, impression of how the aged draw meaning into their lives from their intermingling with relatives.

In contrast, cross-cultural studies of the aged tend to focus on small-scale societies or individual communities within industrial states. This perspective permits comparisons to be made between the complex interwoven whole of cultural systems. One approach centers on highly controlled comparisons where the social units under study are similar except for one or two features. A classic example is S. F. Nadel's (1952) study of two African tribal societies, the Korongo and the Mesakin. While alike in terms of environment and economic, political, and kinship organization, each society differed in the degree of intergenerational conflict and the attitude of males toward aging. The key difference seemed to lie in the greater number of age distinctions recognized by the Korongo and the smoother transition into old age characteristic of this society. As a consequence, there was not only a greater congruence between social and physical aging among the Korongo but also an easier and more cheerful acceptance of old age itself.

Alternatively, the more typical approach to cross-cultural studies has been to maximize the difference between the societies being contrasted. In certain instances, researchers have searched the available literature to see what could be learned about a specific aspect of aging such as: intergenerational relations (Levine 1965; Rubinstein and Johnsen 1982; Akiyama, Antonucci, and Campbell, chapter 6; Simic, chapter 4); age as a basis of social organization (Eisenstadt 1956; Stewart 1977; Foner and Kertzer 1978); widowhood (Lopata 1972, 1987; Luborsky and Rubinstein, chapter 12); and general aspects of female aging (Bart 1969; Datan et al. 1970; Dougherty 1978; Brown and Kerns 1985; Cool and McCabe 1987).

Whichever approach is taken, cross-cultural research on aging is important in at least two ways. First, it may suggest general hypotheses about the aging experience that can be tested by employing larger samples or conducting longitudinal studies. By using a relatively small number of cases it is possible to retain a picture of the qualitative nature of sociocultural variables and thereby (hopefully) avoid overly simple theoretical models. A good example of this is found in chapter 6 where Hiroko Akiyama, Toni Antonucci, and Ruth Campbell contribute to theories of exchange and reciprocity through the cultural comparison of intergenerational support between women in Japan and the United States.

Second, intercultural comparisons can help us to understand in a detailed fashion how aging in the United States varies from that experienced in other places. Such analysis can suggest alternative strategies for developing a better environment in which to grow old. A particularly good example of this is found in chapter 8, where Bruce Zelkovitz contrasts Swedish and American ideologies with respect to state intervention in the life of the elderly. Sweden is proposed as a possible model of the way in which complex industrial nations might actively facilitate the integration of their older citizens as active, healthy, and productive members of society.

One of the significant problems with cross-cultural research, however, is the difficulty of gaining consistency in methods used to study qualitatively the intricate cultural phenomena observed in the societies being contrasted. An attempt at confronting this issue directly is project AGE (Age, Generation, and

Experience). As discussed by Keith, Fry, and Ikels in chapter 13, their cross-cultural comparison of two American communities with Hong Kong combines long-term fieldwork with a precise and consistent research protocol. The methodologies employed in this project were developed in the early 1980s by a working group of anthropologists and other scholars concerned with cross-cultural gerontology. The book resulting from this collaboration, *New Methods for Old Age Research* (Fry and Keith 1986), constitutes the most important handbook available for conducting research on aging in different cultural contexts.

MYTHS OF AGING IN "EXOTIC" PLACES

In taking a global appoach to the cultural contexts of aging, it is tempting to present a number of wildly diverse exotic tableaus of growing old in a West African city or among Yugoslav peasants. Such a perspective would miss the important lessons to be learned by considering such variety in light of common issues that bind the aged in all human groups. It may come as a surprise, and perhaps a comfort to some, to learn that the Tiwi, a tiny, culturally homogeneous non-Western society living in a benign climate, have not escaped confrontation with the physical and emotional burdens of senility or what we call "euthanasia." In sum, while the literature on aging in non-Western contexts contains a good deal of romanticized nonsense, there are several generalizations that are relevant to a realistic consideration of aging in an international perspective. For example:

1. A single cultural system may provide highly successful solutions for some problems of aging but fare miserably with regard to others (Beall and Goldstein 1981). A unidimensional evaluation of the aged based primarily on the concept of "status" is simply inadequate for understanding the multidimensional phenomena of aging in even the smallest of human societies.

2. Not all non-Western, nonindustrial cultural systems provide a better milieu for aging and intergenerational relations than is found in the modern industrial West. Those who yearn for the "world we have lost" or even Reagan's small-town America should think again. While this volume contains various examples of cultural contexts for aging which many North Americans might care to emulate (see especially Rosenberg, Simic, and Keifer in this volume), the ethnographic and historical literature also contains numerous cases of "traditional" societies whose attitudes and treatment of the aged, healthy or frail, provide little to envy (Laslett 1976; Nydegger 1983; Maxwell, Silverman, and Maxwell 1982).

3. Social change does not automatically reduce the quality of life of the elderly. While this proposition follows logically from the previous

statement, it is worth noting that under certain conditions, massive societal change, referred to as modernization, can impact positively on the life of the aged (Amoss 1981, Foner 1984b). We will see this quite clearly in chapter 7 where Philip Olson analyzes the transformation of China over the last several decades.

4. A single cultural system may offer vastly different opportunities for successful aging based on gender, class, or rural/urban variation (Cool and McCabe 1987; Halperin 1984, 1987). All too often descriptions of aging in non-Western societies are based on cultural ideals or a male perspective and have skewed the reality of how intracultural distinctions can alter the meaning of aging within the same societal setting.

5. The potential security and quality of life of the aged is maximized when cultures facilitate (a) *both* community and kin roles for the elderly, and (b) these arenas of interaction are mutually supportive rather than constructed as separate entities (Sokolovsky and Sokolovsky 1983b).

6. Until quite recently there was widespread belief (even in the scientific community) that there existed geriatric utopias where old people existed but the normal aging process did not. Isolated mountain valleys in Ecuador, Pakistan, and especially the Caucasus region of the Soviet Union were thought to contain villages with very long-living people (130–150 years of age) who were free of "old people's diseases" such as Alzheimer's. Despite the long-standing quest for the "fountain of youth," careful studies have now shown that even the most idyllic spots in the world contain roughly the same share of centenarians and a similar incidence of dementing diseases as found in the United States (Rubin 1983; Palmore 1984; Beall 1987).

These six propositions represent a core of ideas which I believe can transcend cultural boundaries. They are linked to the gerontological topics that compose the organization of this book. While these sections do not exhaust the range of important aging studies, I hope the following eighteen chapters will illuminate how the experience of becoming and being old is made meaningful in the cultural context.

NOTE

1. Some of this research that I have labeled "cross-national" (e.g., Arnoff, Leon, and Lorge 1964; Seefeldt 1984) is described by the authors as "cross-cultural." However, the survey questionnaire approach of these studies places them in the methodological camp of what I call cross-national studies and perhaps explains why they find so few differences in the samples they examine.

PART I
CULTURE, AGING, AND CONTEXT

> Every month the net balance of the world's older persons (55 years and over) increases by 1.2 million persons. More than 80 percent of this monthly increase. . . occurs in developing countries.
>
> — Kevin Kinsella

Despite the dramatic statistic cited above, at first glance it might seem that excessive interest by social scientists about aging in the Third World would be a case of misplaced research priorities. In the poorest developing countries, the average span of life from birth remains abysmally low. For example, in Africa thirteen nations in 1980 had life-expectancy projections of forty-five years or less (United Nations 1985:100–101).

In contrast to the almost universally "aged" industrial countries where the elderly account for at least one-tenth of the citizenry, structural population aging is barely apparent in the Third World as a whole. As of 1980 the elderly made up 5.8 percent of the world's population. For developing regions, populations contained a much lower percentage (3.9 percent) of those over sixty-five than was found in the developed world (11.4 percent) (World Bank 1980). Exceptions occur, such as those indicated by Harriet Rosenberg's study of the !Kung (chapter 1) where persons over sixty-five years of age compose about 6 percent of this small-scale preindustrial society. Yet, it is more typically found that the "agedness" (percent over age sixty-five) of such populations is in the 1 to 4 percent range. As of 1988 most Third World nations remain demographically "young," with less than 4 percent of their population over sixty-five — Kenya, 2.1 percent; Guatemala, 3.2 percent — or "youthful," with 4 to 6 percent over sixty-five — Mexico, 4.1 percent; China, 5.5 percent (Kinsella 1988). In the near future some Third World countries are even expected to show a slight decline in the percent of the elderly, as improved health care is likely to have the greatest impact on keeping children alive rather than reducing mortality in adults. This is in contrast to the "grayer" industrial regions designated as either "mature" (between 7.9 percent and 9.9 percent over sixty-five – Hong Kong, 8.3 percent) or "aged" (10 percent or more over age sixty-five – United States, 12 percent).

Yet, this set of statistics does not tell the entire story. By 1988 other Third World countries, such as Jamaica and Costa Rica, already had life expectancies equal to that of the United States. Moreover, much of the difference between low-life-expectancy nations and Western industrial societies (averaging seventy-four years) can be attributed to the very high levels of infant mortality still persisting in the Third World. One can note, for example, that although the expected years of life *at birth* in the United States in 1980 (seventy-three years) exceeded that for Nigeria by twenty-five years, males at age sixty in the United States could only expect to survive three years longer than similarly aged men in Nigeria (Selby and Schechter 1982:208–9).

The 1980s have in fact witnessed a dramatic demographic revolution with the nonindustrialized nations of the world now containing a majority of the world's elders. While over the next two decades these countries will still not reach the level of "societal aging" now faced by North America, much of Europe, and Japan, they will have to contend with an extraordinary increase of 154 percent in actual numbers, going from 200 to 350 million aged. Over the next decade, developing nations are expected to add 9.4 years to life expectancy. By the year 2025, there are expected to be 1.1 billion persons in the world sixty years or older, and China alone will have about as many people of this age as there will be persons of any age in the United States (Nusberg 1982). Some regions of Latin America and Africa are expected to enter the twenty-first century with the world's most rapid increases in both the very youngest (under fifteen years of age) and the very oldest (eighty years and over) segments of their populations! (See Myers 1982; United Nations 1985; Hoover and Siegel 1986; Kinsella 1988; and Okojie 1988 for analysis of demographic data on the elderly throughout the world.)

It is important to note that the most rapid population increases are expected for persons over eighty, those most in need of the types of medical care and services which are virtually nonexistent in many parts of the Third World. While between 1980 and 2000 the number of people over eighty in North America is expected to rise by 56 percent, more substantial increments will be found in West Africa (143 percent), tropical South America (138 percent), South East Asia (113 percent), and China (92 percent) (Myers 1982:26–27). Such changes when coupled with increasing poverty, overurbanization, the accompanying rural exodus of young adults, and alterations in ideological systems may create the greatest problems for the aged in what are now considered "traditional societies."

TREATMENT OF THE AGED

A small-scale traditional society is described by Harriet Rosenberg in this section's first chapter about the !Kung, a formerly nomadic gathering and hunting group in Botswana. Despite the erroneous image created in the recent film, *The Gods Must Be Crazy*, they are not the unchanged people, lacking contact with the outside world.[1] Instead, over the last twenty years they have become a captive group, restricted to a reservation and forced to alter significantly their quite successful foraging lifestyle. Nonetheless, this harsh context imposed by the South African government has not yet destroyed core cultural features of !Kung family, community, and ritual life, forums in which the elderly still perform valued roles. Here we clearly see the benefits of long-term ethnographic research in understanding the cultural mechanisms of caring for the elderly. Without her having lived with the group for an extended period or having had access to her husband's twenty years of experience with the !Kung, Rosenberg might have mistaken the constant "kvetching" (sharp complaining) of most elderly as proof that this is a society that habitually abandons its older citizens in need of care. Instead, her penetrating analysis linking complaint discourse to the egalitarian and communal roots of !Kung society shows that outspoken nagging is part of their package of cultural devices that reinforce values of caring and extreme compassion for even the very frail elderly. Importantly, caregiving is carried out evenly by persons of both sexes avoiding the overdependence on female caregivers typical for industrialized countries.

GLOBAL PERSPECTIVES ON STATUS AND SUPPORT OF THE AGED

One of the promises of a truly cross-cultural comparative gerontology is to gain an understanding of aging divorced from the narrow boundary of a single case such as the !Kung. In fact, it is among such types of society—nomadic, nonagricultural, lacking economic stratification, with bilateral descent—that one is statistically most likely to find the very frail elderly having their lives hastened. The first serious attempt to deal with such issues on a worldwide basis was the massive study by Leo Simmons, *The Role of the Aged in Primitive Society* (1945). However, one must be cautious about his statistical results. As might be expected from one of the first studies using the Human Relations Area Files, the methods were flawed by a poorly drawn sample, inadequate statistical controls, and an imprecise definition of some key variables. Nevertheless, the many insights Simmons provided have served as guideposts to more recent, controlled comparisons and holocultural studies seeking to uncover variables which are associated with high status, deference, and support shown toward the elderly.

Working independently with small, cross-cultural samples, Cowgill (1972) and Press and McKool (1972) proposed similar variables which account for high status in traditional peasant societies. These involve four interrelated clusters of cultural phenomena:

1. an available role set emphasizing continuity, and important responsibilities in a community organization and public life;
2. integration into a residentially viable extended family organization;
3. control of some important material and informational resources;
4. a value system praising a group-oriented ideology while de-emphasizing individual ego development.

In applying these variables to the !Kung people studied by Rosenberg, we can see that their cultural context does not fulfill all of the criteria listed above. This is especially the case in terms of their lack of a residentially stable extended family organization, such as might still be found in rural China (see Philip Olson, chapter 7). Yet the cumulative effect of the important roles the elderly play in kinship relations, control of knowledge, mastery of the dangerous spiritual force called "*num*," combined with the communal ideological orientation, has created a cultural context in which the elderly are well supported.

A series of holocultural studies have corroborated, in many respects, the association of status and deference with the control of informational and administrative roles (Sheehan 1976; Silverman and Maxwell 1987) as well as valued activities and extended family integration (McArdle and Yeracaris 1981). In terms of resource and information control, Silverman and Maxwell have demonstrated that only certain types of control, particularly administrative and consultative, correlate with beneficent treatment of the elderly. Some forms of supernatural information control, especially transformational powers, were in fact a potential threat to the elderly. This is highly relevant to some historically known situations of massive societal change, such as in thirteenth-to-sixteenth-century Europe, where the majority of persons burned at the stake for their "transformational knowledge" (witchcraft) were middle-aged and older females (Bever 1982). As will also be noted in Barker's analysis of the Niue (section VI), being close to one's ancestors does not guarantee a pleasant final abode while still among the living.

A special concern within the growing comparative perspective on being old is confronting the darker side of aging—various types of nonsupportive and even "death-hastening" behaviors directed toward the elderly. This is a particularly apt issue to examine as some leaders in the United States have begun to reconsider moral objections to euthanasia with regard to the most frail aged. As we have already seen in the discussion of the Tiwi, "high-tech" societies are not the only ones to grapple with this dilemma. Anthony Glascock in chapter 2 throws this question into global relief and finds some disquieting results. A majority of the societies in his sample exhibited some form of "death-hastening" behavior, with fewer than one-third providing unconditional support. However, few societies enforce a single treatment of their elderly, and it was commonly found that both supportive as well as death-hastening behaviors coexist in the same social setting. Glascock's study demonstrates that when anthropologists have cared to probe the later stages of the life cycle, they have found cultural distinctions drawn between "intact," fully functioning, aged and "decrepit" individuals who find it difficult to carry out even the most basic tasks. It is persons placed in this latter category toward whom geronticide or death hastening is most frequently applied. In the book's final section the varied cultural responses to the oldest old will be more fully explored.

THE FEMINIZATION OF OLD AGE

Women constitute more than a majority of the aged population in virtually all parts of the world about which data are available.[2] In the less developed nations, the gender ratio over age sixty is relatively close, about 90 men for every 100 women, while in the more developed world there are 20 percent fewer males than females still alive. However, it is in the former type of societies that the social worlds of males and females are found to be most socially and culturally divergent. This is especially the case in patrilineal societies with a good deal of stratification, where men try to control strongly the sexuality and reproductive history of women in their family. In such societies one can "in fact speak of separate male and female subcultures" (Simic and Myerhoff 1978:23).

It is unfortunate that until quite recently the analysis of aging in such societies has largely portrayed the male perspective, despite the importance of older women to the functioning of society. Many authors have begun to document a common pattern in nonindustrial societies of dramatic positive changes of roles, power, and status by women as they pass into the middle and latter adult years (see especially Bart 1969; Kerns 1983; Brown and Kerns 1985; Cool and McCabe 1987; Gutmann 1987:133–84; Teitlebaum 1987). For example, Jane Goodale, in her book *Tiwi Women*, notes that as women become older they often assume more authority, become more assertive. While they are not considered the formal leaders in key rituals, such as a funerals, "the men do consult female members of the patrilineage that is in charge of the ceremony, and the women voice their opinions freely. The nominal male leaders consider these opinions to be important" (1971:228–29).

The chapter by Catherine Coles contributes to the growing body of knowledge about the lives of older women in non-Western societies. Her work shows how the intersection of Hausa tribal culture with Islamic traditions creates a range of contexts in which older women contribute to society. This work is especially important in providing one of the few studies of female elders in an urban African context. Coles shows that older women in the Hausa city are not only crucial to the functioning of households and larger kin grouping but also can act as initiators of changes which have broad importance to the community. It should be noted, however, that class and national variants of Islamic cultural contexts, such as Ellickson (1988) describes for Bangladesh, can provide older women, especially widows, with poorer prospects than are available among the Hausa people.

NOTES

1. While quite popular with the general public, the 1982 film, *The Gods Must be Crazy*, has evoked a storm of protest from scholars. They have criticized the film for depicting an erroneous, benign view of a South African political structure which protects the childlike !Kung living in a pristine state of Stone Age existence. In reality the !Kung have been placed on a fenced-in reservation, their traditional lifestyle has been prohibited, and the men are often conscripted by the South African military to fight guerilla forces in rural areas.

2. While no regions of the world show a majority of older males over older females, a recent study lists four countries for which this is the case for the population over sixty years of age: Bangladesh, Zimbabwe, Morocco, and Tunisia (Kinsella 1988).

1 COMPLAINT DISCOURSE, AGING, AND CAREGIVING AMONG THE !KUNG SAN OF BOTSWANA

Harriet G. Rosenberg

Old people have long complained: it is an old thing. Even if the child did everything for them, they would complain.

Koka, age 80

This chapter explores the social basis of !Kung San caregiving discourses. It looks at how a particular sociocultural formation reproduces the social relations of elder care. It examines the language through which care is negotiated within the context of family, kinship, and community.[1] These are the discourses that locate caregiving (by position in the family/community, by gender); that reproduce the ideology (morality) of caregiving in both its public and domestic realm; and that legitimate caregiving so that it is experienced as "natural."

Despite the changes in economic and social life that the !Kung have experienced in the last fifteen to twenty years (described below), !Kung caring discourse appears to be autonomous, in the sense that it is constructed within the culture itself, with very little influence from state agencies (legal, health, educational, social services) or non-!Kung religious philosophies.[2]

THE !KUNG SAN

The !Kung San of Botswana and Namibia are one of the best-known and documented gatherer-hunter peoples in the world. Although their history of contact has been a complex one, some !Kung groups have lived as relatively isolated foragers well into the 1960s.[3] As gatherer-hunters, the !Kung can provide insights into a way of life that was until 10,000 years ago a human universal.

Studies of the !Kung have been carried out on a wide variety of topics by over a dozen investigators.[4] The Dobe area, where the majority of these studies were undertaken is a line of eight waterholes in the northern Kalahari Desert of Botswana. The area is about 10,000 square kilometers and has in recent years supported a population of between 800 to 1000 people. In 1986, the 663 !Kung speakers shared their eight waterholes with about 325 pastoralists, mainly of the Herero ethnic group. Our studies of aging and caregiving covered both the Herero and the !Kung but the present chapter focuses on the latter.

During the 1960s the majority of !Kung lived in small camps of about fifteen to thirty people, often centered around a core of siblings, their spouses, and children. The groups relied on wild food products for the bulk of their subsistence needs and moved three to six times a year in search of food and water. These camps were characterized by egalitarian social relations and the widespread sharing of foodstuffs—the typical features of a small-scale communal social formation. The language and kinship system were intact and fully functioning.

Missionizing has had little influence in the Dobe area. Indigenous religious practices included belief in two major deities (a high god and a lesser, trickster god) and ghosts of ancestors called *gangwasi*. Trance dancing maintained the health of the community and was used to cure individual sicknesses. At some camps the all-night dances took place two or three times a week. A woman's drum dance was also prominent.[5]

After 1968, conditions began to change rapidly. In 1968, the first store opened, followed by a school in 1973 and a health post and airstrip in 1978. During this period the !Kung began to shift over to small-scale livestock and crop production. They began to settle down into semipermanent villages. Cash became a common medium of exchange which coexisted with the traditional regional gift exchange system called *hxaro*.[6] Migrant labor, livestock sales, and craft production became sources of cash income. In addition, some young men were drawn across the border into the South African military where they earned high salaries as trackers in the war against the South West African People's Organization (SWAPO).[7]

By the mid-1980s, in their dress and economy, the Dobe !Kung have come to resemble the lifestyle of many impoverished southern African peasants. They now receive drought relief, and bags and containers from overseas countries litter the villages. Their children go to school (but usually drop out in the early grades), they seek health care at local clinics or from mobile health units, and they often spend their modest incomes on transistor radios, European-style clothing, tea, sugar, tobacco, and beer.

Their transition to an agricultural way of life has been far from successful. Over half the families lacked livestock, and even the "affluent" herders numbered their livestock in the range of ten to twenty. Foraging continues to be an important part of subsistence activities.

On a deeper level the !Kung are struggling – not without success – to adhere to the values and beliefs of their ancestral culture. It is this cultural context which has continued to generate the motifs, themes, and rationales of the discourses about aging and caregiving which are explored in this chapter.

AGE IN !KUNG SOCIETY

Like most foraging peoples, the !Kung are not interested in and do not keep track of chronological age. Birthdays and anniversaries are not social markers. Age segregation is noticeably absent among the !Kung; there are few social activities which would exclude people by virtue of their age.

Major life transition hallmarks exist at the younger end of the age spectrum distinguishing among infants, children, adolescents, and adults. No ceremonies mark the onset of old age (or menopause), but all elders (including those without children) do bear the honorific *na* in their names, which means "old," "big," or "great." No ritual occasion marks the moment when one becomes *na*, usually in one's mid to late forties.

Old age is divided into three broad categories. All elders are *na*, and those who are very old but still functioning are called "old/dead," *da ki*, a term that designates extreme old age and one that is also a joking term. A sick or decrepit elder may be referred to as "old to the point of helplessness," *da kum kum*. *Da ki* and *da kum kum* do not denote a sharp decline in social status. Unlike many societies described in this volume (see Barker and Glascock), the frail elderly are not a particular butt of ridicule or a source of fear and anxiety. For example, the mention of incontinence in a story is usually the signal for a good laugh, such as the case of someone describing the circumstances of a hunt in which men unexpectedly confronted a leopard and were described as losing sphincter contol as they ran away from the threatening situation. In that circumstance, the audience roared with laughter at the misadventures of the hapless hunters. But in the case of elders, incontinence is associated with imminent death and is not the occasion for joking.

It should be noted that growing old and the changes that accompany it are a constant topic of conversation and a source of humor. Linking sexuality and aging seems to make the best jokes, and much of campfire disucssion features endless jokes about decline in sexual prowess, especially among men. Postmenopausal women also delight in engaging in broad sexual joking (Lee 1985). Frail elders are subjected to a gentler form of joking about their lack of sexual activities. As one informant said, "They lie there like logs."

Although the !Kung do symbolically link old age with degeneration, elders can also be associated with generative and life-giving activities, as Biesele and Howell (1981) have pointed out in their analysis of a beautiful folktale of a grandmother/granddaughter relationship. Nor is death exclusively connected with old age. Historically, the !Kung have had a high infant mortality rate, and now tuberculosis is prevalent in the Dobe area. Thus death can and does occur at any age.

In the realm of sociopolitical power, !Kung elders do have limited prerogatives. They command control over defining kinship relationships. A senior person, male or female, has the right to decide who fits where in the kinship system and to determine an avoidance or a joking framework for social interactions. This system of seniority gives elders power in defining the social universe, but it does not constitute a gerontocracy. For in a propertyless world, seniors cannot wield the threat of disinheritance to encourage compliance.[8] !Kung old people, by dint of their personal authority, may try to construct marriage alliances which seem sensible to them, but young people can refuse marriages, thwarting the intentions of their seniors.

Another arena of personal authority for elders is their role as healers. Not all people develop the power to heal—to sing, dance, go into a trance, and "pull sickness" out of others. Those who do can often go on until they are quite old, teaching other healers and participating in healing the community at large. Richard Katz has described the situation of Twa Na, a woman in her early eighties. "Though completely blind, hard of hearing, and slow moving, needing a walking stick, her *num* [medicine] is slowly accumulating strength. She exemplifies the Kung belief that, for some persons, their *num* keeps them young. In experiencing *kia* [trance] and healing they stay young" (1982:151–52). In the case of Twa Na and a few other elders, their charismatic energy creates around them an aura of exceptional strength and spirituality.

THE CURRENT PROJECT

The discussion which follows is based on field research (participant-observation, formal questionnaires, and open-ended, unstructured interviews) with the !Kung San in 1986 and 1987[9] and on the accumulated work of anthropologists who have worked with the !Kung since 1963. We were thus often able to compare our informants' retrospective accounts with field descriptions of observed behavior over the past twenty-four years. There has been very little systematic research on aging in !Kung culture.[10]

In 1964, 9 percent of the !Kung population was over sixty.[11] By 1973, that proportion had risen to 10.5 percent, and in 1986 the figure was 12.5 percent, with 7.5 percent over age sixty-five. In addition, the birth rate has risen. As of 1986, almost 40 percent of the population was under fifteen years of age. Thus at the time of our field research, 48 percent of the population was between fifteen and forty-nine and supported both young and old.

I will be interested here in issues of aging and caregiving and the role of social change in the experience of aging and in the delivery of care. This chapter focuses on the following aspects of that research mandate—the ways in which caring is mediated by (1) narratives of neglect and abandonment, (2) the concept of entitlement, and (3) the social organization of care.

NARRATIVES OF NEGLECT AND ABANDONMENT

To the observer !Kung elders appear to be hale and hearty and well integrated into the social life of their community.[12] Frail elders are embedded in caregiving networks of several on-site caregivers who provide for their needs.[13] Yet the discourse used by elders to describe their situation is often one of unrelenting complaint and blaming. In general the most common response to the question, "Who looks after old people?" is "Their children." But when we stepped outside the normative system and asked elders, "Who looks after you?" the response was very frequently, "No one. Can't you see that I am starving and dressed in rags?"

Elders frequently complained about the neglected state they were in and told lengthy tales about the deficiencies of those who should be caring for them but were not. While the neglect discourse took on a variety of forms, two common styles will be explored here. One is the nagging style and the other is broad melodrama.

The first style is typified by Chuko, age seventy-two. Chuko lives with her husband, her daughter, and her son-in-law, all of whom share in the caregiving. Yet Chuko describes herself as neglected because she says that her three half-brothers and their children do not provide for her.

I asked Chuko if she could give me an example from her "own memory" of how an old person was looked after until they died. "Do you know of any old person who was abandoned?" Chuko was not interested in the past just then: "I have no story, but the only example that I can give you is my own. I have younger siblings with children. And I am old. I have no niece or nephew who brings food from my siblings. And I just see that they are not looking after me."

The care that she received from her daughter, son-in-law, and husband was scarcely acknowledged. Chuko asserted that caregiving had deteriorated in the present. In the past, she maintained, children were collectively responsible for all elders. "When I say the past was better I mean this: before, the child listened to his/her parents.[14] When children were out to play and an adult who saw an elder ailing came upon them, he scolded them for letting the elder die of thirst and ordered them to attend to [the elder]. Today an adult will merely look and say or think: 'Let his/her children take care of him.' And even the children themselves are not caring by nature." She then reiterated her complaints against her half-siblings.

Two of her brothers agreed to be interviewed, and they defined themselves as being caregivers to their sister and pointed out that they sent food and water to her via their children and grandchildren. Nevertheless, Chuko maintained a persistent patter of complaint. Far from not wishing to seem a burden or a dependent, she went out of her way to publicly blame her brothers and their families as being delinquent caregivers. Her form of expresssion was often a monologue which was quietly declaimed to no one in particular.

Chuko's complaint discourse can be interpreted in a variety of ways. She may be detecting changes in the distribution of social obligations that have accompanied settlement and may indeed be picking up a drift away from sibling care toward a more nuclear pattern. Her family and her brothers had lived together in the past in a traditional sibling core unit. Now the brothers live on the other side of Dobe. Two of these brothers have many children, grandchildren, and elders to care for and may be preoccupied with their immediate situations. The third sibling is often dismissed as a person with no sense who cannot be relied on. Thus Chuko may be complaining about a new experience of social distance. On the other hand, complaining itself is not new.

Anthropologists consider the !Kung to be "among the most talkative people in the world. Much of this talk verges on argument, often for its own sake, and usually ad hominem" (Lee 1979:372). Thus Chuko's stream of complaints is not viewed within the culture as unusual or as a particular attribute of old age. Campfire conversation often swirls around accusations of improper meat distribution, improper gift exchange, stinginess, and the shortcomings of others.

Complaining is an important leveling discourse. It is a public exhortation to keep goods and services circulating, it warns against hoarding. It may allow individuals to unburden themselves about a particular domestic grievance but the complaint discourse is rarely confined to the immediate family.There is no ideological division between public and private spheres among the !Kung; a private betrayal can easily be considered an injury to all.

Complaining rhetoric may also be part of Chuko's individual efforts to keep herself visible. Just as Jewish elders in Barbara Myerhoff's study of a senior drop-in center used narration and "competitive complaining" (1978:146) as a performance strategy to mark their continued presence in the world, so Chuko's constant hum of words may be her way of saying, "I'm still here."

No competing legitimate discourse to the ideology of sharing has thus far emerged among the Dobe !Kung. There is no language yet which expresses a world of personal needs which might be at odds with obligations to others, and there is very little leniency shown to those who may have many conflicting obligations. Those who have attempted to limit the circle of reciprocity when they switched from foraging to agro-pastoralism have found it difficult to explain why they were not sharing their crops or killing their goats and cattle to meet the needs of their kinspeople (Lee 1979:412–14).

One woman in her early sixties, who owns many cattle, has been observed to be among the loudest of complainers, denouncing all and sundry for their failure to share. One day, while following an anthropologist back and forth while he was packing up camp, she delivered a blistering tirade against his hard-heartedness. Back and forth from tent to truck they trudged, the anthropologist silent, carrying bundles of goods, Nuhka on his heels yelling at him. Suddenly, she stopped, and, like a scene in a Brecht play, she stepped out of character, altered the tone of her voice, and calmly said, "We have to talk this way. It's our custom." Then she stepped back into character and resumed her attack.

The !Kung actually have a name for this type of discourse: it is called *hore hore* or *oba oba* and can be translated as "yakkity-yak." In the case above, Nuhka stepped out of character to break the tension of the verbal assault she had mounted. In other cases, the tension can be broken by a joke which leaves "the participants rolling on the ground helpless with laughter" (Lee 1979:372). The neglect discourse is thus not peculiar to elders but may be invoked by anyone at any time to decry real or potential stinginess. However, elders will frequently avail themselves of the opportunity to complain. In contrast to Chuko's nagging style, others recount their complaints with great theatrical flare.

Kasupe, age seventy-four, a skilled storyteller, responded to the question of who looked after him by denouncing his entire family. First, he attacked his children: "My own children do not look after me. See the clothes I am wearing—these rags I'm wearing—I get them from my own work, my own sweat. None of them have done anything for me. Because they do not look after me I, their parent say they are *kwara n* [without sense.]" He went on to discuss his future prospects: "I do not know who will take care of me when I am old and frail. Right now I can manage; I still have some strength. But as I grow old, I cannot point out a child—a person—about whom I can say, 'This one will take care of me.' Perhaps I will perish." Warming up to his tale of woe, Kasupe also denounced his brothers and sisters. In fact, all of his relatives were dismissed as being uncaring. To illustrate the depths of their perfidy, he launched into the following narrative:

Here is proof of the uncaring nature of my children. I will tell you a story. I'd gone hunting with some Herero [men], and we had split up, agreeing to meet later at a certain point. Those Herero warned me that they had set a trap in the direction I was headed. I went on but because it was dark, I could not see and was caught in the trap. It grabbed my ankle. I stayed there and my wife and children were following me. None of them came to see how I was. I was only helped by you, Gakekgoshe [the Tswana/Herero translator], and Tontah [Richard Lee, an anthropologist.] You helped me heal and saw to it that I got better. None of [my family] came to see how I was doing. It was only you. Even my brothers and sisters in Southwest [Namibia] did not come to see how I was doing.

At this juncture Gakekgoshe turned to me and said in English, "A big story." And indeed it was.

After the interview concluded, we returned to camp, fetched a copy of the book, *The Dobe !Kung*, and returned to confront Kasupe. There on page 105 of the book was a photo of Kasupe "on the day of the crisis" lying on the ground surrounded by family and !Kung healers. The text also included a lengthy account from Lee's field notes describing Kasupe's wife and children sobbing and wailing as community members worked on curing him. Lee administered some penicillin. The next day Kasupe began to improve, and within three months he was hunting again. Lee assessed the crisis this way: "What had healed Kasupe? I'm sure it wasn't the penicillin alone. Equally important was the fact that his family and his campmates had stuck by him and the healers of the camp had protected his life with their healing energy" (Lee 1984:104–6).

Feeling some glee in having caught Kasupe in a "lie," we laid the evidence out before him. Here was the story and photograph of his family and community making heroic efforts to save his life. Kasupe's only response was to break out into a loud, long, thigh-slapping laugh which was immediately echoed by the !Kung audience and the anthropologists. Kasupe was completely unabashed and expressed no regret at having accused his relatives of neglect, abandonment, and death-hastening behavior. Whether there was any "truth" to his narrative was quite irrelevant. His version of events made a good story. It was gripping and dramatic; he was impressive as he told it. The listener was captivated by "the utterance" (Eagleton 1983:115).

But like Chuko's less melodramatic narrative, Kasupe's performance also had another side to it. Kasupe had expressed what "might" happen if caregivers were not to do their duty. He had described aloud what the world would be like should the caring system not be reproduced. By saying "the unthinkable" he allowed his audience to imagine the dire scene of family neglect. By negative example, he restated the social contract of caregiving obligations. His laughter, and the audience's laughter, did not mean that the complaint lacked seriousness, only perhaps that he had been topped by a better story this time. But the complaint was important: the !Kung system of mutual responsiblity and caregiving requires constant lubrication, and complaining greases the wheels.

TALES OF "REAL" ABANDONMENT

In a more serious vein, Xoma, a respected elder, who was not given to extravagant rhetoric, pointed out that there were indeed cases of real abandonment in the past. He explained the circumstances of an abandonment a generation ago: "They'd leave him/her and go off, because they didn't know what to do with him/her. Naturally, they had no truck, no donkey, nothing. And they were also carrying her/his things on their bodies. Sometimes they'd try to carry him/her where they were going. Someone else would carry his/her things, if there were many people. But if the people were few, or if there was only one man, they didn't know what to do with the old person. They would admit defeat, leave him/her, and go."

It is quite likely that there have been cases of death hastening among the !Kung in the past. We do not have any sustained ethnographic account of such behavior comparable to Hart's encounter with the Tiwi custom of "covering up" (see the introduction to this volume). The !Kung do use the equivocal term *na a tsi*, to leave in the bush, which implies abandonment. As Xoma's dispassionate analysis implies, "burden of care" was often not a metaphor for a stressful situation but a description of a concrete situation which entailed physically carrying a frail elder on one's back. When this was the only means of transportation, there were likely to have been times when the coping skills of the

Kasupe laughing after telling his story, with his friend /Twi seated.

caregivers were stretched to the breaking point, and the elder was abandoned in the bush.

It is clear that settlement has made a difference. Currently, we have found incapacitated elders being scrupulously cared for by kin and community. The conditions of a settled lifestyle, the availability of soft foods (dairy products and porridge), and access to vehicles in cases of medical emergencies all make it easier to care for frail elders today in comparison to thirty or more years ago. Furthermore, settlement has also meant !Kung practices are now more closely scrutinized by the state than they were in the past. The presence of a legal apparatus and police in the Dobe district has undoubtedly influenced community thinking on abandonment of elders.

The question of what constituted real abandonment was a thorny problem for the researchers, and we have found no easy solutions. About 90 percent of our informants said that they knew of no cases of elders being abandoned in the past. Many described cases of young people carrying frail elders on their backs from water hole to water hole until they died "in our hands." Many others said that they had never even heard of old people being abandoned.

But a few informants recounted explicit stories describing elders being purposely left to perish. A consistent element in these accounts was that those associated with death-hastening activities were always close relatives – a spouse or children. This finding is consistent with Glascock's discussion (this volume) that the decision to abandon an old person is almost always made within the immediate family, although in the !Kung case, elders do not appear to be part of the negotiations. What is unknown but nevertheless very important in these discussions of euthanasia is how long the elder was incapacitated before the decision to terminate life was made. It may be that among the !Kung, if close family members have been seen to be caring for a decrepit elder for a very long period of time, a culturally acknowledged but unexpressed statute of limitations comes into play and abandonment is permitted, especially if it is *not* presented as a premeditated action.[15]

To complicate matters still further, some stories suggest that elders were left temporarily en route but had died before their kinspeople could return from finding water or setting up camp. Whether they intended to hasten the death of an old person or were simply strategizing around the most efficient way to set up camp and meet the needs of that person is unclear.[16]

The discourse of neglect is thus quite complicated. It is used to describe cases in which real abandonment may have occurred. It is used as a social regulatory mechanism to reinforce sharing and caregiving. It is used as a vehicle to tell a good story. What is most apparent about this discourse is that it is words and words alone that have up until very recently been the main social regulators of behavior. The !Kung themselves have no legal/police system with which to coerce behavior or punish offenders.

ENTITLEMENT

I would not want to live with my family. They are nice people, very generous, but it would not be fair to them.

Eighty-two year-old Toronto woman

!Kung elders do not see themselves as burdens. They are not apologetic if they are no longer able to produce enough to feed themselves. They expect others to care for them when they can no longer do so. Entitlement to care is naturalized within the culture. Elders do not have to negotiate care as if it were a favor; rather, it is perceived as a right.

The needs of elders are not defined as being markedly different from the needs of anyone else. The material aspects of caring for elders was uniformly defined by our informants as providing *da, gu, msi* (firewood, water, and food). These are the basics of life which are procured and shared among all members of the community. Obtaining these necessities in the past was not especially onerous, requiring on average twenty hours of work a week in food gathering from the active population, but today those with herd animals do work longer hours. Thus elders have not been experienced as a particular economic burden or a category of people with "special needs."[17] In fact, in terms of health care, elders are both givers and receivers of care. Most healers are elders whose activities and advice are well respected. Even with the arrival of government health workers in the district, healing dances continue to flourish, giving elders a prominent role in community life.

One rarely hears an old person express appreciation for the care which she/he receives, and one never hears elders express the desire to live alone in order not to burden the family with caregiving obligations. In fact the desire to live alone is classified as a form of mental illness. "Only a crazy person would live alone," said one young informant.

The following story illustrates how old people make demands. In the middle of a hot afternoon in 1986 Gumi Na was sleeping in her house next to a small fire.[18] I had never met her before, but she was Richard Lee (Tontah)'s social mother and they have had a close relationship which spans over twenty-three years. At first sight Gumi, age eighty-three, looked to be very frail, weighing perhaps sixty pounds. Her daughter, Sagai, spoke with her by cupping her hand and shouting about four inches from her ear. Although Gumi had awakened from a sound sleep and had not seen her "European" son for over six years, she immediately tuned into the situation, greeted her visitors, and established their place in the kinship system.

Throughout the interview, Gumi gave alert and to-the-point responses to our questions. At the same time she launched her own demanding harangue for more gifts. Her words went like this: "Give me some medicine. . . .Well, I got some clothing. . . Tontah, *hxaro mi cosisi* [give me things]. Give me beads. . . . Give me clothing."[19] At one point during the lengthy interview, her daughter

The elderly Gumi Na clasping the hand of her visiting "European son," Richard Lee, as her daughter Sagai looks on.

interrupted the steady flow of demands and laughingly said, "Oh, stop going on and on about *hxaro*." Gumi was completely undeterred; "No! No! You tell Tontah that I want to still talk about *hxaro*. Hey, give me things."

When we returned to Dobe, we were asked how Gumi was faring. We described her situation and her persistent requests for gifts. Two !Kung elders glanced at each other with knowing looks when we mentioned the demands for *hxaro*, and one said, "Even as old as she is, she still knows how to talk nicely. Her thoughts are still sound."

What I had experienced as demanding ingratitude was culturally interpreted as a sign that Gumi was in good mental health. She "talked nicely" in the sense that her words were considered to be appropriate to a gift exchange situation in which she was an active participant. The ability to make demands is a signal of social connectedness and a symbol of entitlement.

For some, entitlement to care flows directly from the parent/child relationship. Tasa, age sixty-five, describes this process of socialization: "When a child is born you teach that child to care for their parents throughout the time the child is growing up so that when the child is older he/she will willingly care for his/her parents. But if that child has a crippled heart, is a person with no sense, that will come from inside her/him and she/he will neglect the parents." As Tasa pointed out, childrearing techniques provide no guarantee of filial caregiving performance. Many of our informants felt that, ultimately, nothing could be done to compel a child with "no sense" to act appropriately.

Others, however, argued that direct sanctions from the spirit world would occur in cases of filial negligence. According to Gai Koma, fear of ancestors underlies elders' entitlement to care. "We feel under an obligation [to care for our parents] because they brought us up. We've drained all their energies. After they die, we would be left with bad luck if we had not cared for them. We could fall ill."

Many concur that there is a link between elder care and the role of *gangwasi* (the ghosts of ancestors), but the relationship between the two worlds is not clear cut. *Gangwasi* have both a punitive side and a charitable side. These ambiguities are explored in the following exchange with Tsau.

Question: What happens if you don't care for an old person?

Tsau: Take your mother. She nursed you. She looked after you, and when she gets old, if you don't look after her, her heart gets very sad, and that's what kills her. It works like this, if you are neglected and your child is not paying attention to you and your heart is sad, you die and when you are a ghost you will return and kill the child.

Question: Why would a mother or a father ghost do this to a child?

Tsau: Yes, some of the *gangwasi* spare their children but others. . . their heart is so saddened that they take the child.

Gumi Na inside her house with her daughter Sagai at her side.

Question: Is it love or hatred that makes the ghost take the child to the village of the dead?

Tsau: Yes, sometimes, the father ghost wants to kill the child and the mother ghost wants to spare the child. The healers see the struggle. If the child lives, then the one who loved the child has won.

The *gangwasi* are not interested solely in elder care but in all phases of human interaction, and their messages to the living are remarkably contradictory. They visit misfortune and sickness on the living to punish, but they also "long for" the living and wish to take them with them to the villages of the dead simply because they are lonely for their loved ones (Lee 1984:107–9). Thus the reasons for a caregiver's illness or death may be explained either by negligence or devotion; their poor performance may have provoked ancestral anger, or their good deeds may have unleashed yearnings among the *gangwasi* to be reunited with their loved one. This ambiguity about motives of the *gangwasi* ultimately lodges the obligation for caregiving in the land of the living.

THE SOCIAL ORGANIZATION OF CAREGIVING

Caregiving is normatively described as being the responsiblity of all adult children. All but one informant said that the responsiblity should be shared equally among all the children.[20] No elder thought the responsiblity was linked to gender or that daughters should be or were doing more than sons. According to Nahka, a women with many children and grandchildren, feminization of caregiving is not a social norm. "In my household, both my sons and daughters help me. The care they give balances so that I see no difference. I don't think girls are more caring than boys. [Is this the same for others at Dobe?] Yes. I give the example of Nai, who has no daughters, but the care that her sons give her is of the same quality as that which I get from my children."

Most caregivers subscribed to this version, but a few women felt they were doing more than men. Gumi's daughter, Sagai, was particularly angry with her !Kung brother, Toma, and fought with him about his lack of attention to their mother. On the other hand, Toma felt that his sister had not been sufficiently attentive when their father was ill and dying.

For our informants it was not gender which divided the population between active caregivers and delinquents but rather a personal quality or quirk. A !Kung elder noted: "If you have a child and that child has a good heart, regardless of whether he/she is male or female, he/she will look after their parent." Nothing can be done to force a child to be a good caregiver. If a child fails to do his/her duty, then others will pitch in, especially if the old person has no children. The situation of Chwa is illustrative.

Chwa was in her late eighties at the time of the interview, had poor eyesight, good hearing, and could still walk. She had no children and lived with her co-wife, Bau, and their husband, both of whom were in their early eighties.[21]

Throughout our discussion, neighbors dropped by with food and water. Chwa entered a conversation which compared past caregiving of the elderly to the current situation. One of her neighbors commented that she had never heard of elders being left in the bush in the past. Chwa stated that she had "heard of people carrying those who were sick on their backs from village to village," but "today, people do not look after the old sufficiently." Two of her neighbors immediately disagreed and took turns affirming that the young do *nabe nabe*, care for, the old.

Chwa, however was adamant. She pointed out that her nephew, Tsau, was derelict in his duty. (Tsau is her brother's son, a man of about sixty, married and living at another village.) "He wants to," she went on, "but his wife won't let him. But those who do take care of me are this Nisa here [an elderly neighbor] and that woman there, my co-wife [Bau], while our husband tends the cattle."[22]

She then proceeded to recount this positive description of care, one of the very few that I had ever heard from an elder. "Once, when I was very sick, I was burning with fever, she [Nisa] poured water on me, and then she held me in her arms. These women, Nisa, Tankae [an elderly neighbor], and my co-wife cared for me. I slept in their arms. This happened this summer, when the *karu* [wild onions] came out of the ground and the grewia berries were already on the bushes [February-March]. My heart craved bush food, and these women collected it for me." One of the caregivers explained further: "We collected the grewia berries; we sold it to the school people [parents who had children at Xai Xai school and couldn't easily go gathering]. And then we bought sugar and tobacco for this old one." I asked, "What made you think of doing that?" And Bau, Chwa's co-wife, using her hands for emphasis, responded: "What is there to think about? You see an old person. She is your person. She can't walk. She can't do it for herself, so you do it."

Thus, although Chwa has no children of her own she was firmly anchored in a responsive caregiving network. She also felt it her right to demand caregiving from her nephew, even though he had other obligations elsewhere.[23] She dismissed this situation of competing caregiving responsiblities by claiming that it was the nephew's wife who prevented him from doing his duty. From her perspective, he still had a duty to her. He, on the other hand, asserted that she was being looked after by "her people" or *zhu*.

In both cases, the terms "person" and "people" are important in understanding the embedded nature of caregiving. It is often used to designate participation in a group who live together and are said to be attached by kinship relationships. These kin ties, however, can be quite distant as in the case of Chwa's network. Chwa's neighbor, Nisa, calls Chwa an elder sister although they have a very remote kinship connection. She and other caregivers use the language of *zhu* to express an affiliation which incorporates a mixture of sentiment based on ethnicity and residential proximity and is expressed in quasi-kinship terms.

The caregiving role for someone who is "your person" is naturalized, i
something that a person doesn't think about and interestingly enough it is not
feminized.[24] Caregiving is explained as a quality of human, not female, nature.
We have observed male and female carers providing food, firewood, and water,
although the foods may represent a gendered division of labor, with men hunting
and women gathering. Government drought relief food will be carried to elders
who cannot manage to go to the relief trucks themselves by any of "their people."
Both men and women also care in other ways. Massage is an important service
rendered by carers. Both men and women will gather the plants and nuts used
to prepare the ointments that are used during massage. Women are more likely
to provide other, smaller services for female elders, like grooming hair, but both
men and women spend time visiting, talking, and drinking tea with elders.

In the delicate area of toileting old people, there did seem to be a gender link.
Male caregivers would take responsiblity for guiding male elders in and out of
the bush, and female caregivers would look after the needs of women elders.

Children, regardless of sex, were enlisted in caregiving as well. Sometimes the
special relationship of grandparent/grandchild was used to mobilize care. This
relationship is quite expandable into an inclusive kinship mode, which draws in
distant kin. Elders, for example, may invoke the "name" relationship so that
children with the same name as the old person will be regarded as grandchildren
and available to perform services like fetching water, if they are willing.[25]

The web of caregiving thus moves well beyond the limited confines of the
nuclear family.[26] It is located in kinship/community ideology; it is not sentimentalized as a form of self-sacrifice.[27] The web of obligations is also so far-reaching
that there are always those who will be denounced as delinquent carers. Kushe,
the wife of Tsau, for example, had left her eighty-one-year-old mother, Chuko,
in Dobe to be with her son at a health clinic in another village. The mother's
caregivers (her *zhu*) complained about the daughter's absence, even though
Chuko was in good health and was able to gather and fetch water on her own.
Said one caregiver: "My heart [wants to care for Chuko]. We've seen that the
old woman has no more work [in her] and that she's in trouble. Her daughter
left her and went to live somewhere else. What kind of terrible thing is that?
What's wrong with her that she is so terrible? Her mother's old and she doesn't
take care of her! Nahka [a caregiver] and I said this to each other."[28]

This caregiver was herself a long way from Dobe when she made these
remarks and was planning to be absent for several weeks. She also knew that
the reason for Kushe's absence was that she was staying with her sick son at a
health post, but Nisa could not resist making these charges of neglect.

!Kung elders are independent and autonomous (as are all members of the
community) in the sense that can do what they wish when they wish. Able-bodied
elders forage, fetch water, visit, trade gifts, make crafts, dance, sleep, and eat
whenever they choose. They live wherever they choose and do not face fears of
pauperization with old age or the struggles of living on a "fixed income." Their
old age is not filled with anxieties about personal security: they have no fears

about interpersonal violence, robbery, or abuse. They do not lock themselves in their houses at night. Like the "advantaged" elders in a North American study of income levels and aging, they show few signs of depression (Hillebrant 1980). Their discourse is not filled with talk of the "agony of loneliness" (Hillebrant 1980:408) but rather complaints and jokes about the shortcomings of others.

Frail elders are also enmeshed in a web of caregiving. The eight frail elders we interviewed had between four and eight people looking after them, for a total of forty-four people undertaking frontline elder care responsiblities.

Even those who are extremely weak are not segregated from the social landscape. We observed a situation in which Dau, a very sick !Kung man, who slept almost all the time, was placed in the center of social life. Around him gathered family and neighbors who chatted, smoked, and cooked together. Nearby his son hacked up the carcass of a kudu, and the old man's wife, Koka, stirred the cooking pot, children played, and an infant nursed. As the meat cooked, his wife lifted his head every few minutes and fed him a morsel of food. He chewed silently, his eyes shut. When he was done, he rested his head back on the blanket. In the meantime, his wife chatted with those at the fire. Both the old man and his caregivers were rooted in a social matrix which undoubtedly eased the burden of care and perhaps enhanced the quality of this very frail person's last days.

CONCLUSION: THE PARADOX OF SHARING AND COMPLAINING

By North American standards the social circumstances of !Kung elders in Botswana today appear to be quite positive.[29] They have personal autonomy, respect, and a great deal of control over the immediate circumstances of their lives. They live in a culture which strongly values caregiving and support. Old people participate in social, political, economic, and spiritual life. They may regret growing old – and ask someone to pull out the first few grey hairs – but they are also equipped with rich cultural resources for articulating their concerns, fears, and anxieties and for ensuring support.

Yet the !Kung complain all the time. They are cranky, funny, and loud. They live in a moral universe of high caregiving standards, in which the ideal seems to be that every person is directly obligated to meet the needs of every other person all the time. But since such a perfect world is impossible to obtain, they find ample justification for their complaints of inadequate caregiving. Furthermore, personal preferences, personality conflicts, old unresolved grievances also enter into the caregiving equation, making it far from an ideal universe. There is always someone who is not doing enough. And there is always someone ready to denounce that person in terms which are not at all pleasant or polite.

On the normative side, the cultural forms which reproduce respect and care for elders through complaint discourse reflect deep patterns in !Kung culture.[30] Boasting or displays of pride are strongly discouraged. One should not recount good deeds or boast about generous gifts to others. Hunters are self-effacing and downplay their skills and the quality of the animals they have killed. Intense social pressure is brought to bear on those with tendencies towards self-aggrandizement. The !Kung fear arrogance for they believe that it leads to violence and will use insult and ridicule to "cool the heart" of those who boast (Lee 1969).[31] There is no !Kung word for "please," and the term for "thank you" is rarely heard in conversation. People share food, firewood, water, and social and spiritual support as a matter of daily intercourse. They give with an expectation that they will inevitably get; they receive with an understanding that they will inevitably give.[32] The motivation to share is reinforced not by an etiquette of polite phrases but by ". . . rough humour, back-handed compliments, put-downs and damning with faint praise" (Lee 1979:458). The !Kung are competitive in only one area — complaining. And it is hardly surprising that elders are so good at it, they have been practicing their whole lives.

These discourses have not abruptly unraveled with changes in material culture like the appearance of transistor radios, cassette tape players, and bicycles. In other words, cultural formations are resilient, and, contrary to the highly romanticized myth presented in the South African film *The Gods Must Be Crazy*, the world is not turned upside down by the introduction of a minor artifact of Western society. The !Kung of Botswana drink soda pop and still conduct trance dances, complain about those who do not share, and care for their elders.

Of more far-reaching significance for !Kung society in general and elder care in particular are the major infrastructural transformations in subsistence patterns; in integration into state educational, legal, and medical systems; in the outcome of the war in Namibia; and in the role that tuberculosis and alcohol consumption play in the region. The pushes and pulls of these new elements in the !Kung world create challenges and consequences that are unpredictable. For the time being the !Kung are meeting these challenges with a powerful cultural formation of sharing/complaining — one that can still produce the following discourse: "Here are words about caring for an old person. Words like if a person is old, you take care of her. You put your heart into it and scold others, saying, 'Don't you see this person is old? Take care of her today, you take care of her today. Do you say she has strength? She has no strength. Now you put your heart into her.' That's what you say to another person. You're telling him to put his heart into an old person. That's what you say. That's another piece of speech. Now I'm finished."[33]

NOTES

The field research upon which this chapter is based was carried on in Botswana between May and July 1986 and January and August 1987. The "we" used here refers to a team of investigators, research asssistants, and translators. The investigators included Richard B. Lee, who interviewed in the !Kung language, Meg Luxton, and Harriet Rosenberg, who used translators. We gratefully acknowledge the assistance of Nandi Ngcongco, Dorothy Molokome, and Leonard Ramatakwame of the University of Botswana; Makgolo Makgolo, M. A., of Gaborone; and Gakekgoshe Isaaka and Gai Koma of the Dobe region. In addition, Megan Biesele consulted with this project. We thank her for the careful translation/transcriptions she made of interviews she conducted in the !Kung language in Namibia.

The investigators wish to thank the Social Sciences and Humanities Research Council of Canada for providing funding for this project, "Aging, Caregiving and Social Change in an African Population," file number 410–84–1298.

A version of this chapter was presented to the International Congress of Anthropological and Ethnological Sciences, Zagreb, Yugoslavia, July 24–31, 1988. I would like to thank Christine Gailey and Richard Lee for their insightful comments.

1. The !Kung have no written language. Their language contains popping and clicking sounds which are unique to the Khoisan and neighboring languages of southern and eastern Africa. In addition !Kung contains glottal stops and nasalisations. Anthropologists, in committing their words to writing, have developed an orthography to approximate a rendering of these sounds in English. The !Kung language is characterized by four major clicks:

/   dental click, as in the woman's name /Twa. In spoken English this sounds like the mild reproach "tsk, tsk". The name /Twa is rendered in the text as Twa.

\   alveolar click, as in the man's name \Toma. No English equivalent.

!   alveopalatal click as in !Kung. No English equivalent.

//   lateral click, as in the woman's name //Koka. In spoken English this sound exists in some dialects to urge on a horse.

The word *zhu* is nasalized.

2. Influences from Herero practices have been observed among the !Kung. The issue of burial practices is discussed in note 16.

3. By foraging I mean a mode of subsistence entirely based on wild food sources, without agriculture or domesticated animals, except for the dog.

4. See, for example, the works by Marshall (1976); Lee (1979, 1984); Shostak (1981); Katz (1982); Howell (1979); Biesele (in press). Lee and Devore (1976) contains summaries of a number of studies.

5. See Katz (1982); Katz and Biesele (1986).

6. *Hxaro* is a gift exchange system for "circulating goods, lubricating social relations, and maintaining ecological balance" (Lee 1984:97). Receiving *hxaro* implies that you will also give it. See also Wiessner (1977).

7. See John Marshall's film, *Nai, the Story of a !Kung Woman*, for a vivid depiction of the effects of militarization on the !Kung of Namibia.

8. Since the !Kung are beginning to acquire property, they are now faced with the question of inheritance. Most informants claim that the expectation of an inheritance is not a factor in the quality of elder care. Some say that it does make a difference in Herero and Tswana communities, where sons might direct witchcraft against an aged father who wished to remarry.

9. Fieldwork was conducted at the three main villages of Dobe, Xai Xai, and !Kangwa and to a lesser extent in the smaller villages of Mahopa and Goshe. The 1986 population of !Kung in the region was 663, of whom 83 people were sixty or older. The research team interviewed 90 percent of the elders and about thirty caregivers.

10. A notable exception is Biesele and Howell (1981).

11. The !Kung themselves do not mark chronological age. The ages used in this chapter represent estimates make by the demographer Nancy Howell during field work in 1968 (Howell 1979) and revisions made according to census updates by Lee during field trips in 1973, 1983, and 1986–87.

12. In 1967–68, Truswell and Hansen (1976) conducted a health survey of the region. They found !Kung elders to be remarkably fit and not suffering from high blood pressure or other stress-related illnesses.

13. We divided the elderly into five categories of functionality: one was the most fit, and five represented those who were completely dependent. "Frail" refers to those in categories four and five, about twelve people.

14. The third person singular is not gendered in !Kung. Thus the English terms "his/her" and "she/he" are used in the text to translate the !Kung speaker's usage. While he/she may seem awkward to some English speakers, it is consistent with the !Kung language which does not distinguish between male and female in the third person singular, just as English does not in the third person plural "they," but French does in the forms "ils/elles."

15. In analyzing abandonment in foraging societies, it would be useful to distinguish between those in which gathering dominates and those in which hunting dominates, as well as to look at climate. I suspect that one would find a difference between Inuit and Chipewyan on the one hand and !Kung and Mbuti Pygmy on the other, which would be linked to issues of ease of subsistence and gender roles.

16. Acculturation to Herero beliefs about death and burial seem to have influenced !Kung perceptions about death and abandonment. The !Kung way has been to collapse the hut around the person who has died in camp or to dig a shallow grave and leave it unmarked if someone dies on the trail. The Herero, by contrast, have elaborate funerary rituals (Vivelo 1977:127–29) and are particularly offended by !Kung casualness in grave marking. In some discussions with the !Kung, it seemed as if their own funeral customs were now being viewed through the Herero perspective and that statements about the abandonment of the elderly might in fact be referencing "improper burials."

Suicide among the elderly was treated by informants as a rather incomprehensible notion. When we asked if they had heard of an elder saying that he or she was too tired to go on and just wanted to be left to die, we were treated with quizzical looks. "No, I've never heard of that. They [elders] just follow the rest when it's time to leave [move camp] and go with them. They stay with their people."

17. Nor have children been viewed as economic burdens. Until quite recently, children did not participate in subsistence activities until their teens. With settlement and the acquisition of goats and cattle, children now do more work.

18. Old women among the !Kung are thus quite different from the passive "Dear Old Grans" described as commonplace among old women in a long-term geriatric ward "who cheerfully surrender [their] autonomy" and "potential to challenge" (Evers 1981:119–20).

19. See note 6.

20. She said that it was the duty of the first born, "the one who cracked your bones," to look after an aging parent.

21. Polygyny occurs in about 5 percent of marriages among the !Kung. In most socially sanctioned forms, men will take two wives, although cases of more than two have been reported historically. Occasionally, irregular polyandrous unions have also been reported.

22. Later in the conversation Chwa also mentioned a third caregiver who was also very old, a woman who is in fact even older than Chwa. Tankae also acts as a caregiver to her teenage granddaughter who has physical handicaps and has recently been diagnosed as having epilepsy.

23. The nephew, Tsau, lived with his wife and elderly mother-in-law and was preoccupied with caregiving for his adult son and his family while the son was being treated for tuberculosis.

24. In Western societies, where elder care is predominantly done by unwaged women workers in the household and women in the waged workforce, expressing the experience of caregiving in ungendered language poses a problem (Finch and Groves 1983). For example, a young man, in trying to articulate his experience in caring for his lover with AIDS, found that "the closest model with which to compare my seven months with Paul is the experience of mothering. (My mother brought this home to me. . . .) By this analogy I mean the cluster of activities, characteristics, and emotions associated with the *social role* of motherhood. Whether performed by women or men, mothering—and its analogue within the health care system, nursing—involves intimate physical care of another being, the provision of unconditional care and love, the subordination of self to others, and an investment in separation" (Interrante 1987:57–58).

In this context, only the gendered term, "mothering," was found to be able to convey the intensity of commitment Interrante had felt. Interestingly, his insight is substantiated by a footnote referencing three feminist theoreticians—Dinnerstein, Chowdorow, and Eherensaft—all of whom have analyzed the social construction of female caregiving. Mothering carries with it the meanings of long-term unconditional support. "Mothers" are people who do not abandon no matter how demanding the circumstances become. Mothering is thus not only a feminized metaphor for caregiving, it is also highly idealized and sentimentalized.

25. Draper (1976) and Shostak (1981) have pointed out that children are raised in a very nonauthoritarian manner and are not normally expected to do work or do anything for adults that they do not want to do. Even today, with settlement, most parents say that they cannot make children perform work if the children refuse. Children are not seen to owe any special deference to elders.

26. Gubrium (1987b:31–35) describes the conflict which follows an elder's creation of a caregiving network that is perceived to be competing with the rightful caregivers—the adult children. Maida, the old person in question, is described as rejecting her "own" children, whom she has accused of not being her "real" children because they have placed her in a nursing home against her wishes. Maida formed close bonds with a small group of coresidents who have constituted themselves as a "family" including the designated roles of "baby" and "grandma." Both Maida's children and the health professionals identified this alternate caring network as a "problem." The mother's actions were interpreted by the children as a repudiation and described as a sign of mental confusion. The health workers found the group to be cliqueish and divisive to equitable caring on the floor. Thus Maida's stepping outside the discourse of filial caregiving was construed as a contentious and threatening counterdiscourse.

27. Self-sacrifice is not always considered admirable in caregivers in the North American context. Gubrium's 1987b account of a support group for the families of Alzheimer patients reveals a strong counterdiscourse to expressions of wifely devotion. Caregivers are warned not to burn themselves out and to be "realistic" when assessing the burdens of caregiving. One pointed expression of this counterdiscourse was: "Dear, you're not an old man's lover; you're an old man's slave" (p. 31).

28. From Megan Biesele's 1987 transcript of an interview conducted with Nisa at Gausha, Namibia.

29. Their material conditions are far from ideal.

30. It may seem contradictory to argue that elders are respected and well cared for in a work that also discusses senilicide. Here we can draw a parallel to !Kung non-authoritarian childrearing techniques (Draper 1976; Shostak 1981) and the occasional practice of infanticide. The !Kung do not beat their children and, like most foraging people, are extremely indulgent toward their children. But they have also practiced infanticide if twins were born or if a child was born with deformities that would make it difficult for it to survive nomadic life.

31. See also Lee's discussion of violence and homicide in chapter 13 of *The !Kung San* (1979). He found material on twenty-two cases of homicide and fifteen woundings among the !Kung between 1920 and 1969.

32. This pattern of generalized reciprocity is almost universal among foraging peoples (Sahlins 1965, 1972).

33. From transcript of Megan Biesele interview with Nisa in 1987, Gausha, Namibia.

2 BY ANY OTHER NAME, IT IS STILL KILLING: A COMPARISON OF THE TREATMENT OF THE ELDERLY IN AMERICA AND OTHER SOCIETIES

Anthony P. Glascock

The killing of the decrepit/frail elderly, terminally ill individuals, and seriously deformed newborn infants is an issue which has received increasing attention in the last few years. Medical technology now enables people, who only a few years ago would have died relatively quickly, to be kept alive, often longer than the individual or the family desires. Thus, we, as a society, are faced with ethical questions which we are generally reluctant to think about or to discuss until they affect us directly. Then we turn to medical, legal, religious, and philosophical experts in an attempt to reach a decision, but the opinions of these experts are made more difficult by the uncertainties in the law.

Much of this discussion is taking place with the implied assumption that we are the first society which has had to face this dilemma. Emphasis is placed on the advances in medical technology which allow for the prolongation of life beyond anything that has existed in any other society at any other point in time. Experts argue that this medical technology makes our situation unique, and, consequently, we must struggle with these questions without the benefit of comparative data from other societies. This assumption is simply incorrect since people in other societies have also had to face the dilemma of how much effort should be used to cure a person's illness and to prolong the lives of people who are dying. The following discussion is based on the proposition that there are similarities between euthanasia and death-accelerating behavior directed toward the elderly in American society and death-hastening behavior directed toward decrepit old people in many nonindustrial societies. Additionally, the ethical, moral, and legal uncertainties that surround these issues are not unique to American society; people in other societies have had to struggle with them just as we have. Therefore, it is useful to observe how people in less sociopolitically complex societies deal with these issues and to compare their solutions to ours.

AMERICAN SOCIETY

Examples of death-accelerating behavior and euthanasia are becoming abundant in American society. Many of these examples show the contradictions that exist as Americans attempt to reach a consensus as to what behavior is the most appropriate for the decrepit elderly. Perhaps the example which received the widest coverage in 1985 was Roswell Gilbert, a seventy-six-year-old Florida man who shot and killed his seventy-three-year-old wife who was suffering from Alzheimer's and osteoporosis. Gilbert was sentenced to twenty-five years to life for murder, even though an outcry was raised by a wide range of supporters and sympathizers. While Gilbert was sent to jail, two other men who violently killed close relatives went free. In the same courthouse in which Gilbert was sentenced, a seventy-nine-year-old man who shot and killed his wife, also suffering from Alzheimer's, was not even indicted for a crime. In Texas a sixty-nine-year-old man who killed his seventy-two-year-old brother in a nursing home was sentenced to ten years probation rather than prison (*Time*, May 27, 1985:66–67).

Thus, one perpetrator of active euthanasia is sentenced to prison, one is put on probation, and one is not even tried in a court of law. Obviously, there is no societywide agreement as to the appropriate behavior for the treatment of decrepit loved ones. Examples of this societal confusion, however, exist outside the family: How are our health professionals to treat the decrepit elderly? In particular, should hospitals be required to force-feed dying elderly patients and postpone their deaths?

The New York Supreme Court ruled in 1984 that "a nursing home should not force-feed an 85-year-old patient who was in poor health and had been fasting." The court decided that the man was "entitled to die of his own will [and] that the nursing home was not obliged to force-feed the man" (Hirsh 1985:9). In New Jersey, in contrast, an appellate court ruled that a hospital could not remove the nasogastric tube of an eighty-four-year-old man who wanted to die, and in California a hospitalized woman was prevented, through force-feeding, from starving herself to death (Hirsh 1985:10).

The contradictions are also present at the individual level. Angela Holder, writing in *Medical Economics*, advises physicians how to properly write "Do Not Resuscitate" (DNR) orders so that lawsuits are avoided. She suggests that the orders be explicit and that the family members and the patient be consulted, but the results of DNR orders are that elderly patients are allowed to die when they could technically be kept alive. However, some physicians will not write DNR orders under any conditions, while other members of the medical team often find this cruel. A California nurse, Barbara Huttmann, decided on her own that a terminally ill patient should not be resuscitated and has been accused of murder by some and proclaimed a hero by others (Huttmann 1983:15). Even when a conscious decision to let a person die has not been made, subconscious emotions apparently structure the behavior of the medical personnel in such a way as to lead to the accelerated death of the elderly (Watson 1976:115–17).

The publicity surrounding many of these cases has at least led to a more open discussion of euthanasia and death-accelerating behavior within American society. We have reached a stage where a governor, Richard Lamm of Colorado, and an ex-senator, Jacob Javits of New York, can publicly discuss the costs associated with the medical care of the terminally ill elderly, the "duty to die," and "death with dignity." Although denying that they support "mercy killing," both men have called for a national debate on these topics and the development of national legislation which would "allow" the elderly to die when they desired (*Time*, April 9, 1984:68; Krieger 1985:13–14). Also, in an attempt to create a national consensus, the President's Commission for the Study of Ethical Problems in Medicine concluded in 1983 that "hospitals should honor the wishes of patients who do not want to undergo life-sustaining treatments [and] when a patient is unconscious or incompetent to decide his family should be permitted to decide" (*American Medical News*, April 1, 1983:6–8). Yet, the debate continues and no general agreement has been reached.

Euthanasia, whether active or passive, whether defined as withdrawing or withholding treatment, whether based on not starting treatment or stopping treatment, is a topic of concern to a growing number of people both inside and outside the medical professions. This concern has led some individuals to argue that euthanasia, or other death-accelerating behavior, once accepted for some elderly terminally ill individuals who want to die, will become a solution for a series of growing societal problems. In particular, it is argued that euthanasia can be viewed as a solution to rising health costs. This argument is based on the fact that the elderly consume costly amounts of health care as they approach the end of life, and, thus, a health care system that would give "food and tender loving care for the elderly" and little else would save much money and avoid the stresses that appear to lead to other forms of death-accelerating behavior (Golin 1985:4).

One such potentially death-accelerating behavior is elder abuse, which usually takes one of three forms. Physical abuse includes violent acts against the older person as well as extreme neglect and the denial of medical treatment which leads to bodily harm. Financial abuse includes theft or the misappropriation of an older person's valuable property, and psychological abuse is really the dehumanizing of the older person to the point where his or her life is threatened. An extensive study of this behavior conducted by the staff of the House Select Committee on Aging indicated that approximately 4 percent of the nation's elderly, over one million individuals, were subjected to some form of elder abuse (Pepper 1986:24). Since only one of five cases of elder abuse is reported to the appropriate authorities, the extent of the problem is much greater than the study indicates. The victims of elder abuse are usually women over the age of seventy-five who are dependent on others for care. The most common abuser is a son or daughter who is experiencing great stress connected with the care of the older parent and who experienced abuse as a child. There are no easy answers to the question of why elderly individuals are abused, but one can anticipate that the problem will grow as the number of the oldest old, those most dependent upon others for care, increases over the next three decades.

This increase will also necessitate the continued reliance on long-term care facilities. At any point in time, fewer than 5 percent of the nation's elderly are in nursing homes, but the subject of long-term care has preoccupied gerontologists and the general public alike. Horror stories abound concerning the physical and mental abuse of nursing home inhabitants, and the question of whether such institutions accelerate death has been asked for over twenty years. Even though nursing homes are among the most regulated businesses in America, abuse does exist, and certainly in some instances death is either deliberately or accidentally accelerated (Watson 1976; Kayser-Jones 1981; Vesperi 1987).

Regardless of one's own views on the subject, the elderly are definitely killed by various direct and indirect means in American society. The question that an anthropologist must ask when presented with such a fact is, Does such behavior exist in other societies? Further, if such behavior exists, Who is killed? Why are they killed? Who decides that they are to be killed? Who kills them and how? In what types of society are old people most likely to be killed? and finally, How does the behavior found in other societies compare to that which is present in American society? The remainder of this chapter will attempt to answer these questions.

NONINDUSTRIAL SOCIETIES

Methodology

Much anecdotal information is available concerning the killing of the elderly in nonindustrial societies. Almost everyone has heard stories about the old Eskimo woman who is set adrift on an ice floe or the elderly man left behind by his group when he is no longer able to walk. Unfortunately, little beyond this type of isolated, noncomparative data has been available to provide answers for the questions raised above concerning death-hastening behavior in less advanced societies. There have been several notable exceptions to the general lack of systematic analysis of the elderly in nonindustrial societies (Simmons 1945, 1960; Silverman and Maxwell 1978; Maxwell et al. 1982). Although concerned with the status and role of the elderly, these studies are only tangentially concerned with the parameters and causation of the killing of old people.

In order to provide answers to the questions surrounding death-hastening behavior, a study was undertaken which focused specifically on nonsupportive behavior directed toward the elderly. The study employed hologistic analysis, which "is a research design for statistically measuring the relationship between two or more theoretically defined and operationalized variables in a world sample of human societies" (Rohner et al. 1978). The research relied on data drawn from the Human Relations Area Files and utilized Raoul Naroll's HRAF

Probability Sample Files (PSF), which consist of sixty nonindustrial societies (Naroll et al. 1976). For a more complete discussion of the methodology employed, please refer to Glascock and Feinman (1980, 1981).

Definitions

The first finding of the study was that killing, often termed gerontocide or gericide in the literature, was too narrow a concept to employ to describe the behavior directed toward the elderly in nonindustrial societies. A broader concept, death hastening, which includes killing, abandoning, and forsaking of the elderly and is defined as nonsupportive treatment that leads directly to the death of aged individuals, was used. Four brief examples from the literature analyzed illustrate the type of data found in the Human Relations Area Files and the scope of the death-hastening concept.

Killing

Chukchee — reindeer herding people who speak a Paleo-Siberian language and live in northeastern Siberia, principally on the Chukotsk Peninsula.

> Few old Chuchi die a natural death. When an old person takes ill and becomes a burden to his surroundings he or she asks one of the nearest relatives to be killed. The oldest son or daughter or son-in-law stabs the old one in the heart with a knife. (Sverdrup 1938:133)

Abandoning

Lau — a horticultural and fishing people who speak a Malayo-Polynesian language and live in the Lau Islands off southern Fiji in the central Pacific Ocean.

> Informants on Fulanga said that when the *tui naro* (headman) of the Vandra-vandra clan became old and feeble he was taken to Taluma Islet in the lagoon and abandoned.... There is a cave filled with skeletal remains of old people who died there after having left the community. (Thompson 1940:102)

Forsaking—Denial of Food

Bororo — a horticultural people who speak a Ge language and live in the Amazonian forest of Central Brazil.

> It is the same for the old people; after a hunt or successful fishing trip, they are brought a piece of meat or a few fish. But also they sometimes are forgotten. The indigent person is then reduced to going without a meal and all night long, alone, utters ritual lamentations. (Lévi-Strauss 1936:276)

Forsaking—Denial of All Support

Yakut — Yak herders who speak a Turkic language and live in north-central Siberia in the Soviet Union.

> The position of older people who were decrepit and no longer able to work was also difficult. Little care was shown for them, they were given little to eat and were poorly clothed, sometimes even reduced to complete destitution. (Tokarev and Gurvich 1964:277) [A]ged people are not in favor; they are beaten by their own children and are often forced to leave their dwellings and to beg from house to house. (Jochelson 1933:134)

Each of these behaviors leads directly to the death of the elderly within the particular society. The example of killing is self-evident: the elderly are not left to die but are rather dispatched directly by members of the social group. The abandoning example is also fairly clear-cut. The data concerning the abandoning of the elderly ranged from the above description, in which the elderly are physically removed from a permanent community, to societal members leaving the elderly behind as the group moves to a different location. The two examples of forsaking behavior given show some of the range of this behavior. Forsaking is the broadest of the three behaviors and includes the denial of sufficient food, medical care, clothing, and shelter.

These behaviors contrast with supportive treatment, which is defined as the active support of the elderly including the provision of food, shelter, medical care, and transportation. Supportive treatment is more than the expression of deference or respect and must be accompanied by tangible actions that aid in the survival of the elderly individual. Behavior that falls between supportive and death hastening is, for the present study, defined as nonsupportive, nonthreatening behavior and includes such behavior as insulting the elderly, requiring them to give up certain property, and removing them from their normal residence. These behaviors can be unpleasant and may even have long-term detrimental effects on the well-being of the old person, but they do not directly threaten his or her life. Thus, nonthreatening behavior can be viewed as transitional between supportive and death hastening and may eventually lead to death.

A definitional problem was raised by the type of data analyzed: How is elder suicide to be categorized? If an old person asks his sons to kill him, if an old woman wanders away from camp in order to die, or if an elderly individual gives away all of his or her possessions and then wanders from village to village, eventually to die of neglect and exposure, are these examples of suicide rather than death hastening? To avoid the development of numerous coding categories which would prove too difficult and confusing to employ, the decision was made to include such behavior in the existing categories of killing, abandoning, and forsaking. The issue as to who initiates the death-hastening behavior is considered as each of the particular categories is discussed.

Table 2.1
Treatments In Nonindustrial Societies

Treatment	Number of Societies	Percent
Only Support	12	29
Support and Nonthreatening	4	10
Only Nonthreatening	4	10
Only Death Hastening	6	14
Death Hastening and Nonthreatening	4	10
Death Hastening and Support	11	27
Total	41	100

Findings

Data concerning the treatment of the elderly were available for forty-one of the sixty societies in the Probability Sample Files. In twenty-one of these societies, at least one type of death-hastening behavior was present (see Table 2.1). Examining the data more closely, ten societies have a single form of death-hastening behavior, while in eleven societies there is a combination of behaviors (see Table 2.2). Killing is the most frequent means of hastening the death of old people; it occurs in fourteen of the twenty-one societies. Forsaking is found in nine of the societies, and old people are abandoned in eight societies. The most frequent combination of behaviors is to both kill and abandon the elderly within the same social group — five instances. A combination of forsaking and killing is present in four societies, and forsaking and abandoning are present in only a single society.

Importantly, in all but one society in which multiple forms of death-hastening occur, supportive or nonthreatening treatment is also found. The most common pattern is for the killing, forsaking, and abandoning to be present with supportive treatment. Intuitively, it would appear to be emotionally, cognitively, and behaviorally inconsistent for such extremes of treatment — killing and support — to be present in the same society. This is resolved by answering the questions, Who is to be supported? Who is to be denied food? Who is to be killed? A cultural contradiction is apparently avoided simply by directing different treatments toward different categories of the elderly within a given society. The criteria upon which this differentiation is based are complex and will be discussed in detail in the analysis/discussion section.

The data on death hastening provided additional details concerning the forsaking and killing of the elderly. In five of the nine societies in which old people are forsaken, there is total nonsupport. The elderly are denied food,

Table 2.2
Societies With Death Hastening

Death Hastening Alone (N = 6)

Bororo (Forsake)

Chukchee (Kill)

Copper Eskimo (Abandon)

Lau (Abandon)

Mundurucu (Kill)

Truk (Forsake & Kill)

Death Hastening and Nonthreatening (N = 4)

Aymara (Kill)

Dogon (Forsake & Abandon)

Lozi (Forsake & Abandon)

Yakut (Forsake & Kill)

Death Hastening and Support (N = 11)

Amhara (Forsake)

Aranda (Forsake & Kili)

Cagaba (Forsake & Kill)

Iroquois (Abandon & Kill)

Klamath (Forsake)

Lapps (Abandon & Kill)

Ojibwa (Kill)

Pawnee (Abandon & Kill)

Pygmies (Abandon & Kill)

Serbia (Kill)

Yanoama (Abandon & Kill)

shelter, and treatment for illness. Most often, as the previous examples show, the elderly are driven from their homes and forced to either beg or scrounge for food. Interestingly, societies in which the elderly are specifically denied sufficient or "desirable" food tend to be horticultural societies, whereas those that practice total forsaking tend to rely on hunting, fishing, or animal husbandry. The existence of relatively frequent "hunger seasons" in horticultural societies appears to result in the elderly being denied food, or only being provided with foods that are low in nutritional value or not easily chewed and digested (Fortes 1978:9; Ogbu 1973:319–23). Even though these "hunger seasons" appear to occur more frequently than is commonly presumed, it is usually only by chance that a researcher is in a community during a period of a severe food shortage. Thus, the forsaking of the elderly through the denial of sufficient food or the substitution of undesirable food is perhaps under-represented in the available ethnographic literature.

Details concerning the killing of the elderly are largely lacking in the eth-nographic material. An outsider is just not going to easily collect specific information on the killing of societal members—regardless of the age of the people being killed. The available data, though, do indicate several interesting patterns. The elderly are killed violently: beaten to death (three societies), buried alive (three societies), stabbed (two societies), or strangled (one society); and no difference based on sex was uncovered. The decision to kill the elderly individual was made, in all but one instance, within the family. The common procedure was for the children and the elderly individual to decide jointly that the time was "right to die." In two societies the elderly individual appears to decide on his or her own when it is the proper time to die. Among the Yanoama, a South American shifting horticultural society, the decision is removed from the family and placed in the hands of the village leaders. The actual killing of the old person is also a family affair. In six of the seven societies on which data were available, a son, usually the eldest, kills his parent. Once again there is no variation based on sex. Only among the Yanoama is an aged person killed by someone outside the immediate family—a man designated by the village leaders.

Analysis/Discussion

The findings presented above answer three of the main questions posed earlier. The killing of the elderly *does* occur in other societies, and when killing, forsaking, and abandoning are combined into the broad category of death hastening, the elderly are dispatched in 50 percent of the societies with data in the PSF. The sex of the individual does not appear to make a difference, since both males and females have their deaths hastened. Adult children, after consultation with their parents, make the decision, and sons actually carry out the killing. Three questions still remain to be answered: Why are old people killed, forsaken, or abandoned? In what type of societies is death hastening found? How does this behavior compare to the killing of the elderly in our society?

Death hastening is directed toward individuals who have passed from being active and productive to being inactive and nonproductive members of the social group. This transformation of the elderly from intact to decrepit has long been recognized within the anthropological literature, but the connection between it and death-hastening behavior has only recently been systematically analyzed (Rivers 1926; Simmons 1945, 1960; Maxwell et al. 1982; Glascock 1982). Leo Simmons perhaps best described the results associated with the transformation when he stated: "Among all people a point is reached in aging at which any further usefulness appears to be over, and the incumbent is regarded as a living liability. 'Senility' may be a suitable label for this. Other terms among primitive people are the 'overaged,' the 'useless stage,' the 'sleeping period,' the 'age grade of the dying' and the 'already dead' (1960:87). Thus, at least two categories of the elderly exist in nonindustrial societies: "normal old age" (the intact) and the "already dead" (the decrepit). In the most simple terms, it is when people are defined as decrepit that they have their deaths hastened.

In fourteen of the sixteen PSF societies in which a distinction is made between the intact and the decrepit elderly, some form of death-hastening behavior is present. (For a more extensive discussion of the intact/decrepit distinction, see Glascock 1982). In the majority of these cases, both supportive and death-hastening treatments occur. The evidence clearly indicates that the intact elderly are supported and the decrepit elderly are killed, abandoned, or forsaken. This dichotomization of treatments can be most easily seen in several recent ethnographic studies. D. Lee Guemple's research among the Eskimo documents well the change in behavior that accompanies the redefinition of an elderly individual as decrepit as his or her health declines. "They [the aged] suffer a marked reduction in both respect and affection when they are no longer able to make a useful contribution. As they grow older and are increasingly immobilized by age, disease, and the like, they are transformed into neglected dependents without influence and without consideration. In short, old age has become a crisis" (1969:65). At this point, the "practical bent of the Eskimo asserts itself forcefully. To alleviate the burden of infirmity, the old people are done away with" (Guemple 1969:69).

Likewise, Judith Barker (this volume) found, among a population of slash-and-burn horticulturalists living on the western Polynesian island of Niue, that treatment of the intact and decrepit elderly varies significantly. Intact elderly who are in good health are respected within the community and are vital family members and often political leaders. The frail/decrepit Niue elderly, on the other hand, are frequently ignored, ridiculed, and neglected. The key factor for the definition of decrepitude is immobility, combined with a cessation of participation in family and community events. Barker argues that this neglect, which leads to a high incidence of "accidental" death, is not a result of recent modernization. Instead, archival evidence indicates that the variation in the treatment of the elderly is not of recent origin but a pattern of behavior which predates contact with Western societies.

Finally, recent research in New Guinea and its neighboring islands shows the transition from intact to decrepit and the resultant change in behavior. "Van Baal reports that the Marind Amin elderly are respected and well treated as long as they are in good health. When they become helpless and senescent they may be buried alive by their children" (Counts and Counts 1985a:13). Research among the Kaliai of New Britain conducted by Dorothy and David Counts provides an example of an elderly man who, because he was suffering from physical disabilities and declining mental acuity, had, in the eyes of his sons, lived too long. The sons, therefore, conducted final mortuary ceremonies, distributed property, and essentially defined their father as socially dead (Counts and Counts 1985b:145).

Although drawn from widely different societies, the above examples show that death-hastening behavior is directed toward a specific type of elderly individuals — the decrepit who have experienced actual or perceived changes in their health to the degree that they are no longer able to contribute to the well-being of the social group. This inexorable journey is traveled by males and females alike, but there is some evidence in the ethnographic literature that females begin the journey at a slightly later age than males.

Thus, death-hastening behavior is directed toward the decrepit elderly, but is this behavior found equally in all nonindustrial societies? To answer this question a series of variables selected from the *Ethnographic Atlas* were correlated with the killing, forsaking, and abandoning of the elderly. The results indicate that death-hastening tends to be present in societies which (1) are located in areas with harsh climates, in particular, desert and tundra environments, (2) have no horticultural activity or only shifting horticulture in which grain crops predominate, and (3) lack systems of social stratification. Societies which lack death hastening and instead have only supportive treatment tend to (1) be located in areas with temperate climates, (2) have intensive agriculture, (3) have systems of social stratification, and (4) have a belief in active high gods. In other words, death hastening tends to occur in societies which can be characterized as simple — hunting and gathering, pastoral and shifting horticultural — while societies with exclusively supportive treatment are more economically complex — sedentary agricultural.

Although death-hastening behavior tends to be found in more technologically simple societies, it is common for this treatment to be present in conjunction with support of older people and to be directed toward only the decrepit elderly. Likewise, the supportive behavior found in more technologically advanced societies can vary depending upon internal conditions, such as social stratification, residential location, and gender. In many ways it is more desirable to be old in Pygmy society, even if one faces being abandoned and killed, than in some advanced agricultural societies. As long as they are intact, older Pygmies can look forward to respect and supportive treatment, receiving the most desirable foods in an environment that provides abundantly for the general population. In advanced agricultural societies, even though supportive treatment for the elderly is present, it must be put in the context of often harsh environmental and societal conditions; isolated residences, frequent food shortages, and exploitive state political systems can put the elderly in jeopardy even if they are generally supported.

These conclusions are consistent with the results of a recent hologistic study which examined the nature of gerontocide in nonindustrial societies (Maxwell et al. 1982). The authors of this study, which employed Murdock and White's Standard Cross Cultural Sample (SCCS) rather than the PSF, argue that gerontocide "is found chiefly in societies at the lower end of the spectrum of societal complexity" (Maxwell et al. 1982:69). Although their research uncovered no relationship between the presence of gerontocide and climate, their general conclusion that the elderly are killed more often in nonagricultural societies is supported by the present analysis. Further, Maxwell et al. assert "that a causal sequence exists in which a socio-cultural antecedent, namely subsistence techniques that are less complex than most forms of crop cultivation, generates a set of conditions in which the poorer physical performance of the elderly becomes notable, chiefly because of their lessened ability to secure food or otherwise make themselves valuable" (p. 81). This change in physical performance leads to a decline in esteem, which in turn leads to gerontocide. Thus, "physical weakness can be seen as an efficient cause of gerontocide" (Maxwell et al. 1982:74). This conclusion is strikingly similar to the findings discussed previously: the transformation of an elderly person from intact to decrepit brings about the hastening of his or her death. Certainly a decline in physical strength is a contributing factor in the redefinition of a person as decrepit, although other factors appear to contribute equally to this transition, particularly the loss of mental faculties (Eastwell 1982; Glascock 1983).

There is an apparent inconsistency between the results of the Maxwell et al. study and the present research in the reported frequency of gerontocide and death hastening. Maxwell et al. report that gerontocide is present in 14 percent of the societies in the SCCS. This appears to be significantly lower than the 33 percent of the societies in the PSF, in which the killing of the elderly is found and the 50 percent of societies which possess some form of death hastening. Maxwell et al. also found that 9 percent of the societies in the SCCS abandon the elderly, which once again is lower than the 21 percent of the societies in the PSF that practice abandoning. Given that Maxwell et al. did not consider forsaking of the elderly in their study and did not appear to allow for more than one form of behavior within a single society, these discrepancies are not that surprising. The important conclusions that can be drawn from the two hologistic studies are: (1) the elderly in nonindustrial societies are killed, abandoned, or forsaken in societies which can be characterized as technologically simple; and (2) a decline in strength and health that results in old people becoming burdens on the other members of the social group is the reason for death hastening.

CONCLUSIONS

Death hastening, therefore, is a relatively common occurrence in nonindustrial societies but how does the killing, abandoning, and forsaking of the elderly in these societies compare to the killing of the elderly in American society? Also, can we learn from the similarities and differences which exist between these behavioral responses as we struggle to reach some type of societal consensus on this very complicated issue?

There are some clear similarities between death hastening and the killing of the elderly: (1) The behaviors are directed toward old people who have experienced a decline in physical or mental health; (2) the individuals killed are considered burdens to themselves, their family, and to the community; and (3) the decision to kill or hasten death is difficult and involves family members and often the old person. There are, however, some significant differences between the behaviors found in American and nonindustrial societies.

First, examples of overt, direct killing of the elderly in America are still rare enough to produce sensational responses, particularly in news reports. In nonindustrial societies the killing, abandoning, and forsaking of the elderly, although emotionally demanding, do not take on the dramatic character found in American society. Death hastening is part of the culture of these societies; children have personally experienced the death of close relatives, as they age they may be called upon to hasten the death of one of their parents, and they in turn may ask their children to do the same. As a result, death hastening is open and socially approved in nonindustrial societies. In America, on the other hand, the killing of the elderly is usually covert – the turning off of a life support-system, not undertaking a procedure to prolong life, or abusing the old person.

Second, the people who decide and implement the killing or hastening are quite different in the two types of societies. In nonindustrial societies the decisions are made by the family, often with open discussions with the older person. As Maxwell et al. (1982:77) state, "Gerontocide is usually a family affair." The decision is made by family members and usually carried out by a son. In American society it is often unclear as to who decides – children, spouse, the old person, medical staff, courts of law, or some combination. Most often, the decisions appear to be made on an ad hoc basis, with the family brought in at the last minute and the elderly individual often not consulted at all. As the earlier examples of recent legal cases in America show, when the decision is made and implemented by a single person, the consequences can be severe – he or she can be charged with premeditated murder. Thus, it is not surprising that people, especially hospital and nursing home administrators and physicians, are reluctant to take responsibility for accelerating the death of an elderly person. Social sanctions in the form of prosecution and lawsuits are applied inconsistently, with the result being that the killing and accelerating are done covertly and then covered up. In contrast, death hastening in nonindustrial societies is open and direct and people are willing to take responsibility because the rules are known and accepted by the social group.

Perhaps the most significant difference between killing and death hastening is the respective levels of technological sophistication of the two types of societies in which the behaviors are found. As has been shown, death hastening is most prevalent in societies with simple subsistence/technological systems:

hunting and gathering, pastoral, and shifting horticultural. Even though the issues surrounding the killing, abandoning, and forsaking are similar to those found in our culture, the ability to maintain life is vastly different. In addition, the need for the social group to move frequently produces a threat to the elderly, as does the inability of most of these societies to store sufficient quantities of food to allow all members to survive severe food shortages. American society is the most technologically sophisticated society that has ever existed. We have the ability not only to maintain life but also to prolong life beyond the point which many people think is reasonable. We are able to provide physically incapacitated individuals with many technological marvels which allow these individuals to live, if not a productive life, one that certainly extends beyond that even imagined by members of nonindustrial societies. Yet we kill the elderly, struggle over the moral, ethical, and legal questions, and search for a societal consensus which seems to be further away today than a decade ago.

So what conclusions can we draw from these similarities and differences? Arguably, the most significant conclusion is that we are not the first society to struggle with the question as to what should be done to or for older people who are no longer active, productive societal members. Other societies face the same problems of appropriate behavior for the elderly who are burdens to themselves and the social group. The difference between these nonindustrial societies and ours is that they have reached a consensus and we have not. Perhaps we should be pleased that we are at least beginning to discuss the issue openly, since it is impossible to reach agreement as to the appropriate behavior without first being willing to discuss the various options available. However, we are still far from creating a situation where the elderly can live a dignified life in which their rights are respected and in which they are able to control their destiny.

3 THE OLDER WOMAN IN HAUSA SOCIETY: POWER AND AUTHORITY IN URBAN NIGERIA

Catherine Coles

Women in the Muslim world have frequently been described as occupying a subordinate position in male-dominated societies, confined to the domestic realm while males control the public sphere. Women in various life stages have been viewed as links between males and male-dominated kin groups and assumed to be under the control of males. A young girl is described as passing upon marriage from the guardianship of her father or another male to that of her husband; widowed women of childbearing age are viewed as "between marriages" and are expected to remarry, often in accordance with the wishes of male kinsmen; and older unmarried women are analyzed frequently in terms of their ties to adult sons (Antoun 1968; Peristiany 1966; Pastner 1980).

Many of the studies assuming these perspectives have contributed valuable knowledge regarding women's roles by documenting the informal power which Muslim women exercise, primarily in the domestic arena, even though they emphasize the lack of women's participation in formal political structures and processes. Cynthia Nelson, a forceful challenger of assumptions regarding male domination in Middle Eastern society, contends in this regard: (1) that women are actually involved in negotiating rules governing their relationships within particular sociocultural contexts; (2) that their roles within and between kinship groups are particularly important, given the fundamental nature of such institutions in Muslim societies; and (3) that seclusion by gender reserves to women participation in and control of social activities which have significant political and economic effects on the wider society (1974:553, 559; see also Rosen 1978). Nelson makes a further crucial point when she suggests that in some non-Western societies, such as those she describes, Western definitions of political activities and formal political structures may be inappropriate. Clearly, in many Muslim societies the domain of the family overlaps with formal structures through which political authority is exercised and public policy formulated and implemented. Where this is the case, a broader construction of formal political processes and institutions may be required. Furthermore, a close examination of the "informal" power and authority exercised by women might point out the implications of their behavior for the wider society which are distinctly public in nature (Friedl 1967; Lamphere 1975; Raphael 1975).

Outside the Middle East, research in numerous societies documents a wide range of variation in the roles of Muslim women. In sub-Saharan Africa, in particular, studies focusing upon women and gender have investigated the synthesis of Islamic orthodoxy and fundamentally different systems of indigenous cultural beliefs and practices (Barkow 1972; Cohen 1971; Strobel 1979; Ellovich 1980; Boddy 1985) and have illustrated wide variation, both within and between Islamic African societies, in the status of women relative to men, in norms governing female behavior, and in the actual behavior of women.

The possible bases for differentiation in the roles of Muslim women in African societies are many: variation in kinship and descent systems, urban/rural distinctions, participation by women in particular subsistence activities, the degree to which they control wealth and valued items in the society, class, and age are but a few. While it is beyond the purview of this chapter to investigate all these different features as they are related to particular forms of female roles and to the degree of power and authority exercised by women, we consider here the effects of one specific aspect—the aging process—with emphasis upon the movement of women through later stages in the life cycle. Furthermore, we look at aging Muslim women in an urban setting in which rapid and ongoing social and technological changes have occurred during their lifetimes. Our specific focus is middle-aged and old Muslim Hausa women in the northern Nigerian city of Kaduna.

In Muslim Hausa society the greatest degree of power and authority among females accrues to middle-aged and old women. Such a finding is consistent with the results of many, though certainly not all, studies of women cross-culturally (Brown et al. 1985; Foner 1984b; Cool and McCabe 1983). In the words of Judith K. Brown, "Overwhelmingly, the cross-cultural evidence indicates positive changes. Middle age brings fewer restrictions, the right to exert authority over certain kinsmen, and the opportunity for achievement and recognition beyond the household" (1982:143). Among other societies in sub-Saharan Africa, there are numerous examples of elder women with such advantages: Carolyn Bledsoe (1980) describes older Kpelle women in Liberia who manipulate the labor and marriages of younger, less powerful women, as well as controlling them through the Sande secret society. Simon Ottenberg's (1971) account of Afikpo Igbo women in Nigeria presents elders in positions of authority in an extensive age-set system, able to command the labor of younger women, and to regulate their trading activities. !Kung women in Botswana after the age of forty, according to Richard B. Lee, experience considerably more freedom in their sexual behavior than do younger women; gain power through arranging marriages and organizing gift exchanges; and "become central nodes in kinship networks" by acting as the ultimate authorities for pronouncing appropriate kin terms for specific individuals (1985:29).

Certainly such increases in power and autonomy are not ubiquitous in Africa. Claire Robertson's (1984) study of Ga women in Accra (Ghana) suggests an unfortunate fate for female traders who work to educate their sons for member-ship in the elite but are cared for in poverty in old age by their less-educated daughters. And Nancy Foner's (1984b:181–82) classification of inequality among age groups provides examples of African societies such as the Luvale and Ndembu in Central Africa in which dependent old women, as well as old men, are viewed as witches; in earlier times they were burned, and now they may be driven from their villages. Nevertheless, the case of Hausa women represents a trend associated with aging that is visible in many Muslim African societies (Boddy 1985; Landberg 1986).

Historical accounts of the indigenous Hausa political system describe queens of the old walled cities of Daura and Zaria and other roles for royal women such as *Magajiya* (heiress, a state title which brought duties in the court), *Alkaliya* (a female judge), *Iya* (the male ruler's mother or elder sister, who was a fief holder and acted as an intermediary in affairs involving the ruler and his lesser chiefs), and *Jakadiya* (female who carried messages to a male district head or other officeholder inside the female quarters). These roles were eliminated with the coming of Islam, as Mack states:

> Thus it is during the centuries in which Islam gained its foothold in Hausaland that women's names gradually disappear from historical ac-counts. With the formal establishment of a state religion, northern Nigerian women lost their political foothold and their social roles changed profoundly. Queens and women warriors gradually disappeared under increasing Islamic influence, which carried with it the practice of secluding women in the harem [*harim*, Ar.]. The impact of Islam on women's roles began during the fifteenth century, but had its most profound impact through Shehu Usman Dan Fodio's nineteenth century *jihad* [holy war] (Mack, forthcoming; see also M. G. Smith 1955, 1960, 1978).

In the city of Kaduna there are no discrete formal political roles in existence at the present time for females. Yet in many roles — in particular, those involving kin or conjugal relationships, ritual or religious activities, productive or reproductive work, and social or community networks — power and authority are exercised by women in their attempts to control and influence the actions and behaviors of other individuals. In particular, it is elderly women, free of seclusion and often of higher social status than younger women, who may assert substantial influence in interactions with males and females alike. They act as linkages between different social and kin groups which are significant in the larger society and control the behavior of younger females in a social setting segregated by gender.

In the following pages, these and other aspects of power and authority in the roles and behaviors of middle-aged and old Hausa women in Kaduna are explored. It should become clear in the analysis that older Hausa women regularly influence the behavior and choices of male and female individuals and groups in society and that the control exercised by them contributes both to the maintenance of basic social institutions and to the introduction and spread of social change. As independent agents, older Hausa women act to further their own interests and use their power and authority to this end. The following sections include (1) a brief description of the sociocultural and ecological context within which Kaduna Hausa women live; (2) a discussion of the roles of middle-aged and old Hausa women with particular reference to aspects of these roles in which power and authority are exercised; and (3) an examination of implications for the larger society of patterned behaviors and interactions involving the use of power and authority by older women and of some changes in these behaviors which are evident today.

Data presented here on older women were obtained as part of a broader study of roles of women in various life stages, from marriageable age through old age, as these stages were defined by members of the local Hausa community (Coles 1983b). The individual women studied were part of a social network consisting of several generations of females living in two wards (Unguwan Kanawa and Unguwan Shanu) in Kaduna, Nigeria. Data were collected initially over a period of nearly two years in 1980–81, with a follow-up study conducted in July/August 1985. Research activities included participant-observation, recording life histories of women in several generations, and administration of an interview schedule to a sample of 122 women. Of 111 interviews completed during 1980–81, twenty-six were conducted with women forty-one years of age or older, the minimum age of women in the sample who referred to themselves as middle-aged or old (although a number of women suggested in conversation that middle age might begin even earlier). In 1985 approximately twenty-five additional middle-aged and old women outside the original sample but resident in the local community were interviewed, as were those women from the original sample who were living and still resident in the area. At this time, several women in their thirties referred to themselves as middle-aged.

THE ECOLOGICAL AND SOCIOCULTURAL CONTEXT

The Hausa are concentrated primarily in northern Nigeria, although some of the original city-states which were the core of Hausa culture and society lay in what is now Niger. While there are estimated to be approximately 25 million native Hausa speakers spread throughout West Africa and into Central Africa, members of other ethnic groups have for several centuries sought to live in Hausaland, to engage in long-distance trade along with the Hausa who

A Hausa *tsohuwa*, old woman, in Kaduma, Nigeria.

controlled it in large areas and to adopt Islam and Hausa identity along with it. The original Hausa, known as Habe, were settled agriculturalists and specialists in trading and numerous other occupations such as dyeing, smithing, leather-working, and weaving. Hausa society today has emerged through the intermarriage of Habe with Fulani Muslims. It is strongly hierarchical and heterogeneous, with wealth, aristocratic birth, and occupation providing the most significant bases for stratification.

The city of Kaduna was founded early in the twentieth century as a British colonial administrative center for northern Nigeria, in contrast to the traditional walled cities which constitute the indigenous Hausa urban experience. It is situated about twenty miles south of Hausaland proper, in an area originally inhabited by the Gwari people. Attracting both Hausa and non-Hausa migrants, Kaduna continued to grow throughout the early years of the century and, like many other cities in Africa, experienced particularly rapid growth from 1945 onward. From 1965 to the present, growth rates have been estimated at 12 percent per year, resulting in a population of over 600,000.[1] Today the capital of Kaduna state, the city of Kaduna includes residents from all parts of the country. Yet Hausa culture and Islam clearly predominate. The two wards in which research was carried out reflect similar characteristics. High growth rates from 1945 on produced a 1981 population of about 27,500. Ethnically and culturally diverse, the community is roughly 60 percent Hausa and 63 percent Muslim (Kaduna Polytechnic 1981) and clearly is dominated by its Muslim Hausa residents.

Basic amenities are scarce or lacking throughout the two wards: there are only six functioning public standpipes, sewers and drains lie open, roads are unpaved at best and nonexistent in many locations. One maternal and child welfare clinic serves the entire population as the sole local health facility. Most residents live in mud-walled compounds, about 80 percent of which have wells inside outer compound walls and few of which have pipe-borne water. About 65 percent of compounds have electricity. While water and electricity were supplied only sporadically in 1980–81, the situation had improved somewhat by 1985. Given such conditions, residents continue to suffer from many of the diseases associated with urban poverty. While many have radios and material possessions such as clothing, furniture, and extensive collections of pots and dishes and a few possess bicycles or television sets, only a small number of wealthier inhabitants own small refrigerators, motorcycles, or the newest status symbol—video casette recorders.

The Hausa network described here, part of the larger Hausa population in the two wards, comprises a migrant community of which the core is the family of the *Mai Unguwa* (local ward chief) and other residents whose forebears accompanied his father from Kano City to settle here. This core was enlarged by others who joined the settlement in its early years, coming in the late 1920s and early 1930s from other locations. Members of this network today maintain close ties with kin in their locations of origin—frequently, but not exclusively, the older Hausa cities of Kano, Katsina, and Sokoto and the villages surrounding them.

Hausa kinship is traced through both maternal and paternal lines (bilateral), with a strong preference for patrilineal descent. After marriage, the ideal form of residence is with or near the husband's parents, although such prescriptions are not always followed. Marriage is the *rite de passage* to adulthood: most females marry first between the ages of eleven and thirteen, while males first marry in their twenties, by which time they have developed an occupation and can support a wife.[2] Marriage is frequently polygynous (the maximum of four wives being in accord with Muslim law) and usually involves seclusion of wives during the childbearing years. Divorce and subsequent remarriage within a few months are extremely common, with separation usually occurring on the initiative of the wife (Coles 1983b:ch. 4). Women have primary responsibility for nurturing and raising children, cooking, and care of the home. In spite of seclusion, they are active occupationally, earning incomes over which they have complete control, through such activities as trading (cloth, foodstuffs, clothing, jewelry, kola nuts), preparing and cooking food for sale, weaving straw floor mats, sewing, and grinding, most of which are carried on inside their compounds.[3]

An undetermined number of Hausa women do not follow the usual course in the life cycle of marriage and rearing of children. Such women marry once, become single (usually after a divorce), and then take up the status of either prostitute (*karuwa*) or formerly married woman without the connotation of prostitution (*bazawara*). There were no prostitutes in the social network described here (only a single visitor to a compound included in the study where she had kin), although a small number of single women, divorced or widowed but clearly seeking another marriage, described themselves as living in *zawarci* (as a single woman).[4]

THE MIDDLE-AGED AND OLD HAUSA WOMAN: ROLES, POWER, AND AUTHORITY

At about the time childbearing ceases, the adult Hausa woman passes into the life stages in which she is called *dattijuwa* (middle-aged woman) and then *tsohuwa* (old woman). Women become *dattijuwa* in two different ways. First, with the cessation of childbearing and onset of menopause, a woman clearly moves into middle age. The most obvious impediment to her entrance is the continuation of childbearing; yet in 1985, several women in their late thirties who referred to themselves as middle-aged reported that they were using family planning to prevent further pregnancies. For barren or childless women, and for those widowed or divorced, this impediment is not present, and they appear able to move into middle age as they desire at any time during or after their late thirties.

The second mode of entry to middle age occurs as a conscious decision by a woman to assume the status of this new life stage. While menopause and the cessation of childbearing constitute physiological changes which cannot be disputed, there appears to be a period from about age thirty-five to fifty, before such changes have been completed, in which a Hausa woman herself may select her own time of entry to the stage of *dattijuwa*, consciously discarding roles associated with younger, childbearing age and adopting those of elderly women of middle age. An example of selected entry to middle age is provided in this excerpt from the life history of Hajiya Aishatu.[5]

HAJIYA AISHATU

Hajiya Aishatu was born about eighty-five years ago in Kano City, the last child of an *Imam* (prayer leader) and slave trader of the Sullubawa clan who had come to Kano from Sokoto. Her mother was a Fulani from Yola. Hajiya was secluded as a child, and in her Koranic education she completed memorizing the Koran, a mark of special status. She was first married at the age of nine to an old man, a trader from Kukawa in Bornu, who also acted as a landlord and middleman for people coming from there. Hajiya was in complete seclusion for five years after her marriage; after seven years of marriage, her husband took her to Kaduna, where he became the first *Mai Unguwa* (ward head) of Unguwan Kanawa. She was then his third wife. One child born to Hajiya in Kano died; in Kaduna she gave birth to three others (two sons and a daughter) who lived.

Hajiya was divorced from her husband after she left him following an argument: he had used money given him by his wives for the purpose of buying dowry for a daughter in order to obtain a fourth wife for himself. Hajiya beat the new wife, and all three of his wives left him. Hajiya returned to Kano to live with her mother for one year following her divorce, during which time she cooked and sold rice and beans in a shop near the family compound. She then married a Zaria man and lived with him in a house behind the Emir's palace in Zaria for nine years. She was secluded in this marriage also and earned income weaving inside the compound. Finally she decided that she was not happy with Zaria people and asked her husband to divorce her, which he did.

By this time all her children were grown, and her former husband had died. Hajiya went back to Kano, but her youngest son, the new ward head in Unguwan Kanawa, asked her to return to Kaduna. He said people were asking for his mother. Hajiya's mother warned her not to go to live with her son in Unguwan Kanawa but suggested that she go instead to stay in Unguwan Shanu to the house owned by her daughter. The younger sister of Hajiya's first husband had fostered Hajiya's daughter, and this daughter had inherited the house when her foster mother died (see below for a discussion of fostering). So Hajiya went there to live.

When Hajiya went back to Kaduna she was not yet old. Many men asked her to marry, and her two sons wanted her to marry. She had a shop outside her compound where she sold yams, beans, rice, and other food. She refused to marry, telling her sons that a husband would stop her from working at her occupation. She said that since she did not drink liquor or smoke or have "bad friends" (prostitutes), she could refuse to marry. Further, she considered her work as her husband. Hajiya has continued to live in this compound, which belongs now to the son of her daughter. For some time she continued to cook and sell food and to trade in various items to earn an income. She fostered the daughter of her eldest son, and this girl married the son of Hajiya's youngest son, the ward head of Unguwan Kanawa. Hajiya sent the girl to primary school but would not allow her to continue with secondary school, even though her husband attended university. By 1985, Hajiya was unwell and unable to continue any work of her own. She was supported by her daughter and grandson.

As the daughter of a wealthy religious man, an *Imam,* and through marriage to the *Mai Unguwa,* Hajiya was of high social status (as were the men to whom she was related) and thus subject to stricter observance of seclusion during marriage than most women of her age. Following her second divorce, in the face of marriage proposals and urging by her sons to remarry, Hajiya perceived conflict between the expectation for seclusion associated with the role of wife and her own desires to carry out her chosen occupations — cooking, selling, and trading. Instead of remarriage, she chose to assume the identity of a middle-aged woman and thus live alone respectably out of seclusion.

This strategy is used frequently by Hausa women during the transitional stage in which their status changes from that of younger married women to middle-aged women. It indicates that they clearly recognize and anticipate the freedom, independence, and power acquired with passage to middle and old age, and, indeed, they seek to assume this status when it becomes possible and advantageous to their other interests to do so. In manipulating entry to middle age, Hausa women are exercising their right to choose the roles they wish to enact in society and are opting for roles which allocate greater degrees of power and authority with respect to both males and females.

Middle age is assumed to last from the time a woman enters it until about the age of sixty, when she begins to be referred to as an old woman. The transition to old age appears to occur with the onset of physical signs of aging, such as the loss of easy mobility and physical strength. There is not always agreement among women as to whether an individual female should be called middle aged or old. Unlike the clear-cut change in roles which marks the transition from younger childbearing status to middle age, this later alteration in social position represents further movement along a path embarked upon with the passage into middle age and not the assumption of radically new roles.

The passage from middle to old age brings with it increasing freedom from prescriptions for restraint and reserve in female behavior. While younger women are expected to act in a manner restrained, quiet, and subservient to males, old women may — and often do — voice their opinions freely. Old Hausa

women in Kaduna roam throughout the two wards studied: they visit married
children with whom they are not living morè frequently than do middle-aged
mothers and give vociferous (sometimes unsought) advice to children,
grandchildren, and other younger women. Elderly women are accorded increased
respect by males and females alike. Many Kaduna Hausa women in their eighties
remain active in lucrative occupations such as trading and midwifery, perhaps
retreating more into their homes to conduct business as their physical mobility
decreases with age, but no less busy and in some cases equally productive.

In the discussion which follows, the roles of those women acknowledged
publicly as middle aged and old that involve the use of power and authority are
presented within the following domains: kinship and residential relationships,
productive and reproductive work, participation in local society and community, and ritual and religious activities. Role descriptions within the
categories represent emic constructions of roles by adult female actors within
Hausa society, and they apply to both middle-aged and old women unless
otherwise specified.[6]

KINSHIP/RESIDENTIAL ROLES

Unlike kin groups in the older walled cities and rural Hausa society in
northern Nigeria (Saunders 1980; Schildkrout 1986; Hill 1972; M.G. Smith
1955), Kaduna Hausa families have been present for three to four generations
at most. Many have come even more recently. Compounds frequently house
unrelated residents, who rent accommodations, rather than members of extended families, and the full range of kin relations is not immediately present.
Actual kin have priority over nonkin, expressed in the preference for choosing
a relative as one's first marriage partner, in financial support provided to one
another, and in frequent visits made to those living in other cities or rural areas.
Yet a single system of kin terms is used by Hausa residents to address members
of a "kinship/residential" group, which includes both actual and fictive kin,
friends, neighbors, and selected other coresidents. Ritual events such as naming
ceremonies, marriages, funerals, and Islamic holidays are mutually celebrated
by these individuals and family members within the local network.[7]

The importance of marriage in the life of every Hausa woman was addressed
above. The average number of marriages contracted by women who had reached
middle and old age in the Kaduna sample in 1981 was just over two; however, a
number of other women not included in the formal sample (acquaintances of
the author who were living in the areas and who were interviewed informally in
1981 and again in 1985) had married as many as four or five husbands. And, as
Table 3.1 shows, in the age group fifty-one to sixty, 57.1 percent of women had
contracted three marriages.

Opportunities for remarriage decline considerably once a woman is no longer
in her childbearing years, yet a number of women in the Kaduna network did
contract marriages in middle age. If a woman chooses to marry after divorce or

Table 3.1
Numbers of Marriages by Age Groups of Women (Kaduna 1981)

Age Groups	0	1	2	3	4	5	Row Totals
		Numbers of Marriages					
9–15	9	7	0	0	0	0	16
	53.3%	43.8%	0.0%	0.0%	0.0%	0.0%	14.4%
16–20	1*	17	4	1	0	0	23
	4.3%	73.9%	17.4%	4.3%	0.0%	0.0%	20.7%
21–30	1*	18	11	2	2	0	34
	2.9%	52.9%	32.4%	5.9%	5.9%	0.0%	30.6%
31–40	0	3	5	3	1	0	12
	0.0%	25.0%	41.7%	25.0%	8.3%	0.0%	10.8%
41–50	0	4	6	3	0	1	14
	0.0%	28.6%	42.9%	21.4%	0.0%	7.1%	12.6%
51–60	0	1	2	4	0	0	7
	0.0%	14.3%	28.6%	57.1%	0.0%	0.0%	6.3%
60+	0	1	4	0	0	0	5
	0.0%	20.0%	80.0%	0.0%	0.0%	0.0%	4.5%
Column Totals	11	51	32	13	3	1	111
	9.9%	45.9%	28.8%	11.7%	2.7%	0.9%	100.0%

* These women are sisters, both students in secondary schools.

the death of a previous husband, she is likely to contract a marriage of *auren silkiti* or *daukisandanka*, in which there are separate residences for husband and wife. In such a marriage the husband visits periodically, and she has the financial support and social recognition awarded a wife. Yet she is free to carry out whatever activities she pleases. Most middle-aged women in my sample were married in 1985; only three were unmarried, and they were widows. About half the women in old age were married. Old women in Hausa society may, however, choose to live as single women (divorced or widowed) in a compound with family or friends. In middle or old age the term *bazawara* (single woman) is not generally used; instead, a woman simply refers to herself by the age-linked terms *dattijuwa* or *tsohuwa*.

Even when married, older women are not usually secluded except in very wealthy, aristocratic, or religious families, as was the case of Hajiya Aishatu above. This represents a marked difference from the conjugal roles of younger married women. Table 3.2 shows the number of women in the sample of different ages who claimed to be secluded, illustrating the general absence of seclusion for older women. The trend toward fewer numbers of women in seclusion becomes apparent between the ages of forty-one and fifty and is more pronounced between fifty-one and sixty, when most women are no longer secluded.[8]

Table 3.2
Seclusion Status of Hausa Females in Various Age Groups
(Kaduna 1981)

Age Group	Number Secluded	Number Not Secluded
11–20	25	14*
	64.1%	35.9%
21–30	26	8
	76.5%	23.5%
31–40	10	2
	83.3%	16.7%
41–50	5	9
	35.7%	64.3%
51–60	1	6
	14.3%	85.7%
61–70	0	1
	0.0%	100.0%
71–80	0	4
	0.0%	100.0%
Totals	67	44
	60.4%	39.6%

* 11 of these are unmarried girls.

Old women without children at home usually foster children so that they have someone in the home to help with domestic work and to keep them company.[9] Very often these fostered children are grandchildren, nieces, or other female kin of the older woman, and she may decide upon their education (or lack thereof), arrange marriages for them, and even provide much of the dowry for girls she fosters (see M. F. Smith 1981:111–12). In either case, by the time they reach adulthood, the older woman's sons and daughters (whether fostered or natural) who have their own occupations frequently contribute materially and financially to her welfare, providing her a place to live, food and clothing, and money for her to make the pilgrimage to Mecca.

Among her kin by marriage and descent, an older woman's age provides the opportunity for exercising power and authority over both males and females. Elderly female control over males is manifest in many forms. Within families, older women are treated with respect and tolerance from adult male children. They have a voice in the selection of a wife for their sons (particularly in the first marriage), frequently for their grandsons, and in some cases for a brother's children as well. This is especially true when an older woman contributes to the sum needed for bridewealth, as is often the case. Decisions concerning marriage partners are important, as they result in exchanges of wealth among different kin groups and in the creation of social linkages affecting the status of such groups.

A number of women of middle and old age in Kaduna have acquired houses or earnings from an occupation which allow them to be independent of their families. Such women have inherited houses from husbands or kin who have died, or else they have built up lucrative occupations such as midwifery or herbal medicine and bought their own property. This degree of wealth on the part of older women in the Kaduna sample may not represent the usual case for an older Hausa woman, as Enid Schildkrout suggests in her article on widows and divorcees in Kano City (1986).[10] Those women who are wealthy may exercise considerable power over kin and coresidents, however. They may rent rooms in their compounds to other families, and female compound heads settle disputes among their tenants, both male and female, and set appropriate standards of behavior within the compound. Such women may also provide a house within their own compound for a male grandchild and his wives to live. Others send their sons to Mecca and foster male children of their kin. This generosity results in ties of power and influence between a woman and the males involved.

Within the secluded world of women, females control each other through a hierarchy based on seniority with respect to age and relative status. This control is most intense within kin/residential networks, where older women watch over younger secluded married women and reprimand, punish, and praise them for their behavior. Sanctions against improper behavior by younger women are often initiated by elder females within the kin group, with adult males joining in if their interests are involved, as in a wife's breach of seclusion which publicly threatens a man's social standing in the community. The wife of the compound head, whether a senior relative or simply the senior wife of the compound's owner, has authority over other females in the compound. Senior women in the local community perform rituals for those events most important to the kin group's members—births, naming ceremonies, and deaths—and carry and exchange information among secluded women in compounds. In addition, it is only elderly female adults who can move freely in and out of secluded Hausa compounds in the community and who can also move without restriction in the domain of males. They carry news of events in the larger community or from other compounds, purchase needed items for younger women in seclusion, and sell goods for them. This mobility allows old Hausa women to function as links between kin groups, compounds, and, to a large degree, between adult males and females in the society.

PRODUCTIVE AND REPRODUCTIVE ROLES

The older Hausa woman usually has long occupational experience and may be wealthy in her own right from financial success in these activities. This wealth may also result from her freedom to pursue a range of occupations not accessible to younger women, either because seclusion precludes their practice (such as trading in bulk items, which requires frequent travel to distant markets) or because social norms specify that they be carried out only by old women (such as midwifery, *ungozomanci*). Observational data suggest that those Hausa women, such as Hajiya Aishatu, who become "old" women at a younger age relative to other women in the community, are the most active in occupations such as trading and midwifery, which require movement in public places. Many other women who call themselves *dattijuwa* at later ages continue to carry out occupational activities such as preparation of food for sale, weaving, or grinding inside their compounds. All middle-aged and old women interviewed in Kaduna, save those who were physically incapacitated, were engaged in at least one, and often several, income-earning activity.

The most frequent primary occupational activities for middle-aged and old women in the sample in 1981 are shown in Table 3.3.[11] When the sample was expanded to include additional middle-aged and old women in 1985, other lucrative occupations appeared: herbal medicine, work as a commission agent, as a pawnbroker, or running a small shop, usually attached to or outside of the woman's compound. Another occupation frequently, though not exclusively, engaged in by middle-aged and older women is that of *uwar adashi*, the person who organizes a credit association and holds the money which is paid in, receiving for her services a small payment from each participant. While all women engaged in productive activities have felt the consequences of a severely

Table 3.3

Occupational Activities of Middle-Aged and Old Women (Age 41 and Over) by Location of Activity and Seclusion Status (Kaduna 1981)

| | Location of Activity* | | | Seclusion Status | |
| | Inside | Outside | | | Not |
Occupation	Compound	Compound	Both	Secluded	Secluded
Trade	3	0	4	1	6
Weaving/ Sewing	2	0	0	2	0
Peparation and Cooking of Food for Sale	5	1	8	2	10
Midwife	0	1	0	0	1
Other	1	0	0	1	0
Totals	11	2	12	6	19

* Compound refers to the compound of the woman undertaking the occupational activity.

depressed economy in Nigeria which began with falling oil prices in the late 1970s, older women in 1985 appeared to have achieved more stability in their occupations than their juniors and to have weathered the years of economic crisis more successfully. None had been forced out of their occupations entirely, as had many younger women (Coles, forthcoming).

Financial success in her occupation brings a Hausa woman increased power, particularly over her own life. If a woman can support herself from her earnings, she has greater freedom of choice about whether and when she wishes to live as a single woman and, if she chooses to remarry, in negotiating the conditions of marriage with a prospective husband. She may wish to contract a marriage which does not require her seclusion or in which she may remain in a home she owns, with her husband either joining her there or living elsewhere. A woman who has achieved a secure financial base through her occupation may have made the pilgrimage to Mecca, thereby increasing her prestige and social standing in the community. She may also have the resources to send other relatives (such as a daughter or granddaughter) to Mecca or to pay school fees and expenses so that they may attend non-Koranic school. By giving gifts and sharing her earnings and resources with others, particularly her own kin, a woman increases her power and authority over them and, consequently, their responsibility to her in the future.

Old women continue to take part in the nurturing and raising of children, although by the time they are elderly and their physical capacities diminish, they are often relieved of domestic tasks such as food preparation, cooking, cleaning, and washing clothes, which younger women in the compound usually perform.

RITUAL/RELIGIOUS ROLES

Unlike younger women, who pray alone at home, old Muslim Hausa females (not those in middle age) may pray in the mosque as do males. However, most other aspects of their ritual and religious roles do not differ from those of younger women. With the increase in available wealth and the growth of a wage labor economy, women of childbearing age are as likely as older women to have made the *hajj* to Mecca and thus to have acquired the increased prestige which accompanies such an experience. While old women had not in 1985 enrolled in the new Islamic schools which appeared in 1982–83 in Kaduna and throughout northern Nigeria's urban centers, many middle-aged women were joining younger married women in attending.[12]

The most significant exercise of ritual power and authority for women lies in the practice of midwifery, an occupation which is available only to elderly women. In the case of Hajiya Asabe, which follows, we see the development of her participation in this occupation, the types of activities associated with it and changes in their arena, and the wealth and high status in the community which her ritual activities have brought.

HAJIYA ASABE

Hajiya Asabe was born over eighty years ago in Kano City. Her mother and father were both Kano Hausa, and their large family compound was near Dalla Hill. Hajiya's father was a *mallam*, who conducted a Koranic school in their house; her mother finished the Koran and was strictly secluded. When Hajiya was a child, she was taught in her father's Koranic school and was not allowed to go out much herself, being the daughter of a *mallam*.

Hajiya was first married to the son of her father's brother in a marriage between kin (*auren zumunci*). Her husband was a Koranic scholar and teacher, and she was his only wife. Before coming to Kano, Hajiya gave birth to two children, both of whom died when very young. In Kano, Hajiya was strictly secluded. Her occupation was trading and selling food from inside her compound. In 1926, when Hajiya was in her twenties, she came with her husband to Unguwan Kanawa, along with the first group of Kano settlers, including the first ward head. Her husband built a compound directly behind that of the *Mai Unguwa*, where Hajiya still lives today. Another compound next to Hajiya's was built by a man from Sokoto and his family. Hajiya gave birth to two more children in Unguwan Kanawa: a daughter who lives nearby today and a son who died as an adult. About thirty-five years ago Hajiya's first husband died of an illness. Following Hausa custom, Hajiya stayed in her compound for five months following his death (*idda*).

When she finished the five months and could leave her compound, Hajiya was approached by a man staying in the compound of her neighbor from Sokoto, who asked if she would marry him. This man was a laborer who had worked for the Sardauna of Sokoto, the most important leader of the Hausa states. When Hajiya agreed to marry him, he joined her in her house in Unguwan Kanawa, which had become her own after the death of her first husband. Hajiya was the only wife in her second marriage.

When Hajiya married for the second time, she was no longer bearing children, nor was she secluded. She had begun practicing *ungozomanci* (midwifery). She had been introduced to this skill when she was younger and had been left alone in her compound with a woman giving birth. She continued to learn from other women in her family. She also learned to treat women and children for sickness, gathering herbs and making her own medicines. Today she also sells henna (used for cosmetic staining of women's hands and feet) and kola nuts and receives income from renting rooms in her compound. Hajiya's work as a midwife includes the delivery of infants (she must be the first to touch a newborn child), cutting of the cord, and initial washing of the baby. She then returns to wash a newborn infant twice daily for a week and takes part in the naming ceremony (*suna*), for which she receives the head, skin, and legs of the ram which is killed. She is paid for her services with money, cloth, and food or other small personal gifts. She also instructs young mothers in the proper techniques for washing themselves with nearly boiling water for several weeks after the birth.

Hajiya is now one of the oldest and most respected members of the local Unguwan Kanawa and Unguwan Shanu Hausa community. When deaths of women or children occur, she is called to prepare the body, supervise the organization of the estate of the deceased, notify members of the family, and carry out various rituals associated with the death and burial. Hajiya's close friends are all other elderly women in the area — the mother of the present ward head, the mother of this ward head's first (now deceased) wife, the former cowife of his mother (to whom Hajiya has given a room in her compound rent-free), and two other women who live nearby and have been resident in Unguwan Kanawa for almost sixty years, like herself. Hajiya Asabe's company is sought so often by others in the community that she is nearly always carrying out her midwife duties, visiting other friends or residents, or being visited in her own home. She can rarely be found alone. She travels frequently to Kano to visit members of her own family at their home and brings news to many in the local Hausa community of their own relatives in Kano. She has fostered the daughter of her elder brother's son, a young girl of thirteen who is soon to be married, having recently finished primary school. Hajiya has made three trips to Mecca, all within the last ten years. She has paid for all her trips and also paid for her daughter to make the pilgrimage two years ago.

Hajiya's ritual/occupational duties have brought her prestige and status in the local community and provided her with the means of obtaining an income sufficient to make several trips to Mecca, to be financially independent, and to give freely to other members of her family, both male and female. She provides rooms rent-free to several old friends and has also done so for several granddaughters after they have been divorced. Usually she has been involved in arranging for their remarriages as well. In 1985 she was building two new rooms inside her compound to house her grandson and his new wife, after having played a major role in arranging their marriage.

Other middle-aged and old Hausa women in the local community practice herbal medicine associated not with Islam, but with *bori*, a Hausa spirit possession cult. *Bori* predates the acceptance of Islam in Hausa society, and many adepts are female (Besmer 1983). One middle-aged woman in the area, Hajiya Mai Magani (literally, the owner of medicine), has an international reputation as an herbal practitioner and bori specialist and treats both physical and mental illness. She, like Hajiya Asabe, has become extremely wealthy, owns several compounds locally, and is considered a powerful and influential woman by area residents. Both Hajiya Mai Magani and Hajiya Asabe have cooperated with orthodox medical authorities in testing local herbal medicines and in establishing programs to improve maternal and child welfare in the state. The ritual roles of these women obviously merge with their occupational roles; the power, authority, prestige, and status which accrue to them arise out of both aspects.

SOCIAL/COMMUNITY ROLES

Hausa women of all ages in Kaduna regularly contract asymmetrical client relationships and equal bond friendships with other women. These relationships express relative social status between women. Older women are frequently sought as senior partners in hierarchical patron-client relationships. As *uwar daki* (mother of the house) to *'yar arziki* (daughter in wealth), the senior woman advises her younger female friend in matters of marriage, divorce, and children, provides occupational assistance, and gives her gifts. In return, the older woman will have the help and assistance of her "daughter" in ceremonial events (such as a marriage or naming ceremony). A younger woman would be greatly honored by the attendance of her *uwar daki* at one of her own family ceremonies. Age, occupational success, and social status may all attract younger female clients to particular older Hausa women. Bond friendships are formed between women of the same age and social status who become *kawaye* (formal female friends). Such women engage in ritual gift exchanges on occasions of ceremonial events known as *biki* (for example, naming ceremonies, marriages, and celebrations ending the feasting of Ramadan). Many of the middle-aged and old Hausa women in the wards studied speak of each other as "sisters" and are closely bound in these friendships (M. F. Smith 1981:191–206).

Females are influenced, though not controlled, through these two types of relationships, which may join both kin and nonkin. As Vanessa Maher (1976:222) notes, for Moroccan women, such female-female relationships are particularly important for the emotional and material support they provide where marriages are unstable. For Hausa women, female friendships may last a lifetime and often provide them much greater continuity and stability than do marriages. In the case studies presented here, Hajiya Asabe and Hajiya Aishatu are extremely close friends, and Hajiya Asabe herself provides free accommodation and food to another of her close female friends who is now elderly and without male support. Such social relationships overlap to some extent with the kinship/residential relationships which Hausa women form with other females; however, it is the formal bond and client relationships which provide for the exercise of greater influence by women with respect to one another.

IMPLICATIONS OF FEMALE POWER AND AUTHORITY IN A CHANGING SOCIETY

Older Hausa women in Kaduna exercise considerable power (the ability to control and influence behavior) as well as formal authority (the socially recognized right to exert this control). Before middle age this control over others is more circumscribed for women. However, while fathers, husbands, and brothers have the power to marry women to other men, especially when women are young, and to some degree regulate female access to Western education, women can and do resist such control (see Coles 1983a). During childbearing years they escape unacceptable marriages by leaving husbands and seeking a court divorce; they attempt to contract their own marriages as they grow older; and, less frequently, they remain single after the conclusion of a marriage and assume the role of unmarried woman or prostitute. As they enter middle and old age, however, women become increasingly free of male attempts to dominate their marriages; they become more independent and autonomous, and their influence over the lives of younger women grows considerably.

While male control of women tends to be exercised periodically and lessens as women grow older, female control over other females increases with age at a fairly consistent pace. The influence and control women have over each other is thus in many ways more pervasive and longer lasting in Hausa society than control by males. The control of younger women by elderly females is especially significant within the context of a Muslim society which holds the seclusion of younger women as an ideal: segregation by gender enhances the control and influence which women exert relative to each other, since seclusion prevents male intrusion into the activities of women (Pittin 1979).

We may assume that these particular powers of older women are not a new development in Hausa society (M. F. Smith 1981). Yet in other ways the power and authority of older Hausa women in Kaduna appear to be increasing over that experienced by women generally in the last two centuries. For Kaduna women in the sample, new experiences and increasing influence are related directly to opportunities arising from wider social and technological changes. For example, the availability of family planning services may allow women who use them to enter middle age sooner than if they continued to bear children into their late thirties and early forties. For such women, and for those whose lives have been lengthened because of improved medical facilities, the time they spend as middle-aged and old women may surpass the number of years they will have spent in life stages which presented greater restriction of their autonomy.[13] Some women with occupations in herbal medicine and midwifery have markedly increased their influence in the local community; their association with external governmental and medical authorities has elevated their authority and prestige by "validating" their knowledge and competence in indigenous medical treatment, while at the same time it links them to a second source of healing recognized as powerful in its own right—orthodox medical practitioners and government hospitals. Financial reward has followed public recognition and contributed to the economic power of such women, with subsequent increase in their influence over the behavior of others. They are able to pay for trips to Mecca for themselves and members of their families, for the education of grandchildren, and for lavish gifts. Because the occupational success of these women involves ritual activities, their power and authority have increased beyond that which normally accrues to women who have lucrative occupations.

The development of fast and inexpensive automotive transport has made it feasible for middle-aged female traders to travel by taxi every day to periodic markets outside of Kaduna to buy bulk foodstuffs which they take back to the local community and resell to younger women who process, cook, and sell the food. Changes in Islam leading to an increased emphasis on literacy and adult Koranic education for women have made it possible for them to contemplate careers as Koranic teachers—indeed, a small number of middle-aged women attend classes in the new Islamic schools in hopes of preparing for this profession. Independent wealthy women even play public roles by supporting and donating funds to particular community development projects of their choosing, which are organized by Kaduna local goverment and undertaken by local male residents.

Cases such as these dispute the assumption that the prestige and well-being of elderly individuals — in this case, women — decline with increases in urbanization, literacy, widespread education, and the introduction of orthodox medical technology (Cowgill 1972). They also document the fact that middle-aged and old women in Kaduna have not merely responded to the far-reaching changes which have occurred during the present century, but they have frequently been initiators of change in their society. Innovative female herbalists such as Hajiya Asabe and Hajiya Mai Magani, a number of newly middle-aged women who are seriously pursuing Islamic studies, and other local women whose behavior departs from prevailing cultural norms have through their activities extended the range of variation in female roles and provided new role models for all women in the area. These individuals are not recognized publicly either as advocates of change in women's roles or as resisters of those forces which control females in Hausa society. Instead, most Hausa women innovate by initiating change in one particular role (and perhaps others closely related) but follow local behavioral practices in others. Older women are likely to be innovators in certain areas, while they are also conservative and supportive of other behaviors which serve their own self-interests. For example, Hajiya Asabe supervises and enforces adherence to normative roles in the behavior of younger women in the local community through her activities as a midwife and as a key ritual participant in naming ceremonies and funerals. Yet her daughter and granddaughters, although married, are secluded only nominally and already have extraordinarily active occupations in trading—they too appear to be innovators.

Middle-aged and old Hausa women identified in Kaduna as initiators of change generally have high status and prestige in the local society among both men and women. This status is based not upon the position of husbands or fathers but on the achievements of women themselves in an occupation or religious education, wealth, social relationships with other women, ritual/religious activities or having made the *hajj*, the number and achievements of their children, and their age.[14] Status and prestige are only loosely associated with class; a woman may marry a member of the hereditary elite, be divorced from him, and subsequently marry a laborer with no loss to her own social standing (M. G. Smith 1959; Yeld 1960).

Monica Wilson (1977:172) has pointed out that innovators who are members of a local community can provide powerful examples to others, especially if they are serving as reference individuals. In Hausa society, seclusion structures interaction so that most relationships in which women engage are with other females, and the reference groups of which they are members or whose values they take into account are composed only of women (primarily female kin and coresidents, bond friends, members of patron-client relationships, and other women well known in the local community, many of them middle aged or old). Relationships between women within these reference groups, particularly with their most significant reference individuals, provide linkages or paths of influence along which role change proceeds and replication of new behavior patterns occurs. Women in three positions act most frequently as reference individuals for Hausa females in Kaduna: the woman raising a female child (either *mahaifiya*, female who gave birth to her, or *marikiya*, female who fostered her); the *kawa* (close female friend) or *uwar daki* (senior woman in a client relationship); and elderly respected women with ritual powers (midwives or herbalists) who are well known in a community. It is within these particular relationships that senior women are most likely to attempt to influence the behavior of their "juniors" and that younger, less influential women are most likely to adopt the changing behavior patterns of senior, more powerful women.

CONCLUSION

It is in many of the newer urban centers such as Kaduna that forces for change impinge most dramatically upon Africans today. Culturally, ethnically, and religiously plural, these cities and towns attract large numbers of migrants because of the available services and facilities and employment opportunities in both the formal and informal sector. Hausa in Kaduna — young and old, male and female — experience regular contact with non-Hausa and non-Muslims. They have adopted the technology of the city and have begun to identify with a larger political community, assisting in local community development programs, voting in federal elections, watching news and film events from around the world on television. Exposure to a variety of educational programs and institutions, both secular and religious, has led to rapidly rising literacy rates, particularly among adult women and children.

Yet change in Hausa society is tempered by strong adherence to customary norms and behaviors (many of which are linked to the practice of Islam) and a persistent hierarchy based upon status, occupation, and age. The continuing significance of kinship in Muslim Hausa society in Kaduna and its relevance to public life are evident in the high status which the family of the *Mai Unguwa* (ward head) commands in the local community. In formal recognition of his historical right to exercise authority over the local community, the *Mai Unguwa*, son of the first ward head (who founded the area), has been designated a local government official. He and several of his brothers live together and operate lucrative businesses jointly. His eldest son is a university graduate, and others are still attending secular schools; his daughters have married members of wealthy local families; and his mother, as noted above, is highly respected in the community. For other Kaduna Hausa families in the sample whose oldest members have been in the wards since their origins, patrilineal kin groups continue to form the basis for residence and participation in local social life. These families are linked through numerous marriages.

Clearly, older Hausa women in Kaduna play major roles within and between kinship and descent groups. For example, the earliest initiatives in marriage negotiations frequently are made by an elderly woman related to the male as she approaches an elderly female relative of the prospective bride to chat informally. Furthermore, older Hausa women are custodians of Hausa cultural values and important actors in processes by which social control is maintained throughout the entire community. Their presence is as important to newer residents who establish themselves as nuclear families, renting rooms within large compounds owned by older families, as it is to longer-established Hausa residents. Upon becoming part of the kinship/residential system described above, recently arrived male migrants rely heavily on local, older women for overseeing the behavior of married women in seclusion (just as such women would do in their own kin groups) and even for assistance in contracting further marriages with local women.

But the influence of elderly females in Hausa society is not limited to the preservation of cultural values and long-accepted behaviors. Such women are also innovators and independent agents, acting in their own self-interest and in many ways benefiting from their control over secluded, immobile, younger women while experimenting with new social forms. They do not exercise power by holding formal political roles either in the new governmental structure or in a traditional royal court or political bureaucracy. Rather, their influence is informal, exerted as senior members of kin groups, through activities that link gender-segregated sectors of society, in pivotal positions within the secluded world of women, through ritual and occupational activities which they monopolize, and as wealthy individuals influencing others through distribution of favors. The pervasiveness of elderly female influence enables most older women in Hausa society to exercise considerable power and a few to be recognized publicly as having significant authority.

These are the sources of power and influence, and the processes by which they are exercised, recognized explicitly by Cynthia Nelson (1974) in her study of Middle Eastern women. In Hausa society, segregation by gender provides older women the opportunity to maximize their power both within the kin group and in the wider society. As the only adult links (other than male kin or husbands) between the domestic arena of secluded younger women and the extradomestic world, older women monopolize an important communication system, controlling both the substance of messages and the manner in which they are transmitted. For example, elderly women bring to secluded women news of the availability of certain goods and firsthand observations of events in other areas of the town; to males, they may relate information about secluded women relevant to a future marriage. Through such activities they engage in impression management between males and females and in negotiation of rules for female behavior. Hajiya Asabe regularly counsels young women to remain secluded, yet she has arranged nonsecluded marriages for several of her granddaughters, convincing their husbands that the women's intentions are honorable and that their occupational earnings will benefit the men. Control of information and impression management can be powerful in influencing the behavior of individuals in society, particularly when combined with a monopoly of occupational and/or ritual activities, which are both lucrative and crucial to the life of the community.

The life histories provided above document the activities and concomitant power of relatively affluent women in the local community. There are, however, many middle-aged and old women in the sample who are poorer and less influential, although they are certainly not powerless. These women live in compounds along with family members or wealthier acquaintances, and although some have fewer material possessions (clothing and furniture), this is not an accurate indicator of degree of wealth. All such women known to the author in this community either could provide for their own subsistence and accommodation or were living with and receiving subsistence from family or friends. Furthermore, every elderly woman was able to influence other women, to control communications as described above, and to exert power in a kin group if she was living with her kin. Affluence and aristocratic birth may increase the power of a woman but are not the sole bases for it.

Hausa society has been described as a prototype of complex, stratified societies, with the argument that male and female systems of status can be analyzed separately (Yeld 1960). In historical and political accounts, scant attention has been paid to the exercise of power or authority by women, and recent studies which focus on changes in Hausa society emphasize the oppressed condition of women in seclusion. The evidence suggests that not all Hausa women are equally powerful or influential (Schildkrout 1986; Coles 1983a, 1983b; Pittin 1979). Yet in contemporary urban contexts such as Kaduna, it is clear that some women, predominately older females, are sources of power with which males as well as younger females must reckon, and some are becoming increasingly influential. The exercise of this power extends beyond the boundaries of kinship groups into the public sector. It begs for greater attention to processes (rather than formal systems) by which control is exercised and attests to the need which Nelson sees for a renewed attempt to conceptualize political activity and roles to reflect the realities of a society in which males and females participate differently while sharing in systems of influence and control.

NOTES

An earlier version of this chapter was presented at the Annual Meetings of the African Studies Association, Boston, Massachusetts, December 7, 1983. Subsequent research was made possible by Goodman Funds from the Department of Anthropology, Dartmouth College, and further data analysis was supported by a Faculty Research Grant, Dartmouth College, both of which the author gratefully acknowledges.

1. Estimates by urban planners in Kaduna vary from 500,000 to 750,000. I have used a conservative estimate provided in verbal communications by several planners, taking into consideration the 12 percent per annum growth rates they suggest. No recent census figures are available. Statistics for the wards studied are derived from Kaduna Polytechnic (1981).

2. The stages in the life cycle of Hausa females are: *jinjirniya* (infant), *yarinya* (girl), *budurwa* (marriageable young girl), *amariya* (bride), *mace* (woman, wife), *dattijuwa* (middle-aged woman), and *tsohuwa* (old woman). For a comprehensive description of roles in the life stage of Muslim Hausa woman of childbearing age (*mace*), see Coles (1983b:ch. 5).

3. In a previous paper (Coles 1983a) I have described processes of role negotiation by Hausa women of childbearing age who manage their images in social interaction so that they appear to be supportive of norms which enforce adherence to seclusion while actually behaving in a manner contrary to them. Their strategies and behaviors influence the actions of other females (and males) in the society.

4. The term *karuwa* (prostitute or courtesan) tends to be used by males to refer to all unmarried women of childbearing age who are not kin, while it is used by women more specifically to refer to a woman who actually practices prostitution; *bazawara* is used by males to refer to single women who are kin and by females to identify women who are not practicing prostitution but are living without a husband. As prostitutes tend to move away from their natal families, it is not surprising that none were present in the network of women studied here (see Pittin 1983).

5. The use of the term *Hajiya* signifies that she has made the pilgrimage (*hajj*) to Mecca.

6. Categories were delineated for analytic purposes after data had been collected. Clearly, they overlap and are not meant to be considered rigid and exclusive.

7. The idea of looking at a single social system based both upon kinship and residence was suggested by Dr. Jan Vansina. Pierre Bourdieu (1977) has argued along similar lines (see chs. 1–2).

8. A few women choose to remain secluded or are expected to do so by husbands who are Muslim scholars or prayer leaders, very wealthy, or of extremely high status. But even these characteristics do not insure seclusion in old age.

9. Hausa distinguish between a child who is fostered (*riko*) and one who is adopted (*agola*). Either males or females of any age may foster children, that is, raise them until the time of their marriage. The genitors may or may not exercise continued control over children fostered with relatives or close friends. Adopted children are those whom a male agrees to accept and support when he marries a widowed or divorced woman with children from a previous marriage.

10. Ongoing data analysis (which has not yet been completed) may show such differences in Kaduna as Pittin has found in Kano for widows and divorcees. However, because

a number of women in the Kaduna sample were married to, or widows of, former soldiers, the existence of pensions may also provide a source of income not necessarily found among the general population of older Hausa women.

11. Hausa women generally have several different income-earning activities which vary seasonally, with market conditions, as they can obtain needed assistance in the work from other individuals, and as they are able to finance them.

12. Most Koranic scholars teaching in Islamic schools are males, although there are a few Hausa women teaching. In the single school located in Unguwan Kanawa, two married women of childbearing age were teaching in 1985. Boyd and Last (1985) describe the roles of Hausa female Islamic scholars around the time of the *jihad* (1804–1806) and make the case that this is a historical tradition which has not been adequately recognized by contemporary scholars in Hausaland.

13. This change will be felt fully in the society only in long-range terms as life expectancy increases. However, in looking at the experiences of individual older women today, improved medical care has lengthened their lives in a number of cases and provided for their being in old age for a longer period of time.

14. A number of characteristics describe innovative middle-aged and old women in Unguwan Kanawa and Unguwan Shanu. Not all these qualities are present in each individual referred to here as an innovator. First, several had married men employed in the military, police, or civil service and had lived in various locations in Nigeria to which their husbands had been posted. A second characteristic appears to be the development of a successful occupation such that a woman can support herself and, as she grows older, to allow her to refuse to marry. Finally, a group of "marginal" women, primarily those who do not have children, may be innovators. Hajiya Mai Magani, the local herbalist, is one such individual. Younger Western-educated Hausa women, particularly those who attended secular schools through secondary levels and above, also tend to be innovators, perhaps by necessity. Frequently, such women had fathers employed in the military, police, or civil service.

PART II
THE CULTURAL CONSTRUCTION OF INTERGENERATIONAL TIES

While most other primates live in multi-aged communities, only human societies have developed systems that require high levels of prolonged material and social interdependence between generations. This connection of people in different parts of the life cycle is universally recognized by age-linked language categories, such as child, adult, and old person. The variable definitions of when and how persons move through such markers of age-based status and the expectations attached to each category strongly shape the culturally differentiated perceptions of time, aging, and generation (Smith 1961; La Fontaine 1978; Fry and Keith 1982; Kertzer 1982; Fortes 1984). In section IV Jane Peterson shows that chronological age and even the words old age and aging have little cultural meaning for African American women in a Seattle community. Rather, "maturity" and having reached the "age of wisdom" are the key linguistic markers for older, adult women who are called "the wise." This designation of "wise" is given to women who have not only borne but also have raised children, who in turn have their own offspring. Women who might be in their eighties but have not accomplished these social tasks of maturity will be considered in the same generation as teenagers.

Social boundaries associated with age-based statuses show great variation in the degree to which they allot power and esteem to the differently named categories of persons. For example, the Mbuti pygmy hunter-gatherers of Zaire have four loosely defined age grades (categories): children, youths, adults, and older persons. There are neither elaborate rituals marking the passage from one grade to another nor barriers to easy interaction between those in different age categories. However, there are well-known norms of the behavior and responsibility assumed to be the reserve of a given grade. Despite having great regard for the aged, who as a category of person are called *mangese*, the great ones, the

Mbuti have one of the most balanced, egalitarian systems of linking generations that is known in the ethnographic literature. Unlike the Tiwi there is no hoarding or "sanctified keeping" (Maxwell 1986) of esoteric knowledge by the elderly or attempt to control the lives of the younger generations among the Mbuti. As Colin Turnbull notes:

> The responsibility allocated to childhood was that of ritual purification, most specifically in the daily act of lighting the hunting fire. The youths had full control of the political arena, and the adults were fully occupied with all the major economic responsibilities. The role of the elders was the one, as vital as all the others, of socialization. During the daytime, when youths and adults were off on the hunt, the elders mostly stayed behind in the camp, looking after the young children. By playing with them, acting out great sagas of the hunting and gathering days of yore, or just by lying back under the trees and telling stories, old women and men, the *tata* of the camp, filled the youngsters with their own love of the forest, their trust in it, and their respect for the forest values that made life so good. (1983:55)

In contrast, one can find societies where age grades are transformed into sharply ascribed age sets, where different spans along the life cycle are sharply set apart by spectacular ritual, distinct dress, specialized tasks, modes of speech, comportment, and deferential gestures. Here persons move through the life cycle collectively and form tightly bound groups performing specific tasks. While societies where age plays such a powerful role in ordering social life have been found in Africa, among certain Native American groups, Australian aborigines, and in Papua New Guinea, their occurrence is relatively rare (see Stewart 1977; Hinnant 1986). The most elaborated forms of such cultural systems are found among East African nomadic herders, such as the Samburu of Kenya (Spencer 1965; see also Legesse 1973; Baxter and Almagor 1978; Sangree 1986, 1988 for other East African groups). Here age sets of males initiated together move through the life cycle collectively. Over time and through elaborate rutual they progressively enter, as a group, age-bounded roles of herders, warriors, and finally various levels of elders who exert control on the lives of younger community members. Elders in their fifth and sixth decades gain substantial power through maintaining large polygynous households, holding wealth in their numerous cattle, and having a ritual link to the ancestors, whom they can call upon to supernaturally curse younger persons who misbehave. As is the case for most such age-based societies, a Samburu woman's social maturation is accomplished through individual life-cycle rituals, and her status is much more tied to her place in the family unit (see Kertzer and Madison 1981 for the rarer case of women's age-sets).

All too often such cultures have been held up as exemplars of places where the elderly are truly respected and are well-off. It is important to note that this is frequently accomplished at the expense of intense intergenerational conflict, of exploiting and repressing the young and preventing women from gaining an equitable place in the community. Among the Samburu, older women in fact do not share the very high esteem accorded to old men, and, especially when widowed, they suffer both materially and socially.

FAMILIES AND GENEALOGICAL GENERATIONS

A basic structural difference between kin-based small-scale societies such as the Tiwi or the !Kung and the United States is that in the first type of society the elderly have available a life-span continuity with access to essential resources derived from membership in kinship groupings. In such cultural settings, the wide embrace of family frequently provides what Simic (1978b) calls a "life-term arena" — a stable setting for the engagement of an entire life. Even in the age-set societies noted above, the intense ties among age-mates or the ritual bonds across "social" generations do not destroy the links between what Baxter and Almagor (1978) call "genealogical" generations — forged from the developmental cycle of family formation.

In capitalist, industrial societies, it is more typical that access to resources and status over the life-span requires productive participation outside of one's kin group and the transit through numerous "short-term arenas." However, over the last two decades many gerontologists have marveled at the "discovery" that our system of urban industrialism had not, as had been predicted by some sociological prognosticators of the 1930s, totally destroyed extended family contact and intergenerational bonds (Sussman 1965). Pointing to facts such as that almost 80 percent of the elderly live within one hour's drive of a child and have contact at least once a month, various studies have decried any easy assumption that the elderly are socially divorced from their younger kin (Shanas 1979). Although fewer than one in ten of our elderly live in three-generation households, research has shown the persistence of a so-called modified extended family composed of partially independent, nuclear families engaged in frequent contact and support among the generations (Sussman 1965). Nevertheless, relatively little attention has been paid to understanding the cultural factors shaping such interaction (Rubinstein and Johnsen 1982). The three chapters in this section seek to remedy this situation.

In the first selection, Andrei Simic examines value systems and socialization processes to draw a strong qualitative contrast of intergenerational relationships between South Slavic peoples of Yugoslavia and those of the United States. Here two opposing models are analyzed: a white, middle-class American pattern of self-realization, independence, and generational replication is compared to a Yugoslav ideal stressing kinship corporacy, interdependence, and generational symbiosis. In making this analysis, Simic draws not only upon his many years of research in Europe but also on quite recent fieldwork among Yugoslav-Americans in California.

As Simic notes, the replication of genealogical generations in the United States tends to permit only certain types of exchanges which would not impinge upon the independence of individuals. This can be relaxed somewhat when the interaction of alternate generations such as grandparent and grandchild is considered. However, performance of this role relationship among middle-class Euro-American background families still must not interfere with the perceived roles of the middle generation as independent self-reliant parents. It is especially important to cross-culturally examine roles of the elderly, such as grandparenthood, which are universally embedded in family relationships. In such an examination, one can show both the potentials and limitations of this oft-noted dimension of older adult life.

By focusing on Native Americans in California and a reservation in South Dakota, Joan Weibel-Orlando makes a strong contribution to our knowledge about how cultural context affects the grandparenting role. Compared to Euro-American background families, less restricted boundaries between genealogical generations often provides the possibility for grandparents to have crucial roles as "cultural conservators"; they may even request that they bring up as their own one or more of their grandchildren. However, in her sensitive portrayal of contemporary Native American life, Weibel-Orlando shows that there is a variety of grandparenting models among the peoples she studied. These different ways of being an Indian grandparent reflect not only ancient, indigenous patterns but needs generated by poverty-imposed stresses placed on the parenting generation. The lessons from her study as well as from Simic's discussion of Yugoslav-American can be profitably added to the later chapters on the ethnic aged in section IV.

THE FAMILY CONTEXT OF CAREGIVING TO THE ELDERLY

One of the central issues in gerontological research on intergenerational relations is the degree to which the elderly can expect to receive various types of support from their younger relatives (Springer and Brubaker 1984; Bass 1987; U.S. Select Committee on Aging 1987; Kendig, Hashimoto, and Coppard, in press). Leo Simmons, in his examination of the role of the aged in seventy-one nonindustrial societies, observes that "throughout human history the family has been the safest haven for the aged. Its ties have been the most intimate and long-lasting, and on them the aged have relied for greatest security" (1945:176). In Third World nations this is still generally the case, even in urban areas in which a majority of older adults reside with younger relatives and must rely exclusively on familial resources for survival. For families in these countries the capacity for care of the aged is shaped not only by values and kinship structures but also by demographic conditions producing an adequate number of *potential* caregivers. Here the mean number of persons aged 45 to 49 per hundred individuals aged 65 to 74 was 163 in 1975 compared with a figure of 92 in the industrialized countries (Giele 1982:44). However, as Sokolovsky and

Sokolovsky (1983b) have shown in their study of a peasant village in Mexico, the specific nature of kinship systems and how they link up to public domains of support for the aged greatly influence the family's capability for support in rapidly changing Third World contexts.

Although many of the world's poorest countries — such as Afghanistan, Chad, Mali, India, Haiti — have legislated some type of public pension system, often less than one-third of the economically active population is eligible for benefits which when applicable amount to only 40 to 50 percent of pre-retirement wages (U.S. Department of Health and Human Services 1982; Petri 1982). Such entitlement programs seldom reach rural sectors, where 75 percent of the Third World elderly live. Commonly, the rationale for the lack of extending pension programs to peasant populations is that the family can tend to the needs of all its members. However, in just the last decade certain changes, particularly urbanization and economic dislocation, have radically changed the kin-centered basis for support in many developing countries. For example, "in Malaysia, the Philippines, and South Korea, rural households were found to be smaller and less likely than urban households to include elderly persons living with their offspring" (Kinsella 1988:29). Caused by the mass migration of young adults to cities, such a situation can be particularly stressful on middle-aged and older women in rural areas, for they often bear the brunt of both agricultural labor and care of their older spouses and kin (M. J. Gibson 1985; Doty 1986a).

Even where the structure of the extended family persists in "traditional societies," policy makers should not harbor unqualified optimism about intergenerational kindness or the capacity of family systems to ensure the well-being of aged relatives (Levine 1965; Nydegger 1983). This was illustrated by a study by Goldstein, Schuler, and Ross (1983) of Hindu households in Kathmandu, Nepal, where 61 percent of all aged individuals lived with at least one son. It was noted that while the ideal *form* of the patrilineal extended family existed, the material and psychological foundations of filial support were rapidly disintegrating. The authors found it particularly ironic that given the Hindu ideal value of depending on a male child in old age, "the most truly miserable elderly parents were the very ones who objectively were completely dependent upon a son" (p. 722).

In industrialized and highly urban societies, the realization that the elderly are not as isolated as previously thought has stimulated a large body of work exploring "natural" or "informal" systems of support, particularly those generated within the bounds of family relationships (Little 1983; M.J. Gibson 1984; Wenger 1984, 1986; Doty 1986b).[1] To a large extent much of this new work has been accomplished by replacing the traditional approach to social structure, that of examining normative roles, with a social network approach, which looks at the actual transactions that pass between and within generations and the cultural mechanisms which regulate that flow (Kahn and Antonucci 1980; Wentowski 1981; Francis 1984; Antonucci 1985; Sokolovsky 1986; Sokolovsky and Cohen 1987; Kart and Longino 1987; van Willigen 1989). The relatively few attempts to conduct cross-cultural studies of family support systems for the aged have been marred by a lack of attention to the qualitative, internal mechanisms that may belie superficial similarities measured by frequency of interaction or ideal statements about the desire to support one's parents. The final selection of this section seeks to avoid such a limited perspective. Using a variety of qualitative and quantitative approaches, from individual case studies to national surveys, Hiroko Akiyama, Toni Antonucci, and Ruth Campbell provide a pathbreaking study of intergenerational exchange among women in Japan and the United States. A comparison of these two societies is particularly important as it allows us to hold relatively constant the factor of urban-industrial development while comparing the effect of dramatically different cultures on the life of the elderly. Here we see that in Japan the statistic of extremely high elderly coresidence with adult children (70 percent versus 19 percent in the United States) is embedded within a cultural system with different values and perspectives on the nature of intergenerational reciprocity (Maeda and Shimazu, in press).

NOTE

1. In the 1983 volume of the *Gerontologist*, where Little's introductory article appears, there are numerous other articles from many nations, including Israel, Japan, China, Egypt, Poland, Australia, Sweden, and the United States.

4 AGING, WORLD VIEW, AND INTERGENERATIONAL RELATIONS IN AMERICA AND YUGOSLAVIA

Andrei Simic

This chapter will explore aging and seniority in mainstream Anglo-American and Yugoslav culture in terms of contrasting value systems and the behavior they engender. In this respect, the American ethos will be characterized in terms of individualism, generational independence, and self-determination, while Yugoslav world view will be stereotyped as stressing kinship corporacy and intergenerational symbiosis. In this context, aging will be conceptualized not simply within the framework of old age, but as a process subsuming the entire life-span. Thus, such phenomena as childrearing practices, the family developmental cycle, attitudes toward money and work, and residence patterns will be shown to reflect overarching values that profoundly affect the position of the elderly.

The model of middle-class American culture that will be described here is largely an impressionistic one but, nevertheless, one that is consistent with the opinions of a number of scholarly observers of life in this country and other Western industrial-urban societies. The contrasting description of Yugoslav intergenerational and family relations has been derived from fieldwork carried out on five occasions since 1966 in both rural and urban settings in Yugoslavia and among Yugoslav-Americans since 1974. Research was conducted in both Catholic and Orthodox parts of Yugoslavia, as well as in both Serbian and Croatian immigrant communities in California,[1] and includes interviews with more than 300 individuals.

This comparison of aging in two contrasting cultural contexts will strive not only to contribute to our understanding of the variability of the aging process but also to shed light on the perplexing theoretical problem regarding the fit between abstract values and actual behavior. What will be suggested is that culture constitutes one of a number of influences present in the social environment, and that the individual must often make critical choices between opposing imperatives (Simic 1978a:9–22). Thus, culture will be interpreted as largely channeling behavior rather than determining it. Similarly, although the discussion will focus on social and cultural regularities, this should not be conceived as a negation of the active and frequently unpredictable role of the individual, nor of the dynamics generated by the interplay of relatively static mores and ever-changing situations.

VALUES AND INTERGENERATIONAL RELATIONS IN AMERICA

In a recent study focusing on nonindustrial societies, Nancy Foner (1984) has noted that age inequalities have crucial implications for old people's lives and their relationships with younger people, in that they form the basis of structural inequalities. However, her research also makes it clear that the ramifications of this will vary from culture to culture and that it is not always to the detriment of the elderly. Similarly, in a study of parent-youth conflict, Kingsley Davis (1940) observes that, although such conflict appears to exist in all societies, its extent and severity depend on such variables as the rate of social change and the complexity and degree of integration of the culture. In this regard, Davis contrasts contemporary urban-industrial society with rural communities of the past, where the family was the primary unit of production and socialization. He characterizes intergenerational relations in this setting in terms of a gradual and culturally predictable emancipation of children from parents with little competition for status. Davis's essay is representative of a vast sociological literature dealing with intergenerational conflict in our society (for a summary of these, see Bengtson, Furlong, and Laufer 1974). It is significant that there are few comparable studies from Yugoslavia. Thus, one possible interpretation of this is that such conflict constitutes a relatively more important facet of American life, and since it is an artifact of intergenerational relationships, it will have special significance for the elderly. Undoubtedly, its causes can be attributed to a variety of factors including the high level of social and spatial mobility that has characterized the United States since its inception. Regardless of its historical origins, it is my contention that this behavior is perpetuated by cultural imperatives reflecting a distinct world view.

What is probably most remarkable about American culture (as well as that of a few other highly industrial and urbanized Western countries) is its uniqueness, a uniqueness that characterizes our way of life as a distinct societal type in opposition to a spectrum of technologically less developed and more "traditional" nations. This quality does not stem entirely from our high level of economic and technical acumen, nor from our material prosperity, but rather it is rooted in the most basic ideas regarding the nature of interpersonal relationships, especially those pertaining to the family (Simic 1982:51–52).

There seems little doubt that self-determination, independence, and individualism are among the most widely accepted values in our society. Recently, these abstractions, together with their derived behavioral manifestations, have assumed an increasingly prominent role. Nowhere is this more evident than in family life, with its deemphasis on corporacy and the orientation of its constituent members away from the household toward the external world, each with his or her own unique set of interests and concomitant social network. These centrifugal characteristics have been noted over and over by a spectrum of observers. For instance, Thomas Meenaghan (1986:4) comments that the postindustrial period in America can be described in terms of the "highlighting of the individual as the basis for organization of the society." Similarly, with greater specificity, David Riesman (1972:38) notes in an essay dealing with American character in the twentieth century that children, through the influence of their peers, the school, and the mass media, are oriented towards imperatives that are not in harmony with parental ones. Yugoslav anthropologist and psychologist Vera Stein Erlich (who lived and worked in California for over ten years) has made similar observations: "The desire for complete independence has become so strong during the past few decades that it has emerged as one of the principal causes for the isolation of older people, and although the entire American life style from its incipiency placed personal independence on a high rung of the value scale, the desire for independence has become so absolute in recent times that it is threatening family life" (1972:55) (my translation).

This problem is also recognized by Edward Levine, who laments the adverse affect of individualistic cultural values on childrearing practices in our society: "Among the most important cultural changes that have come in the wake of the transforming forces of urbanization and industrialization has been the growing emphasis on impulse-gratification, self-centeredness, and an orientation to the present, as well as the increasing interest in individual fulfillment" (1982:198).

The causal role played by such rampant individualism in undermining intergenerational relationships is stressed by Peter Uhlenberg and David Eggebeen, who state: "As men and women increase their commitment to their own self-fulfillment, they necessarily reduce their commitment to sacrificing personal pursuits for their children's welfare" (1986:36).

If self-fulfillment and unfettered individualism are indeed central values driving a rift between children and parents and subverting family solidarity, then what are the behavioral correlates of this world view? At least in part, the answer to this question can be illuminated by reference to the middle-class American socialization process, the family developmental cycle, patterns of authority and affect in the family, and, most significantly, underlying assumptions about the content and conduct of interpersonal relationships in general. Significantly, these are topics traditionally treated by anthropologists; thus, as an ethnographer I will attempt to describe these as much as possible from an alien perspective, that is, focusing critically on phenomena that we as natives commonly take for granted.

The short developmental cycle of the American family can provide a starting point for understanding the culture of aging in our society since the behavior that contributes to its brevity also shapes the roles that its members are destined to play in later life. In this regard, the experience of the elderly cannot be interpreted in solely historical, economic, or situational terms. Rather, we must turn to cultural values and the socialization process by which they are inculcated from a child's earliest years. Of particular significance is the concept of independence, which provides a central childrearing theme. Closely related to this is the idea of privacy with its connotation of the right, pleasure, and necessity of being alone. The expression, "I need my space," should not be interpreted entirely metaphorically, but also as a serious statement of American ethos. For instance, this value is reflected in the strong desire for the exclusive control of individual space within the household and in the stress on personal, rather than familial, ownership of material possessions. It is significant that the word privacy cannot be translated into Serbo-Croatian (nor into a number of other languages including Spanish), but can only be glossed by such terms as *tajnost* (secrecy), *osamljenost* (loneliness), and *povuchenost* (withdrawal), all of which have highly negative connotations (Filipovic 1966:764). Thus, privacy is what Paul Bohannan (1963:11–12) has labeled a "key term," that is, an expression identifying an important category within a culture, one which usually cannot be directly translated into other languages but must be explained contextually.

The American concept of privacy, with all that it implies, is inculcated from a very early age, often when a newborn child is given a room apart from its parents and siblings in recognition of a culturally assumed need for individual space. Underlying this are the beliefs that each child's uniqueness transcends the commonality of the family group and that brothers and sisters will inevitably develop divergent interests, values, and extrafamilial ties that will not be shared with other members of the household. In contrast to these prevalent American attitudes, Levine stereotypes the family ideal in "traditional societies": "Children helped parents with their tasks, adopted their family's culture and religion as a matter of course, and learned family roles, values, and standards that were essentially consistent with those of the community. They also knew that deviance from them quickly brought harsh sanctions" (1986:4).

Underlying the socialization process of many American children are a belief in the desirability of peer-group solidarity and a stress on relationships achieved through the sharing of narrowly defined interests. What is evident is that family ties are given no special preference over extrafamilial ones and are, in fact, frequently subverted to them. This early orientation toward the world outside of the home is reflected in the realization of such rituals as birthday parties, where parents and other family members remain discreetly in the background, sometimes not actually partaking in the festivities at all, while active participation is limited to the child and his or her invited peers. This behavior reaches its most extreme form during the teens, when young people unabashedly, even righteously, exile their parents from the home during gatherings and parties which sometimes reach orgiastic proportions in the proclamation of filial independence. This phenomenon appears to be broadly, though certainly not universally, accepted as part of the normal segregation of the generations. At least in part, these attitudes can be attributed to the fact that adolescents in modern societies spend a great deal of their lives in school isolated with their age-mates. Moreover, the orientation of American children is further directed away from the home through their participation in a spectrum of clubs, classes, sports, and other planned activities. Thus, they are influenced to a greater extent by their peers than by their parents (Coleman 1961). At the same time, the parents themselves frequently orient their interests toward concerns having little to do with their families as a whole. The reality is that in many American homes children and parents actually see very little of each other during the most formative period of a young person's life.

While this outward direction of young people away from the home is surely facilitated by middle-class prosperity (Elkind 1986:44), it is also clear that this is in total harmony with our expectations that children will not spend a significant part of their leisure time interacting with family members. And when they choose to do so, they are as often as not regarded apprehensively as "odd," and corrective efforts are usually made to encourage greater participation in peer-group activities. For instance, "social adjustment," which seems to signify "getting along with one's peers," has long been a concern of American public education. This same focus continues throughout life, and adults, like their children, join with their own age-mates in a sometimes frenetic and exhausting round of benevolent, civic-minded, and recreational activities that have little or no relationship to the needs and welfare of their families as a whole (Banfield 1958:15).

The appearance some time ago of the term "youth culture" simply represented the institutionalization of the long-standing idea that age groups were characterized by distinct and largely exclusive interests and traits. This phenomenon has clearly had an impact on the elderly as well as on the young. For example, Christie Kiefer (1971) has described the aged as a "social minority," while Arnold Rose (1962) has portrayed them as "the carriers of a distinctive subculture." One implication is that the elderly have been forced to live lives apart from those ideas and activities deemed most significant by those younger than themselves. However, what must also be considered is that the elderly are simply following the dictates of a world view to which they themselves also subscribe.

Another value profoundly affecting American family life is the democratic ideal. This is reflected in a stress on the equality of rights and equal participation in decision making within the limits of each member's skills and knowledge. At the same time, there is a concomitant deemphasis of hierarchical principles based on either age or sex. Therefore, lacking clear-cut rules for the wielding of power within the home, the decisive factor rests on the nature of the various personalities. This is not to say that parents do not exercise authority over children, especially young ones, but simply that the rights of adults vis-à-vis children are only vaguely defined, and that most, if not all, formal signs of deference toward older persons have disappeared. Moreover, those parental prerogatives that do remain are usually eroded as children approach adulthood. Similarly, in contrast to many traditional cultures, older siblings are rarely given lasting authority over, or responsibility for, their younger brothers and sisters. On the contrary, efforts by older children to dominate younger ones are most often discouraged, even regarded as an unfortunate form of antisocial behavior.

Closely related to the issue of authority is that of affect within the family. In this case, the striving for personal autonomy tends to limit the nature of affectual exchanges since these also constitute a medium for the exercise of power and/or control (Simic 1978b:18). Effusive displays of affection are characteristically limited to interaction between husbands and wives (and in many families this, too, appears to be a rare occurrence) or to attentions directed towards very young children. With the beginning of adolescence there is an expectation that most forms of physical affection between children and parents will diminish, and marriage signals the almost total transfer of loyalties and sentiment from the natal family to the newly created household. It is implicitly assumed that the most lasting bonds will be those linking husband and wife, who constitute the only potentially life-term corporate unit within the family. Today, even this relationship is problematical, and recent currents of thought suggest that husband and wife should also be free of entangling mutual obligations, each to pursue his or her individual interests and fulfillment.

In few areas of family life is corporate sentiment more lacking than in the realm of economics. From a very early age children are encouraged to earn money, a practice, for instance, that in many other areas (such as Yugoslavia and Latin America) is typical only of the peasantry and urban poor. Among the American middle class this is usually rationalized as "learning the value of money." However, there is also the implication that "money can make one free." Thus, children are rarely expected to contribute their earnings to the family coffers. In other words, a child's money is private property to be disposed of according to his or her own desires. This same kind of compartmentalization continues into later life, and it is not uncommon that husbands and wives in two-earner families maintain individual rather than joint control over their finances. Implicit in this value system is the presumption that the economic fate of one family member is not necessarily the concern of others. This can be seen in the exchange of money within family groups, which is frequently phrased in terms of a "loan" rather than the sharing of joint resources. While parents frequently aid their children financially, this is as often as not rationalized as helping them achieve "independence." Thus, such exchanges are not intended to create lasting reciprocal ties and obligations between the generations. This same ideology prevails in old age, and what the American elderly seem to fear most is "demeaning dependence" on their children or other kin. Rather, the ideal is to remain "one's own person."

Outside the household, behavior is greatly influenced by values focusing on universal standards and an ideological aversion to personalism and nepotism. This ethos by its very nature tends to blur the boundaries between family and nonkin. The result is that in America, unlike many other parts of the world, the kinship group does not provide the focus of a rigidly defined moral universe characterized by a double standard differentiating behavior considered characteristically "good" and associated with close kin from that permitted in the "amoral" sphere of the larger society (Simic 1975:48–50). Thus, in our culture, although actual practice deviates considerably from this model, ideally the same general standards should be applied to kin and nonkin alike. Even such previously venerable concepts as a parent's responsibility for the actions of his or her child have recently come under question. All of this reflects a conceptually weak corporate image of the family and fails, in many cases, to provide the basis for a lifetime of cooperation and reciprocity linking the generations.

If the family now provides a diminished arena for social and moral engagement and for the definition of individual identity and esteem, what does? One explanation can be found in the familiar concept of *work* and its middle-class correlate, the *career*. Reference is made here to the familiar ideas associated with Protestantism, and in particular with its Calvinist variant (Weber 1930). The secular expression of this ideology has been commonly associated with the concept of work as a moral commitment containing its own intrinsic rewards in addition to any material remuneration. Perhaps in few other areas of the world has this idea enjoyed greater currency than among the American business and professional classes, where, for many, it has taken on the aspect of an absolute, sometimes compulsive imperative. Moreover, what in recent times appears to have been a movement away from this ethos in the direction of a variety of popular philosophies centering on transcendence, self-improvement, self-realization, and pure hedonism has, in fact, been functionally quite similar to the Puritan ethic in its stress on the realization of self as a moral absolute.

No matter what guise it may assume, the work ethic has become a cliché of American national character and as such merits reexamination in the context of family life. It is indicative that in our society occupational markers of identity have largely replaced those derived from kinship. Observing this, an anthropologist of Hindu birth, Triloki Pandey, once commented to me that upon meeting a stranger in India, one does not first ask the given name and occupation, but rather the identity of the person's kinship group.

These observations underscore the primacy of both individualism and work in America, and draw attention to the tendency to regard the family as little more than a logistic mechanism supporting its members in their disparate occupations and interests. Thus, activities outside of the home are not usually regarded as part of a common effort uniting the family, but rather constitute the fulfillment of unrelated personal aspirations and the moral obligation to strive for individual psychic well-being and emotional fulfillment. At the same time, it should not be concluded that work is valued in American culture and not in others, but simply that the values associated with it in our society differ from those typical of other cultures where work is largely regarded as a means to an end, not as an activity of intrinsic value unto itself.

VALUES AND INTERGENERATIONAL RELATIONS AMONG THE SOUTH SLAVS

Yugoslavia's present cannot be understood adequately without reference to the past. This is probably true to a greater extent in the Balkans than in most other parts of Europe, because here modernization in the form of urbanization and industrialization occurred only very recently — since the close of the World War II (Simic 1973:28–34). In this respect, Yugoslavia can be described as an intermediate society, that is, it has not yet completed the transformation into a contemporary nonagrarian nation. Such cultures are typified by the coexistence of traditional and modern elements, elements that sometimes interact in harmony and, at other times, in sharp conflict. For example, in Yugoslavia not only do traditional forms of kinship and household organization survive in the countryside, but even in the urban centers traditional kinship ideology has persisted, structuring family and other relationships alike.

Until the 1960s the majority of Yugoslavia's population was rural with the peasant family constituting the basic unit of production and social identity. In much of southern and central Yugoslavia the prevailing model of the village family was the *zadruga*, a patrilocally extended household controlling land, livestock, equipment, and other material and ritual property communally. In some cases these households were quite large with as many as eighty or more coresident members (Hammel 1968:14–15). Even today some households with over one-hundred members persist among the Albanian minority in southwestern Serbia.

In the period prior to World War I, a closely related, and perhaps more ancient, form of social organization prevailed in the rugged Dinaric Mountains of western Yugoslavia. Here relatively small and often isolated households were organized into patrilineal clans called "brotherhoods" (*bratstva*), which constituted the maximal units of kinship organization. These were also political bodies articulating power through the medium of the blood feud (Djilas 1958; Simic 1967; Boehm 1984). Both the Dinaric tribal system and the *zadruga* reckoned descent through the male line, and although there were elements of democracy in both variants of family organization (Buric 1976), this was within the limits of a hierarchy based on seniority and male dominance.

In contrast, in the northern and coastal parts of Yugoslavia (especially in Dalmatia and Slovenia) the family structure was under the influence of Italy and Central Europe and more resembled its counterparts in the West. But even here, there appears to have always been a patrilineal bias and a stress on kinship solidarity beyond the nuclear family.

In areas formerly characterized by the *zadruga*, since the turn of the century, there has been a decline in the size and economic significance of large extended families. However, these changes appear to be less in function or ideology than in form. Joel Halpern and Barbara Kerewsky-Halpern (1986:16–44), for example, report that what has occurred is a shift from lateral to lineal extension of the household. In other words, rural families now contain more generations than previously, although their overall size has diminished. In the case of highland Dinaric tribal society, while kinship groups have largely lost their political role due to the encroachment of governmental authority, the stress on kinship has survived and developed new functions.

In the face of the enormous social, political, and demographic changes that have taken place over the last four decades, including massive peasant migration to the cities, South Slav culture has shown great tenacity and adaptability (Hammel 1969; Simic 1974). This phenomenon contradicts the contention by many social scientists that kinship fails to play a significant role in urban-industrial society. Yugoslavia, at least, provides a counterindicative case substantiating Lewis's (1952:40) assertion that "urbanization is not a simple, unitary, universally similar process," but rather one that "assumes different forms and meanings, depending upon the prevailing historic, economic, social, and cultural conditions."

The model of the contemporary Yugoslav family that will be suggested here is one that strives to illuminate those traits which transcend both regional and ethnoreligious differences as well as the rural-urban dichotomy. As an introduction, I would like to assert that the cultivation of social ties with kin and nonkin alike constitutes a kind of South Slav national vice. In fact, the preoccupation with interpersonal relationships is an all-absorbing one, often so extreme as to inhibit the functioning of ostensibly universalistic economic and governmental institutions (Buric 1976:117–18; Simic 1983a).

Of all the arenas of personal social engagement, family and kinship are the most intense, highly cultivated, and morally obligatory. A major difference between the South Slav family and its American counterpart is a processual one. The developmental cycle of the Yugoslav family is generally not marked by the same sharp breaks and discontinuities characteristic of the American household. The family in Yugoslavia frequently spans a number of generations without total cleavages in its composition, and even in death members continue to exert their influence and project their presence on the living. It is difficult to place temporal boundaries on the South Slav family since, in many cases, one generation simply flows into the roles occupied by the previous one. Thus, replication takes place, not in the context of newly formed family units as in America where premarital and postmarital neolocality prevail, but through the gradual replacement of members within the same social entities.

Postmarital neolocality, although it does occur, is neither in harmony with traditional Yugoslav values nor with the exigencies of city life in this rapidly urbanizing country with an acute housing shortage. In the countryside, patrilocality is still the rule, especially in the more conservative areas such as Serbia. Therefore, it is common for a bride, at least initially, to join her husband's household, while in other cases, a newly constructed house on a plot of land adjoining the groom's father's, or even grandfather's, farmyard will constitute the couple's new residence. Frequently, some child, usually a son, will remain with elderly parents until their death and then continue living in the same home with his (or sometimes her) family of procreation. In many cases, sons continue to work the same land as their fathers, land which may be shared with brothers as an undivided patrimony. Thus, while there is some sloughing off of family members through death or other forms of separation such as migration to urban centers or abroad, households tend to exhibit continuity over a number of generations. In other words, the family cycle of fusion and fission is not usually punctuated by abrupt separations, as is so commonly the case in the United States. Rather, the transition from generation to generation tends to be an imperceptible and gradual one.

In 1969 a survey by the Institute for Social Policy in Belgrade (Nedeljkovic 1970) studied 1798 elderly peasants (over sixty-five) in various parts of Yugoslavia, and a similar group of 878 urbanites from six cities. It was discovered that in 66 percent of the village cases and in 47 percent of the urban ones a child was living with his or her parent. Only 10 percent of the peasants and 17 percent of the urban group lived alone, and fewer than 3 percent of those who were physically unable to carry out normal household tasks in both rural and urban settings lacked some family member or kin to aid them. Thus, kinship provided an invaluable resource for elderly peasants and urbanites alike.

In village and city alike, unmarried individuals, of whatever age, expect in the normal course of events to live with parents or other kin whenever possible. Although economic conditions and housing problems usually preclude premarital neolocality, cultural considerations appear paramount. For example, not a single respondent from among fifty-six young adults from a spectrum of social classes whom I interviewed in Belgrade during 1968 and 1969 voiced the desire to have his or her own personal residence. The idea was simply alien to them, and my impressions from a 1988 trip to Yugoslavia indicate that these attitudes had changed little over seventeen years. The response of a twenty-two-year-old university student to the question as to whether she would like to have her "own apartment" was typical: "What a strange idea! It would be so lonely without my parents." Also clear from interviews with people of all ages is that the American concept of "privacy" is not only unfamiliar, it strikes Yugoslavs as somehow deviant and antisocial.

Even when household members are physically separated, this does not necessarily result in the loosening of family ties. In response to the increased spatial mobility of the Yugoslav population, dual or even multiple residence is not at all uncommon. For example, older people frequently spend the warm summer months in their native villages and the cold winters in the greater comfort of their children's urban apartments. Another common phenomenon is the exchange between kin of urban and rural children during school holidays. In this respect, of the hundreds of urban Yugoslavs I have interviewed and known over the past twenty years, only a few lacked or failed to maintain ties to rural relatives.

Another sign of the corporate mentality that continues to unite members of recently separated households is behavior associated with the celebration of the lineage patron saint, the *slava*. Among the Serbs, the *slava* is observed by all those who trace common descent through the male line from the founder of their lineage. Observances take the form of ritual feasts held in each independent household, while lineage solidarity is symbolized by the veneration of a common supernatural patron. However, many adult males living apart from their fathers do not hold an official commemoration in their own homes as long as their fathers are alive. The explanation offered by one Belgrade informant was simply, "one household, one *slava*." The implication is that, in spite of spatial separation, the family is still conceptually regarded as a single social unit with two loci of residence.

Family corporacy is particularly reflected in economic behavior. This is especially true of rural migrants in the cities who continue to engage in both ritual and material reciprocity with their village kin long after having established residence elsewhere. The same kind of reciprocity also links family members abroad with their kin at home. There is, for example, hardly a Yugoslav village that does not evidence numerous new modern homes built by remittances from "guest workers" in Germany and other parts of Western Europe. Similarly, jet travel has made possible exchanges between immigrants in the United States and their kin in the homeland. The case of a Croatian family in California is not atypical. After almost fifteen years in this country, there appears to be no diminution of ties to family in Yugoslavia. For example, some member of the household has visited kin in their native region almost every year, and the American family has financed numerous visits by relatives to California.

Visiting patterns provide a good indication of family sentiment and commitment. In this regard, E. A. Hammel and Charles Yarbrough (1973:132) found that in a sample of 326 Belgrade males who did not reside with fathers or brothers also living in the Yugoslav capital, there was a mean rate of contact between fathers and sons of every other day, and a frequency of 159 yearly visits between brothers.

Even in death the deceased continue to exert a strong psychological presence among the living, and generational continuity is perpetuated in the form of mortuary customs that include elaborate funerals, the erection of imposing monuments, regular visits to the graves, yearly religious and/or secular observances on the anniversary of death, and, among the Serbs, feasting in the cemeteries on the Days of the Dead (*zadušnice*) and the honoring of deceased ancestors as part of the celebration of the lineage saint's day (the *slava*). However, the death of one's parents does signify the assumption of full adult status since children often remain emotionally tied to their fathers and mothers

Mate Buljan, from California, visits his aged mother in Imotski, Dalmatia, Yugoslavia.

Slava Buljan, from California, visits her aged father in Imotski, Dalmatia, Yugoslavia.

far into adulthood. This is especially true of the relationship between mothers and sons (Simic 1983b), and to a lesser extent of that between mothers and daughters, since women, at least in rural areas, usually marry into their husband's households and are thus separated from their own parents.

The continuity between generations which typifies South Slav families can be understood with reference to childrearing practices just as the middle-class American predisposition toward individualism can be interpreted in light of the way the young are socialized in our society. In most Yugoslav households there is an early stress on the reciprocal relationships children will maintain with parents and other kin throughout their lives. As mentioned before, the concept of privacy is notably lacking, that is, the recognition of a need to be periodically alone and to control private space and possessions. In fact, such tendencies are not only actively discouraged, but are sometimes regarded as signs of hostility or emotional imbalance. It is probable that many Yugoslavs have never spent any prolonged period alone. To cite but one of many possible examples from my fieldwork: "Mirko came to the United States with his wife and two children to spend a year at a California university doing research in electrical engineering. Near the end of this sojourn, his wife and children decided to return to Sarajevo

Three-generational household in the village of Podi, Boka Kotorska, Yugoslavia (Montenegro).

four weeks earlier than Mirko. At two in the morning of the first night of his family's absence, Mirko called a colleague in a state of extreme agitation asking if he could sleep at his house because he had never been alone overnight in his entire life."

The socialization of Yugoslav children deemphasizes peer-group solidarity, and young people are presumed to identify more strongly with members of their own families than with their age-mates. By American standards, they are expected to spend a large part of their leisure time at home or in the company of family members. This reflects a strong emphasis on age-specific roles, roles that are perceived, however, as symbiotic rather than autonomous in the context of intergenerational relationships. It is significant that when I questioned informants about the kinds of things children and old people did, the reply was frequently, "Old people do old people's things, and children, children's things." Thus, although there is a strong consensus regarding the activities thought appropriate to young people and the elderly, these are not seen as a divisive medium for the expression of individualism, but simply as predictable aspects of a family solidarity based on a sexual and generational division of labor. This ideology is expressed in crisis rites in which kin of all ages are expected to participate actively in their realization. For example, birthday parties (which are a rather recent phenomenon in Yugoslavia) are not viewed primarily as an opportunity for the child to interact with his or her extrafamilial peers, but rather as an occasion to strengthen kinship ties.

The principle of seniority tends to dominate within the Yugoslav household, and most expressions of independence are discouraged among the young. Childrearing is shared by all older family members, including siblings who are given both responsibility for, and authority over, younger brothers and sisters. Grandparents are particularly influential in the rearing of children, and they play an important economic role in urban families by freeing working mothers from household tasks. Similarly, in rural settings, the participation by the elderly in childrearing is an expression of the traditional division of labor. In fact, in many village homes, the young wife can be regarded as a kind of apprentice to her mother-in-law. As Gunhild Hagestad (1985:46) has suggested in a general context, "The presence of grandparents, especially older grandmothers, may also serve as a catalyst for wider family cohesion." In this respect, it is older Yugoslav women who take a leading role in the control and manipulation of family and other social relationships, as well as acting as the safeguarders of traditional mores (Simic 1983b:66–67).

While individualism and self-determination in the American sense are discouraged in Yugoslav children, they are encouraged to perfect their skills and talents and to perform tasks assigned them with excellence, as part of the fulfillment of reciprocal obligations within family and as a sign of filial respect. Economic individualism is also antithetical to the ideal of kinship corporacy, and, in many cases, even adult children contribute their earnings to a common household fund. More generally, there is the expectation that among family members and close kin, good fortune will be shared, reflecting communal rather than personal interests.

Affect in the South Slav family tends to link the generations rather than centering on the husband-wife dyad. In this respect, one should not be unduly influenced by apparent structural similarities between the contemporary South Slav household, particularly its urban variant, which is frequently nuclear, and its stereotypic American counterpart. For example, to understand the lines of affect and authority in the American household, there is usually no need to transcend the boundaries of the nuclear family. In the Yugoslav case, a broader network of kin must be considered, one usually consisting of at least three generations. While in our society marriage constitutes a logical starting point for describing the developmental history of a household, in Yugoslavia, as often as not, marriage simply signifies the addition of a new member to an existing social unit. During the traditional period in the Balkans (which lasted well into this century), in most areas marriages were arranged, and the bride and groom may have scarcely spoken to each other before the ceremony. Even after marriage, there was little expectation of communication, positive affect, or companionship between husband and wife. Moreover, overt signs of affection between a couple were perceived as a threat to the solidarity of the larger kin group, at best interpreted as a sign that the man had become a henpecked husband (*papuchar*). For instance, Halpern calls attention to such behavior in the Serbian village of Orašac where he carried out fieldwork during 1953 and 1954: "Although a great deal of affection is shown children, and from children to parents and grandparents, parents are never openly demonstrative toward one another. In fact, it is still common for couples to refer to each other as He and She or My Husband and My Wife" (1958:202).

Even today, marriage is widely viewed in Yugoslavia as an economic and procreative union, and in most cases husbands and wives do not look to each other for friendship-based companionship (Buric 1976:135). Rather, parents are linked by mutual concern for their children who will remain emotionally attached to them throughout their entire lives (Hammel 1967:57). Thus, intense affection typifies the relationship of children of all ages toward their parents and, by extension, to grandparents as well.

A variant of the South Slav parent-child relationship is what may be called the "sacrificial child syndrome" (Simic 1983b:78–79).[2] This refers to an unmarried son or daughter who remains with aged parents until their death. Probably the most common form of this behavior is where a son renounces marriage in order to care for his mother. Although this also occurs in Anglo-American society, among the Yugoslavs it is considered a valid alternative. It is interesting to note that this phenomenon appears to take place with greater frequency among Yugoslav-Americans than it does in Yugoslavia, where postmarital patrilocality is widely accepted. In contrast, few American-born women seem willing to live with their mothers-in-law. Family histories collected among Serbs and Croats in both Yugoslavia and America suggest that in many instances mothers deliberately select a particular child to be socialized for this role. As a California Serbian Orthodox priest explained it, "What wife could make such a man feel like a king from the moment he enters the house when in reality he is only a common laborer or peasant?" The frequency of this behavior among American Yugoslavs is suggested by my 1976 census of a California Serbian Orthodox parish. Of 119 households surveyed, there was a total of fifty-seven married couples or individuals with living adult children. In twenty-four of these cases, an unmarried son or daughter (a number of them middle-aged) lived with his or her parents or parent; in one case, a married son and his wife lived with his mother; and, in another, an adult grandson lived with his paternal grandmother and greataunt. Thus, in almost half of all those instances where it was possible, the sacrificial child syndrome occurred. Also, this failed to take into account those cases where children lived in close proximity to their parents and saw them on an almost daily basis.

The South Slav family functions to a great extent in terms of a moral double standard, that is, with reference to personalistic values rather than universal ones. Therefore, in relationship to the external world, family members are expected to use their positions and/or influence to aid kin. By extension, relations with close friends are structured according to the same model. Thus, the social universe is divided between those toward whom one has moral obligations and those toward whom one has none.

Among the Yugoslavs, few transcendental values can vie with those associated with kinship and family. For example, work is seldom regarded as an end unto itself, but rather as a means to support and enhance social relationships, both familial and extrafamilial. Therefore, occupational statuses can be seen as secondary to those associated with position in a kinship system. Even the intense nationalistic sentiments which typify the various groups in Yugoslavia are inseparable from family origins. In a similar way, religion is intimately related to both ethnic and kinship loyalties. For instance, national flags and other ethnic emblems are prominently displayed at weddings and other family rituals. Similarly, grave monuments are frequently decorated with both religious and national symbols. Thus, there is a constant reinforcement of kinship ideology through the appeal to both religious and ethnic loyalties.

As in other Mediterranean societies, the Yugoslavs tend to view men and women as "separate orders of creation" (Campbell 1964:150–72; Peristiany 1965). In the same way, the young, the middle aged, and the elderly are perceived as characterized by distinct abilities, predilections, knowledge, and skills. Thus, intergenerational relations are typified by the same kind of complementarity and reciprocity as is the sexual dichotomy. In this respect, there exists an underlying rule of family life: *only likes may compete or occupy identical positions in the same social arena*.[3] In the normal course of events, children do not vie with adults, nor do women strive for the roles of their male kin. Even in contemporary urban settings where the majority of women are employed outside the home, wives and mothers continue to manage the household arena, setting and main-

Ninety-eight year-old Marija Kirincic and two of her daughters, on the island of Krk, Yugoslavia.

taining the moral tone while also manipulating the course of events in the ouside world through the affectual influence they exert over their sons, brothers, and, sometimes, husbands and fathers.

The South Slav family exhibits what may be characterized as long-term dynamics related to different male and female life trajectories (Simic and Myerhoff 1978:236–40). Mothers, for instance, eventually age and die, and wives become mothers and then mothers-in-law and grandmothers. At the same time, men experience profound changes in their later years, when there is a sharp decline in physical strength and aggressiveness, qualities highly valued in males by Yugoslav culture. Moreover, the death of a mother leaves a son with an affectual void that somehow must be filled. Thus, a middle-aged wife is frequently able to assume the role previously occupied by her mother-in-law and in this way reverse the asymmetrical power relationship which typified an earlier period in her life. While the elderly male is no longer able to engage in public demonstrations of machismo, he nevertheless retains the structural position of authority in the family and may even gain prestige in the eyes of his children due to the closer relationship to their mother.

In summary, the evidence points to the expectation of intense and continuing reciprocity between parents and children at whatever point in the life course they may find themselves. Thus, not only do children regard their filial obligations as a lifelong moral imperative, but parents appear to accept these ministrations without feelings of what might be regarded by many Americans as debilitating dependency. Rather, both parties view these intense relationships as further opportunities to engage in the kinds of exchanges that have punctuated their entire lives.

CONCLUSIONS

Two contrasting views of intergenerational relationships have been suggested here, each reflecting a different constellation of overarching values. Nevertheless, this comparison should not be interpreted as an absolute one, but rather as one of degree. It would be naive to deny that individualism, as we conceive it in the West, is utterly lacking in Yugoslavia or that intense family solidarity is unknown among the American middle class. Furthermore, the comparison is not meant to be an invidious one; rather, it is my intention simply to reiterate that each culture must be interpreted in terms of its own value structure. In this respect, aging can be regarded as a kind of career in which most people succeed, to varying degrees, in achieving the goals set out by their cultures (Simic 1978a:77–105). In the Yugoslav case, success in aging depends largely upon the skillful management and manipulation of family relationships throughout the life course. On the one hand, great security can be derived from this, while on the other, personal ambitions frequently must be modified or sacrificed for the collective good. Moreover, in a society that functions largely on the basis of personalism, to lack family and kinship resources is to be at a severe disadvantage. Thus, those who by accident of birth, happenstance, or their own miscalculations find themselves without significant family or kin are destined, especially in old age, to experience a profound sense of alienation from the South Slav value system and its associated rewards.

In America, it seems inevitable that many of our elderly – caught up in a world view stressing individual economic and psychological independence and evaluating excellence in terms of skill and dedication in the carrying out of occupational roles – once deprived of their work statuses and lacking a strong ideology of intergenerational reciprocity, will experience a deep sense of isolation and anomie. It is also not surprising that old people, excluded from these routes to prestige, security, and meaning, in many cases either simply withdraw from active competition for goals that they can no longer hope to achieve (Clark and Anderson 1967) or create age-homogeneous social arenas where they can dramatize their own sense of worth within the context of new or reinterpreted values (Myerhoff 1979; Simic 1982:62). It is significant that such folk aphorisms as "Stay active" and "Be independent" are so frequently heard in our country among the elderly. These maxims simply restate what are core values of our culture as a whole. Nevertheless, it should be noted that, in spite of their sense of alienation and ostensible loneliness, many of the elderly actually subscribe to the very world view that has contributed to their own sense of isolation. In effect, they are unwilling to forgo the reputed pleasures of individualism and independence to commit themselves to the kinds of intense reciprocity that typify family and other social relationships in more traditional societies such as Yugoslavia.

NOTES

This chapter represents an expansion and reinterpretation of a previous article (Simic 1983c).

1. Fieldwork was most recently conducted from 1984 through 1986 among Serbian and Croatian Americans in Northern California as part of a three-year study, "Ethnicity and Successful Aging," financed through the University of Southern California by the National Institute on Aging.

2. I would like to thank my wife, Jacquelene Simic, for recognizing this phenomenon and contributing the term, "the sacrificial child syndrome."

3. See Friedl (1962:87–91) regarding this phenomenon in Greece.

5 GRANDPARENTING STYLES: NATIVE AMERICAN PERSPECTIVES

Joan Weibel-Orlando

Much of the grandparenting literature and especially the small collection of works specifically about Native American grandparenting examine shifts in statuses and roles which aging women experience in relation to their parents, children, grandchildren, and society in general (Amoss 1981; Nahemow 1987; Shanas and Sussman 1981; Schweitzer 1987; Tefft 1968; Teski 1987). Primarily focused on social, cultural, and psychological outcomes for aging women of the status, grandmother, these studies, with a few noteworthy exceptions, assume grandparenthood to be shaped largely by social and biological factors over which the aging woman has little personal control. Grandparenthood, however, is neither defined by the narrow constraints of biological and reproductive attainments nor executed solely within the parameters of cultural consensus. Rather, grandparental roles among contemporary North American Indians are expressed across a range of activities, purposes, and levels of intensity. The ways these components fit together are so varied as to be identified as distinct grandparenting styles. These five grandparenting styles are identified below as: cultural conservator, custodian, ceremonial, distanced, and fictive.

Freedom of choice in the creation of one's particular brand of grandparenthood is considerable. Some American Indian grandparents petition their children for the privilege of primary care responsibilities for one or more grandchildren with considerable success. When parents are reluctant to relinquish care of a child to its grandparents, individuals who relish continuing child care responsibilities past their childbearing years activate alternative strategies of both traditional and contemporaneous origin. Establishment of fictive kinship, provision of foster parent care, and involvement in cultural restoration programs in the public schools are among the alternative roles available to older

American Indians whose grandchildren, either because of distance or parental reluctance, are not immediately accessible to them.

The findings presented here are based on the reflections of the North American Indian grandparents with whom I have worked since 1984 and my observations of their interactions with their grandchildren. The grandparenting styles listed above are defined by seven factors: (1) the quality and intensity of the relationship across the grandparent/grandchild generations; (2) the grandparents' perceptions of what grandparenting goals should be *vis-à-vis* their grandchildren; (3) accessibility of the grandchildren by the grandparents; (4) social and familial integration of the grandparents; (5) personal life course goals of the grandparents; (6) social, economic and psychological stability of the children's parents; and (7) the age at which grandparenthood is attained.

While custodial, fictive, ceremonial, and distanced grandparenting styles are evidenced cross-culturally, I suggest that the cultural conservator grandparenting style, if not particularly North American Indian, is essentially a phenomenon of general ethnic minority-group membership. Fearing loss of identity as a people because of the relentless assimilationist influences of contemporary life, many ethnic minority members view their elders as cultural resources for their children. Grandparents as cultural conservators constitute both a cultural continuity in that reponsibility for the enculturation of the youngest generation was traditionally the role of the grandparents across American Indian tribal groups (Amoss 1981; Schweitzer 1987). Cognizant of the heady influences which attract their urbanized, educated, and upwardly mobile children away from tribal pursuits, many contemporary American Indian grandparents understand their roles as conservators and exemplars of a world view and ethos that may well disappear if they do not consistently and emphatically impart it to and enact it for their grandchildren. The ideological, enculturational, and behavioral components of this grandparenting style are particular foci of this chapter.

DESCRIPTION OF THE SAMPLE

Contemporary North American Indian life has been an abiding interest of mine ever since I first "discovered" American Indians living in Los Angeles (Weibel 1978). In the ensuing years I chronicled the effects of the Federal Indian Relocation Program and urban life on the thousands of American Indian families who migrated to Los Angeles since the 1950s particularly as it impinged on family life, health, and ethnic identity.

To my surprise and delight I found that at least half of the people I had met during early fieldwork periods were no longer living in Los Angeles. Upon retirement strong family, economic, friendship, and aesthetic ties pulled increasing numbers of older, "urban" American Indians back to tribal homelands. Retirees' reduced incomes go further in American Indian communities where the cost of housing, utilities, medical services, and some foodstuffs are federally subsidized. Rural family lands and ancestral homes provide the older American

Indians much relished sanctuary from the hustle-bustle of urban city life. And lifelong friends and family provide easily accessed affectional supports, in contrast to the increasingly attenuated ones in urban centers. Recognizing this unexpected phenomenon, I happily shifted my research efforts to where the exurbanite, American Indian elders had "gone home."

Since the summer of 1984, when this study began, I have interviewed twenty-six North American Indians who had lived for at least twenty years in either the West Coast urban centers of Los Angeles or San Francisco or in rural areas at least 500 miles away from their original homelands.[1] All of the interviewees had returned to their childhood homelands less than five years before they were interviewed.

The shift of research sites to South Dakota and Oklahoma was predictable. Aside from being two of the three most heavily represented territorial groups in Los Angeles, the Sioux and the Muskogeans were also among the very first relocatees to come to Los Angeles (Weibel 1978). It was reasonable to assume, then, that they would be most heavily represented in the retirement age American Indians I could identify. Aside from widely separated traditional territories the Sioux and Muskogeans represent two distinct cultural traditions (Kroeber 1939).

The Sioux, who at the time of European contact were nomadic, big game hunters of the northern plains, contemporarily maintain seven tribal reservations in North and South Dakota. No one has written more persuasively about Sioux personality development than has the psychoanalyst Erik Erikson (1963). Yet, in over fifty pages of text dealing with Sioux childrearing patterns, Erikson provides no clue as to the role of the grandparents in the enculturation of the Sioux child. There are, however, lengthy discussions of the mother's role in shaping the world view of the developing child. William Powers (1977) suggests that the bilateral nature of contemporary Sioux kinship reckoning masks an earlier matrilineal pattern. From my observations of contemporary Sioux childrearing practices and the predominance of both mother and grandmother and the shadowlike nature of fathers' and grandfathers' involvement in the enculturation process, I suggest that now, as then, the Sioux family presents a strongly matrifocal profile.

Traditionally, the clear division of labor by sex (men did the hunting, women maintained the hearth and home) resulted in the absence of the Sioux men from the hearth for long stretches of time. When the men were on the hunt or off on raiding forays, the women were left to their own devices in the rearing of the young. With work of her own to do on behalf of her husband and family (preparing hides, gathering seeds and tubers, and curing meats), young Sioux mothers often left weaned toddlers in the care of their older siblings or other female members of the three- or, occasionally, four-generation band or residential unit. Often from the same generation as the children's biological grandmothers, these women as well as the biological grandmothers who shared their daughter's *tipis*, would be addressed by their charges as *unci*, the Lakota term for grandmother. It is assumed, then, that Sioux grandmothers had as much input into the enculturation of the young child historically as they do today.

The Muskogean-speaking people (Creeks, Chickasaws, and Choctaws) of this sample were originally village farmers from the southeastern states of Georgia, Alabama, and Louisiana (Driver 1969). In the 1830s, however, their ancestors were summarily removed from their thriving communities and resettled in the territory which now comprises most of Oklahoma's southeastern quadrant (Foreman 1934).

Again, what data we have about childrearing practices and grandparenthood among these tribal groups are extremely sketchy and provide only hints as to possible enculturation practices during historical times. We do know that all three tribal groups were clearly matrilineal. Families were matrifocal as well as matrilocal. The typical family constellation consisted of three generations living in the ancestral village home or in its near vicinity and carrying out a yearly round of agricultural chores on behalf of the most senior female head of household. Use of large agricultural plots were passed through the matrilineage, though husbands and brothers worked the gardens outside the protection of the village palisades. When the men were not gardening or holding elaborate fertility rites around the agricultural calendar, they engaged in the many and continuing intertribal skirmishes and, by the eighteenth century, numerous wars with offending European interlopers (Driver 1969; Foreman 1934).

As with the Sioux, then, the Muskogean men were usually otherwise occupied and, therefore, took minimal interest in the care of the young children. We can assume that, as among the Sioux, much of the parenting responsibility of young children fell under the purview of "women's work." The younger Muskogean women, too, had their quota of work. Smaller family gardens within the village compounds were the responsibility of the women (Driver 1969). It seems likely that grandmothers would be expected to tend children while their parents gardened and prepared food.

Though the two culture areas represented by the people in this sample are widely disparate traditional ecological adaptations, they share several important cultural traits: division of labor by sex, predominance of the three-generation extended family residence pattern, and relative absence of male involvement in the care of offspring during early childhood. I, therefore, suggest that childrearing patterns and, particularly, the role of the grandparents in that process in these two culture areas were probably as similar historically as they are contemporaneously.

The twelve Indian men and sixteen American Indian women in the sample ranged in age from fifty-six to eighty-three in 1984. Twelve people (seven women and five men) are Sioux and were living on the Pine Ridge Reservation in South Dakota when I first interviewed them. Fourteen participants live in the area traditionally known as Indian Territory in southeastern Oklahoma. Five of these (two men and three women) are members of the Creek and Seminole tribes. Six (three women and three men) are Choctaw, and one man and two women are Chickasaw.

The twenty-eight participants represent seventeen households. Five women and one man were single heads of households. Out of fourteen families who had biological grandchildren, only five did not have grandchildren living with grandparents. Of these five families, all had grandchildren who still lived on the West Coast or at least five-hundred miles away, with their parents.

Seven families live in the type of three-generational family setting Harold Driver (1969:236) described as the modal North American Indian household configuration. One family had at least one member from each of its four generations living under one roof. Eight grandparents were the primary caretakers for at least one grandchild. In seven cases, the parents of the grandchildren were not living in the primary caretaking households at the time of the interviews. In an eighth case, the mother lived at home but worked full-time. Here, the resident grandmother was the primary caretaker of the three grandchildren in the household during the workweek.

The number of grandchildren in the household ranged fairly evenly between one and five. One family cared for a great grandchild at least half of the day while his mother attended high school classes. All fourteen biological grandparents had other grandchildren who were not living in their homes at the time of the interview.

These demographics illustrate that a substantial percentage of American Indian grandparents still assume primary caretaker responsibility for their grandchildren. Additionally, the multigenerational household still appears to be the modal family composition in the two focal tribal groups.

GRANDPARENTING STYLES

What little literature there is on the role of the North American Indian grandparents in the enculturation of their grandchildren during historic times (sixteenth to nineteenth centuries) tends to be sketchy, ambiguous, and highly romanticized. Grandparents are depicted as storytellers (Barnett 1955:144), mentors to girls about to become socially acknowledged as women (Elmendorf and Kroeber 1960:439) and to boys old enough to embark upon the first of many vision quests (Amoss 1981), and caretakers of children left orphaned by disease, war, or famine (Schweitzer 1987). In all cases the literature depicts Indian grandparents as protective, permissive, affectionate, and tutorial in their inter-actions with their grandchildren. Only most recently has Pamela Amoss (1986) offered an intriguing analysis of the ambiguous nature of Northwest Coast Native American myths about grandmothers. In these legends the old women have the power both to protect and to destroy their progeny.

The generally acknowledged model of Indian grandparenting presented above fits most closely the cultural conservator and custodial models to be discussed. In both cases, I suggest that such grandparenting styles in contemporary American Indian family life spring from the same conditions and concerns that shaped historical grandarenting modes: practical issues of division of labor and the efficacy of freeing younger women so that they can participate more fully in the economic sector of the tribal community; nurturance of unprotected minors so as to maximize the continuance of the tribe as a social entity; and the belief that old age represents the culmination of cultural experience. Elders are thought to be those best equipped to transmit cultural lore across generations, thus ensuring the cultural integrity of the group.

In the sections to follow, five observed grandparenting styles are defined and illustrated by excerpts from life-history interviews with individuals who exemplify a particular grandparenting style. These grandparenting styles are not mutually exclusive categories. Rather, the grandparents who shared their life histories with me, over time, have manifested attributes of several caretaking styles both with the same children and across their assortment of other grandchildren, both biological and fictive. The case studies presented represent the individual's modal executions of grandparenting which constitute their most consistent grandparenting style.

Although this chapter deals mainly with women as grandparents, there are ten men in the study who interact on a continuing basis with their grandchildren, so it seems more precise to label these relational styles grandparenting, rather than grandmothering, styles. The grandfathers, although present in the homes, are much less absorbed in the ordering of their grandchildren's lives than are their wives. As described in nineteenth-century ethnographic accounts of American Indian family life, the grandfather, like the father, is more likely to be the soft, affectionate, shadow figure in the family constellation who leaves the discipline and socialization of the grandchildren to his wife or her brothers (Pettitt 1946). Rarely, and in this study only in the case of two men who were religious leaders, did grandfathers take on assertive roles *vis-à-vis* their grandchildren's socialization. Today, as in the nineteenth-century accounts of North American Indian family life, raising children is women's work.

The Distanced Grandparent

Of the seventeen families in this study, only three are best described by the term distanced grandparent. In all three cases the grandchildren are living either on the West Coast with their parents or far enough away to make regular visits difficult. Nor do summer school vacations herald extended visits from the grandchildren in these families. Occasionally, the grandparents will make the trip west to visit their grandchildren. These visits, however, are infrequent and do not have the ritual qualities of the scheduled visits of the ceremonial grandparents. The distance between grandparent and grandchild is geographical, psychological, and cultural. For the most part, the distanced grandparents understand the lack of communication with their grandchildren as the effect of changed lifestyles on their children and grandchildren. As one Choctaw

"Grandpa Whitecloud" (Pueblo) and his great-grandsons prepare to fancy dance at a Saturday night Many Trails Club powwow in Long Beach, California.

grandmother told me: "Oh, they've got their own thing in the city. You know, they have their friends, and their music lessons and school activities. They'd get bored out here if they couldn't get to a mall or the movies."

In one case, the grandfather had had a child from a failed first marriage whom he has not seen since her birth. He has been told that she has had children of her own whom he also has not seen. This instance of both geographical and psychological distance, while more common among American Indian men, is highly unusual and almost nonexistent among American Indian grandmothers. For example, one Sioux grandmother not only knew all of her grandchildren from her children's formal marriages or publicly acknowledged, long-term liaisons but also all of her biological grandchildren from her sons' informal sexual encounters. In fact, the issue of grandparental responsibility to a new grandchild was such a strong cultural tenet that she sought out the assistance of a medicine man in determining the truth when a young woman presented herself as the mother of one of her son's children and the young man refused to acknowledge the paternity of the child. Of importance to the Sioux grandmother was that the child would know who his family was and that she would not shirk her grandparental responsibilities to the child because of her son's indifference.

The distanced grandparent, then, is a relatively rare phenomenon among North American Indian families. I find no reference to this kind of grandparenting style in the literature on traditional American Indian family life. If it occurred, it /as usually viewed as a cultural aberration due to separation of family members through capture by enemies, death, or marriage out of the group. Rather, the distanced grandparent appears to be an artifact of an earlier (1950s to the 1970s) migration of American Indians into urban centers. The distancing is gradual, accumulative, and only exacerbated by the second and third generations remaining in the cities to work, go to school, and become . acclimated to urban life when grandparents decide to return to their homelands upon retirement.

Most American Indian families would still view this relative lack of contact between extended family members as an aberration. American Indians speak proudly of their familistic propensities, often comparing themselves favorably to what they see as the more nucleated, individualistic, and isolated Anglo-American family configuration. Indeed, the popular literature on American family life tends to perpetuate this comparison (Holmes 1986). That three of seventeen families exhibit this grandparenting pattern suggests countervailing tendencies; the continuing vitality of cultural tenets which promote strong intergenerational ties in both culture areas versus the growing negative influence of postmodern migration patterns on intergenerational cohesion.

The Ceremonial Grandparent

Only two cases of this grandparenting style were identified. In both cases the grandchildren live some distance from the grandparents who, as with the distanced grandparents, have returned to their ancestral homes after living for many years in urban centers. The quality, frequency, and purpose of their family visits, however, distinguish their grandparenting style from the distanced grandparent. These families tend to visit with regularity. Every year, summer vacations are planned to include a sojourn with the grandparents. Flowers, gifts of money, clothes, or plane and bus tickets are forwarded to the grandparents at most holidays and birthdays.

When grandchildren visit grandparents, or vice versa, the host communities are alerted. The entire family attends a steady round of ethnic ceremonial gatherings and social activities at which announcements of their visits are made and applauded. Frequently, the public announcements make references to the distances traveled and the venerable ages of the visiting or visited grandparents. That these features of intergenerational visits are equally and enthusiastically applauded by the spectators underscores the importance of cultural values, such as family cohesion and reverence for one's elders, which are ritually enacted and legitimized by these public displays of the ceremonial grandparents.

Ceremonial grandparenting is expressed in other public forms as well. Grandparents are often asked to say prayers, lead honoring dances, or stand and allow the community to honor them in ceremonies which dramatize the traditional attitudes of respect and reverence for those who have had the spiritual power to live to old age. Families gain honor and visibility in their communities for fostering the health and well-being of their ancient members. Therefore, the ceremonial prerogatives of old age are sought out and perpetuated both by the elderly person as one way of maintaining a public presence and by the elderly person's family as one way of enhancing group membership and family status within their ethnic group.

Ceremonial grandparents provide ideal models of "traditional" (correct) intergenerational behavior for their children, grandchildren, and the community. In time-limited interactions with their grandchildren, the venerated grandparents embody and enact those behaviors appropriate to their age and prestige ranking in the community. By watching the ceremonial displays of age and family cohesiveness, the children learn the appropriateness of veneration of the elderly and how adherence to community mores qualifies older individuals for displays of respect and love in old age. The children are taught to display appropriate ceremonial behavior toward their elders: assisting the unsteady of gait to the dance floor, fetching food and cold drinks for them, and formally presenting them with gifts and performance in special ceremonies such as the Siouan powwows and giveaways and the Muskogean church "sings."

The ceremonial aspect of contemporary American Indian grandparenting is certainly consistent with historical accounts of public behavior toward tribal elders (Schweitzer 1987). In fact, insistence on public veneration of the elderly may now be exaggerated so as to underscore, once again, what is assumed to be the more positive approach to aging in American Indian culture *vis-à-vis* Anglo society. Both American Indians and non-Indians are aware of mass-media ruminations about the American preoccupation with youth and the warehousing of its elderly. As a counter to this, there is an insistence on elder spiritual leaders at Sun Dance processions and communal prayers at powwows and sings. In general, both aged men and women are expected to be in attendance at public events so as to be recognized and honored simply for being there at their advanced age. Such events tend to convince community members and non-Indians alike that American Indians know how to treat their elders.

The Fictive Grandparent

Fictive grandparenting is an alternative to the lack or absence of biological grandchildren. All three examples of fictive grandparenting in this sample are women. Two of the women had biological grandchildren living on the West Coast whose parents would not relinquish their care to the grandmothers. Solutions to their grandchildless homes included a variety of ingenious strategies. One Sioux woman applied for and received foster home accreditation. During the first two years of her return to reservation life she harbored seven different, nonrelated children in her home for periods of four to eighteen months. At one time she had four foster children living with her at the same time.

> Well, I got to missing my grandchildren so much. And none of my kids would let me have one of their kids to take care of so I decided I had to do something. And there's so much need out here . . . you know . . . with all the drinking, and wife abuse, and neglect of the children and all that . . . so I felt I could provide a good home for these pitiful Sioux kids whose families couldn't take care of them. So I applied for the foster parent license. I was scared that maybe they would say I was too old at sixty-five. But, you know, within a week after I got my license I got a call from them. And they had not one, but two kids for me to take. (Sioux woman, sixty-seven, Pine Ridge, South Dakota)

One Choctaw woman, a teacher's assistant in the public school system, became involved in the development of teaching materials designed to introduce American Indian and non-Indian students to traditional Choctaw life. Simple readers and instructional sheets in English that provide study outlines for the acquisition of traditional Choctaw dances, games, and foods have now evolved into a full-fledged Choctaw language-learning course. The grandmother's skill as a Choctaw-speaking storyteller has allowed her access to dozens of kindergarten to third-grade children who fill the widening gap she recognizes between herself and her West Coast-based grandchildren.

> I think it is very important for the young children, both Choctaw and non-Indian, to learn about traditional Choctaw culture. In this way they have something to be proud of. They won't think of themselves the way

the non-Indians think of them — dirty, dumb savages — but as people who had a rich and beautiful culture which they can be proud of and that was taken away from them for no good reason. I feel as if I am passing on my heritage to not only my grandchildren as it would have been done traditionally but to all of the grandchildren who will ever have me as a teacher. (Choctaw woman, sixty-five, Broken Bow, Oklahoma)

One grandchildless woman had an informally adopted son living with her who was young enough to be her grandchild. (She was eighty-three and he was twenty-five when interviewed in 1984 and still living in Los Angeles.) He subsequently accompanied her to Oklahoma when she decided to return to her hometown in 1985. "He needed a home. And he didn't want to live with his mother no more. And we didn't know where his dad was. And all I had was my daughter, who works all day and is practically blind, so she isn't much help around the place when she gets home at night. I needed someone around here who can look after me, drive me places, help me with the shopping, and all that. So I adopted him when he was around seventeen and he's been with me every since" (Creek woman, eighty-three, Los Angeles, California).

Fictive grandparenting was not initiated by any of the men in this study. That is not to say, however, that men do not facilitate these types of relationships upon occasion. In fact, some older men, particularly if they are in command of medicinal or spiritual lore, will apprentice young men who they later adopt as kin if there is no blood tie between. Older women tend to initiate fictive kin ties for the broader personal, emotional, social, cultural, and purely pragmatic reasons stated above.

The Custodial Grandparent

As Linda Burton and Vern Bengtson (1985) rightly and importantly point out, grandparenthood is not a status to which the universe devoutly aspires. The ease and enthusiasm with which the status is acquired depends, to a great extent, on timing, personal career paths, aspirations of both parents and new grandparents, and the relative stability of the extended family structure. Though Burton and Bengtson's findings are based on black family studies, much the same can be said of the range of responses to grandparenthood among the American Indian grandparents I have interviewed. Marjorie Schweitzer points out that, "It is customary for [American Indian] grandparents to raise grandchildren who have been left without a father or mother or both. It is also customary for grandparents to raise grandchildren when parents work, a parent is sick, away on a job relocation or when it eases the burden of too many children" (1957:173). I suspect custodial grandparenting can be identified across cultures where unanticipated family trauma (divorce, death, unemployment, abandonment, illness, neglect, or abuse) separates child and parents.

Three families in this study are best described by the term custodial grandparenthood. In all three cases, the grandchildren were children of daughters who had either died, had their children taken from them by the court system, or had been abandoned by the children's fathers and could not keep the families intact with their meager earnings or child welfare stipends. In all cases, the grandparents' roles as primary caretakers were solicited either by the children's parents or the courts, not by lonely grandparents rattling about in their empty nests.

In one family the grandmother was not only caring for a daughter's three children but also one son's child, as well as a great-grandchild, when I interviewed her. The custodial role essentially has been forced upon her by the misconduct or lack of interest of two of her children. She begrudgingly accepts the role as the duty of a moral Christian woman and in the best interest of her several troubled and abandoned grandchildren.

> When is it ever going to end, that's what I would like to know? All my life I've had these kids off and on. Especially with my daughter's kids. . . Atoka has been with me since she was a year and a half. Her mother would go out and would be partying and someone was left with the child. But that person took off and left Atoka by herself. And the neighbors called me to tell me the child was all by herself, crying. The judge wouldn't let her [the daughter] have her back so he gave her to me. Lahoma, she's been with me since she was born, I guess. Pamela went with somebody. I think she was placed in a home, then she would come to stay with me for a while, then her mother would take her back, and then get into trouble again and the whole thing would start all over again. (Choctaw woman, fifty-seven, Broken Bow, Oklahoma)[2]

Recognizing that her children, and especially her drug-dependent daughter, take advantage of her nurturant nature, this woman explains the moral responsibility she feels for the welfare of her grandchildren: "In L.A. sometimes I would go out to one of the Indian bars just to do something else besides working and taking care of kids. So I'd pay someone to watch the kids and I'd go out for a few hours. But every time I was at a party or a bar in the back of my mind I'd think, 'What if something happened to me? What if I get in an accident? What's going to happen to those kids?' You know, most people don't think like that."

For the cultural conservator, having a houseful of grandchildren is an expected privilege of old age. In contrast, the custodial grandmother is often relatively young and unprepared to take on the caretaking responsibilities culturally appropriate to the status of grandmother. In this case the woman's perceptions of her custodial grandmothering range from an appreciation of the comfort and companionship she received from her favorite grandson to annoyance and frustration with having to assume the extra burden of her sixteen-year old granddaughter's unwanted pregnancy. These child-care responsibilities are particularly irksome as they are thought to be inappropriate to the current stage of her life career trajectory: "I shouldn't be doing this [taking care of children]. Not at my age. I should be just taking it easy and going here and there. Now Donny, he's no problem. He's real sweet and bright – he's got a brain. He's a lot of company for me. But, then, there's my sixteen-year-old granddaughter. She's going to have a baby. And guess who's going to take care of that baby when it comes?"

The bitter inflection of the grandmother's last words underscores her resentment and sense of futility in this matter. Pressured by cultural norms and familial needs, this fifty-seven year-old soon-to-be great-grandmother feels powerless to act on her own personal behalf. Suffused since childhood with fundamental Christian values (charity, self-denial, motherhood, the sanctity of the family) and spurred on by the promise of heavenly rewards to those who endure an earthly martyrdom, she resentfully accepts her custodial great-grandmotherhood as her "cross to bear."

The Cultural Conservator Grandparent

Being raised by one's grandparents is not an enculturative phenomenon unique to either twentieth-century rural or urban American Indian experience. In fact, grandmothers as primary caretakers of first and second grandchildren is a long-established native American child-care strategy. Leo Simmons tells us that "old Crow grandmothers were considered essential elements in the household, engaged in domestic chores" (1945:84) while helping young mothers who were burdened with work. And Marjorie Schweitzer explains that "within the framework of the extended family a special relationship existed between grandparents and grandchildren which began at birth and lasted a lifetime. Children were cared for by grandparents and, in turn, the family cared for the old when they were feeble" (1987:169).

The cultural conservator role is a contemporary extension of this traditional relationship. Rather than accept an imposed role, the conservator grandparents actively solicit their children to allow the grandchildren to live with them for extended periods of time for the expressed purpose of exposing them to the American Indian way of life. Importantly, the cultural conservator is the modal grandparenting style among the families in this study.

Six families are best described by this term. One Sioux woman, who had two of her grandchildren living with her at the time of the interview, exemplifies the cultural conservator grandparenting style. The enthusiasm about having one or more grandchildren in her home for extended periods of time is tempered by the realization that, for her own children who grew up in an urban environment, the spiritual magnetism of reservation life is essentially lost. She regards their disdain for tribal life with consternation and ironic humor and consciously opts for taking a major role in the early socialization of her grandchildren. She views her children as being just "too far gone" (assimilated) for any attempt at repatriation on her part. Her role as the culture conservator grandmother, then, is doubly important. The grandchildren are her only hope for effecting both personal and cultural continuity: "The second- or third-generation Indian children out [in Los Angeles], most of them never get to see anything like . . . a sun dance or a memorial feast or giveaway or just stuff that Indians do back home. I wanted my children to be involved in them and know what it's all about. So that's the reason that I always try to keep my grandchildren whenever I can" (Sioux woman, sixty-seven, Pine Ridge, South Dakota).

She recognizes the primary caretaking aspects of her grandmotherhood as not only a traditionally American Indian, but also as a particularly Lakota thing to do: "The grandparents always took. . . at least the first grandchild to raise because that's just the way the Lakota did it. They [the grandparents] think that they're more mature and have had more experience and they could teach the children a lot more than the young parents, especially if the parents were young. . . . I'm still trying to carry on that tradition because my grandmother raised me most of the time up until I was nine years old."

She remembers her grandparents' enculturative styles as essentially conservative in the sense that those things they passed on to their grandchildren were taken from traditional Sioux lore. The grandparents rarely commanded or required the grandchild's allegiance to their particular world view. Rather, instruction took the form of suggestions about or presentation of models of exemplary behavior. "Well, my grandfather always told me what a Lakota woman wouldn't do and what they were supposed to do. But he never said I had to do anything." She purposely continues to shape her grandmotherhood on the cultural conservator model of her own grandparents. "I ask [my children] if [their children] could spend the summer with me if there isn't school and go with me to the Indian doings so that they'll know that they're Indian and know the culture and traditions. [I'm] just kind of building memories for them."

Those cultural and traditional aspects of Sioux life to which this grandmother exposes her city-born grandchildren include a wide range of ceremonial and informal activities. The children go everywhere with her. An active participant in village life, she and her grandchildren make continual rounds of American Indian church meetings, senior citizens lunches, tribal chapter hearings, pow-wows, memorial feasts, sun dances, funerals, giveaways, and rodeos. The children attend a tribe-run elementary school in which classes are taught in both English and Lakota. The children actively participate in the ceremonial life of the reservation, dancing in full regalia at powwows and helping their grandmother distribute gifts at giveaways and food at feasts. Most importantly, those grandchildren who live with her for long periods of time are immersed in the daily ordering of reservation life. Through the grandmother's firm, authoritative tutelage, complemented by their gentle and affectionate grandfather, and through the rough-and-tumble play with rural age-group members who, for the most part, can claim some kinship with the urban-born visitors, they learn, as did nineteenth-century Sioux children (through observa-

tion, example, and experimentation), their society's core values and interactional style.

As stated earlier, the grandparenting styles are not mutually exclusive
categories. Rather, this woman's primary caretaking responsibility, at times,
has taken on elements of the custodial model. She describes her reservation
home in relation to her children's Los Angeles homes in much the same way
she remembers her own grandparental home. Her modest prairie ranch home
takes on qualities of sanctuary — a place of calm, regularity, and wholesome-
ness. She sharply contrasts the stability of her home with the characteristic
turbulence of her children's urban social and psychological context: "I think
I have a stable home and I can take care of them. Especially if the mother and
father are having problems. This next June, Sonny [her daughter's son] will
be with me two years, and last November Winoma was with me one year, so
she's been with me a year and a half. That's how long I've had them. But this
is an unusual situation. The parents. . . are going to get a divorce. That's why
I didn't want them around there [Los Angeles] while this was going on. I think
they're better off with me."

On the occasion of the great-grandmother's ninety-first birthday, four generations of Seneca women were called forward to be honored at a Saturday night
powwow in Long Beach, California.

Marjorie Schweitzer (1987) suggests that adults, especially women, welcome becoming a grandparent and are proud to claim that status. For the cultural conservator, primary caretaking is a role eagerly negotiated with children. For the Sioux woman in question, having her youngest grandchildren in her home and under her absolute custody for extended periods of time is just one more example of her acceptance and enactment of behaviors expected of properly traditional, older Sioux women. Her active grandmotherhood fulfills what she sees as an important cultural function not only for herself but also for her future generations. She exercises that function in ways that would have been familiar to her arch-conservative grandparents — a cultural continuity she finds particularly satisfying. "I think it's a privilege to keep my grandchildren. When they're grown up, they'll remember and talk about when I lived with my grandmother. . . . Like I talk about living with my grandmother."

CONCLUSIONS

The five divergent perceptions and expressions of grandparenthood presented here are clearly consequences of the individuals' sense of personal control and initiative in shaping the style in which they would carry out their grandparenthood. Clear parallels to the distanced and custodial grandparenting styles can be found in the descriptions of contemporary American grandparenthood (Cowgill and Holmes 1972; Myerhoff 1978; Stack 1974; Burton and Bengtson 1985; Simic 1987). I suggest that those factors which prompt these interactional styles among American Indian families — migration, psychological estrangement between the parental generations, and relative psychological and economic stability of the parental household — also produce instances of these grandparenting styles among non-Indian families. Interestingly, neither style is the cultural ideal for either American Indians or non-Indians. The popular literature deplores the psychological distance between generations, yet also finds the child reared by grandparents as culturally and psychologically disadvantaged. While American Indians equally deplore the distanced grandparenting style, the child in the custody of a grandparent is seen as potentially advantaged by that experience.

Incidence of the ceremonial grandparenting style among non-Indians is not clearly indicated in the literature, although, I suggest, it does exist in some form (the inclusion of grandparents in national and religious holiday celebrations, for instance). Where ceremonialism between grandparents and grandchildren occurs in Anglo-American families, however, it is prompted by different motivations. As the literature suggests, the noninterfering, affectionate grandparents who live independently in their own homes at some distance from the nuclear parental family is the Anglo-American cultural ideal (Holmes 1986; Simic 1987). In contrast, the ceremonial grandparenting style among North American Indians is a compromise — at once pleasing and incomplete. It is symbolic behavior, enactment of one aspect of American Indian family life, in the wake of missing others.

Both the fictive and cultural conservator grandparenting styles are particularly American Indian adaptations. Neither of these grandparenting styles is apparent in the literature on Anglo-American grandparenting. Current motivations for both styles are consistent with historical ones. Pragmatic concerns for providing emotional and economic supports in the absence of biologically mandated ones prompt fictive kinship designations today as in the nineteenth century. And the need to care for children while parents work and to fulfill a sense of continuing participation in family and community life prompted the cultural conservator grandparenting style then as now.

Today, however, presenting one's grandchildren with traditional cultural lore has become a critical issue of cultural survival *vis-à-vis* a new and insidious enemy. Faced by consuming cultural alternatives and unmotivated or inexperienced children, American Indian grandparents can no longer assume the role of cultural conservator for their grandchildren as practiced historically. Rather, grandparents, concerned with continuity of tribal consciousness, must seize the role and force inculcation of traditional lore upon their grandchildren through a grandparenting style best described as cultural conservation.

The status, grandparent, is imbued with considerable sociostructural weight in that it, across cultures, automatically confers both responsibility and rewards to the individual upon the birth of the grandchild. The roles associated with grandparenthood, however, can be and are negotiated. Satisfaction with both status and role is an artifact of the individual's sense of creating a grandparenthood consistent with both personal and cultural expectations.

NOTES

This research was funded by grant 1RO1 AGO 3794–2 from the National Institute on Aging.

1. There are, however, twenty-eight people in the sample. One woman is Caucasian and married to a Creek man. They lived in Los Angeles for eighteen years before returning, in 1976, to his hometown, a small city in south-central Oklahoma that is the administrative center of the Creek/Seminole Nation. One man is Mexican-American and married to a Sioux woman. They moved back to his wife's ancestral land on the Pine Ridge Reservation in South Dakota in 1981 after living for twenty-six years in Los Angeles.

2. In all cases fictitious names have been used to protect the privacy of those people who so generously shared their life stories, current activities, and views on grandparenthood with me.

6 EXCHANGE AND RECIPROCITY AMONG TWO GENERATIONS OF JAPANESE AND AMERICAN WOMEN

Hiroko Akiyama, Toni C. Antonucci, and Ruth Campbell

The purpose of this chapter is to explore exchange patterns and exchange rules of social support between two generations of women in the United States and Japan. In particular, we focus on the relationships between older mothers and their middle-aged daughters and daughters-in-law. The relationship between mothers and daughters in the United States and mothers-in-law and their daughters-in-law in Japan have been traditionally considered important sources of support for older women. Consequently, these relationships have a significant impact on adjustment to aging in both societies. Since a higher proportion of social interactions of older people is likely to take place in the family, the central role of women in kinship networks makes a focus on them particularly appropriate.

We explore here the exchange of support between two generations of women by focusing on the concept of *reciprocity*. We believe that the norm of reciprocity affects how individuals accept and provide social support and that reciprocal support relationships contribute in complex but important ways to successful aging in both the United States and Japan. To determine this, we begin with a consideration of the concept of reciprocity and its manifestations in the two societies. We then present relevant data from three studies conducted in the United States and Japan. The differences in the intergenerational roles of women and the patterns of support exchange offer interesting insights into how the reciprocity rule operates in the two societies. The data, from very different sources, suggest that the concepts of exchange and reciprocity are vital parts of the lives of these women, but operates in strikingly different ways in the two societies. Finally, the data also offer evidence that gradual changes in exchange rules are taking place in both societies.

RECIPROCITY NORM OF SUPPORT EXCHANGE

Our definition of the term reciprocity is most consistent with that proposed by Alvin Gouldner (1960) in his early, seminal article on the norm of reciprocity. By the term reciprocity, we refer to equal or comparable exchanges of tangible aid, emotional affection, advice, or information between individuals or groups. This limited definition is generally accepted without controversy, referring simply to the notion of exchange, that is, of giving and receiving.

Recently, several researchers have begun to explore the concept of reciprocity and aging. The work by James Dowd (1975, 1980, 1984) is particularly pertinent to this chapter. He has suggested that the norms of reciprocity, beneficence, and other social exchange notions are critical to an understanding of the status of the elderly in the United States. His central argument is that old age includes a necessary reduction in the possession of valued exchange commodities. This decrease in valued goods results in a lessened ability of older people to interact successfully with younger people who do have valued goods and who like to seek valued goods from others.

Gary Lee (1985) has extended the work of Dowd by considering intergenerational supportive interactions and their consequences for the well-being of older persons within the context of social exchange theory. For example, referring to Elane Brody et al.'s study (1983) on attitudes of three generations of American women toward the care of older parents, he noted that younger people were much more willing to provide supports to older family members than older people were to accept them. Lee has argued that studies of informal support networks have ignored the tremendous value placed on independence and autonomy by the American elderly. Older persons, even if they really need help, are hesitant to accept it if they feel unable to reciprocate. Unbalanced exchange relations which develop dependence could have seriously detrimental psychological or emotional consequences. "Thus while older people may experience many concrete benefits from the services their childern and other kin provide, and while these benefits may be instrumental in maintaining their quality of life, ironically the receipt of these benefits may detract from their quality of life in other ways" (Lee 1985:31).

In Japan the norm of reciprocity has also been demonstrated as a useful frame of reference for understanding social behaviors (Befu 1968; Lebra 1976). For example, the concept of *on*, which refers to a favor or benevolence granted by A to B and to a resultant debt B owes to A, is clearly defined in terms of reciprocity. It has been widely documented that the concept of *on* permeates almost every area of Japanese society and has played an essential role in explaining various social relations in Japan (Doi 1971; Lebra 1976; Reischauer 1977). Every individual owes limitless *on* to his or her parents for life, for care received, and, therefore, for what he or she is today. And he or she feels urged to repay even a small portion of this debt for a lifetime. For many Japanese, this urge to repay the *on* to their parents is a steady source of drive for lifelong achievements. "Successful" employer-employee relationships in Japan are also bound by the sense of *on*, in which *on*-governed employees show persistent loyalty and devotion to their father-figure employer. Moreover, the rich vocabulary of Japanese language which expresses one's indebtedness to another and the frequent use of those terms in daily conversation are indicators of the cultural emphasis on the reciprocity norm in Japan.

It is not clear, however, if the same reciprocity norms which Dowd and Lee have observed among the American elderly can be applied to explain the support exchange among the Japanese elderly as well. In the following sections we examine empirical data from three studies, each of which provides information about the intergenerational support exchange between mothers and their daughters or daughters-in-law. In particular, we attempt to identify and compare how the reciprocity norms operate in the primary groups of older individuals in the United States and Japan and how those norms distinctively affect the adjustment to aging in the two societies.

RECIPROCITY AND EXCHANGE: RECENT FINDINGS

The first study was originally conceived as a comparative study of the rules for reciprocal exchange of six kinds of basic interpersonal resources (money, goods, services, information, status, and love) in the Japanese family and the American family (Akiyama 1984). There were two parts to this project: the first, an extensive questionnaire study of the views of 500 American and Japanese female college students on resource exchanges in various dyadic family relations; the second, an in-depth interview of thirty-two female elderly respondents in each country which focused on the cognitive rules underlying exchange behaviors of older women.

In the initial part of the study, the college students in each country were asked to indicate whether certain resource exchanges were acceptable in various dyadic family relations. Discriminant analyses of the two samples identified two distinct exchange patterns. College students in Japan reported that the exchange of different kinds of resources was acceptable and common in family dyads, whereas American college students reported only the exchange of similar resources was acceptable. Specifically, compared to the United States, expressive resources such as love and status are granted a much broader range of exchangeability in Japan. They can be exchanged not only with other expressive resources but also with material resources such as money and goods. Material resources and expressive resources are unlikely to be exchanged for one another in the United States. We examined family dyads relevant to this chapter and asked what the appropriate response might be to the receipt of various resources in mother (hypothetically aged 70)/daughter (hypothetically aged 45) and mother/daughter-in-law dyads at similar ages. In both types of dyads, the Japanese were considerably more likely than their American counterparts to feel that love or status was the appropriate resource to reciprocate with, regardless of type of resources originally received. Americans were significantly more likely to feel that the exchange of similar resources was appropriate. Thus, the Japanese might report that one responded to the receipt of goods with love, but Americans were likely to feel that the appropriate response would be a return of the same resource, that is, goods.

The in-depth interviews of the elderly Japanese and American women replicated the findings from the questionnaire study. In the interviews the respondents were given hypothetical situations involving older women and their daughters or daughters-in-law and asked whether or not the exchange was typical, appropriate, fair, and emotionally satisfying. A content analysis of the interviews from each country identified two exchange rules distinctive to each of the two family systems and evidence for more acceptability of elderly dependence in the Japanese system than in the American system.

Analysis of these interviews suggests that the American family system prescribes one exchange rule, symmetrical reciprocity, which mandates immediate repayment by a resource in kind and of equivalent value. This American rule suppresses one-way transactions characterized by the failure of equivalent repayment and thereby reduces the development of dependence which not only embarrasses a debtor but may also disrupt the relationship between a debtor and a donor. When one cannot maintain reciprocity, it leads to disturbance of stable relationships. Even in casual exchanges of services or goods between mother and daughter (also between mother and daughter-in-law), reciprocity needs to be carefully maintained in order to secure a good relationship.

The following responses in the interviews with older American women demonstrate such characteristics of the American exchange rule. Receiving a small gift from her daughter-in-law, a woman said, "Of course, I would accept it with love and a thank you. But I would also find a way to return a gift. You can't always accept without returning." Given a hypothetical situation in which a married daughter came a couple of times to do some chores around the house when her mother had a bad cold, another woman responded by saying, "If that happened to me, I would offer my daughter some kind of help such as staying with her children when she and her husband go out. I would feel better if I could reciprocate, even though I know my daughter is not expecting anything in return for what she does for me. Just receiving would hurt my spirit . . . or pride, you know. Reciprocity is very important even between mothers and daughters."

The following case of a seventy-two-year-old American respondent, a retired store clerk, exemplifies how the same exchange rule operates in a somewhat more deprived situation. Mrs. B. raised thirteen children. All of them completed college and are doing quite well. She proudly showed their pictures to the interviewer, pointing out who is a physician, accountant, teacher, rancher's wife, and so on. She is now widowed and living alone in a one-room converted-garage apartment. Due to severe arthritis and heart problems, she is confined to a wheelchair and requires help in daily domestic chores such as cooking and cleaning. During the interview, a volunteer of the local meals-on-wheels program delivered a hot lunch. She repeatedly apologized for the mess of her apartment. After completing the interview, she pointed to one of the shoeboxes piled up in a corner of the room and asked the interviewer to open it. In the box, the interviewer found a stack of uncashed checks sent from the woman's children, along with birthday cards and Christmas cards. She was tickled to report that, on her birthday a couple of years before, the children surprised her by presenting a blueprint of a small house designed for a wheelchair-bound person and also how creative her daughters and daughters-in-law were to make excuses for bringing leftover food and for offering to scrub the floor and to do other household chores because they needed to lose several pounds. All of this she had gratefully declined to accept. She explained that she would not feel comfortable accepting a gift or favor when she could not reciprocate and that, even if she sometimes experienced inconvenience or scarcity of resources, she preferred living in this way.

As shown in such interview cases, the American women appear to apply basically the same exchange rule, that is, symmetric reciprocity, to both daughters and daughters-in-law. This finding is also supported by a national survey study of social support of older individuals in the United States (Kahn and Antonucci 1984; Antonucci and Akiyama 1987) in which detailed data were collected on six types of supportive behaviors: confiding, reassurance, respect, sick care, talk when upset, and talk about health. Respondents over age fifty were asked to provide specific information about who they provided each type of support to and from whom they received each type of support. Focusing on support exchanges between older women and their daughters and daughters-in-law, an analysis revealed a quite similar exchange pattern in the two types of family dyads. The older respondents reported they *exchanged* supports and maintained reciprocal relationships with both their daughters and daughters-in-law. In general, however, they were much more likely to exchange supports with their daughters than daughters-in-law. In other words, the support exchanges in those two family dyads in the United States differ in frequency or quantity but they appear to be quite similar in terms of the exchange rule.

By contrast, the Japanese family system applies two clearly distinct exchange rules for family members and for nonfamily members. The rule for family members is asymmetric reciprocity wherein expressive resources hold high value and broad exchangeability. On the other hand, the rule for nonfamily members is one of symmetry and equal exchange within a prescribed time period. This is similar to the American rule. The single exchange rule in the United States and the double rules in Japan may derive from the different family structures in the two countries. A nuclear family, defined as the favored basic unity of organized relationships in the American family system, usually forms strong bonds with its close kin through frequent contacts and mutual aid. Thus a kin network emerges, which has been conceptualized as the "modified extended family." It assumes equal partnership and autonomy and often results in strong collateral relationships among members (Sussman 1976).

A ninety-year-old grandmother with her two-year-old and one-month-old granddaughters.

The traditional Japanese family system, however, has the stem-family structure in which descent and inheritance pass from the father to the eldest son. The eldest son remains in the family home with his wife and offspring, while younger sons form branch houses. In such stem-family systems, "family members" consist of the members of a three-generation stem household and its branch households. Others are regarded as "nonfamily members." The fact that in Japan family and nonfamily are formally defined may be particularly relevant here. Formally, for an older woman, her daughter-in-law is clearly a family member and the mother and daughter-in-law relationship is completely governed by family-member rules. However, again formally speaking, her married daughter is not considered to be a family member. Since the married daughter formally belongs to her husband's family, the mother and daughter relationship is expected to abide by the nonfamily exchange rule.

The exchange rule for family members in Japan prescribes repayment for virtually any type of resource by an expressive resource. Repayment by a material resource in the family is often perceived to imply distance or even insult toward a partner in an exchange. Resource exchanges governed by such exchange rules are both diffuse and lacking in specificity in terms of equivalence of return within a specific time period. Reciprocity involving expressive resources is difficult to recognize, because love and status are not always quantifiable. Due to this unquantifiable nature of expressive resources, one can never feel the debt is completely discharged. This indeterminateness of debt discharge was demonstrated by interviews on mother-in-law and daughter-in-law relationships, in which older women reported that they were uncertain of fairness when they repaid their daughter-in-law's services with love and/or status, although they considered such exchanges to be quite common, appropriate, and satisfying. With a certain amount of ambiguity as to whether the debt has been repaid, one is never free psychologically from the obligation to reciprocate with more expressive resources such as affection and appreciation. Before one debt can be repaid, more material resources usually are received, so that the recipient can easily be placed in a *perpetual debtor* position in which one must be continually vigilant for another repayment opportunity.

Therefore, it is quite common that resource exchanges in the Japanese family are carried out over time. A classic example is the repayment by adult children to their aged parents for what they received as dependent children decades before. Futhermore, under certain circumstances where direct repayment within a dyad is difficult or inappropriate, a third party, sometimes fourth and fifth ones, could be involved as an intermediary of resource exchanges. More than a few older Japanese women reported in the interview that, in repaying the devoted services of a daughter-in-law, it was more rewarding to address affection toward grandchildren than to address it directly to the daughter-in-law. However, to be fair, these daily family interactions are not usually perceived as a flow of resource exchanges. Although also evident among American exchanges, the prevalence of these long-term indirect exchanges among the Japanese is another factor which contributes diffuseness to the Japanese family exchange rule. Such diffuseness and indeterminateness of the Japanese exchange rule acts as a mechanism that inhibits complete repayment, thus maintaining indebtedness and dependence. It consequently serves to regulate and sustain family solidarity based upon dependence.

The following case exemplifies how the mother-in-law and daughter-in-law relationship works in a typical working-class family residing in an urban area of Japan. Mrs. M. is a relatively healthy seventy-one-year-old widow who is living with her son, a taxi driver, and his family in a small, four-room house in a suburban community outside of Tokyo. She shares a room with her granddaughter. On typical days, she gets up at 5:30, sweeps around the house, and waters the shrubs. Her daughter-in-law calls the family to breakfast when it is ready. After breakfast Mrs. M. usually goes to a local senior citizen center. She told the interviewer that since she started going to the center the amount of family dissension, particularly between herself and her daughter-in-law, had significantly decreased. "Our house is too small for two women," she said. On her way to the center, she often buys some candies or fruits to share with her friends at the center. "I receive 100,000 yen [about $700] yearly from the government. Although the amount is small, receiving it is something new. My mother did not have any money of her own. I can buy snacks to take to the center and can occasionally give my grandchildren extra spending money. It is a really good feeling to have my own money," she said with a smile. She spends most of her time at the senior citizen center talking with her regular group of friends and participating in a few of the activity programs such as folk dancing and dollmaking. Her favorite part of day is soaking herself, along with her friends, in a hot tub which is heated by the city garbage. After dinner, she usually helps her daughter-in-law clean up the table and watches television with her grandchildren.

In her household, as in those of most women interviewed, the daughter-in-law does most of the domestic chores. Mrs. M. helps, as expected, whenever she is needed. A couple of years before the interview, she had surgery to remove blood clots in her leg. During the entire period of hospitalization and recuperation at home, her daughter-in-law spent countless hours caring for her. She has reciprocated these hours of service by her daughter-in-law with appreciation and praise. She always tells her neighbors, friends, and relatives how caring and diligent her *yome* (daughter-in-law) is and how happy she is to have such a wonderful *yome*. Responding to a question of whether or not she reciprocates her daughter-in-law's services in any other way, she said she had never thought of giving a gift or doing something special for her. "She [daughter-in-law] enjoys her reputation of being an ideal *yome*. The good reputation and respect from others, not a piece of jewelry or clothes, are the most rewarding things you get from your hard work, I think," she added.

While resource exchanges between mother-in-law and daughter-in-law are prescribed by the family exchange rule, a married daughter is formally defined as nonfamily and the mother-daughter relationship is expected to be governed by the nonfamily exchange rule. In fact, women reported in the interviews that it is not common in Japan for a married daughter to provide her mother with services. The daughter is expected to maintain certain distance from her parent's "family" as a measure of her respect for the wife of the brother with whom her parents live. It is not appropriate for a mother to visit her married daughter to provide help, either. This is particularly true for the daughter who lives with her parents-in-law, although it is becoming more acceptable for a mother to visit and help married daughters who are not living with their in-laws. The relationship between mothers and daughters has been undergoing substantial change during the past few decades. It is now more acceptable to provide each other with some degree of support beyond that traditionally prescribed.

Interestingly and perhaps indicative of a new trend, the exchange rules for such informal transactions of resources between mothers and married daughters have not been clearly defined. It appears to be common and acceptable for a mother to reciprocate her married daughter's minor services, if she receives any, only with affection and/or respect. However, when the daughter provides a considerable amount of services such as spending several days caring for her sick mother, the mother reciprocates with a material gift to both her daughter and her daughter's family in acknowledgment of her services and the patience of her family for the inconvenience caused by her absence. On the other hand, a mother would not reciprocate her daughter-in-law's services with a similar material gift, because the mother and daughter-in-law belong to the same family. It is considered *mizukusai* (lack of intimacy) to reciprocate any kind of resource with material resource such as goods and money within the family.

Similar revisions of the traditional exchange rules in the Japanese family system have been observed in the transaction of goods between mothers and married daughters. Gift giving among nonfamily members is a minor institution in Japan, with complex rules defining who should give to whom, what occasions require a gift, what sort of gift is appropriate on a given occasion, and how the gift should be presented (Befu 1968). It has been a custom for a mother and her married daughter, or in a more restricted sense, their families, to exchange gifts on specified occasions. Such gift exchanges are strictly governed by the rule of symmetric reciprocity. Besides such formal gift giving, more informal transactions of goods between mothers and daughters are now becoming increasingly common. In the interviews, the older Japanese women reported receiving small gifts such as a box of their favorite candies, kitchen scissors, and a new hairbrush from their daughters. Those gifts were often given without the knowledge of the daughter's husband and in-laws. Unlike formal gift exchanges, both mothers and daughters seem to apply the exchange rules for family members to such informal gift giving. It is most appropriate for a mother to reciprocate such small gifts only with affection and appreciation.

Clearly, the mother-daughter relationship in Japan is undergoing transition. The trend is that mothers and daughters are choosing to maintain continuously close relationships and frequent support exchanges as family members even after the daughter's marriage. It is obvious that such changes in the mother-daughter relationship are affecting the current mother-in-law and daughter-in-law relationship. There are various factors which contribute to these changes in family relations. Above all, gradual changes in family structure in Japan, particularly the increase of older people living separately from their children, are altering the resource exchange patterns and exchange rules in the Japanese family.

This is demonstrated in the findings from a third set of data which compared the family relations of two groups of older Japanese women, those who live in three-generation households and those who live independently from their children. We can see here the direction of the future changes in family exchange relationships in Japan. In this study (Campbell and Brody 1985), two groups of women were compared: (1) a joint-living group composed of 128 mothers-in-law and 136 daughters-in-law and (2) a separate-living group of 136 mothers and their daughters. The findings reported here pertain to the older women's relationships with their daughters and the younger women's relationships with their mothers. About 80 percent of the older women living with their sons and daughters-in-law also had daughters living separately.

When asked about visits within the past month, women living apart from their children report both paying more visits to and receiving more visits from their children than did those living in joint households. Consistent with the discussion above, mothers appear reluctant to visit their daughters who are living in joint households. Only 9 percent of daughters living with the husband's parents report receiving visits from their own mothers, as compared to 31 percent of daughters living separately. However, it is important to note that over half the women living in joint households were visited by their own daughters within the past month. The women living in joint households are, on the average, older than those living separately and perhaps would have more difficulty going out to visit their daughters. That many of them receive visits from their daughters demonstrates the diminution of traditional norms of distance between households. Although the traditional structure of intergenerational relationships still carries considerable force in Japan, the more "natural," affective ties seem to be gaining in strength.

In relation to concrete help such as housekeeping, assistance with a family business, care when ill, care of grandchildren, and help with errands, the mothers living separately exchange substantially more help with their daughters than do those living with their daughters-in-law. In the joint-living households it is clear that the daughter-in-law takes charge of most of the household responsibilities. Doing the laundry is the only activity for which the older women take more responsibility than do their daughters-in-law.

In the area of gift giving, there is somewhat more gift exchange reported by women living separately. The exchanges of food and clothing are high and relatively equal between the two groups, supporting the findings from the previous study that informal exchanges between mothers and daughters in joint-living households were gaining in frequency. A striking difference appears when daughters are asked if they have had dinner with their mother within the past month. Forty-four percent of those living separately reported having had dinner with their mother as compared to only 9 percent of those living with their husband's parents.

The question of living arrangements came up frequently in interviews with both generations. Although the majority of older Japanese live with their children, the percentage of those living separately has increased from 13 percent in 1960 to 31 percent in 1980. Recent surveys indicate that Japanese of all ages view living separately as a reasonable option when the older couple is healthy. As parents become ill or are widowed, people are more likely to prefer living together with children. Overall, although the Japanese seem to be widening the boundaries of what is possible, the staying power of traditional patterns of support exchange, despite modernization, is remarkable.

EXCHANGE RULES AND AGING

From an exchange theory perspective, the problems of aging are essentially problems of decreasing exchange commodities. Older people as a statistical aggregate suffer from lower income and poorer health than younger people. Consequently, they are physically and financially limited in entering into exchange situations. They might not be able to afford to exchange holiday gifts with children and grandchildren in the way they used to do or to watch grandchildren in return for the help which they receive from their daughters or daughters-in-law. This is particularly true for the very old. Many of them have very little to exchange which is of any instrumental value.

How do the exchange rules affect the support relationships of older persons in the two societies? As described in the previous section, the American rule is characterized as symmetric reciprocity, which prescribes repayment by a resource in kind and of equivalent value within a relatively short time period. Under this rule, faced with diminishing instrumental resources, the American elderly would find it difficult to repay with resources in kind in order to maintain reciprocal relationships. There is a widespread fear that the failure of equivalent repayment develops dependency.

On the contrary, the exchange rule in the Japanese family prescribes repayment by an expressive resource regardless of the kind of resource received. Since expressive resources are essentially inexhaustible for any individual, Japanese elderly are expected to be better able to cope with declining instrumental resources by reciprocating with expressive resources.

Thus, due to their exchange rules, American elderly seem to have more difficulty than their Japanese counterparts in adjusting to their decreased instrumental resources. How do American elderly cope with this difficulty? There are several observations and explanations for changes in support exchange behaviors as well as exchange rules among older persons in the United States. For example, it is commonly observed that older individuals withdraw from exchange situations. This is clearly considered to be a coping strategy in which older persons still maintain the norm of reciprocity and simply choose not to enter exchange situations to prevent nonreciprocal relationships when they do not have resources to reciprocate.

Other explanations suggest modifications of exchange rules applied to older people. Antonucci (1985) suggests the concept of a Social Support Bank to explain support exchanges across the life-span and help clarify the reciprocity issue in old age. The notion of a Social Support Bank emphasizes the enduring aspect of interpersonal relationships and long term reciprocity in a continuing series of exchanges of support with significant others. It suggests that individuals utilize a generalized accounting system in the supportive exchanges they experience. That is, they maintain a mental record of supports they have provided and to whom, as well as supports received and from whom. This accounting system is thought to be informal and, for the most part, a cognitive activity conducted with little conscious attention on the part of the individual. This cognitive support account can be considered in a manner analogous to an individually maintained savings account at local banks. One can think of the Support Bank account in a similar fashion, as an attempt to "save up for a rainy day." One strives to maintain, at minimum, a balance between what is deposited and what is withdrawn, but the development of a support reserve, which can be drawn on in time of need, is optimal. Thus, one is motivated to maintain exchanges that help significant others. These essentially constitute deposits. On the other hand, receiving support from others is similar to making withdrawals from one's savings account. In time of need, one can rest assured, at least if deposits have been made in the past and interest accumulated, that support will be available. It is conceivable that, with diminishing exchange commodities, older people (and probably their social networks as well) come to emphasize this long-term reciprocity notion of a Social Support Bank and define their support exchange by this norm, so that they can receive a great deal of support from close and important others, potentially for an extended period of time, and yet feel relatively unindebted.

James Dowd argues that a completely different rule governs the exchange of social support involving older people, particularly the very old. Even in this contract-oriented society of reciprocity, noncontractual elements are not completely absent. No longer bound by the norm of reciprocity, older people are entitled to benefit by the norm of beneficence. "The norm of beneficence requires individuals to give others help as they need and without thought of what they have done or can do for them" (1984: 103). It is acceptable, in other words, that the very old receive more than they are owed under the norm of reciprocity.

These observations and explanations for support exchange involving older persons are obviously not exhaustive or mutually exclusive. They offer interesting hypotheses but are far from conclusive. An important question is: Do the oldest old continue to maintain the norm of reciprocity as their exchange rule? If they do, future research should examine how they can manage to maintain reciprocal relationships with limited exchange commodities; if they do not, what alternative exchange rules do they adopt? It is also important to learn whether or not the other party in an exchange relationship, such as a daughter or daughter-in-law, also revises her exchange rules when the exchange involves older persons. In short, future research should be designed to further specify the nature and changes of reciprocal relationships in old age.

PART III
AGING, MODERNIZATION, AND SOCIETAL TRANSFORMATION

THE MODERNIZATION MODEL AND ITS CRITIQUE

The dramatic upsurge of older citizens remaining alive in Third World countries is a legacy of the last two decades. This demographic change has been inter-twined with alterations in economic production, distribution of wealth, or-ganization of families and communities, the very structure of states and their link to major industrial powers. How has this effected the life of the elderly? A simple answer was provided by Leo Simmons's terse dictum, "Change is the crux of the problem of aging" (1960:88). Few could doubt the power of this statement after reading Nancy Scheper-Hughes's (1987) poignant study detail-ing the demise of the rural Irish "gerontocracy." One could also point to the case of the Ik of Uganda where government-mandated change from hunting and gathering to sedentary agriculture turned their society into a leaky lifeboat and the elderly into shark bait (Turnbull 1972).

On the other hand, studies of Samoa (Rhoads 1984; Holmes and Rhoads 1987), China (Treas 1979; Davis-Friedman 1983; Olson, this volume), and the famous Abkhasians of Soviet Georgia (Benet 1974) demonstrate that significant social change is not always a disaster for the aged. In fact, a careful examination of the history of the Abkhasians reveals that substantial alterations in their societal structure since the end of the nineteenth century have in fact improved what was already a strong situation for the elderly (Inal-Ipa 1982).

Until quite recently the primary model for considering how massive worldwide change has affected the elderly has been the "modernization" theory. Most briefly, modernization theory has developed as an extension of a functionalist interpretation of societal evolution from relatively undifferentiated rural/traditional-based societies with limited technology to an urban-based entity. This shift is marked by the use of complex industrial technology, in-animate energy sources, and differentiated institutions to promote efficiency and progress. Third World countries are said to develop/progress as they adopt, through cultural diffusion, the modernized model of rational/efficient societal organization. While such a transformation is often viewed as an overall advance for such countries, a strong inverse relationship is suggested between the elements of modernization as an independent variable and the status of the aged as a dependent variable. Donald Cowgill, first by suggesting a number of discrete postulates (1972) and later in developing a more elaborate model (1974, 1986), has been the most dominant writer on this subject. The hypothesized decline in valued roles, resources, and respect available to older persons in modernizing societies is said to stem from four main factors: modern health technology; economies based on scientific technology; urbanization; and mass education and literacy.

Validation of this model has been uneven and has spurred a small industry of gerontological writings, which debate the proposed articulation of modern-ization and aging (see Finley 1982 for an excellent review). Historians have sharply questioned the model, saying it is not only ahistorical but that, by idealizing the past, an inappropriate "world we have lost syndrome" has been created (Laslett 1976; Aschenbaum and Sterns 1978; Fischer 1978; Aschen-baum 1982; Quadagno 1982). Goldstein and Beall (1981) argue that the concept "status of the aged" must be constructed as a multidimensional variable with no necessary assumption of covariance between the different dimensions of status. Examination of ethnographic studies has suggested the need to consider varia-tions within given elderly populations based on such factors as class (Harlan 1964), values (Holmes 1987), gender (Roebuck 1983; Cool and McCabe 1987; Counts, in press), kinship systems (Sokolovsky and Sokolovsky 1983b), and age-cohorts (Foner 1984a).

Perhaps the most far-reaching challenge to modernization theory stems from "dependency" or "world-systems" models of global development. Such theorists as Amin (1976), Chase-Dunn and Rubinson (1977), Frank (1979), and Wallerstein (1979) contend that the lack of development in Third World countries is not predicated on a failure to adopt "modern ways" but is determined by a historic process of continuing "underdevelopment." This is based on an international division of labor which allows capital accumulation to take place in core nations of a capitalist world system while these countries control the developmental process in semiperipheral and peripheral areas. Overall, it is contended that the tie of dependent nations to core industrial powers through multinational corporations and foreign aid has resulted in the enhanced position of favored urban elites at the cost of growing rural impoverishment and internal inequalities. Jon Hendricks (1982), one of the few writers to consider aging from a world-systems perspective, suggests that the situation of the elderly will be determined by their "use-value" relative to the demands of the core sector or the extent to which they "embody old ways inimical to core interests" (p. 341).

SOCIETAL TRANSFORMATION AND AGING

Particularly important in our understanding of how massive structural change affects the elderly is the study of socialist societies such as China which have taken non-Western paths to societal development (Ganschow 1978; Cherry and Magnuson-Martinson 1979; Treas 1979; Davis-Friedmann 1985; Tsai 1987; Schulz and Davis-Friedmann 1987; Aimei, 1988; Ikels, 1988). Based on repeated trips in the last several years to the People's Republic of China, sociologist Philip Olson examines in chapter 7 the awesome transformations in the life of the elderly. Sparked first by the revolutionary reordering of society following World War II and more recently in the wake of the post-Mao "four modernizations," the case of China forces us to take into account the nature of the state as a key variable in assessing the impact of change on the situation of the aged. Some of the most dramatic changes have been in the lives of women, whose feet are no longer bound and whose futures cannot be readily sold in arranged marriages. Especially in urban areas, we see how new roles and supports in neighborhood committees and workplace associations have created for older women a world of possibilities that now extends beyond the household. Nevertheless, the most recent changes in breaking up the commune system present special challenges in supporting the childless aged who appear to be the most vulnerable members of any Third World population (Donner 1987; Husby-Darvis 1987; Rubinstein 1987; Sangree 1987; Zimmer 1987).

Third World countries are not the only societies undergoing change which affects the elderly. In the industrialized West, since World War II, radical changes in labor markets, the growth of the welfare state, and seemingly instantaneous alterations in lifestyles have created new contexts in which aging is experienced. Added to this is the growing "agedness" of these countries, where up to 18 percent are over sixty-five (in Sweden), and of these persons typically eight out of ten are no longer employed. Given that the United States is still one of the least "aged" of the industrialized nations and has barely begun to define national policy on the elderly, it has the fortuitous possibility of learning from efforts of other nations addressing this issue.

In just such a way Bruce Zelkovitz analyzes in chapter 8 Sweden's attempt to use its "middle way," between United States-style capitalism and centralized, planned socialism to enhance the quality of life of the aged. He uses a political-economy approach to show how one Scandinavian country has created state mechanisms of support which seek to be positively "transformative" rather than the defensive, crisis management type of welfare system in the United States. Recognizing that in the past a major problem has been "overcare" in institutions and "undercare" within households, Sweden has embarked on a national program to promote the independence, integrity, and meaningful participation of the aged in community life.

Another important national level comparison is provided in Christie Kiefer's study of how attitudes and behavior toward the elderly have fared in contemporary Japan. Rapidly becoming the wealthiest and most urban country in the world, Japan currently has little more than one-half the "agedness" of Sweden in its population. However, Japan already has the world's second highest life expectancy and between 1980 and 2000 will undergo the most rapid aging any nation has ever experienced. Potentially buffering the negative effects of such changes on the aged is the high status and prestige accorded the elderly in traditional Japanese culture (Benedict 1945; Smith 1961b; Plath 1964, 1972; Palmore 1975). This is promoted by cultural patterns which include: the Japanese version of Buddhism with its linking of the aged, and even the dead, to a family system stressing filial devotion; an age-grading system favoring seniority; and a corporate emphasis which strengthens the place of the elderly in extended family settings.

Kiefer's chapter engages the very controversial debate over the ability of Japan's traditional culture to resist erosion of the status of the elderly in light of extensive modernization (see especially Sparks 1975; Plath 1980, 1987; Maeda 1983; Palmore and Maeda 1985). Here he argues that the typical measures of status employed in most analyses of modernization are too simple and fail to allow us to appreciate the diversity of impact such change can have in a single society.

7 THE ELDERLY IN THE PEOPLE'S REPUBLIC OF CHINA

Philip Olson

Zhang Jinwen, seventy-one years old, lives in a small three-room apartment in northwest Beijing City with his wife, to whom he has been married for fifty-five years, his married son and daughter-in-law, and their two children. Married by arrangement between his and his wife's parents when he was sixteen years old, he had never seen his wife prior to the marriage.

> We lived together in the same room and I worked at a nearby university as a ball boy, chasing tennis balls on the courts of the university, earning two *jiao* an hour. We eventually had children, two sons and a daughter, and we lived in a very small three rooms. My wife took care of the home and the children, and I worked for the university, mostly cleaning up one of the buildings, but sometimes running errands for the officials. When I got married I had to move out because there was no more room. My wife was always a good wife. She took care of the children and the house, and she seldom complained; that is because I always gave her a certain amount of money each week to buy food and household items and clothes; if she ever needed money I gave it to her. Once she said something to her sister about never getting any gifts from me. I don't know why she would want any gifts because I always gave her enough money to buy anything she needed.

"Lao Zhang," as he is called by younger people for whom the word *lao* (old) denotes respect for elders, is now retired from the university where he worked for fifty-five years as janitor and handyman. He lives on a pension of 130 *yuan* a month. (The average wage of a factory worker is now 75 yuan a month — a yuan is about $.35.) Since his retirement in 1976 at the age of sixty-one, he has been given another job at the university as night watchman in a building on campus, where he has a small room in which he spends the night. It is furnished with a cot, chair, table, ceiling light, and radio. During the day he goes home to be with his wife, married son, and grandchildren. For the night watchman job, he is paid 60 yuan a month. His married son also works and brings home 70 yuan a month, which is considered part of the household income because the meals are prepared in the one kitchen and all eat as one family. The son wants to move out, but the unavailability of housing forces him to remain in his parents' home. Lao Zhang now has more income than he can spend on his needs; his three rooms cost him 5 yuan a month, electricity and heat average about 6 to 10 yuan a month, and the combined food bill for the whole family is no more than 30 yuan a month. So, Lao Zhang lavishes his six grandchildren with gifts, such as toys, clothes, and a 50-yuan pair of ice skates.

I am happier now than I have ever been; I enjoy still working, and I do not have to worry about food and clothes for my family. My married daughter lives nearby and I see her two daughters often; and my younger son also lives in Beijing and they come to visit us on Sunday, when we all have dinner together in my apartment. Usually we have a fresh chicken; before I retired we seldom had chicken to eat, because it was too expensive. Now we eat as we like, and my wife goes to the street vegetable market every morning to buy vegetables and a little meat or eggs or fish. She does all the cooking and also takes care of the two grandchildren while my daughter-in-law goes off to work; she works in a factory, operating a machine, the same place where my son works. I get home in the morning after my son and his wife have gone to work, and I usually spend a little time playing with the grandson who is three. Perhaps I am a bit unusual because I have spent a lot of time over the last fifty years teaching myself English. Even though I have no education, I can speak English better than many college-educated students here on this campus. But I am the only one in my family who can speak it, except my grandson, whom I am teaching a few words. In the morning I take a walk in the park and spend some time talking with some of my long-time friends who gather around a table near the lake to play chess; now we are again playing *Mah Jong*, but of course we do not gamble, only for fun. After my wife fixes lunch for me, I take a short nap, and sometimes in the afternoon my wife and I talk a little about the grandchildren. Then at five o'clock I walk to the campus to my room where I spend the night.

Lao Zhang typifies a generation of elderly who are experiencing a new era in Chinese culture. The 1980s is an era of dramatic change for the Chinese people, but especially for the elderly who were raised under conditions extremely different from the younger generations of Chinese. It is the culmination of forty years of political, economic, and social reform, which began with "Liberation" in 1949 by the Chinese Communist Party (CCP). In order to understand the meaning of the current conditions in which Lao Zhang and other old people are living, it is necessary to understand the impact of industrialization and urbanization on the social structure of China, an agrarian society.

THE MODERNIZATION OF AGRARIAN SOCIETY

One of the principal areas of interest in the study of such societal changes, often labeled modernization, is the question of how it affects the elderly population. The theory of modernization predicts that the traditionally high status of the elderly tends to change under industrialization (Cowgill 1974, 1975, 1986). It postulates that the proportion of elderly increases as a result of advances in medical and hygiene practices which contribute to lower mortality rates and a longer life-span. It further suggests that, under these conditions, the status of the elderly (status includes both economic well-being and level of prestige) changes as the society places a priority on younger workers who possess the job skills necessary in a technologically advanced society (Rosow 1967; Palmore and Manton 1974). Under these conditions the elderly decline in prestige and may or may not decline in their standard of living. As they play a lesser role in the production system, they actually drain resources from the society rather than adding to its output. Those examining the development of the welfare state under industrialization (Cutright 1965; Jackman 1975; Wilensky 1975) assume that the demand grows for a social security system for the elderly, made possible by an increase in economic surpluses. In this view, the economic status of the elderly does not necessarily decline under modernization. However, there is a collision course between the growing size of the elderly population and the rest of its population: the elderly compete with the rest of the society for resources and thus the social and economic conditions of the elderly become politicized. To what degree they come to occupy a central place on the political agenda of the modernizing society is a crucial element in the theoretical debate over the changing role of the elderly in industrializing societies. It remains a largely unanswered empirical question, even in cross-cultural research (Palmore and Whittington 1971; Bengtson et al. 1975; Maxwell and Silverman 1970; Press and McKool 1972).

In this examination of changing conditions of the Chinese elderly, we will expand the theory of modernization by exploring the role of the political economy in shaping the impact of modernization on the elderly. We will add an element called the "state." In an attempt to identify the state as a crucial variable in understanding political agendas, Theda Skocpol (1985; Orloff and Skocpol 1984) dismisses the "simplistic" explanation that economic surpluses and the changing demography of industrializing societies cause the development of welfare systems, including those directed at the elderly. Instead, she calls for assessing the role of the state as a factor in establishing the political agenda, independent of the issues deemed important to the members of the society (Orloff and Skocpol 1984:729–30).

Whereas the theory of modernization argues that economic and social factors eventually force the elderly into a declining social position and into an ambiguous economic position, the addition of the state as an element in the process offers to explain "how" the status of the elderly changes through the interplay of competing interests within the society, and thus, how it is possible to trace both increases and decreases in their economic and social status over time as the society modernizes. The state as "actor and institutional structure" affects the political arena, and thus, can influence the future of the elderly. This is particularly true in a society like China with its centralized, one-party system.

The state and political structure in the People's Republic of China (PRC) under the regime of the Chinese Communist Party since 1949 gives the Party control over all governmental units at every level from the locality to the state (Lieberthal 1983). The Party Secretary and the Political Bureau influence the State Council, the most powerful governmental unit in China (Liu 1986; J. Wang 1985). Thus, the direction of modernization is shaped by the centralized command of a small group of people, and, though attempting to be accountable to the "people" through mass organizations, it can and does establish policy in all sectors of society. It can, then, affect the influence of modernization on the elderly (Olson 1988). Indeed, there is good evidence that the Party agenda for modernization has positive outcomes for the elderly, and so we are able to trace the changes in conditions of life for the aged to the political agenda of the Party and state. We will explore this matter in a later section.

THE TRADITIONAL ROLE OF THE ELDERLY IN CHINA

Agrarian China was characterized by the centrality of the family and the reverence for the elderly. Indeed, the two are related and form an essential base upon which the social structure of China was substantially built. As an agrarian society, China in the premodern period (before the Republic was founded in 1911) was rooted in a tradition of ancestor worship and filial piety. It was a patrilineal society, meaning that family descent was through the male side of the family, and it was dependent on the land. One's future resided in the male offspring, for he carried on the family name, inherited property, cared for one in old age, and himself produced offspring that carried on the family lineage, ensuring continuity with both the past and future. A man was seen as a link in an unending chain of kin stretching back as far as ancestors could be traced and forward into the future through his descendents. To break the chain by not having male children was a failure to honor his obligations to both past and future generations (Baker 1979; Chai and Chai 1969).

Confucianism built on this premise of ancestor worship and provided a moral and intellectual foundation for revering the elderly; older persons, by virtue of their number of years of study and their accumulated experience, were the moral and ethical models of their society. They were to be respected, honored, and followed. Because this idea was so central to Confucian philosophy and because this philosophy was so central to Chinese society during the two millennia preceding its entry into Western industrialization, it is understandable why the elderly have played so large a role in the history and development of the Chinese social structure (Ganshaw 1978). This veneration of both age and the past served to preserve the importance of the family over the single person, the dominance of male over female, and the power of age over youth.

However, Confucianism was not widespread among the Chinese (Freedman 1961; Ikels 1975; Leslie 1979); it was limited to the upper segment of society, perhaps no more than 20 percent. For the vast majority of Chinese, the Confucian practice of venerating the elderly was an ideal rather than daily practice (Yin and Lai 1983). Yet children were important, if not for veneration, at least for security in one's old age. The agrarian society depended on the family for its social security system.

Underpinning the importance of the family and reverence for the elderly was Chinese folk religion, which forebode the dangers of Hungry Ghosts wandering alone in the Underworld. One became a Hungry Ghost if he or she failed to leave descendents. Descendents were vital in the role of worshipping the ancestor after his demise. To face old age and death without natural or adopted descendents was indeed a grim prospect (Sankar 1981). To avoid this prospect, unmarried persons or childless couples went to great lengths to ensure having some descendents who could care for them after death. As Andrea Sankar points out, there were thousands who found themselves in this position, and they coped with their dilemma through a variety of cultural solutions. Sometimes nephews were adopted. The two most common means for unmarried women to avoid this outcome were to become servants within a home where they established familylike relationships or to enter a secular sisterhood (Sankar 1981:32).

THE ROLE OF THE ELDERLY AFTER LIBERATION

The triumph of Mao Zedong on October 1, 1949, marked the beginning of the Chinese Communist Party era and the historic redistribution of wealth, property, and power in China.[1] The economic ups and downs of the Mao years had their impact on the elderly, who, as relatively weaker producers in the system, depended for their well-being on the overall prosperity of the society. Among those who have observed the role and status of the elderly during these years, there is little consensus over whether the elderly fared better or worse under Maoism. Although some argue the status of the elderly has declined under Communism (Ganshaw 1978; Woon 1981; Cherry and Magnuson-Martinson 1981), there is considerable evidence for the equal or increased status of the aged under Mao (Tien 1977; Kinoy 1979; Treas 1979; Yin and Lai 1983; Davis-Friedmann 1981, 1983). Perhaps the clearest analysis of the increased status of the elderly is provided by Yuan Tien who states: "Their life is characterized by 'no wasted years and no isolated existence' plus respect" (1977: 6). In addition, he cites work done in the early 1960s by D. Lazure (1962) which points out the respect youth show for elderly and in the 1970s by A. Chen (1970) who examined the literature of China for evidence of generational attitudes. Tien concluded that the literary image of grandparents was wholly positive for the first time since the 1930s.

Undoubtedly, the enactment of the new marriage laws in 1950 and their revision in 1981 heralded the new attitude toward elderly parents and women. Men and women are considered equal under this new law; monogamy is the only recognized marriage form; parents are responsible for proper care of their children; and children are responsible for the proper care of their parents in old age. Though it is certain that the passage of this new law did not instantly transform millions of relationships within existing families across China and did not compel all young people to obey the spirit of the new law, it did set the public ideology and level of expectations of the new generations of Chinese. In the thirty-nine years since its enactment, there have been changes in family relationships, especially in urban areas: women have greater rights and freedoms; children marry later and have more freedom in choosing partners; and women have greater economic independence. In traditional family life, the wife had no property rights and remained unskilled except in domestic work. Now she is more likely to have a skill, an income, and a participatory role in the society, especially in the urban neighborhood, where she is likely to serve on a neighborhood council (called "Resident's Committee"). Also, in her work role she may have some responsibility and authority. The younger women, in their positions of greater autonomy, are now becoming especially visible to the older women. Later, we shall look at how this affects older urban women, such as Madam Liu, whose story is later included.

Mao's personal attitudes concerning elders and youth were unquestionably a factor in the state policies toward the elderly following Liberation. Those who have examined closely his writings and his political career conclude that he was not Confucian in his outlook: he looked not so much to the elderly for leadership or wisdom, but to the vigor and enthusiasm of youth for the success of the economic and political revolution he mounted (Ganshaw 1978:307–9). Though there is debate over the precise role Mao played in launching the Cultural Revolution, there is little doubt that he believed in purging the system of traditional values (i.e., the sacredness of age, the importance of the "old," and the inviolateness of tradition) and replacing them with continued new revolutions. As he said in 1969, "The dead still rule" (Mao 1969:368).

Yet it seems quite certain that Mao never intended that the old should undergo such vilification, and as the Cultural Revolution unfolded, efforts were initiated to redirect the attack away from the elderly, who were themselves no longer defined as evil, but only as having lived through periods of an evil political economy. Thus the elderly were called upon to join publicly with the young and form a "three-in-one" alliance: "The old cadres and the young cadres must acquire each others' strong points, unite as one and do their work still better together" (quoted by Ganshaw 1978). In addition, the old were called upon to bear witness to how bad the "old" China really was (Ganshaw 1978:318; Davis-Friedmann 1983:8; Woon 1981:253). This activity was undertaken by bringing old people to the schools to tell children stories of their past: the evil practices of the past eras in which old people especially were poorly treated and where general conditions were miserable.[2]

In rural China, despite the economic gains made through collectivization, the primary responsibility for the aged remained with the family. William Parish, in his analysis of rural family life, notes, "the welfare system is still based on the family" (1975:616); this has been largely accomplished "through the ability of the elderly to share the rewards earned by younger family members, and not through increases in direct state intervention" (Davis-Friedmann 1981:53). So rural care of the elderly depended upon the economic successes of the communes, and although there were almost no pension systems for older farm workers during this period, the wealthier collectives provided better medical care and other benefits to retired persons. But for the masses of rural elderly there were no major programs or policies to look after their needs. This condition, called "urban bias" by Michael Lipton (1977), is typical of developing societies because resources are first put into urban areas.

For the childless elderly and those who bore only daughters—because daughters always moved to the household of their husband and tended to take no responsibility for the care of their own parents—the rural communes developed a system of relief. In 1956, during the era of expansion of the collectives, the system of "Five Guarantees" (*wu bao*) was developed, providing food, clothing, shelter, medical care, and for the young, education, or for the elderly, a burial. Although it was far from uniform in its formative period (Dixon 1981:191–95), this system did provide the childless elderly with a degree of assurance that they would be cared for regardless of their ability to work. By the end of 1958, a massive development of old age homes had occurred: 100,000 homes in the countryside with a resident population of two million elderly (Dixon 1981:198–99). But these homes were short-lived, and after the failure of the "Great Leap Forward" in 1958–59, there was no comprehensive welfare program for the rural elderly, except the Five Guarantees for the childless and a few homes for the aged. For those elderly with children, the family remained the principal welfare unit.

In urban areas the care of the elderly under Mao was quite different than in the countryside. The development of retirement programs and pensions for workers began on a small scale in the mid-1950s and grew rapidly during the 1970s (Davis-Friedmann 1981). The development of pensions for retired workers removed the burden of care from the children of older workers, and the retirement of workers at ages fifty-five and sixty opened the way for younger, more vigorous workers to fill the factory jobs of the often less skilled and less efficient older workers. Medical care and other benefits to the aged were also considered better in urban areas than in the countryside.

On balance, then, Deborah Davis-Friedmann's observations are warranted: "The overall security of the aged has markedly improved since 1949" (1981:52), and "the Communist revolution has thus strengthened rather than weakened traditional views of old age and the elderly have benefited from government support" (1983:13).

CHINA'S GROWING ELDERLY POPULATION

All modernizing societies are characterized by an increase in their elderly population, the result of a decline in the mortality rate brought about by improved sanitation and medical care practices. China follows this general pattern, and Table 7.1 shows the population of China between 1953 and 1982. Because modernization has only just begun there, it is not yet possible to obtain accurate data on the growth of the population. However, since those people who will be over sixty-five by the years 2000 and 2025 are now already living, it is possible to project with some reasonable accuracy how many will be living then if current mortality rates continue; however, what percentage they constitute depends on the birth rate in the coming decades.

The proportion of elderly will dramatically increase by the year 2000, when the percentage sixty years and over will be 11 percent; and by 2032 it will rise to 15.7 percent. This increase is an important reason why China is now preparing for its elderly through policies of medical care, pensions, and social support programs encouraged by the National Committee on Aging.

Of the total population of China in 1982, approximately 80 percent lived in rural areas. The urban population was 206,590,000 and the rural 801,532,000. The number of persons over 60 years of age, estimated for 1985, is 85 million;

Table 7.1
Population of China, 1953–1982 (in thousands)

	1953		1964		1982	
Age	No.	%	No.	%	No.	%
0–14	206,845	35.7	281,650	40.5	337,251	33.5
15–64	347,558	59.9	388,608	55.9	621,506	61.6
65 & over	25,401	4.4	24,687	3.6	49,366	4.9
Total	579,804		694,944		1,008,123	
60 & over	42,142	7.3	42,427	6.1	76,749	7.6

Source: Anonymous 1984a.

of these, 68 million (80 percent) are rural and 17 million are urban. Whereas the percentage of rural elderly over the age of sixty is 7.7, the two largest cities in China, Shanghai and Beijing, have 11.5 percent and 8.5 percent, respectively, of their populations over age sixty, evidence of the pattern of more rapid aging of the urban population found in other modernizing societies, and in China reflecting the policy of restricting migration of rural youth to cities.

Of particular interest in understanding aging patterns in China and the problems they raise for the society is the proportion of childless elderly. The childless represent those elderly who do not have the traditional supports (children) for themselves in old age. There is no reliable census of the number of childless elderly in China, but the number has been estimated to be between 7 and 12 million. Of these, nearly 3 million are receiving some kind of economic assistance in the countryside through a program known as the Five Guarantees, and about 50 thousand in the cities are receiving some form of economic aid from the government. The lack of a rural retirement system accounts for the relatively large number of rural households receiving government aid. Whereas 75 percent of all urban workers who are retired receive a pension from their work unity, fewer than 1 percent of all farmers over sixty receive a pension.

MODERNIZATION POLICIES IN THE POST-MAO ERA AND THEIR CONSEQUENCES FOR THE ELDERLY

The death of Mao Zedong in 1976 brought an end to one era in Chinese history and the beginning of another. During this current period, full-scale modernization has been occurring. The impetus for this accelerated modernization lies in the January 1975 announcement by then-Premier Zhou En-lai of the Four Modernizations Program to be achieved by the year 2000. The program outlined the development of agriculture, the military, industry, and science and technology. The adoption of this program in 1978, together with the downfall of the "gang of four" following the death of Mao, ensured that China would develop through technological advances rather than through class struggle, as the Cultural Revolution had promoted.

There are three major policies as part of this modernization process: (1) economic reform, (2) Party reform, and (3) population reform.

Economic Reform

The political successor to Mao, Deng Xiaoping, has "encouraged unity through increased economic interdependence, through reliance on effective, planned allocation of material goods and capital, and through a regularized promotion and personnel management system" (Oksenberg 1982:170). This decade has witnessed a remarkable reform of the entire economy, including the abolition of the farm commune, the opening of "free markets" for many goods and services, the institutionalization of a work incentive policy, greater decentralization of enterprise management, implementation of a mixed controlled and market economy, and greater reliance on Western technology, capital, and markets. Every economic indicator available suggests that these reform efforts have resulted in economic growth of the entire system, large-scale improvements in the standard of living, inflation, and greater "Westernization" of the lifestyles of the Chinese peoples, especially those living in urban areas.

Party Reform

Developed in the early 1980s, it includes: abolishing life tenure for cadres, encouraging retirement of veteran cadres, and promoting younger cadres to leading posts (An 1982). In a speech delivered in 1981 on the occasion of the sixtieth anniversary of the founding of the CCP, Party Chairman Hu Yaobang said, "It is now a pressing strategic task facing the whole party to build up a large contingent of revolutionary, well-educated, professionally competent and younger cadres. . . and they [old, veteran cadres] should free themselves from the onerous pressure of day-to-day work" (Liu 1986:355). A major thrust of this reform was to streamline the bulging bureaucracy that has often been cited as a cause of the sluggishness of the reform, the major impediment to efficiency, and a drain on the economy.

This policy was launched in 1982 when the Party Central Committee passed a resolution establishing a veteran cadre retirement system (Zhao 1987). In the words of Deng, the goals are "to make the ranks of cadres more revolutionary, younger in average age, better educated, and more professionally competent" (Deng 1983). In 1984 it was announced that over 800,000 veteran cadres had retired by the end of 1983, signaling that the retirement policy was well launched (Ding 1984).

Population Reform

This was among the first policies developed in the period following Mao's death. Its aim was to reduce the growth of population as a necessary step in economic reform (Saith 1981). Unless the population could be contained at its then present level, the chances for economic development could never be realized because the growing population would erode gains in economic growth. Thus was launched the "one child" policy that attempted to limit population growth. In the decade since its inception, it has reportedly shown signs of success, most dramatically in urban areas and in those rural counties closely linked to urban centers along the eastern coast of China (Bianco 1981; Poston and Gu 1984; Chen 1985).

These three policies, though aimed at economic and political reform, have significant consequences for the elderly population. The success of the reforms depend on the success of well-orchestrated policies and programs for the elderly, and thus reform policies of the State necessarily include policies toward the elderly that appear to favor improved conditions for older citizens. For example, the policies of economic reform in urban areas include bringing younger and better trained workers into the work force, but limited economic growth cannot make new jobs available at a fast enough rate for the growing, young labor force. Retirement policies for older workers were introduced, setting retirement for men at sixty and women at fifty-five, that resulted in the opening up of jobs for younger, trained workers. In addition, the policy of *dingti*, or a child's right to get the job of his or her father or mother if he or she retires, is widely encouraged (Liang 1985:13) and further enhances retirement rates. Increased retirement has led to a major problem in the system: inadequate funding for a retirement plan (L. Liu 1982). A major agenda for the state in the late 1980s is finding a feasible and realistic way to provide economic support for the millions of urban workers who will retire in the coming decade. Between 1982 and 1984 the total amount reportedly paid in pensions rose from 7 million to 14 million *yuan*, while the total number of urban retired workers rose from 14.5 million workers in 1984 to 16 million in 1986 and is projected to increase by 1 million each year until the year 2000 (Tao 1986).

The veteran cadre retirement policy has also had a significant impact on policies toward the aged. As the number of veteran cadres who retire increases, greater pressure exists to focus attention on what to do with this enlarged "idle" population, and as part of the political agenda of encouraging more veteran cadres to retire the Party must show positive inducements to those wavering.

The population containment policy also bears on the aged. Even though a major impediment to the success of the "one child" policy remains the strong preference for having a son, an overriding consideration is the inevitable question, Who will take care of me in my old age? Already the concept "one-to-four" has appeared; one couple will be responsible for the care of four elderly parents in the future (J. Liu 1983; W. Wang 1986).

INSTITUTIONALIZING SUPPORT FOR THE ELDERLY

The first substantial effect on the elderly of this post-Mao modernization campaign was the revision of the Constitution, adopted on March 5, 1978. Article 50 states: "Working people have the right to material assistance in old age, and in case of illness or disability. To ensure that working people enjoy this right, the state gradually expands social insurance, social assistance, public health services, co-operative medical services, and other services. The state cares for and ensures the livelihood of disabled revolutionary army men and the families of revolutionary martyrs."

Through this Constitutional change, the state undertook the task of developing a pension system for the urban elderly. It also undertook to develop a welfare system and health services in a more substantial commitment than under previous constitutions.

A revision of the Constitution, adopted on December 4, 1982, expanded the welfare and retirement benefits for the elderly. Though it did not spell out how such benefits would be funded, it proposed greater relief for more people. The degree to which it will be implemented depends on a solution to the vast economic burden this new constitutional mandate creates for a society that is in transition from a predominantly agricultural to an industrial society.

A second major institutional change favoring the elderly was the establishment of the China National Committee on Aging, formed in 1983 as a result of a directive from the State Council, the most powerful governing unit in the government. The task of this committee is to reeducate the public to the importance of the elderly and to help develop ways to use the "leftover energies" of the elderly (Wu 1983). In pursuit of its tasks, it has established local committees on aging in every province, every large city, and in thousands of counties throughout China. These committees work with local groups to find ways to promote the general welfare of the elderly, and they collaborate with local governmental units to ensure that programs for the elderly are implemented. The National Committee also sponsors a monthly magazine, *Elderly Chinese*, and distributes over 400,000 copies each month.

The institutionalization of medical care for the elderly is another important way in which the state shows support for its elderly. In urban areas all retired workers are covered by a national health insurance program that provides care to most elderly. This includes preventive health measures as well as treatment for illness at clinics and hospitals. In addition, there are numerous special programs set up through Resident's Committees, trade unions, and Street Stations. Some hospitals have established special geriatric units (*lao ren ke*) that offer a no-waiting privilege for elderly. In rural areas, similar kinds of care are offered, but the remoteness of some areas and the poverty of some counties restrict the quality of care to many rural elderly, and in general the quality of medical care to rural elderly is not as high as for urban elderly.

The most powerful support for the elderly now underway is the redesign of a national social insurance plan that will provide retirement income for all persons over fifty-five years old. During the years 1984–86, the Chinese government sent government officials to several nations throughout the world in search of effective ways that those nations have solved the problem of supporting their elderly population. Recognizing that they are dealing with a nation of nearly 80 percent peasants, the Chinese government plans to phase in a retirement plan over several years that will gradually include those rural elderly who are not covered by existing retirement plans. The major obstacle to achieving this objective is the lack of surplus wealth necessary to create the large fund needed to provide pensions for so many rural elderly. At present any surpluses are being used for additional economic development, thus postponing any massive program of retirement pensions for China's elderly.

THE DAILY LIFE OF THE URBAN ELDERLY

In present-day China the urban elderly person is likely to be retired from his work unit (and receiving a pension), which had been during his work years the second most important unit in his daily life; the family has always been the center of his life. With or without children, one's family unit, which includes parents, their brothers and sisters and families, grandparents, and the immediate family of one's spouse, forms the core of daily life. Because housing is in short supply and because one traditionally lives with one's eldest son and his family, the household is a complex of at least two or three generations living, eating, and sleeping in the same rooms. For example, according to the 1982 Census, in Beijing only 19 percent of the households contain one generation, 64 percent contain two generations, and 17 percent contain three generations. And in the traditional manner, the eldest male is head of that household. If it is an elderly couple, the husband retains his role as final authority over disputes and decisions, except those in the kitchen and those concerning household chores, for which the wife is in command; the daughter-in-law is expected to obey her mother-in-law's rules.

Liu Yin-wei

Madam Liu, a seventy-six-year-old widow, lives in two rooms in a crowded section of older housing in Harbin, a city of more than one million in northern China. Her husband of fifty years died five years ago, leaving her alone. Her oldest son lives in Guangzhou with his wife and children, and her two daughters are married and living in Beijing with their husbands. Madam Liu's husband had been a cadre, working in a government office in Beijing. He was transferred a few years before his retirement to Harbin. The children were raised in Beijing and the daughters are living there because their husbands are from Beijing.

I don't have any education. I am a common worker who has spent all my life raising children and taking care of my husband and his needs. He was a good man, but, of course, he expected me to keep his house. Now my son is urging me to remarry so I will not be so lonely, since all my children are living away from here. There is a matchmaking organization nearby and some of my friends have kidded me about giving it a try, but I don't want to remarry. Why should I get myself back into the servitude I had when my husband was alive? All a man wants is to be waited on; I am enjoying my freedom too much to return to that kind of life. Every morning I go to the Children's Park, which is just down at the end of this lane, at about five-thirty, where I meet a group of women. We practice *Qi Gong*, a slow movement exercise routine, with a larger group for about half an hour, and then we sit in an area where there are tables and benches and we talk; some of the women have to leave pretty soon to go to the vegetable market and then home to fix breakfast for their husbands who will be returning from their early morning exercises or their get-togethers with companions who raise birds. These bird raisers, they are crazy when it comes to birds; always tending to them, trading them, breeding them, comparing their songs, fixing up the cages, and training them to be good singers. These men meet every morning in certain places in the park with their birds, and when they come home afterwards they expect breakfast to be ready for them. So those wives can't stay as long visiting with us in the park in the morning, but the rest of us chat until maybe eight o'clock, talking about simple things like our grandchildren, what our children are doing, troubles we are having with our daughters-in-law, cooking, some sewing we are working on, and sometimes about things we read in the newspaper. Once a week I go to the office where my husband worked and get his pension; it is not very much because he was not a very high-ranking worker, only 35 *yuan* a week, but it is enough to keep me satisfied. Usually after my breakfast I go to the Resident Committee office, which is in this lane, where I chat with the other women there. The Resident Committee is an important local group that is responsible for the management of many affairs in the local neighborhood. I am a member of the Committee and my main job is to work with the young married women; we are very interested in helping them realize the importance of having only one child, so we talk to them a lot, help them get birth control, and if they want an abortion we arrange it for them. In the households under this Committee I am proud to say we have had 99 percent success in the one-child households of young couples. The overall Committee is made up of elected persons from this neighborhood, and we receive some funds from the Street Station office of government. We meet weekly, and we discuss problems of street cleanliness, family quarrels that need attention, and any matters of theft or other small disturbance. We also run a small business, providing a laundry service in a room nearby, from which we raise a small amount of money that we can use to improve our neighborhood or give some help to a family that has an emergency need for help. We also provide a small business of taking a few small children to school on a bicycle owned by the Committee. When both parents work and are unable to see their children off to school, they arrange with us to transport them in the morning and to watch over them after school until they get home from work. There are not very many of these because in most cases there is a grandmother who can watch them after school. We also have a telephone in the Committee office; because most families do not have their own phone they come here regularly to use this one. And we provide for the morning distribution of milk; still many households do not have refrigerators and so fresh milk delivery is done daily through our Committee office. Some of the other retired women help with this task. The

Committee has fourteen persons; all of us, except two, are women like myself, retired and willing to work on these matters.

Madam Liu, because she is widowed and living alone, is a "special" person to her husband's work unit; at least once a month a worker from there pays her a visit to see that she is all right and to inquire whether she has any unmet needs. He may also deliver some tickets for her to attend a movie or special performance, and once a year he will help her arrange a visit to Beijing or Guangzhou by train to see her children. In July she will travel with a group of retired workers from that work unit to Beihaide, a seaside resort that is a favorite of summer vacationers. The work unit will also see that she gets medical care through its own small clinic and hospital, and should she require extended care it will provide that for her.

If she becomes ill and needs some regular care, the Resident Committee will set up a team of three workers who will visit her house regularly to see that she is all right, that she receives necessary medicine, that she has food to eat, and that her house is kept clean. If necessary, one person will cook meals for her until she is able to care for herself, and, knowing that she has been ill, a woman living in the same building will stop by daily to see that she is well even after she has recovered. For the most part it is the women, and usually the old ones, who run the neighborhood and who take the responsibility for the welfare of those not looked after by family members. Madam Liu states: "Sometimes I feel envious of the younger women in the neighborhood; they have jobs and a skill to earn their own money; and they have freedom from the daily household chores by hiring someone part-time or by letting their mother-in-law do them. So when they get old like me they will not have to depend on their husbands to provide for them; they will have the satisfaction of their own career."

Madam Liu is typical of older urban women in many ways and unlike most in some. Being apart from her children, though not typical, is not a rare occurrence, and it allows us to see the plight as well as the support systems already in place for those older people without family. From studies undertaken in recent years, the attitudes of older women toward their husbands, their careers, and their roles as housewives reveals that as many as half share the views of Madam Liu (Yue 1986). The work unit plays a central role in the care of retired workers, though it varies with the size and prosperity of that unit. In cases where old people without immediate family reach the point where they require too much care, they will be encouraged by members of the Resident Committee to enter one of the nearby homes for the aged. Most will resist this option, thinking the home is a poor place to live, a symbol of their failure to provide for themselves. But increasingly this attitude is changing, the number and quality of such homes is improving, and in some urban areas such homes are being established to provide alternative living arrangements for retired workers irrespective of whether they have children who could care for them.

OTHER SOCIAL SUPPORT SYSTEMS FOR URBAN ELDERLY

The major social units, other than the family and work unit, that provide support for the elderly are voluntary organizations, educational units, and the army. Many organizations sponsor physical exercise programs such as *taijiquan* and *qigong* in most urban areas (Anonymous 1984b). One such organization is building a high-rise that includes dining facilities, a club, living quarters for single elderly, apartments for retired couples, and a reception center for visiting elderly. Universities of the Aged have been in operation since 1983 and offer courses in health, nutrition, horticulture, physical exercise, and calligraphy (Anonymous 1984c).

On special occasions such as Youth Day and during Spring Festival, the Communist Youth League organizes the youth to carry gifts, flowers, and foods to disabled elderly and elderly without family, or who are in other ways isolated. Urban middle-school children visit elderly households, where they clean walls and windows and do other chores. During March, set aside by the state as *wen ming yue*, "civilized month," all people, including students, are asked to do things for the elderly as a way of showing their concern for the society. Every work unit is expected to do good things for others; and all know the slogan, "Everyone should do at least one good thing for someone."

The Peoples' Army plays a role in providing services to the elderly, too. Although they perform services for all sectors of the society, they have an important role in serving the elderly. On special occasions, such as Spring Festival week, members of the Army pay special attention to the childless elderly by cleaning the walls and windows of their living quarters, cleaning the courtyards, and repainting walls and ceilings. In addition they perform personal services such as giving haircuts, trimming nails, and bathing old persons.

THE RURAL ELDERLY

The population of China will remain predominantly rural for several generations, since the industrializing process of agrarian systems takes a long time to urbanize a peasant society. Political bias in industrializing societies tends to favor development of urban areas, often perpetuating the relatively poor living conditions of rural areas (Lipton 1977). As we have already noted, China is about 80 percent rural. Rural and urban areas have approximately the same percent of elderly. Unlike the urban population in China, the rural elderly are almost entirely dependent on the family for their economic and social support; fewer than 1 percent of the rural elderly are supported by pensions, and only about 5 percent receive public welfare (Five Guarantees). Thus for the 60 million rural persons over sixty years of age, the family is the core of their support. In Hebei Province, one of the most rural in China, only 16 percent of the households contain one generation, while 67 percent contain two generations, and 17 percent contain three or more.

As part of the economic reform program begun in the late 1970s, the farm commune system has been dismantled and individual households now lease land from the state and farm it according to quota agreements. Surpluses beyond these quotas can be kept by the household, and they serve as an incentive to increase agricultural productivity. The elderly play an important role in this process, since they participate in the overall household production process. It is common practice for the eldest married son to live with his parents and for other sons to live nearby, often in the same building. They thus form an economic production unit, mutually interested in the total income produced by this extended family. The elderly parents play an important role: they continue to work, regardless of age, at the farming enterprise, and they also manage the household economy by tending small garden plots, raising chickens, repairing broken household items, watching small grandchildren, preparing meals, making clothing, doing the marketing, and other necessary chores attendant to keeping a household running smoothly. Because of these indispensible roles, most rural elderly are not seen as a burden or problem to the society, but as an essential and integral part of the social and economic fabric of the society. Even in the small towns where everyone does not farm, every household has a garden plot and depends on it for part of their livelihood. In some very wealthy rural collectives, especially those surrounding Beijing and Shanghai, older workers receive pensions similar to those found in cities, and for some small manufacturing enterprises in rural areas pension systems have also been established.

A primary problem among the rural elderly is the care of the Five Guarantee families. In 1983, there were 2.5 million such households containing 2.9 million persons. Not all Five Guarantee households are elderly; the program supports the handicapped, orphaned, mentally disabled, and others unable to care for themselves. Most Five Guarantee households live within the rural communities in which they have spent most of their lives; a small proportion are institutionalized, however, and that number is increasing dramatically. In 1978, there were about 7,800 old age homes throughout all of rural China that housed about 170,000 persons. By 1986 it had risen to 27,000 homes with 276,000 residents. A major campaign by the government to increase support for the childless elderly was launched to show the young that the one-child policy would not leave them vulnerable in their old age. These homes for the aged have become an important part of that campaign. Jilin Province became the first to have a home for the aged in each of its 859 townships, in 1983 – a goal the government set in its campaign. Of the 2,400 counties in China, 140 had succeeded in establishing old age homes in every township by 1983.

THE FUTURE OF THE ELDERLY IN CHINA

We have seen that the elderly have fared quite well under the new modernization drive that began in the late 1970s. As part of the economic, Party, and population reform movements, the elderly have benefited in many ways. A pension system for the urban elderly now exists for about 75 percent of all retired workers, and the state is working toward expanding it to include all other workers, including rural elderly. Widespread campaigns have been conducted to ensure the elderly of consciously planned programs designed to make their life better, and more attention is being paid to the childless elderly in both urban and rural areas. This politicization of the elderly is a natural outcome of the struggle of a traditionally "age-oriented" society to abandon many of its older values in an effort to modernize. Because China has a one-party government with a highly centralized decision-making system, it is perhaps somewhat easier to structure the political process in ways that benefit the agenda of the Party. The theory of modernization predicts that the conditions of the elderly will deteriorate as the society reaches more advanced industrialization and resources are channeled into the younger generations and into productive activities. This does not appear to be the situation in China: modernization theory is not adequate to interpret conditions there. However, when the variable of the state is added to the equation it becomes possible to interpret the changing conditions of the elderly in China: because the larger political and economic agendas of the state happen now to benefit the elderly, it would appear that the elderly will not suffer under modernization. Yet the future holds many unknowns for the elderly. As the agendas shift over time, and as the State reassesses its goals, the consequences for the elderly can shift from positive to negative. For example, should economic conditions in China deteriorate and resources be called upon to bolster the economy, it is likely that the elderly will be among the first to relinquish some of the perquisites they have garnered from the system. And the retired veteran cadres who now live in reasonable luxury may be strained in the future should the economy worsen. The loosening of the family system, an almost inevitable outcome of industrialization and urbaniza- tion, will certainly jeopardize the elderly care system that still rests primarily on the family. And the rapidly changing values attendant to industrialization, the focus on increased consumption of domestic goods and materialism, already evident in every segment of Chinese life, will threaten the priorities now placed on tending to the elderly. So long as Lao Zhang brings home a good pension for his children and grandchildren, he will be well regarded. Should that situation change and his care fall to those children who have become accustomed to maintaining their own standard of living, Lao Zhang could well suffer the consequences. Until the Chinese economy has stabilized and institutionalized a permanent support system for its elderly, the present circumstances for the elderly, though positive, are vulnerable. As the agendas of the state shift, so too will the security of its elderly.

NOTES

1. The Republic of China was founded in 1911, and it marked the beginning of the influence of Western industrialization on China, resulting in significant changes in family

structure, especially in urbanized areas (Lang 1946; Levy 1949). The importance of ancestor worship declined, especially in cities, and economic advances for many contributed to the unlocking of family solidarity and some decline in intergenerational households. The family, however, remained the major social security system for old age.

2. During the recantings of how bad it was in the past, recordings were made and later transcribed into books that were commonplace during this period. Such books, generally titled, *Yi ku, si tian* (Recollections of the Miserable Past and Thinking about the Happy Life Now), were part of the propaganda of the period. Because nearly everyone had a relative, or knew of a relative, who had experienced miserable times in the pre-1949 period, this form of propaganda was a powerful force in calling attention to the past role of the elderly.

8 TRANSFORMING THE "MIDDLE WAY": A POLITICAL ECONOMY OF AGING POLICY IN SWEDEN

Bruce M. Zelkovitz

> Good government consists of knowing how much future to intro-
> duce in the present.
>
> — Victor Hugo

A recent development in the social scientific study of aging is the application of the political economy perspective. This approach goes beyond conceptualizing aging as an individual phenomenon and as a problem of individuals in society; it situates aging in a concrete and dynamic context linking the past, present, and future and delves into the "problems behind the problem" (Minkler and Estes 1984:10). It is defined as "the study of the interrelationships between the polity, economy, and society, or more specifically, the reciprocal influences among government ... the economy, social classes, state, and status groups. The central problem of the political economy perspective is the manner in which the economy and polity interact in a relationship of reciprocal causation affecting the distribution of social goods" (Minkler and Estes 1984:11).

This perspective builds on the anthropological tradition of connecting age-related phenomena, such as ageism, to industrialization by locating this process within the context of capitalist welfare states. From the vantage point of political economy, social policy on aging is largely determined by "competing social forces and the visions they carry of the good society" (Myles 1984:4).

While marshalling evidence that sheds light on the social policy on aging and its relationship to capitalist welfare states, the political economy perspective has been applied to the United States and such Western

European nations as Great Britain, France, Germany, and Italy (see Estes 1979; Guillemard 1983; Minkler and Estes 1984). Scandinavia, however, has remained a significant lacuna in the analysis of social policy on aging of Western capitalist welfare states. For reasons beyond the scope of this chapter, such policy in Denmark, Norway, and Sweden has rarely been subjected to systematic political-economic scrutiny. This chapter takes up such a task by focusing on Sweden.

There is a growing body of literature on aging in Sweden, including government publications and scholarly studies (see Sundstrom 1983; Svensson 1984; Daatland 1985; Sundstrom 1986), but it remains "scattered" and is primarily descriptive in nature, indicating services provided and occasionally comparing them to services in other countries (see Little 1978, 1982). Few extant studies attempt to analyze policy on aging with political-economic concerns in the forefront. This chapter utilizes a political-economic framework to examine two crucial aspects of the Swedish "aging enterprise"[1]: the official aging ideology currently promulgated by the national government, and the application of that ideology to residence options for the aged.[2] I shall clarify how the official aging ideology and its implementation reflect broader political and economic currents in Swedish society.

Important as it is to understand how aging policy is shaped by such currents, my research suggests that it would be a mistake to view the aging enterprise as only a passive "mirror" of broader trends. Instead, aging policy actively creates changes in Swedish society, at once shaping and being shaped by other socioeconomic formations in a dialectical interplay. These changes are not accidents, for as currently formulated, aging policy is consciously intended to reform Swedish life. A second intent of this chapter, therefore, is to highlight this unique and significant characteristic of Swedish aging policy—what I call its transformative character—and to describe and analyze its manifestation in residence options.[3]

Virtually all of the scholars cited above argue that aging policy in capitalist welfare states is essentially reproductive; it perpetuates inequities associated with capitalism by segregating the elderly while ensuring that their survival needs are met just minimally enough to defuse potential political resistance. The pervasiveness of this conclusion leads one to surmise that all welfare states must inevitably and inexorably generate aging policies characterized by a conservative bias. I shall argue that Sweden provides an exception in that its aging policy, here represented by official ideology and its implementation in residence options, is transformative in three important ways: (1) it seeks to transform itself, (2) it attempts to transform the elderly, and (3) most importantly for long-term political-economic trends, it provides an infrastructure with the potential to transform Swedish society into a more democratized and integrated society. That such a national ideology can be framed, promulgated, and put into practice with impressive effectiveness in a capitalist welfare state is worthy of note and suggests that aging policy is able to play a far more dynamic role in the transformation of such societies than has been generally assumed.

METHODOLOGY

This study is based upon fieldwork carried out in Sweden during a six-week stay in the summer of 1984. Open-ended interviews were conducted with twenty officials in the aging enterprise and with twenty-one elderly Swedes, as well as with the younger family members of five elderly Swedes. On-site visits were conducted at fifteen facilities of different types, including both residences and day centers, and participant-observation was carried out for a two-week period in the home of a Swedish family that had several elderly members living in three different types of residences – a single apartment, a nursing home, and a home with adult children.[4] During my six-week stay, I visited three Swedish cities. Stockholm, on the Baltic coast, is the cosmopolitan capital – the seat of the national government. Boras, in the west, is located close to the port city of Gothenburg and is known as the "Manchester of Sweden" because of its tradition of textile production. And Linkoping, two and one-half hours inland to the south of Stockholm, is a commercial city dominated by the production of computers and aviation technology; it is often characterized as the most progressive city in Sweden in terms of innovation in welfare state social policy for the elderly.

SWEDEN: POLITICAL-ECONOMIC BACKGROUND

Sweden is a northern European country about the size of California (173,731 square miles), bordered by Norway, Denmark, and Finland. With about 8.3 million citizens, Sweden is the most populous of the five Nordic nations and also has the largest percentage of its population over sixty years of age (see Table 8.1). The majority of its population is urban and is concentrated in the southern part of the country. Ethnically, as of 1985, the nation was 95 percent Swedish, with a small Finnish minority (2 percent) and some 600,000 immigrants of various ethnicities. Some 95 percent of the population belongs – at least nominally – to the state Lutheran church, though vibrant evangelical sects and minority religions enjoy complete freedom of worship. The government is a constitutional monarchy, with King Carl XVI Gustav its titular head. Five major political parties spanning the spectrum from Right to Communist compete through direct election for 349 seats in the single-chamber Swedish parliament (Riksdag), with national political leadership vested in the prime minister.

A complete sketch of Sweden's historical development lies beyond our scope.[5] What is interesting for our purposes is that industrial capitalism developed late in Sweden, compared to the rest of Europe. After 1870, however, social reformers and an active, rapidly organizing proletariat joined forces to combat what were perceived as the "evils" of the new industrial order, culminating in the founding of

Table 8.1
Age and Demographics in Nordic Nations

	Sweden	Norway	Denmark	Finland	Iceland
Total Population	8,348,000	4,152,000	5,105,000	4,908,000	241,000
Breakdown by Age (in percent)					
0–14	18.4	20.7	18.6	19.6	26.7
15–59	58.7	58.3	61.1	63.4	59.5
60 +	22.9	21.0	20.3	17.0	13.8
Percent Urban Residents	85.0	80.0	84.0	59.9 (1983)	88.9 (1983)
Population Density (per sq. mi.)	48.0	33.0	307.0	38.0	6.0
Life Expectancy at Birth (in years)					
Males	73.1 (1984)	72.5 (1984)	71.5 (1983)	70.1 (1982)	73.5 (1984)
Females	79.1 (1984)	79.7 (1984)	77.5 (1983)	78.1 (1982)	79.5 (1984)

All figures are 1985 estimates, except as noted.
SOURCE: *The World Almanac*, 1987.

the Social Democratic Party in 1889. During the worldwide Depression of the 1930s, Social Democratic leaders helped to enact various Keynesian measures such as government-subsidized employment for the jobless which "set the tone" for the subsequent expansion of the welfare state. In 1938 a historic agreement between labor and capital — the "Pact of Saltsjobaden" — laid out the parameters of what Marquis Childs (1980) calls Sweden's "Middle Way" between capitalism and socialism. In essence, Swedish workers promised a minimum of strikes or strike threats in return for expanding taxation to finance a wide range of social welfare programs.

The Swedish economy today includes a network of cooperative enterprises and significant government holdings in pharmaceuticals, alcohol, railroads, shipping, and other sectors. There have been efforts — such as the "Meidner Plan" of 1976 — to transfer a greater share of profits and/or ownership to workers.[6] An aggressive union policy of "wage solidarity" has reduced disparities of income between workers. However, 90 percent of the economy still remains privately owned.

Thus, Sweden is still a capitalist economy; even though income has largely been equalized, wealth has not. The Social Democrats themselves have retreated from the more Marxian orientation of early leaders. They have concentrated more on workplace democracy, wage solidarity, and "co-deter-mination" of technological change than on ownership per se, leading one sociologist to characterize them as "reformist socialists" (Korpi 1978:55).

Still, tangible gains for workers under the Social Democrats have been impressive: major benefits in medical care, family and child care support, old age pensions, and living facilities. Sweden has managed to cushion the worst effects of global economic fluctuations by developing a "societal corporatist welfare state" (Ruggie 1984:16), demarcated by "social bargaining" among employers, workers, and the state bureaucracy. Industrial productivity is high, and unemployment holds steady at 3 percent. One recent study, comparing the United States, Japan, West Germany, and Sweden, rated Sweden first in terms of quality of life (*Topeka Capital-Journal* 1986), attaining a standard of living "roughly 30 percent higher than that in the United States" (Bowles, Gordon, and Weisskopf 1984:40). Infant mortality, for example, is lower, while life expectancy for both men and women is higher (see Table 8.2). There are no homeless people or "slums" in Sweden. Health care is universal, inexpensive,

Table 8.2
Selected "Quality of Life" Indices

	Sweden	United States	Japan	West Germany
Population	8,348,000	238,631,000	120,731,000	60,950,000
Gross National Product	$88 bill. (1983)	$3,855 bill.	$1,200 bill. (1984)	$655 bill. (1983)
Per Capita Income	$14,821 (1980)	$13,451	$10,266 (1984)	$9,450
Life Expectancy at Birth (in years)				
Males	73.1 (1984)	71.6 (1983)	73.0 (1983)	67.2
Females	79.1 (1984)	76.3 (1983)	78.0 (1983)	73.4
Infant Mortality (per 1,000 live births)	6.3 (1984)	10.5	6.0	13.5
Hospital Beds	116,688 (1983)	1.3 mill. (1983)	1.3 mill. (1981)	668,747 (1984)
Physicians	19,300 (1983)	527,900	167,952 (1982)	153,000

All figures are 1985 estimates, except as noted.
SOURCE: *The World Alamanac*, 1987.

and of high quality. Concerted efforts are being made to deal constructively with the recent influx of foreign workers. Meanwhile, Sweden supports one of the highest ratios of social welfare costs to gross national product of all major industrialized nations (Bowles, Gordon, and Weisskopf 1984:46).

Yet Sweden is not without problems. Alcoholism and crime are on the increase, and ageism persists (Bergstrom 1982). There is evidence today of a burgeoning of "utilitarian" individualism, (Bellah et al. 1985), manifested in growing resentment among youth of their obligations to the social welfare system and a corresponding yen to "make a killing" on the stock market. And though Swedes have historically done well in combatting the ups and downs of the global business cycle (Logue 1986), there are mounting concerns about Sweden's ability to maintain its gains in a future of worldwide "belt-tightening."[7]

In the face of these economic pressures, a rhetoric of "lowered expectations" is creeping into government ideology. At the same time, the Social Democrats retain a commitment to social transformation which still lists firmly toward greater democratization and integration. None of my respondents indicated that they foresaw or desired a serious abandonment of governmental support for housing, health care, and other social-welfare programs, and—as I shall discuss—policy makers in the sphere of aging expressed support for the "transformative" ideology of the Social Democratic party.

At least five main political-economic factors shape Swedish social life today: first, Sweden is a capitalist country, with all that that implies about lingering divergence of interests between labor and capital; second, its capitalist economic forms are mediated through a political universe in which workers enjoy an unusual degree of organization and, consequently, influence; third, worker influence has led to a "pact" between classes which includes the assumption that all Swedes, regardless of class background, are entitled to have their survival needs met in a manner which preserves both dignity and "quality of life"[8]; fourth, government has been expected to take a major role in providing the services necessary to fulfill such needs; and fifth, Sweden is currently beset by several economic pressures that are beginning to alter political dialogue. Related to each of these points, and important to bear in mind during the ensuing discussion, is the fact that the Swedish government in general, and the ruling party in particular, continue to espouse an explicitly transformative ideology—something which makes Sweden unusual in the industrial capitalist West.

I shall now consider how these political-economic forces are refracted by the lens of the Swedish aging enterprise, particularly by its official ideology and residence options, highlighting the transformative character of both.

THE OFFICIAL IDEOLOGY OF THE AGING ENTERPRISE

The official ideology is based on five "guiding principles" expressed in the Social Services Act of 1982. While articulated by the state through Parliament and the Ministry of Health and Social Affairs, which control the direction and funding for social welfare and medical services, the guiding principles are implemented nationally by the National Board of Health and Welfare and on the local level through two bodies: municipalities and county councils. Municipalities handle social welfare needs, and county councils minister to medical care. The guiding principles are:

1. Normalization, which means that to the greatest possible extent each individual should be given the opportunity to live and function in as normal a setting and under as normal conditions as feasible.

2. Viewing a Person as a Whole, which means that the overall psychological, physical, and social welfare needs of a person are assessed and dealt with in a single context.

3. Self-Determination, which means that personal integrity is respected. People should have the right to determine their own lives and make their own decisions. The right to personal security and the right to decide things for oneself must be combined in old-age care.

4. Influence and Participation, meaning that individuals should be able to influence not only their own environment but also society as a whole. Elderly people, too, want to assume responsibilities and feel that they are needed.

5. Properly Managed Activation, which implies meaningful tasks carried out in close partnership with other people in a normal stimulating environment. (The National Commission on Aging 1982:17)

These five guiding principles are explicitly transformative in nature as they are all geared toward increasing the democratization and integration of Swedish society. Democratization refers to promoting greater control over decisions in one's own life – decisions of both personal and political nature. Integration refers to promoting less separation between groups in society, including both physical separation and status (prestige) separation.[9] These transformative components are viewed by policy makers as reducing existing social inequities in this capitalist welfare state, hence encompassing the Swedish welfare state vision of the good society. The "good" society is always in a state of becoming; it exists in part yet needs to be achieved.[10]

National and local officials argue that past social policy was dominated by inadequate care for those remaining in their homes and excessive care in nursing homes, making the elderly "uninterested, immobile, and passive." Even with the addition of new forms of residence options and assistance for those old persons who wish to remain in their houses or apartments, too much was "done for them." An official of the National Board of Health and Welfare believes, "We need to train staff of all kinds to see the elderly as human beings and to keep away from doing everything for them." Such sentiments are echoed by a geriatric physician in a Boras hospital who asserts that, "We want to treat the whole person, to take a more humanistic approach."

Emphasis upon a "normal setting" helps to account for the relatively recent reorientation of official ideology away from "closed-care" and toward "open-care" — that is, away from "closed" institutions like nursing homes and geriatric wards and toward programs that encourage and enable the aged to remain in their own homes or in setttings as autonomous, as "homelike," as possible (see Amann 1980; Little 1978, 1982). A commune official in Boras states, "If we can mix the young and the old, it will be like going back to older generations where people lived together in close communities." He continues, "We want to build all kinds of apartments — for the young, old, and the disabled — so that they and others can live together," as well as to remodel and restructure existing facilities for the same purpose. With pride, he emphasizes that elderly and disabled persons from all class backgrounds should have equal access to residences — residences desired by wealthier persons as well, even though "palatial" options are available in the private sector.

One Linkoping official stressed the importance of spontaneous initiative, not coercing the elderly but providing them with contexts in which different groups would be simultaneously present. The Boras official, comparing Sweden and the United States, takes this notion even further: "In the United States, isolated people create possibilities. In Sweden, we create networks that create possibilities." In other words, lifestyle options of a social, political, and educational nature are being built into living arrangements. Various social groups are present, offering possibilities for interaction and fostering democratization and integration, as a Linkoping commune document notes: "Within the Social Welfare Services, we basically believe that people themselves have an ability to create a good society, but we will give them the preconditions to get into contact with each other" (*Jonsson Gardens Document* 1983:11).

These guiding principles did not materialize in a vacuum. They reflect political and economic forces permeating Swedish society. The principle of properly managed activation is an illustration of the government taking responsibility for the needs of Swedes — not leaving the elderly to fend for themselves, but arranging for premises, staff, and networks encouraging and providing preconditions for activity rather than fostering passivity. Certainly normalization and wholeness of person have been shaped by the "social bargaining" of classes that has resulted in emphasizing dignity and quality of life for all — herein making further efforts at reducing status differentials through a vision integrating different ages and lifestyles. The principles of self-determination, influence, and participation are an extension of a historical process through which labor has been able to exert a strong impact on democratizing and integrating the workplace.

Some officials see clustered complexes, discussed in the next section, as a promising vehicle for the guiding principles. However, growing economic constraints may force cutbacks in building new facilities. If this happens, the government is still committed to offering inexpensive technological support to the elderly. But such support, however helpful, cannot replace the transformative potential of new and creative residence options.

In sum, the official ideology of the aging enterprise has a nondoctrinaire transformative direction. It stands for democratization and integration in both open-care and closed-care systems. It presents a real alternative to past aging ideology, replacing "care" with democratization and integration. Hence, it seeks to transform policy itself, the elderly, and Swedish society.

RESIDENCE OPTIONS: THE OFFICIAL IDEOLOGY OF THE AGING ENTERPRISE IN PRACTICE

Since ideology merely refers to a systematized set of ideas, it is instructive to scrutinize the fit between ideology and practice. To this end, I shall examine the official ideology as it is embodied in available residence options and supportive facilities and services, describing these options and assessing their transformative thrust.

Elderly Swedes reside in a variety of dwellings, including (1) one's own house or apartment; (2) pensioner's apartment or one in a pensioner's building; (3) room in an old-age residential home (nursing home); (4) room in a geriatric hospital; (5) apartment in a service house; and (6) apartment, including service apartments, in a clustered complex.

According to the government, 90 percent of Swedes sixty-five and older live in a rented apartment or a one-family home. In such cases, the integrated living seen by the official ideology as necessary for increased democratization and integration occurs through day centers, home help services, and home nursing. The same can be said for the approximately 30,000 pensioner's apartments. To offset the isolation of the elderly, officials are committed to day centers. Such centers, whether they exist as independent facilities or are linked to service houses or other residence options, are seen as facilitating the possibility of the elderly remaining at home. Although day centers offer the aged a context for interaction primarily with other elderly people, the national government wants to make them available eventually to all age groups.

Older people can come together in day centers for leisure pursuits, such as cards and other games. In one day center attached to a Stockholm service house, there are multiple game rooms; one can be used for those who want to play cards or other games at a fast pace, and another for those who prefer to engage in similar activity but at a slower pace. In addition, as reading books and newspapers is popular, a day center attached to a service house in Linkoping provides readers for those unable to read.

Another popular activity is weaving, with many looms present in all cities visited and all day centers observed. Day centers are also a locus for eating meals, having political discussions and meetings, attending entertainment, and obtaining medical services such as a pedicure. Also, district nurses are available at these centers.

According to government officials, plans are underway to expand home help services and home nursing. This includes but goes beyond support in cooking, cleaning, shopping, and other daily life needs as well as health care. Providers are envisioned as part of psychosocial teams trained to assess and to help the elderly identify and meet their needs while spurring them on to initiate more activity. Such services are based in a library in one community in Linkoping; they offer age and activity integration as an incentive for making contact with local teams.

As of 1984, 55,000 persons lived in residential homes, with about 70 percent of them eighty years old or above. These homes, accommodating more than one-hundred pensioners, are being phased out, as they are judged to be too large and too dominated by excessive care. For elderly Swedes who are very ill and cannot engage in the independent living fostered by service houses, there are geriatric wards and geriatric hospitals where efforts at transformation continue despite the unresponsiveness of many patients.

"In 1984, there were about 30,000 apartments in service buildings. Three percent of people over seventy lived in this type of housing" (The Swedish Institute 1986). Service houses are seen as facilities that promote independence and self-determination. They provide apartments equipped with alarms and convenience technology for pensioners who can no longer maintain their own dwellings or are experiencing extreme loneliness. Such facilities are smaller than living environments built in the past, such as nursing homes and residential hotels.

Service apartments, in addition to being located in service houses, are also available in a variety of contexts. In Linkoping, several living facilities combine apartments of this kind with ones occupied by people and families of various ages, a common dining hall, and a day nursery. Day nurseries are placed in many facilities so that the elderly may spontaneously take an interest and a part in child care.

Clustered complexes are seen by aging enterprise officials as the "wave of the future" – the most developed embodiment of the transformative thrust of the official ideology. Two illustrations of this option are Vasa Hills in Stockholm and Jonsson Gardens in Linkoping.

Built in the mid-1970s, Vasa Hills has been described as "a community center with integrated social welfare facilities including apartments for the elderly" (*Vasa Hills Document* 1976). It contains three service houses with a total of 172 apartments that have one, two, or three rooms and a kitchenette. They are connected to a cultural area (with restaurant, music rooms, photo laboratory, and a ceramics workshop), a library, a nursery, a primary and a secondary school (and, soon, a senior high school), a sports center with gymnasium, ice rink, ice hockey rink (in the summer converted to tennis courts), a sauna, cafeteria, a conference room, and a hospital.

Jonsson Gardens was built during the late 1970s and early 1980s and contains two types of housing: six conventional five-story houses with a total of 108 apartments and a collective housing part with "184 apartments in houses built together... of height varying between three apartments and seven apartments" (*Jonsson Gardens Document* 1983). "The collective housing part has eleven different kinds of apartments from one room and a pantry to five rooms and a kitchen" (Jonsson Gardens Document 1983). Thirty-five of those apartments are service apartments for pensioners, while nine are for the mentally or physically disabled. There are common premises on the ground floor, with a restaurant, study/meeting rooms, a library, coffee room, gymnasium, workshops, and entertainment facilities. Day nurseries are also part of the center. The collective housing segment of Jonsson Gardens represents a concerted effort to integrate young families, the elderly, and the disabled in a socioeconomic mix.

The success of the official ideology of the aging enterprise within the context of residence options is not easily evaluated. Disappointing results exist side-by-side with triumphs, while other efforts at transformation through residence policy are too recent to evaluate. But given these caveats, we can conclude that while the transformative thrust of the ideology has been uneven, it is strongly held; structural efforts to put it into place are proceeding apace; and its implementation has had positive results.

As I have pointed out, aging policy has employed the guiding principles initially to transform itself. Such a policy transformation is evident in attempts to democratize and integrate both open- and closed-care. In open-care contexts, the burgeoning of day centers and the commitment to train and increase the numbers of home helpers and home nurses is promising. A home services coordinator in Linkoping spoke glowingly about efforts to convert those persons operating in the homes of the elderly into "self-governing psychosocial teams." Yet, she admitted that social service workers face obstacles like low pay and low status. An additional source of optimism is the spread of service houses on the periphery of metropolitan areas, locations that had previously resisted similar development. Location of service apartments and regular pensioner's apartments in varied integrated contexts — contiguous to nurseries and libraries, for example — is in progress, and if Svensson (1984) is correct, construction will continue despite concerns about economic stagnation.

Vasa Hills and Jonsson Gardens bring the goals of democratization and integration to life. Yet, the fact that such models are still a tiny segment of residence options for the elderly indicates that there is a long way to go to put the guiding principles on firm footing. New construction will be subject to the same political-economic forces that generated the official ideology.

With respect to closed-care, aging enterprise officials spoke persistently of the need to remodel, reshape, and restructure closed-care. They recognized that, though closed-care produced problems for the elderly in the past, all societies still have some need for closed-care. A positive example of the application of democratization and integration to closed-care occurred in Boras, in the geriatric ward of a hospital. Two advanced Alzheimer's patients were bedridden in a large room — spotless, well and naturally lit, tastefully and traditionally furnished, and well supplied with greenery. A geriatric physician apologized for "crowding" two patients into the room. He emphasized that even though these patients were virtually comatose, they still deserved the same normal, private surroundings that others would choose.

Yet, in their unevenness, efforts to empower elderly persons in residential homes have a long way to go. For example, Greta S., living in a well-kept residential home outside of Boras, had her self-determination circumscribed. Greta could not cook in her room, though she had access to a large communal dining room for meals, and an alcove located on her wing of the facility is equipped with a stove and cooking utensils. She enjoyed preparing food for guests but had no way to shop — a task too difficult for her to manage alone. She relied on her children to bring food to her, but she was dependent on them and their schedules. In contrast, a Stockholm service house has a small grocery stand in the lobby where residents can shop for food — empowering them in an important area of Swedish cultural life.

This type of situation brings us to the issue of transforming the elderly. Here I encountered mixed results. Facility officials expressed significant disappointment over difficulties they experienced. At a service house outside of Boras, one cannot but be impressed with the way each hallway and end-of-the-hall alcove is set up with traditional furniture, replicating living rooms from cozy homes ripe for interaction and discussion. Yet, to the dismay of officials, these areas often remain deserted and were so during my visit. People more often head for weaving or playing cards or just stay in their rooms. Even at Vasa Hills and Jonsson Gardens I was informed by an official and a resident that "integrated activity is not all that it had been played up to be" and that many of the elderly either do not like the presence of the young or see them as a "nuisance," which undercuts the democratic and integrative thrusts.

Of course, such resistance to aging policy initiatives are not surprising, given the impact of past socialization and current ageism in Sweden — attested to by Kurt S., an official of a pensioner's organization in Stockholm. In addition, this can be seen as reflecting past top-down, centralized social policy in other spheres of social and economic life where, even though Swedes made gains, the emphasis was not on individual empowerment and integration. Hence, despite the workplace successes noted previously, it has been difficult to activate rank-and-file workers in decision making. Similarly, in the context of child care relations, state policy has been to encourage fathers to take an increasing role in parenting, even to enable them to share extensive parental leaves from work to care for young children at almost full pay and with job protection. Yet few males have bothered to take advantage of the parental-leave option. In all of these areas, including that of the elderly, there has been a substantial cultural lag between the consciousness of the principal actors involved and the architects of the policies.

There are elderly individuals who do participate in transformative activity. Peter G., a Jonsson Gardens resident, was politically active through the residence administrative council and the activities that were part of the tower in which he lived. He felt that he was an effectual force in decision making and that he had an impact on how younger residents view the elderly. And Jock D., a pensioner confined to a wheelchair, received daily communal support, along with his wife Anna, to work for the rights of the disabled. But, as indicated by Britt O., an official at Vasa Hills, it was apparent that it would take time for the elderly to participate in their own transformation.

The impact of official ideology through residence options on social transformation brings the political-economic focus linking past, present, and future to the fore. Difficult as it is to evaluate, this may be the most crucial transformative thrust of aging policy. For in aiming to reduce social inequities associated with capitalism, it not only presents the possibility of further enhancing the quality of life, but also of reducing some of the harmful effects of capitalism. Two illustrations prefigure this "good society" in the realms of both democratization and integration.

During one interview, Lena S., a young professional living with her husband, also a professional, and their two children in Jonsson Gardens, described the development of her son Leif. Their tower includes healthy elderly persons, elderly in service apartments, and disabled persons. Each week they have a collective meal with responsibilities rotating among tower residents, and they engage in other weekly activities among themselves and other residents at the Gardens. Lena indicated that Leif had remained aloof from older and disabled residents at first but, through integrated and democratized activities where they all exercised choice and control, he had come to regard them as "normal" people and now has no hesitation in viewing them positively during interaction in such contexts as parks and train stations. She felt that respect for the elderly and the disabled had been engendered and that Jonsson Gardens had struck a blow against ageism and ableism. She hoped that a proliferation of these types of experiences would form a microcosm for the "good society."

In the day nursery at Jonsson Gardens, a teenager sat reading one afternoon while I was walking through the facility. He told me that he used to think that little children were of no use and that the elderly were excess baggage. But through hanging around at the nursery near his apartment's tower — he said that it was "just there" — his views changed as he took to interacting with small children and the elderly who stopped in. We both watched Olle J., an elderly man in a wheelchair, playing with a few of the small children. The teenager put down his book, excused himself, and joined them in a game of tag. Such a context served as a precondition for a change of consciousness and contributed to the prefigurative articulation of a more fully democratized and integrated future.

Finally, lest the last two illustrations seem overly optimistic, officials committed to the importance of the spontaneous generation of possibilities for prefigurative interaction point out that all too often they have to provide the impetus for such interaction. This is hardly surprising. For despite the successes in the implementation of the transformative thrust of aging policy through residence options, we must not forget what the political economy perspective makes clear: the successes and failures of such efforts reflect the fact that the present is a confluence of past and emergent political-economic forces. In essence, the aging enterprise in Sweden is making transformative aging policy but not under conditions fully of its own choosing (see Marx 1963).

WHAT CAN THE UNITED STATES LEARN FROM SWEDEN?

Attempting to identify areas in which one society can "learn lessons" from the experience of another in any area of social policy is risky. When comparing any two nations, historical and cultural differences aplenty emerge, so that the analyst is often in the proverbial situation of comparing apples and oranges. Indeed, many of my Swedish respondents expressed the conviction that "Sweden and the United States are very different" and were unsure as to whether any facets of the Swedish experience are transplantable to American soil. Thus it is with caution—but also with the conviction that "learning" from other cultures is part of the anthropological enterprise—that I shall briefly compare the current state of aging policy in the two countries and suggest a few areas in which Americans concerned with the elderly might put Sweden's example to use.

I have tried to show how the aging enterprise in Sweden is geared towards the reduction of social inequities. Estes (1979) and others have argued persuasively that the thrust of the aging enterprise in the United States throughout its history has been to perpetuate such inequities—inequities of wealth and income, status, and power. The "harder" form of this argument stresses ways in which powerful interests have striven to "divide" the American masses along lines of sex, race, religion, and age, the better to rule them (see Gordon, Edwards, and Reich 1982). The "softer" form—and the one which is frequently used to explain flurries of social reform which, on their face, appear to enact real improvements in the position of the elderly, such as the New Deal and the social legislation of the 1960s—contends that the American ruling class has occasionally allowed reforms in order to "shore up" foundering capitalist institutions by defusing popular discontent. Scholars who see aging policy through this "softer" lens are, however, quick to point out that such reforms have always been kept within careful bounds (Piven and Cloward 1982).

Scholars in both camps concur that the American "welfare state" has never enjoyed the stability, acceptance, and working-class control of its Swedish counterpart. Thus, three of the political-economic forces identified earlier as lending Swedish aging ideology its character—assumption of government responsibility, entitlement of all citizens, and a strong voice for labor – have been absent in the United States. I think it is their absence that accounts for the fact that American social welfare policy has never transcended what Kurt Samuelsson (1975) calls a "defensive," as opposed to a transformative, posture. Rather than explicitly challenging and seeking significant long-term change in existing social inequities, American aging ideology has used a rhetoric of "helping" the elderly, encouraging "more respect" for them, "cushioning" them from the worst socioeconomic vicissitudes, and encouraging them to keep "contributing to society."

The other two political-economic forces I identified as pivotal in shaping Swedish ideology, capitalism and the newly perceived "era of limits," are, of course, shared by the United States. Reaganomics has, if anything, magnified the effects of both these forces on American social welfare ideologies. The inequities of capitalism are no longer sources of polite liberal embarrassment but rather have been elevated to philosophical heights undreamed of since the palmiest days of Social Darwinism, in an ethic which Irving Howe (1987) glosses as "possessive individualism." Instead of unfortunates to be "helped," those on the lower rungs of the inequities ladder have, in official pronouncements, become deadbeats who buy vodka with food stamps or quixotics who perversely prefer to sleep on grates than in warm, affordable housing units. While lip service is still accorded the need to "respect" and "protect" our elderly, this pejorative view of social welfare recipients cannot but tar them as well.

The economic problems faced by the United States as the leader of the capitalist world compound the situation. If anything, the economic challenges it faces – a record deficit, a soaring trade imbalance, declining industrial production, and increased competition from other nations – are more acute than Sweden's. Without strong working-class representation, and in the face of Reaganomic assaults on government responsibility and citizen entitlement, American social welfare programs are assailed on every front. Far from taking a transformative lead, social welfare ideologues of the Left fight a rearguard battle to keep from losing more funds, while those of the Right engage in ironic efforts to undermine their own programs. Despite efforts by a small American democratic Left, one is hard put to identify any countervailing transformative trends in the ideological climate these days.

What all this signifies is that if American citizens want an aging enterprise that is transformative rather than "reproductive" or "defensive" in its thrust, the Swedish experience suggests that the Gray Power movement should align itself closely and vigorously with a broader labor movement and that both must strive to substitute an assumption of citizen entitlement and government responsibility for the present philosophy of possessive individualism and state "minimalism." Whether this is a realistic possibility in the present political climate and in the face of Democratic Party disarray is an open question, but it is one which those seeking to learn from the Swedish experience cannot avoid confronting.

SUMMARY, SIGNIFICANCE, AND IMPLICATIONS

This chapter has attempted to sketch the ways in which the ideology of the Swedish aging enterprise in general, and of its residence policies in particular, reflects larger political-economic forces in contemporary Swedish society. I have argued that the Swedish aging enterprise is unusual in the industrial capitalist West in that its ideology is explicitly transformative, that is, conducive to greater democratization and integration. Furthermore, in the limited cases I was able to observe, it seemed that the implementation of this ideology was meeting with impressive results.

The full significance and implications of these findings, and of a complex social phenomenon like Swedish aging policy, can be addressed in only the most preliminary fashion.

One obvious conclusion is not original but deserves to be emphasized anew: the way any society deals with aging and the aged cannot be examined in isolation but as part of a complex web of social institutions, processes, and attitudes. The comprehensive lens of a political-economic framework thus seems crucial for real understanding. For example, it would be impossible to understand the apologies offered by the doctor in Boras for having two Alzheimer's patients in a single hospital room without knowledge of the assumption of the "entitlement" of all Swedes to dignity and quality of life, which in its turn would be incomprehensible without knowledge of the unusually powerful social voice that the Swedish working class has won for itself in the years since 1889.

It is also important to recognize that Sweden, which despite its "Middle Way" still stands squarely in the capitalist world, has developed an official ideology of aging that is transformative in both spirit and, to at least a limited extent, in practice. This recognition defuses doctrinaire assumptions of both the Left and the Right about the role that the aging enterprise can play in the capitalist welfare state. On the one hand, appreciation of Sweden's accomplishments in this regard refutes what Frances Fitzgerald (1979:126) has called the "crabgrass theory" of social phenomena, the notion that certain problematic features of capitalist society "just happen." When Robert Binstock, for example, referring to United States aging issues, writes that, ". . . the absence of well-developed, well-defined public policies, and the fragmentation, non-coordination, and under-financing of public services are endemic features of America's political system and culture" (1986:333), he seems to imply that these features of the American aging enterprise are natural and inevitable. The Swedish experience suggests that it would be more useful to go beyond discussions of "endemic" American characteristics to unveil the specific political-economic arrangements that account for such things as "non-coordination" and "under-financing" of programs essential to older persons' health and well-being.

At the same time, Sweden's success, however inchoate and fragile, in creating a transformative aging enterprise gives the lie to the formulations of those "radical" social thinkers who argue that substantive social change cannot be engendered under capitalism. The very real gains which have already been secured by and for elderly Swedes and the promising developments occurring in places like Vasa Hills and Jonsson Gardens indicate that it is not necessary to wait until "after the revolution" to begin the work of social transformation as it affects and involves older persons.

Sweden offers opportunities for study of the aged and age-related issues that have been only cursorily indicated here. It is to be hoped that further work will be done on these subjects within the Swedish context, so that people throughout the world will be better able to understand and to learn from the Swedish experience.

NOTES

I extend my appreciation to those persons whom I interviewed and to those who made my observations at various facilities possible. In keeping with anthropological tradition, I use pseudonyms for informants and facilities. I am grateful to The Swedish Institute—especially to Ms. Catharina Mannheimer—an agency that most efficiently and willingly promotes and facilitates the research of foreign scholars, and to family members in Boras who labored hard to make my stay a fruitful one. My thanks go out to Dr. Jay Sokolovsky for his patience and most helpful comments and suggestions; to Dr. Ken Wagner for his support and considerable insight into Swedish social structure; and especially to Dr. Karen L. Field, without whose inspiration, knowledge, and significant contributions this chapter could not have been completed.

1. The term "aging enterprise" refers to "the congeries of programs, organizations, bureaucracies, interest groups, trade associations, providers, industries, and professionals that serve the aged in one capacity or another" (Estes 1979:2). As used here, the term should be understood as referring in particular to the governmental programs and bureaucracies (both national and local) which serve the aged, since these play such a pivotal role in the Swedish context.

2. The term "ideology" here refers to J. Bailey's definition: "an organized set of convictions... that enforces inevitable value judgments [and that] hold major implications for power relations, for in enforcing certain definitions of the situation, they have the power to compel certain types of action while limiting others" (Estes 1979:4).

3. I use the term "transformative" in this context to refer to that which is conducive to liberatory social change, that which tends to empower the individual and to allow the development of each citizen's potential independent of limitations linked to class, physical disability, ethnicity, sex, or age. The meaning is thus similar in meaning to "emancipatory," as used by many radical social scientists. I prefer the term transformative because, while still implying some value judgments about quality of life, it is less closely aligned with a political doctrine and seems to me to connote a more "open" future—one in which there may be no single, static state of "emancipation," but rather a continuous struggle for greater human freedom. Central to my use of the term in the present chapter are two analytically separable aspects of liberatory social change, democratization and integration, which I define more fully in the section on "The Official Ideology of the Aging Enterprise."

4. The formal interview sample was generated for me by Ms. Catharina Mannheimer of The Swedish Institute. Members of the informal interview sample included friends and associates of that initial group contacted in "snowball" fashion, as well as contacts made during residence in Sweden. The family chosen for participant-observation is related to the researcher's wife.

5. Useful historical materials on Sweden include Heckscher (1954), Andersson and Weibull (1973), Koblik (1975), Childs (1980), and Lofgren (1980).

6. The Plan, developed for the Swedish unions by German economist Rudolf Meidner, proposed that companies with more than fifty employees should place twenty percent of their profits into a fund to be administered by the unions. The Plan was an issue in the 1976 campaign, when it was denounced by Swedish capitalists as exacerbating the problem of "corporate flight" and as placing a unfair burden on smaller businesses. Late Prime Minister Olaf Palme himself did not vigorously promote the Plan, and some political observers feel that its rejection by the electorate indicated that Swedes were not "ready" for such a significant shift in the "ownership" of corporate profits. Others, however, argue that such a conclusion may be unfounded, particularly since the fortunes of the Social Democrats in the 1976 election were damaged by a hotly debated referendum on the future of nuclear power.

7. Marquis Childs (1980), for example, cites as serious economic threats the quadrupling of world oil prices during the 1970s, a drop in exports coupled with increasing competition in key areas from Third World nations, Japan, and West Germany, and inflation (including large, and frequently resented, increases in taxation).

8. As Eli Heckscher put it as early as 1954: "More than in most countries. . . society is held responsible for providing a decent minimum standard to its members" (1954:282).

9. Kurt Samuelsson concurs that "integration" has long been a philosophical keystone of social welfare ideology in Sweden, and that the Social Democrats have conceptualized it as being gradually accomplished ". . . through 'social transformation'; in the long run, integration would be fully realized in a society different from the one in which the work was begun" (1975:342).

10. For one scholar's attempt to sketch more definitively the minimal characteristics of a "good society," with particular reference to the Swedish experience, see Schnitzer (1970:Ch.9).

9 THE ELDERLY IN MODERN JAPAN: ELITE, VICTIMS, OR PLURAL PLAYERS?

Christie W. Kiefer

The approach of death, which always accompanies old age, and the weakening of the organism, which usually does, pose universal problems for human individuals and societies. The weakening of the organism places ever greater emphasis on the elder's symbolic status at the expense of his material output as measures of his social worth. At the same time, the approach of death means the loss of time in which the individual might amass the attributes of status. At some point or other, one's life is judged essentially complete and evaluated as a good life or a bad one. Apparently, very few if any societies attach value to old age per se, and the childless, the deviants, and victims of plain bad luck are apt to end up without honor or security (Beyenne 1985; Barker, this volume; Simic 1978). Anthropologists have long been interested in these facts and have catalogued the ways in which people store up symbolic merit (or fail to do so) in the course of growing old. Silverman and Maxwell (1983) and Gutmann (1980) for example, have documented the importance of goods, offspring, supernatural power, and knowledge as sources of merit.

Likewise, in the study of urban industrial societies, we have been bemused by the apparent difficulty of achieving a successful old age – that is, a respected and secure one – at all. In this chapter I hope to contribute to the literature on the status of the aged in urban industrial society by contrasting two societies with similar economic structures but very different histories and values regarding the status of the elderly – the United States and Japan. More specifically, I am led by this comparison to question a common assumption of cultural gerontology, the belief in a monolithic or integrated cultural pattern which determines the conditions of the elderly. The comparison at hand suggests some kind of pluralistic structure to the "culture of aging"; it also suggests that the tripod which supports benign old age — prestige, power, and security — might be more usefully treated as three analytically distinct issues.

Our American view is usually that our own elderly are bereft equally of all three benefits, and we tend to blame the triple loss on technological progress. This view is embedded, for example, in "modernization theory," which sees industrialization in America as a special case of a universal modernizing trend (Cowgill and Holmes 1972). The idea I am suggesting, that this view may be tainted with the sin of culture-bound thinking, is not new. Modernization theory has been challenged most strenuously by Erdman Palmore (1975), and by Palmore and Daisaku Maeda (1985), a challenge armed as mine is with the pointed statistics of Japanese gerontology. As you will see, though, the direction and outcome of my attack are very different from those of Palmore and Maeda.

By the time anthropology took up the systematic study of aging, gerontology had already developed some of its own traditions. In keeping with a social ethic that stressed self-reliance and equality of opportunity, the aged in industrial society were already seen as a social problem, as members of the "deserving poor," whose plight resulted less from bad character than from their blameless inability to find or to perform work (Quadagno 1982). This view was true enough and painful enough that it demanded remedies. Remedies, in turn, demand explanatory models, and the so-called golden age model soon set up its successful shop in the central mall of gerontology. Before industrialization, people had lived in large families and/or small villages which took care of their aged. Technological change was slow, and the wisdom of elders was valued; power and prestige were based on structural position in a tradition-rich society over which the aged presided as ceremonial masters. Wealth was measured in goods, land, and family labor, over which the elderly often kept control. Since life expectancy was short, old people were in short supply and were carefully husbanded. Industrialization ruined all this at one fell swoop with the introduction of wage labor, small families, rapid change, cities, secularism, and sanitation. With Darwinian predictability, the young cast the now abundant and superfluous elderly on the ash heap along with their handlooms and folk remedies.

The image had, of course, a good deal of truth in it; but it turned out to be much too simple. David Fowler et al. (1982) and Edward Bever (1982) argue that the superannuated aged, those who no longer led productive lives, were generally despised in premodern Europe as elsewhere. Andrew Aschenbaum (1978) and Peter Stearns (1982) show that few families in colonial America could be called gerontocratic and that such reverence for old age as the average colonist had seems to have pretty well disappeared *before* the first smokestacks had begun to darken the preindustrial skies. The golden age was really brass and was quickly turning green in the corrosive atmosphere of the Enlightenment.

It was quite natural that American anthropology took up the golden age model as a principal framework for the cross-cultural study of aging. That model nestles snugly alongside our belief in the functional integrity of cultures. Ruth Benedict writes: "A culture, like an individual, is a more or less consistent pattern of thought and action. Within each culture there come into being characteristic purposes not necessarily shared by other types of society. In obedience to these purposes, each people further and further consolidates its experience, and in proportion to the urgency of these drives the heterogeneous items of behavior take more and more congruous shape" (1934:53). Under the circumstances, a lack of apparent fit between, say, the prestige of the elderly in a society and their economic security is evidence of a temporary distortion of the cultural pattern: "Within any one civilization, the various styles constituting its value component not only coexist in the same society, region, and period; they also tend toward a certain consistency among themselves. . . .This assumption seems validated by the simple consideration that consistent and coherent civilizations would on the average work out better and get farther, and presumably survive better, than inconsistent ones dragging on under malfunction and strain" (Kroeber 1951:621).

It would of course follow that technological changes that downgrade a segment of society will be accompanied—or soon followed—by ideals and expectations that fit the new pattern; and this is what the golden age model says happened. The recent findings that tarnish the model thereby raise in the context of gerontology a question that has been raised in many other contexts: Is the assumption of cultural integrity a useful one? The case of Japan seems to bear on the question, and I will return to it after a look at the cultural facts.

JAPAN: HISTORICAL BACKGROUND

Today Japan is in the forefront of industrial technology, enjoys a fully democratic government, and has a living standard, a gross national product, a public health record, and a per capita income that are the envy of much of the world. Aside from its high population density, its unique language and art, and certain features of interpersonal relations, there is little on the surface of Japanese life that distinguishes it from that of any advanced Western industrial nation. However, two unique features of modern Japanese history must be mentioned before we can discuss the condition of the Japanese aged. They are (1) the late start of industrialization and (2) the official propagation of Confucian values.

By 1868, when the feudal government of the Shogunate finally fell, Japan had already developed many features of a capitalist society: a money economy, national markets, credit buying, large ramified commercial corporations, extensive urban life, and specialized cash farming. Still, many features of an industrial economy were largely missing: there was little foreign trade, little practical education, few political freedoms, poor nutrition and public health, and a rudimentary and labor-intensive technology. Although there was a prosperous merchant class in the large towns, the great mass of Japanese people were nonliterate peasants and laborers with a low standard of living. Infant mortality was high, and life expectancy at birth was short.

By the early 1900s, Japan was a world power whose exports threatened American and European competitors. It was also a political rival of the industrial nations, seeking to protect its stakes in the world economy. The speed of this transformation meant that it was less a deep social transformation than the grafting of a technology onto a traditional way of life. Respect for traditional forms of social relationship remained strong: master and disciple, patron and client, priest and parishioner, trader and partner, neighbor and neighbor continued many ancient forms of exchange and expressions of mutual respect that had been corroded by free markets and economic mobility in the West. Even today Japanese social relationships show a kind of resilience and integrity that few if any advanced industrial societies can match.

The speed of this transformation, paradoxically, gave the industrialization of Japan a kind of orderliness. Starting late, the Japanese inherited an economic and political system that had already suffered and corrected a good many mistakes. They were careful to build a sound national financial policy, to control labor unrest, and to preserve traditions that kept social life stable and protected the economic casualties. There were, of course, strikes, riots, intrigues, and abuses of power, but revolutions, famines, coups d'etat, and military defeats there were not.

One of the mechanisms consciously used by the government to preserve social order was the propagation of traditional values, both through education and through the legal codification of the rights and obligations of family members. Before I examine these codifications of custom and their effects, however, let me briefly examine what some of the relevant customs were.

CULTURAL BACKGROUND

Much has been written about the group-centeredness and hierarchical organization of Japanese society, and space does not permit a satisfactory summary here. The work of Chie Nakane (1972) provides a good introduction. Here I want to mention three powerful features of Japanese culture that closely affect the status of the elderly: age-grading, Confucianism, and corporate emphasis.

Age-grading

The traditional Japanese kinship system was based on the patrilineal clan, or *ie*, a strong hierarchy of interrelated households, within which seniority, primogeniture, and male dominance characterized authority. Like many societies with a strong descent-based social organization, the Japanese also maintained age grades. Although the details of the age-grading system differed according to locale, in a typical configuration the rank of "elder" was reached by males at the age of sixty, whereupon they assumed ceremonial roles in village life, especially religious life (Norbeck 1953). An increased freedom was granted from the constraints of younger adult roles, so that old people were expected to enjoy leisure, strong drink, and bawdy humor. This license was signalled by the wearing, after retirement, of red clothing, a symbol of childhood. Since the dominant residence pattern was patrilocal, women entered at a somewhat younger age the powerful domestic status of mother-in-law and commanded the duties of their son's wives.

The rights and duties of the elders were often explicit and formal, and to some extent they assured the social integration into wider society of at least those elders who had fulfilled the normal familial roles appropriate to their younger years. Individuals who had led exemplary lives were able to retain their prestige and power in late life through the performance of age-grade functions. The role of the artist, scholar, priest, or politician, for example, still tends to confer increasing prestige as the individual ages. The Japanese government's naming of very old artists as "living cultural treasures" formalizes this custom.

Confucianism

Confucianism was borrowed from China by the Japanese in the fifth century, along with writing, Buddhism, and many other trappings of "civilization." Central to Confucian values are the virtues of consideration, support, obedience, and respect shown to parents, regardless of the ages of the generations in question. These values, still so pervasive in Japanese culture, are difficult to convey with a few examples. A Japanese proverb says, "The words of the elders never fall to the ground" (*Toshiyori no kotoba wa chi ni mo ochinai*). It is a source of public shame to be thought negligent toward one's parents, materially, symbolically, or emotionally.

Corporate Emphasis

All was not hierarchy in traditional Japan, however. A second value that guided social life was the subordination of the individual, regardless of formal office or authority, to the well-being of the group. Although households were theoretically ruled by the oldest active male, for example, decisions were often made for the household by the most competent member. A person in authority who wielded that authority unfeelingly or neglected the well-being of subordinates came in for general social disapproval, and sometimes punishment at the hands of the community. Even today, this value regulates not only families but many other types of groups, including businesses, voluntary organizations, and communities. Consensus is considered the ideal form of group decision making. This feature of social organization, called "corporate emphasis" by Harumi Befu (1962), to some extent separates power and prestige. The older person who fails in his or her responsibilities is not exempt from ridicule and even rebellion. As we shall see, this cultural complex is expressed today in the strong sense of obligation that older people bring to their work and family roles.

To return, now, to the process of industrialization in Japan, the values of family solidarity and Confucian filial piety were drawn upon to modulate the disruptive nature of social change. In 1871 the system of family registers was established, requiring the details of residence, employment, and marriage of every citizen to be recorded in the *koseki*, or family register. It also gave the household head power to expel persons from his residence. In 1899 the civil code was revised to require families to care for their aged members. In this new law, the parents of household heads had legal priority over wives and children and parents-in-law over brothers and sisters (Kinoshita 1984).

The effect of these policies was to give the strength of law to the already-respected position of the aged in Japanese society. As noted, traditionally, household heads carried responsibility for the well-being of household members and could not be neglectful or cruel to wives, parents, siblings, servants, or children without risking strong social censure. The laws gave an added measure of security to dependents and helped to build a safety net under the "deserving poor" – at least those who escaped the terrible misfortune of losing membership in a family. Luckily, it seems to have been a rare misfortune.

THE ELDERLY TODAY

In the past, then, the prestige and power of the Japanese elderly has been relatively high, compared with their age-mates in Western societies. Although Japan was a relatively poor society until the 1960s, it also appears that the material security of the elderly was reasonably good relative to other age groups, a condition which varied among Western nations at any given time and which shifted precariously from era to era within nations. But what about these qualities of late life in Japan today?

Although it is difficult to get agreement on indices of prestige, power, and security, we can get an overall feeling for the general levels of these qualities if we compare statistics on the elderly in different societies and have a sense of what is behind those statistics. This forces us to ignore very important differences among the elderly themselves – differences between the well-to-do and the poor, the young-old and the old-old, the urban and the rural, and so on. In homogenizing the aged for purposed of cross-cultural comparison, we are creating a fiction; we can only hope it is a useful fiction.

Let us then compare, in this admittedly artificial way, modern Japan and the United States. What we find, I believe, is that the Japanese elderly enjoy comparatively high prestige but are currently neither more powerful nor more secure than their American age-mates.

PRESTIGE

The compressed industrialization and modernization of Japan have inevitably led to a compressed population explosion, from 30 million in 1860, to 46 million in 1900, to 120 million today. Since World War II, greatly slowed birth rates and the advent of high-technology medicine have assured that much of that growth has been in the over-sixty-five population. Life expectancy at birth rose to 74.8 years for men and 80.5 years for women in 1985, the second highest in the world (Ministry of Health and Welfare 1987), and the over-sixty-five share of the population more than doubled from 4.9 percent in 1950 to 10 percent in 1985.

One would think that the sudden appearance of this great new sea of wrinkled faces would assault the values of even a gerontocratic society, and to some extent this is true. The speed of change has caused serious economic and social dislocations in Japanese society, and the aged are increasingly seen as a problem population. But much like youth in the United States, the Japanese elderly are generally seen as a problem worthy of serious attention. In contrast to the United States, for example, basic medical services for all those over 70 in Japan are virtually free, even though this places a serious strain on the public economy (Kiefer 1987). The difference between Japan and the socialist countries of Europe, moreover, is that the elderly are singled out for this benefit only in Japan.

If one looks for specific attitudes and behaviors that express this relative prestige in daily life, they are not terribly obvious. Contrary to the impression one gets from reading pre-World War II works on respect for the aged, such as those of Lafcadio Hearn (1955 [1920]) and Ruth Benedict (1946), there is not a lot of reverential bowing and unusually polite speech; old people are expected to keep their place and are singled out for criticism if they make unusual demands or expect a free ride. Legislated collective expressions of respect like Honor the Aged Day (*Keiro no Hi*) undoubtedly evoke, as does Veterans' Day in the United States, different feelings in different people and do not make good measures of prestige.

Still, young Japanese are more inclined than Americans to express gratitude toward their elders for the benefits of life, to include them in family affairs if possible, and to smile at their eccentricities. Family honor depends more on the fulfillment of obligations toward those who have given one life, and personal reputation depends more on family honor. There is also a relative scarcity of direct and indirect hostility toward the aged in Japan. Derogatory expressions like *baba* (crone), *umeboshi-baba* (dried-plum crone), *yakamashii baasan* (noisy old woman), *ojin* or *jiji* (codger), *jiji kusai* (like an old codger, said of young people who are stuffy and opinionated), and *gokei typu* (widow-type), as well as terms of address (using the familiar *chan* instead of the formal *san* or *sama*) and derogatory jokes all exist, but are usually held to be in bad taste; it is quite rare to see older people scolded or scoffed at in public. As a young fieldworker in a provincial Japanese city, I was once taken in tow by an eighty-year-old, retired petty official who wanted to help me collect data. Dressed in a red windbreaker and baseball cap, he strode into one city office after another and more or less ordered the staff to get me the material I needed. Although I detected a few ironic smiles, I was amazed that nobody told us to get lost. Moreover, the "successful" elder, one who has played his or her role in life unusually well and has thereby amassed honors, wealth, grandchildren, or disciples, is given reverential treatment of the sort seen more often in Europe than in the United States. Accomplished artists and intellectuals, for example, can expect to enjoy public honors in late life.

In short, the prestige of age in both societies comes variably depending on individual biography and momentary situation, but its general range and mean seem to be noticeably higher in Japan than in the United States.

POWER

When I speak of the power of the elderly, I mean not only their political and juridical power in society but also their ability to control the circumstances of their own lives, their ability, relative to other groups, to make decisions. That power and prestige are loosely linked is clear from a number of examples of social norms. In sex-role-stereotyped societies, for example, women often carry low prestige but have considerable power over their sons and even their husbands by virtue of their control of crucial resources within the home. Likewise, hereditary aristocrats in constitutional monarchies may retain a good deal of prestige while lacking any powers worth mentioning.

Like prestige, power is difficult to measure in a complex society. Statistics alone might give the impression that the Japanese elderly enjoy a higher degree of economic, political, and social power than their American counterparts, but I do not believe this is true. If one questions the elderly themselves, as I have, about their preferred status in the health care system, for example, one finds that a large segment actually oppose the preferential law, which they see as patronizing and destructive of their relations with the broader society. "Most of us can pay for our own health care," they will say. "That's what we'd prefer to do."

Another misleading indicator is the proportion of the elderly who live with children. In Japan the figure is 70 percent, exactly five times the American rate. To the golden age theorist, this conjures up images of the traditional geron-tocrat, lovingly supported in the bosom of his or her family—but is this an accurate picture? In an urban-industrial society where there is little work for an older person to do in the home (in contrast to peasant society where there is much for old hands to do), is the old person's presence likely to be very welcome? In both Japan and the United States, a majority of older people see their children at least once a week. When children are only minutes away by car or bus and seconds away by phone, what does "living separately" actually mean?

It could mean a welcome increment of privacy. Some statistics are interesting in this regard:

- While 38 percent of the Japanese elderly say they prefer living separately from their children, only 30 percent actually have such a residential situation. At least 8 percent then, are dissatisfied with their "privileged" situation. About 4 percent of Americans who live with their children also would like to live elsewhere.

- Coresidence is significantly more characteristic of men than of women, of those over seventy-five than younger, of those in poor health, of those without spouses, and of those with a combination of these characteristics (Prime Minister's Office 1982; Koyono et al. 1986). Given the scarcity of supportive independent living situations for the aged in Japan and their relative abundance in America, this suggests that physical necessity may be more important than personal taste, as a determinant of coresidence.

- Elderly Americans of all ages and both sexes are about six times as likely to participate in social activities outside the family as are Japanese. This again suggests a preference for, and a richness of, independent living in America that is supported by a relative abundance of opportunity (Prime Minister's Office 1982).

The fact that congregate housing for the elderly is in short supply in Japan has both a historical and an economic basis. Because of the cultural expectation that families should care for their elderly members at home, there is an absence of a tradition of decent alternative housing. Until very recently the only type of collective housing for the aged available in Japan (other than acute hospitals) were the so-called *yoroin*, poor houses for the destitute and familyless old. These fearful places evoked such feelings of shame that few who could arrange to live any other way would consider anything remotely like them, regardless of quality. Although attitudes are finally changing, semi-independent living arrangements are still in very short supply.

The economic side of the problem is the cost of land and construction in a very crowded country. Entry fees for such congregate housing as does exist are very high by American standards, and most elderly who have children lack sufficient savings and are reluctant to sell family property to raise funds.

If we look at the availability of work and income as indications of power, again the Japanese statistics are ambiguous. About the same proportion of Japanese (44 percent) and Americans (42.1 percent) over the age of sixty, including those who do and those who do not have jobs, say they need to work for money. Thirty-nine percent of Japanese in this age group have jobs, whereas 24 percent of Americans do. This would seem to indicate that jobs are more available to the older Japanese. However:

- Pensions in Japan are still well below American levels, although the difference is narrowing. Some Japanese pension programs now show the same wage replacement rate as one finds in America, but as yet most elderly are not covered by these pensions (Palmore and Maeda 1985: 77–78). Kiyoko Okamura (1987) found that 34.5 percent of a sample of 501 retirees from companies with fixed-age retirement rules had no pensions at all! Even for those who have pensions, the statistics are deceiving, because many Japanese "retire" twice — first from their career jobs and finally from jobs that pay much less. Michiko Naoi (1987) found that 62 percent of 179 retirees who took second jobs suffered major cuts in pay. Does "wage replacement" refer to the wages of the career job, as in America, or those of the lower-paying second job?
- Elderly American male workers are three times as likely as Japanese to be in managerial jobs rather than blue-collar or service jobs or the trades.
- Elderly American male workers are four times as likely as Japanese to say they work *for enjoyment* (Prime Minister's Office 1982).

It appears that work as a form of recreation is more popular and more available among the American elderly. Japanese values are more family-centered and community-centered, and work is seen more as a duty (38 percent of Japanese workers say they work to preserve their health, versus 14 percent of Americans). My impression from talking with elderly Japanese also is that work is often seen as moral activity and that for this reason the elderly are more serious about finding work and willing to do less interesting, less prestigious, and less well-paid work. The availability of jobs is just one of many factors contributing to employment rates.

There remains the crucial area of old people's ability to influence the decisions of young people. Useful data on this are hard to come by, but at least they do not unambiguously point to a Japanese edge. There is some indication that Japanese expectations of respect are considerably higher and that they are therefore more often frustrated. Several older Japanese I have interviewed have proposed their own version of the golden age theory, saying that they had to obey their parents and parents-in-law when young, but that now they must obey their children and children-in-law.

- When asked to rate their children's attitudes toward their well-being, 83.7 percent of American elderly chose "very interested," while only 67.7 percent of Japanese gave that response (Prime Minister's Office 1982).

An overview of Japanese old people's power to direct their own lives, then, reveals that their lives have improved quite dramatically since the beginning of industrialization, but that they have gained fewer options than have others. Both compared with the American elderly and compared with younger people in their own culture, the Japanese elderly seem to have suffered a relative decline in power. Norms that grant prestige to the aged also saddle them with responsibilities: to avoid unnecessary dependence on others (and hence, for example, to protect their health), to refrain from making undue demands, to protect family honor through decorous behavior, to contribute to family well-being through thrift and hard work, and to preserve family property. Young people, while constrained to show respect and care for their parents in late life, also have the power that attends their economic role in the family. The demands of career and young parenthood are severe but also offer significant choices from time to time—where to live and with whom, what to do for a living, when and whom to marry, when to have children, and many details of lifestyle. The relative dependency of the aged requires them to consign most such choices to the sentiments of the young.

SECURITY

As the human life-span has a definite upper limit somewhere around a hundred years, the closer one approaches that limit the less secure one is, as measured in the likelihood of dying. All old people share to various degrees an insecurity of life. When I speak of the "security" of the aged, then, I mean something other than sheer survival. I mean the security of values, the assurance that what remains of life, including the manner and circumstances of one's death, will be *meaningful*—just, decent, comprehensible, or at least acceptable. The absence of this assurance, in my experience, leads to greater anxiety in the old than the threat of death itself. When I ask old people in American *or* Japan what they fear most, the answer is usually the same, a long, helpless, hopeless illness. It has various names: stroke, cancer, senility, or just *hen na kako* (the ugly decline).

The assurance of a meaningful "home stretch" is of course related to the prestige and power of the aged, but in modern society this relationship is steadily declining. A level of public health and nutrition that greatly prolongs productive life, together with a high-technology medicine that restores acceptable functioning in the aged, has added many meaningful years to many lives. At the same time, our skill in postponing death *without* the maintenance or restoration of acceptable function has greatly reduced the value-security of the aged as a group. The appearance of greatly increased numbers of frail, chronically ill, or medically and psychologically incapacitated old-old stands as a constant threat to the healthy elderly that their lives may well lose most of their value long before the end and that there might well be nothing they themselves can do about it. This is why Japan has *pokkuri jinja* and *pokkuri otera*, "popping-off" shrines and temples, visited by a steady stream of old people who have come to pray for a speedy death.[1] Health care statistics dramatize the situation:

- In 1980 more than a fourth of all hospital beds for the acutely ill in Japan were occupied by people over 70 – a quarter of a million people (N. Maeda 1983). In the United States, about a third of the hospital beds were occupied by people over 65, amounting to about ten million (Shanas and Maddox 1976).

- Including those living at home, about half a million Japanese elderly are bedfast (D. Maeda-1983). Seventy-four percent of these have been incapacitated for more than six months (Soda and Miura 1982). This compares with about eight million American elderly who have "major activity limitation" due to chronic illness (Health Insurance Association of America 1984).

- In spite of the *yoroin* tradition and the consequent Japanese distaste for nursing homes, Japan is now experiencing a nursing home boom. Between 1977 and 1983, for example, the number of beds nearly doubled, from 55,000 to 97,000 (*Asahi News* 1983). There are about a million beds in the United States.

Given the similar levels of medical science in the United States and Japan, it would seem that the effects of health care on value-security in the two cultures should be about equal. However, there is some cause to believe that the Japanese elderly suffer more than Americans in this respect. On a tour of treatment programs for the elderly in Japan in 1983, I saw almost no attention to the rehabilitation of disabled patients with fractures, strokes, sensory loss, and other conditions that can be alleviated through physical and occupational therapy. A 1977 survey revealed that in that year only 7,251 old people in Japan received any kind of rehabilitation service, fewer than 3 percent of the "bedfast" population. Only 4.4 percent of nursing home patients were receiving rehabilitation therapy (Prime Minister's Office 1980). I have argued elsewhere that the reason for this inattention to rehabilitation is partly cultural (Kiefer 1987). Without repeating that argument in detail, let me summarize the probable reasons for the problem:

Rapid growth of the elderly population. Japan has had relatively little time in which to develop adequate services for such a large population.

Power of the medical profession. Physicians' organizations command great political power in Japan and tend to exert a conservative influence on health care planning and delivery. Rehabilitation on the needed scale requires policy commitment to the training of allied health professionals and to the concept of teamwork between physicians and other professionals in the treatment of the disabled. Such a system is seen by many conservative doctors as a threat to their autonomy and status.

Cultural roles of caretaker and patient. Rehabilitation often requires the caretaker to cause the patient discomfort or stress or to be firm in overcoming the patient's resistance. This attitude violates some features of the traditional caretaker/patient role set. Passivity is relatively accepted in the patient in Japan, and caretakers are supposed to be as concerned with the patient's need for nurturance and emotional support as with his or her need for recovery.

This is not to say that the situation is better in America. I emphasize the rehabilitation problem to point out that the image of disability which haunts the Japanese elderly is one that offers little hope of escape, and many seem preoccupied with feelings of insecurity as they contemplate the last decades of their lives.

As in the case of the power of the old, industrialization in Japan seems to have brought absolute gains in the area of material security but to have offset these gains with relative deprivation. The approach of death shifts emphasis away from the material, toward the spiritual and symbolic. In Japan as elsewhere in the industrial world, artificial extension of life threatens the elderly with a new symbolic insecurity that often appears more troubling than material want.

INDUSTRIALIZATION AND AGING RECONSIDERED

The golden age model of industrialization and its twin, the assumption of cultural integration, suggested to early students of cultural gerontology that modern capitalism deprived the elderly simultaneously of the triple benefits of prestige, power, and security. Enlightened public institutions of education, welfare, and health care were needed, the model suggested, to restore equal justice to all age groups (Bellah et al. 1985:256–71). The historical comparison of Japan and the United States suggests some modifications in this view:

1. In America the elderly lost prestige and power *before* the main social and economic changes of the industrial revolution had set in. Economic security became a serious problem considerably later but has been under gradual restoration through improvements in pensions and in public responsibility for health and housing in the twentieth century.

2. In Japan the prestige and power of the elderly were maintained at fairly high levels throughout the industrialization process. Material security, although less than optimum, was about as good as that of other age groups. Recently the elderly have not shared equally in the great improvements in power that economic affluence has brought to their society. They can be said to suffer from relative power deprivation.

3. In Japan and the United States (and other modern industrial societies) the prolongation of life has led to large populations of chronically ill and disabled elderly. This has created a general sense of insecurity among the aged concerning the survival of their values in late life, an insecurity that may be greater in Japan than in the United States because of the relative inattention to rehabilitation in Japan.

These facts are best encompassed in a pluralist model of modernization—a model that portrays the elderly as one of many subcultures, each of which attaches different meanings to, and each of whose well-being is affected differently by, specific aspects of the changing culture. The subcultural composition of every industrializing society is a bit different, and the interest positions and relative power of the various subcultures also differ.

In the West, particularly in England, industrialization was the brainchild largely of a growing commercial class, in alliance with a growing bourgeois intelligentsia, both bent on freeing themselves from the autocratic traditions of the past. Gerontocracy was early equated with other "irrational" principles of rule and fell into disrepute. In Japan, by contrast, industrialization was led by a coalition of the feudal aristocracy and the equally traditionalist *zaibatsu*, or merchant prince families. Their aim was not so much political transformation as political survival through economic reform. Reverence for the aged was therefore seen as a valuable brake on the political transformation that must inevitably accompany the rise of public literacy and wealth.

The Japanese government has continued, on the whole, to support prosenior policies, yet the overall conditions of the aged are not much in keeping with their relatively prestigious position in the value structure of the society. The relative declines in power and security of the aged have resulted from the appearance of other subcultures with their own agendas, especially the subcultures of corporate management and of science.

Corporate management would seem to have two main interests which conflict with the power of the aged. First, the need for Japanese business to create and sustain high levels of domestic demand for innovative consumer goods has led to a gradual shift of emphasis from the values of the traditional extended family to those of the autonomous, style-conscious (and usually young) couple. Second, competition for markets requires large organizations to demand intense loyalty from employees, including willingness to change residence often (including foreign travel) and to regulate marriage, child-rearing, and consumption habits to fit the needs of the company. In a work-centered society, the elderly have little choice but to take whatever commitment is left over from career. Family and kin are not denigrated in the corporate culture, quite the opposite. But when hard choices have to be made, it is often the economic outcome that counts most.

Most of the values of the aged and those of the scientific subculture would seem to be mutually supportive. The comfort and affluence that devolve from applied science to society are usually not targeted for a particular age group.

However, the interest of science in the application of biological knowledge to the prolongation of life, can and does undercut the value-security of the old. This conflict comes about through the peculiar moral position of science in modern society. Because value neutrality is widely held to be an essential prerequisite of scientific research and innovation is taken to be a valuable end in itself, scientific research in all technologically advanced societies suffers from a lack of moral constraint and moral self-consciousness. The old are victimized by science, not because anyone wants this outcome, but because there is a lack of mediating values which link the subculture of science with any other subculture in the society, except the purely economic values of corporate industry.

This, then, summarizes the pluralist model of the aged in industrial society. Note that this picture differs from the golden age theory in that it recognizes structural strains as inherent in the makeup of the culture. To the extent that a young worker has commitments to both the traditional extended-family subculture *and* the corporate subculture, he or she may experience occasional acute personal dilemmas. To the extent that a scientist foresees possible social calamity resulting from the fruits of research, she has a conflict of roles on her hands. Any plural society embodies such strains; it is only when a particular kind of strain reaches pandemic proportions that the society can be said to be dis-integrated.

NOTE

1. Japanese Shinto and Buddhism have many elements of folk religion in them, including the tendency of worshippers to ignore the official deity and function of a shrine or temple and adhere instead to informal traditions. *Pokkuri* shrines and temples are so named in the informal, not the formal, traditions.

PART IV
THE ETHNIC DIMENSION IN AGING

Few topics better reflect this book's prevailing theme of culture and context than the issue of the ethnic aged. Ethnicity is the manifestation of a cultural tradition in a heterogeneous societal framework. The expression of ethnic identity or the performance of ethnically rooted behaviors in industrial societies invariably takes place under new conditions and places from whence the traditions sprang. Therefore, the cultural manifestation of ethnicity is almost always a creative act meshing the ancestral "native" patterns with demands of broader societal units and the exigencies of the local environment. Anthropologists working in urban sub-Saharan Africa in the 1950s and 1960s found that some of the "tribal" groups they were studying in industrial cities were actually new cultural phenomena forged in the crucible of places dramatically different from their rural homelands. Similarly, Barbara Myerhoff in *Number Our Days* (1979), describes how a very old Jewish population, disconnected from kin and the surrounding ethnic community, establish an unusual local variant of *Yiddishkeit* (Jewishness) centered around their own interpretation of Jewish ritual and personal performance.

Despite a prevailing notion of the United States as an effective melting pot, homogenizing immigrant cultures into an invariant social soup, cultural plurality remains a powerful element of national life (Gelfand 1987). Not only is this manifested in the recent ethnic revival among groups long settled into America, but a new immigrant wave, sparked by the 1965 immigration act, ended over forty years of restricted and ethnically skewed migration. For example, "during the last decade, alone, some 800,000 Southeast Asians, 100,000 Soviet Jews, and 125,000 Cubans have been granted safe haven in this country" (Gozdziak 1988:1).

However, only a tiny number of groups in our society have maintained over a long period of time sociocultural systems that are not only more highly variant from the American cultural norms but also stress factors that foster high status for the aged. Among the most distinct are people such as the Amish, Hasidic Jews, and certain native American groups such as the Navaho and Zuni. The long-term positive maintenance of their ethnic divergence has been possible so far as they have remained economically independent of outside groups.

One of the clearest indications of sociocultural distinctiveness comes from the studies of old-order Amish who have largely rejected the "worldly" nature of our industrial society (Hostetler and Huntington 1971; Brubaker and Michael 1987). In their tight-knit agrarian communities, old age is defined functionally, with a varied timing of a retirement process which is voluntary and gradual. Movement into the "grandfather house" adjacent to younger married children provides a transition into a valued, active, and responsibility-laden role-set, bolstered by an ideology in which "old-fashioned ways" are revered and a knowledge of these ways is perpetuated by the older people. Moreover, prestige resides with age because elders retain not only adequate economic resources (such as their own buggy to drive) but also purposeful religious roles, which end essentially with death. Tying these factors together is a strong emphasis on the welfare of others, which overshadows self-absorption and preoccupation with personal needs and comforts. In these respects the distinct culture of the old-order Amish provides a near-idyllic, supportive milieu for the aged that incorporates the key factors associated cross-culturally with beneficial conditions for the aged (Tripp-Reimer et al. 1988)

The Amish stand as a strong contradiction to the rule. Most other immigrant groups have not been able to maintain such a close integration of ideology, social organization, and economic tradition. Thus the manifestation of ethnicity varies tremendously, from the establishment of powerful corporate groups which can satisfy most material and spiritual needs to having a small repertoire of subjective identity markers (food, clothes, music) and a vague sense of belonging to a historically felt past. In this volume, besides the chapters in this section, the variety of America's ethnic aged who are discussed includes Serbs (Simic), American Indians (Weibel-Orlando), and Hispanics (Henderson).

THE REALITIES OF ETHNIC COMPENSATION

A major theme in researching the cultural diversity of America's aged has been ethnicity as a positive resource for the aged – a form of compensation for the problems associated with aging (Cool 1987). In our own societal context a positive dimension of ethnic attachments can promote a nondenigrating component of identity to balance out the potentially negative impact of retirement or the "empty nest syndrome." We have already noted in Weibel-Orlando's study of Sioux native American elders how the reemergence of their ancestral identity in old age served as a source of a key family role for them as cultural conservators. Especially with the recent focus on informal systems of support for providing social services, there has been a general assumption that the traditional ethnic family and community could serve as a model for solving virtually all the problems of the aged (Jackson and Harel 1983; Ikels 1986; Rempusheski 1988).

In chapter 10, Jay Sokolovsky looks at the available data to try to assess the limits of ethnic beliefs and support as a compensator for aging in our urban industrial society. He shows that even among Asian groups, renowned for their filial devotion, certain immigration contexts can result in a very low perceived quality of life by the elderly. Sokolovsky, in line with Henderson's later discussion (section VI) of the Hispanic family's approach to Alzheimer's disease, also finds that when dealing with difficult medical problems, the traditional ethnic response sometimes actually exacerbates the problem. Among the more important points made in this chapter is that the female perspective on family support of the aged can be dramatically different from that of ethnic males.

In the United States the cultural dimension of ethnicity must also be comprehended within the framework of a class system that has created minority groups. These are persons who are "singled out for differential and inferior treatment on the basis of such characteristics as their race, sex, nationality, or language" (Jackson 1980:2). Thus while United States minority populations discussed in this book—blacks, Hispanics, and Native Americans—have a considerably smaller proportion of elderly than Euro-American groups (8 percent, 5 percent, and 5 percent versus 12 percent, respectively), their income, education, access to quality housing, and health care are far below that of the majority of older Americans (Jackson 1985; R. Gibson 1986). After a period in the 1960s and 1970s of gradually improving the "safety net" for the minority aged, the current decade has witnessed deep cuts in programs such as food stamps, low-income housing, and energy subsidies—entitlements that were targeted toward helping the poorest elderly (Navarro 1984). This took place at a time when impoverishment was actually *increasing* among the minority aged, whose rates of poverty (about 20 to 30 percent) are two to three times that of white aged (Torres-Gil 1987). The impact of inequality is particularly severe among older black women in terms of their lower income, greater displacement from the work force by technology, and higher rates of illiteracy than other segments of the minority aged.

One historical response of African American peoples has been to establish community-based mechanisms of support which could buffer the shock of long-term discrimination on the individual. Employing her dual background as professional nurse and medical anthropologist, Jane Peterson explores the participation of older women in two key institutions in an African American community in Seattle. Despite the ever-present spector of multiple jeopardy—being black, aged, and female—a family-based role combined with the more public arena of the Pentecostal church provide a valued context in which successful aging can take place.

Through the experience of Mrs. Lottie Waters we see that mature women in their grandparenting role fulfill a classic "kin-keeping role": nurturing and disciplining children; being the repository of family history; serving as a key decision maker and convener of family ritual.

Despite the patriarchal nature of the Pentecostal church these women belong to, "wise" women can also become church "mothers" who are leaders in a nondomestic sphere and can influence the male "elders" of the religious community. Such women add to the typical characteristics of wise women a devotion to spiritual needs, and some in the role of "nurses" apply a holistic system of healing based on herbs and faith.

In the study of aging it is tempting to focus on ethnic groups that markedly differ in cultural traditions from the predominant Euro-American traditions. Still, a number of researchers have pointed out the need to understand the diversity among "white" elderly (Gelfand and Fandetti 1980; Holzberg 1982). All too often bunched together as a homogeneous body of ethnics, those of European background retain some substantial differences which reflect on how these populations deal with the aging process. In the chapter by Luborsky and Rubinstein, the authors address the difficult problem of widowhood and how variations in ethnic identity and values among Irish, Italians, and Jews in Philadelphia relate to how men cope with such tragic loss. While similarities are noted in the way ethnic values provide a means of overcoming loss, substantial divergence was found in the way loss is conceptualized, how social connections are remade, and how a sense of self is reconstituted. This is one of the few comparative studies of widowhood from the male perspective, although a more extensive literature exists on response of women to this situation (Lopata 1972, 1973, 1987; Folta and Deck 1987; Palmore 1987; Sered 1987).

10 BRINGING CULTURE BACK HOME: AGING, ETHNICITY, AND FAMILY SUPPORT

Jay Sokolovsky

The broadest-based examination of the relation of ethnicity and aging centers on the premise that varying ethnic lifestyles will alter the way old age is encountered, perceived, and acted out. Describing precisely how much subcultures alter the conditions of aging is to say the very least, controversial. I will address this point by asking the basic question, Do ethnic differences make a difference in the elderly? On a more specific level, I will concentrate on the extent to which an overidealization of ethnic subcultures has led to a policy error which places too much emphasis on the ethnic family and informal supports as the savior of the ethnic elderly.

CULTURE, ETHNICITY, AND AGING

To a cultural anthropologist, seeking the answer to this question requires examining the general relationship between cultural variation and aging. The consideration of ethnicity as a factor affecting old age brings the question of sociocultural variation back home to our own doorstep. Ethnicity is commonly understood as social differentiation derived from cultural criteria such as a shared history, a common place of origin, language, dress, food preferences, and values that engender a sense of exclusiveness and self-awareness of membership in a distinct social group. Viewing the variations of aging in our country within the context of ethnicity seems mandated by the continuing cultural pluralism of our nation. While by the beginning of the 1990s only about 5 percent of the ethnic elderly will be foreign-born, throughout the twenty-first century there will be large numbers of American-born ethnic elderly from Indo-China, Asia, and Latin America (Gelfand 1982; Gozdziak 1988).

CULTURE VERSUS CONTEXT

When dealing in general with ethnic segments of the United States we are almost never confronting "culture in the raw," unburnished from Old World or other indigenous origins. Despite such designations as "Moscow on the boardwalk" of Brighton Beach, Brooklyn, "Little Havana" in Miami, or the Chinatowns clinging to numerous downtown, urban districts, there are precious few ethnic groups whose traditional lifestyles and values have not been shattered by the reality of special immigration histories and the continuing social, economic, and political constraints imposed by American class stratification and ideology. In examining a number of transplanted Asiatic ethnic groups, each with a strong "ideal" emphasis on filial devotion, one can see the impact of context on culture. For Chinese-American elderly, migration to the United States in the early twentieth century was largely a movement of young, single males who planned to return to China. Despite living in well-defined ethnic communities, these males, studied in old age, have the smallest family networks of any Asian-American group, and relatively few express high satisfaction with life (Weeks and Cuellar 1981). Older Japanese-Americans, in contrast, came to this country primarily in family groups which intended to become United States citizens. These elders are not only more likely to be more deeply imbedded in kinship networks than the Chinese but exhibit higher levels of social and psychological success. While a majority (54 percent) of Japanese-American elders in a San Diego study (Cuellar and Weeks 1980) said they were very satisfied with their lives, only 18 percent of older Chinese claimed this level of contentment. We will see later on, however, that being surrounded by relatives in an ethnic enclave does not ensure passage to a geriatric Nirvana.

MULTIPLE JEOPARDY OR ETHNIC COMPENSATION

Understanding the context of ethnic aging also requires an understanding of the minority aged, those who "have been singled out for differential and inferior treatment" (Jackson 1980:2). In this particular clash of culture and context there have emerged in the ethnicity and aging literature two key themes that on the surface seem contradictory. One theme stresses how minority group membership creates "multiple jeopardies" in the context of structured inequality and thereby intensifies the problems of growing old (Federal Council on the Aging 1979, 1981; Manuel 1982). The other theme underscores the benefits or resources accruing to those elderly who remain attached to an ethnic identity and subculture (Cool 1987).

From this first perspective Ron Manuel notes that "the distinction of the minority aged is not so much a function of the novel conditions of their aging as it is the dire circumstances of their existence" (1982:xv). Numerous studies have repeatedly demonstrated that in terms of income, housing quality, education, and rates of chronic illness, the minority aged encounter harsher conditions than the majority of older Americans. Not only are these problems more severe, but the "aging network" set up to provide services, typically by uniform bureaucratic standards, often creates barriers preventing the minority ethnic aged from obtaining resources to which they are entitled (Cuellar and Weeks 1980).

The second theme, which I will refer to as "ethnic compensation," often creeps into the discussion of minority aging in an ambivalent fashion. Manuel, after making the statement quoted above, goes on to write, "While relatively more disadvantaged because of the minority experience, the aged have often adopted distinguishable strategies for successfully coping with their problems" (1982:xv). This sentiment corresponds to the prevailing anthropological writings on aging and ethnicity, which largely echo the statement of Linda Cool, "rather than providing yet one more obstacle to be overcome in the aging process, ethnicity can furnish the elderly with a source of identity and prestige which they can manipulate to make a place for themselves in society" (1981:185).

The two themes do not logically exclude each other, but the policy implications of each could be applied to dramatically opposed viewpoints. Ethnicity as deprivation calls for strengthening federal/state resources to overcome lifelong deficits. Ethnicity as compensation or resource could be construed as a rationale to decrease or at least not radically to shift material resources toward the ethnic minority aged. However, a major point I hope to make here is that much of the literature on ethnicity as a resource has been overly optimistic, especially in the area of informal social supports and family networks of exchange.

I concentrate here on the theme of ethnic compensation not because I think it is more important, but because it has been relatively ignored. By stressing this approach, one can also ask significant questions about the nonminority ethnic elderly. Moreover, it is often in this area of aging research that the ways of testing whether the "differences make a difference" have not been up to the questions asked. All too often, ethnic distinctions are measured by mass survey questionnaires, appropriate perhaps for measuring variations in health complaints, the frequency of contact with friends, or the proximity of children to an elderly parent's house. Such measures tell us little about how ethnic differences influence the way illnesses are dealt with, how they affect the perception of old age, if they lead to institutionalization, or how the action of social networks actually contributes to or diminishes the successful functioning of the elderly in the family and the community.

This is especially the case in studies of the aged of European background where statistical documentation can potentially mask subtle ethnic differences. Quite instructive is the work by Cohler, Lieberman, and Welch (1977) studying Irish, Italian, and Polish-Americans in Chicago. Despite a statistical similarity in levels of social contact, the authors showed how subtle differences in value orientations between the Italian and Polish communities related to the nature of support systems affecting the elderly.

In their study, the Polish were found to perceive a greater sense of isolation, and they were more likely to feel no one was available to them for aid in problematic situations. This greater degree of perceived social isolation was related to traditional Polish concerns for privacy, self-containment, and formality in social relations. The authors suggest that what appears to be greater social isolation among the Polish-American respondents may be a reflection of their preference for formal rather than informal relationships and a tendency to look to the community rather than to the family for support. Hence, they argue that there is a tendency here to undervalue informal relations of the family as a source of support in deference to resources through formal links to the community. In contrast, the Italians, who emphasize a traditional value of "family centeredness" and use chain migration to link up with fellow townspeople in the same urban neighborhood, have put an inordinate stress on family relationships. Thus, in contrast to Polish respondents, the Italian aged were more willing to seek out family and close friends in crisis situations. In this case, Italian women were noted as gaining higher status with age, as they were much in demand to mediate problems in the family network. As we shall see below, however, there are costs attached to this "mediating Madonna" role.

While ethnic differences are apparent, the ultimate question remains: do the differences make a difference? Cohler, Welch, and Lieberman (1975), in fact, suggest that for the groups mentioned above ethnic saliency for explaining variant patterns of behavior decreases in old age, with middle-aged cohorts more distinct than aged ones. Nonetheless, this does not mean that general cultural differences among the nonaged ethnic will not have an impact on the elderly. This can be especially important in socially patterned decisions about caring for one's aged parent. An indication of this is a study by Donald Fandetti and Donald Gelfand (1976) comparing Italians and Poles in Baltimore on attitudes toward institutionalization of the elderly. As one might predict from the previous discussion, the authors note that "Italian respondents expressed a significantly stronger preference for using family arrangements than their Polish counterparts." Here is an ethnic difference which not only directly affects differential treatment of the aged, but may also argue for awareness of such differences at some level of policy making.

The general problem of understanding the implications of statistical survey variables often occurs in the discussion of informal social interaction and exchange in family and neighborhood contexts. Numerous studies now exist purporting to compare subculturally variant "network" behavior. With the predominant use of so-called sociometric techniques for gathering data, one is hard-pressed to know if statistically significant differences (or lack of variation) mean anything. A case in point is the well-known "Social and Cultural Contexts of Aging" study conducted in Los Angeles (Bengston and Morgan 1987). Here whites were compared with blacks and Mexican-Americans in terms of social interaction with children, grandchildren, other relatives, and friends. Mexican-Americans were considerably more likely than white elderly to see children and grandchildren on a weekly basis, although no difference was found for contact with other relatives. The Mexican-Americans were much less likely to see friends and neighbors frequently. Older blacks and whites were shown to have almost identical frequency of contact with grandchildren or other relatives, although smaller percentages of blacks reported seeing children and neighborhood friends frequently.

What use can be made of these facts with regard to the function of the aged in familial and community networks? Just because approximately 40 percent of both whites and blacks in Los Angeles see "grandchildren" and "other relatives" weekly does not mean the aged in each ethnic group fit into kinship networks and use such resources in the same way. Various other studies, such as that by Jane Peterson in this book or by Nellie Tate (1983), have given us clues to some of the significant differences. One of these distinctions is a greater flexibility in kinship boundaries among African American families, which results in the absorption of young grandchildren and "other relatives" into households headed by the elderly. This is particularly pronounced for older black women who are four times as likely as older white females to live with young dependent relatives under eighteen years of age (Tate 1983: 98). In her study of Philadelphia's black elderly, Tate suggests how this difference makes a difference: "It appears that absorbed nonindependent younger blacks are more likely to accept their aged who become functionally impaired as a result of chronic conditions" (1983:99).

Various other studies have shown qualitative differences in the nature of nonfamilial and family network exchange which remain after class and other situational factors are taken into account. My own work among the aged in New York City single-room occupancy (SRO) hotels not only shows that informal networks are the core of survival mechanisms in a very harsh environment, but also that subtle differences could be discerned on the basis of ethnic background. In general, most networks are relatively small (fewer than ten people) and do not include much functional contact with relatives but rather focus on residents and neighborhood social ties. However, the structural and dynamic qualities of the networks of older black residents (especially women) were consistently different from those of the aged from European backgrounds. Unlike older white women who maintained moderately sized networks with almost no interconnection between members and little depth in the exchanges, black women generated slightly smaller, more articulated networks where contacts involved a greater variety and depth of instrumental and emotional types of support. This difference is significant because the black women's networks were more successful in dealing with acute medical, psychological, and other daily living crises. Under conditions of physical decline, white women were more apt to become socially isolated.

Other studies have documented substantial ethnic-based variation in familial and nonfamilial support systems. One of the most comprehensive is the research of John Weeks and José Cuellar in San Diego comparing the elderly in nine ethnic groups to an "Anglo," nonminority sample. Variance from "Anglo-white" norms was most prominent among "filiocentric" Asian and Pacific Island groups: Korean, Chinese, Japanese, Filipino, Samoan, and Guamanian. To cite the most dramatic case, 91 percent of elderly Korean parents lived with their children, and over 80 percent said they would first turn to family members to satisfy all eight categories of need. Contrast this with white aged, of whom only 10 percent lived with their children and among whom fewer than one in ten expected their family network to deal with all of their basic needs (Weeks and Cuellar 1981:391; Weeks 1984:101). Furthermore, important and substantial differences were noted in comparing the Asian groups among themselves.

I could proceed with other examples showing the impact of the ethnic family in the life of the elderly, but I have already painted myself into a corner, if my intent is to argue against policy makers putting too much stress on ethnic support systems and the family.

THE LIMITS OF ETHNIC COMPENSATION

Whence springs my pessimism? As I interpret studies now available, the evidence indicates that the capacity of the ethnic family for dealing with the most difficult problems of its elderly members is limited. In the context of rapid demographic and economic changes over the last decade, rural ideals are rapidly giving way to urban realities. As of 1978, 55 percent of black elderly and 84 percent of Hispanic elderly resided in urban areas (Weeks 1984). A case in point is the Hispanic-American elderly. Many writers have described the ideal value structure of this group as involving (1) profound family loyalty, (2) dominance of males, and (3) subordination of younger to older persons. Certain studies confirm some elements of this ideal. Marjorie Cantor's (1979) triethnic elderly study (whites, Hispanics, and blacks) in New York showed that Hispanic elderly received the highest levels of assistance in terms of tasks of everyday living and the receipt of gifts. Similarly, Bengtson and Morgan's study (1987) in Los Angeles showed considerably greater levels of family interactions for Mexican-Americans than among whites and blacks.

However, authors such as Maldonado (1975), Cuellar (1980) and Gratton (1987) argue that much of the literature on the Chicano elderly is of limited utility due to a tendency to overromanticize, distort, and stereotype critical elements of the Hispanic life experience. Using their own research and other work undertaken in the late 1970s, they question the popular assumption that older Chicanos can find significant emotional and social support in the extended family. Various studies by Valle and Mendoza (1978) and Weeks and Cuellar (1981) in San Diego and Korte (1978) in Denver describe situations where, despite the continuing ideal of intense intergenerational family concern and the actual availability of a large kin network in the respective urban environment, obligations and expectations of kin support were radically declining.

In San Diego, even though Hispanics who lived alone had four times more extended kin in the local area than whites, they were found to be less likely to turn to family members in times of need (Weeks and Cuellar 1981:392). They preferred to "suffer in silence." The consequences of this appear to be high levels of alienation, low life satisfaction, and other psychological problems. Part of the problem stems from unmet expectations of family interaction. Indeed, even in those studies in Los Angeles (Bengtson and Morgan 1987) and New York (Cantor 1979) showing high levels of family interaction and support for the elderly Hispanic-American, these aged were more likely to show symptoms of mental stress than either whites or blacks. In both cases the main sources of concern were children and family. This should be particularly disturbing to policy makers, as a recent study showed the use rate of community-based services for Mexican-Americans to be significantly lower than three other ethnic groups surveyed (Holmes, Holmes, and Terisi 1983).

THE GENDER DIMENSION OF ETHNIC KIN SUPPORT

An interesting facet of research on Hispanic elderly is that the negative consequences of needs unmet through the kinship network more likely touch the lives of women than of men. Markides and Vernon's (1984) study in San Antonio corroborates this by showing that, of those elder Mexican-Americans who maintained a very ethnically traditional sex role identity, only among women were there signs of psychological distress. They were found to have significantly higher levels of depression than those older women who were more flexible in their gender role and less traditionally ethnic.

This work, and another I will now discuss, suggest the unsettling proposition that "although it has been assumed that social relations are inherently satisfying and reduce the impact of life stress it appears that, at least in some instances, *such social ties may enhance rather than reduce feelings of distress*" (Cohler and Lieberman 1980:462, emphasis added). Bert Cohler and Morton Lieberman base this statement on their study of Irish, Polish, and Italian families in Chicago. These findings parallel those for the Hispanic elderly but are even more dramatic with regard to gender, ethnicity, and psychological stress. Cohler states that among women "living in communities characterized by particularly dense social networks and complex patterns of reciprocity and obligations with adult offspring and other close relatives, there is a significant negative relationship between extent of social contact and both self-reported life satisfaction and psychological impairment" (Cohler 1983:118). This relationship among a kin-keeping role, ethnic embeddedness, and personal maladjustment is strongest for Italian- and Polish-American elderly but does not hold in the Irish-American case. Interestingly enough, for older men of Italian and Polish descent, the effect of ethnic embeddedness is opposite to that found for the women — they seem to benefit greatly in terms of adjustment to old age.

In the case of the Italian-American aged, where this bipolar gender effect is most notable, one sees structural, gender-based differences in the nature of the social networks by which persons are linked to the local environment. Compared to females, older adult males, even after retirement, are active in a more diverse array of communitywide social contexts outside of the family unit. In this case, men's social clubs have been a long-existing traditional arena where older Italian males could gain public status, recognition, and support. This opportunity to enter old age with vital connections both to lifelong friends in ethnic neighborhood associations and to relatives is seldom obtained by women. Most of the elderly women in this Chicago study appear very much encapsulated within the sphere of kin. As one might predict, it was found that older women who exhibited the lowest levels of psychological stress were those actively involved with friends as well as family (Cohler and Lieberman 1980:454). That is, they had networks more like men in maintaining important social relations both inside and outside the realm of domestic/kin ties.

At a time when younger married women are entering the labor force, the traditional "kin-keeping" role of older women is often nervously mocked by the refrain, "How is it that one girl can bring up ten kids, but ten grown-up kids cannot care for one little old lady?" Analytically, I think the evidence is quite convincing that in terms of material and emotional exchange, women are most often left holding the short end of the stick—giving considerably more through informal kin support networks than they ever receive. The implications for policy makers are clear. Emphasizing certain ethnic family support networks as a primary service mechanism would be of likely benefit to aged males, but may be a disaster for females who make up the majority of older ethnic citizens.

This observation is reinforced by studies of the most family-dependent of America's ethnic aged, Asian- and Pacific Island-Americans. Recall the previously mentioned Korean aged in San Diego, where nine in ten lived with children and almost that number expected to depend on their family to provide for all of their needs. Yet one is surprised to read in John Weeks's analysis of his qualitative data that "among all the groups interviewed the Korean elders were least satisfied with their lives" (Weeks 1984:190). Being poor, primarily female, lacking strong English language skills, and having been followers of their earlier migrating children, they were isolated and lonely within a small, exclusive, family life arena. Sadly, the vast majority found life hard, and one-quarter reported having contemplated suicide.

ETHNICITY IN LIFE-SPAN CONTEXT: JAPANESE-AMERICANS

However, San Diego's Korean aged offer an extreme example and tell us little about some very positive Asian cultural features which greatly enhance the experience of aging in the United States. Perhaps the clearest demonstration of this is by anthropologist Christie Kiefer (1974) in his study of how the Japanese-American *issei* (first generation migrants) handled the problem of aging in the context of the rapid Americanization of their children and grandchildren.

Much has been written about the high standards and prestige accorded the elderly in traditional Japanese culture (Palmore and Maeda 1985; Kiefer, this volume). Many have focused on the Japanese version of Buddhism, with its linking of the aged and even the dead to a family system emphasizing filial devotion, an aged role infused with loving indulgence, and an accepted dependence in this "second privileged period." There is also a traditional emphasis on formal socialization into the retired role (*inkyo*) with its greater freedom but also the expectation of increasing skill and wisdom. While strict maintenance of these ideals has not been possible either in modern Japan or among Japanese-Americans (Plath 1987), studies of the latter group clearly show the salience of Japanese ethnicity for the elderly (Kiefer 1984; Osako 1979).

Despite the significant generational differences noted by Kiefer (1974) and Masuda et al. (1970), most Japanese elderly still live with or near their families, who encourage the *issei* to be involved in family activities and outings. To a great extent, their lives remain focused on core Japanese values such as *kansha* (gratitude), *gaman* (forbearance), *makoto* (sincerity), and *giri* (duty), which culminate in a style of life Kiefer refers to as structural intimacy. This involves valuing cohesiveness and privileges. Seen from the perspective of the individual, psychological and material security are to be achieved through the cultivation of mutually binding relationships more than through the competitive pursuit of individual goals and abstract ends. Kiefer demonstrates how such ethnic perceptions of the self contribute to successfully dealing with specific concerns of the aged such as increased dependency and impending death.

In sum, the practical meaning of ethnicity for *issei* aged hinges on core values that, although somewhat discontinuous through generations, maintain the elderly in nonstigmatized family roles. Just as important, however, is that much of their socialization into old age (Rosow 1974) is provided by age-peers who share these strongly held values and allow their traditional basis of self-esteem to guide them through old age. This later aspect of Japanese ethnicity, linking the *issei* into age-peer-dependent mutuality, may be more important than the rules of filial piety most often alluded to.

A particularly important aspect of Kiefer's work is his discussion of how the high cultural value placed on maintaining harmony in the extended family unit can, in fact, be a substantial problem for the elderly under certain conditions. He found that if elderly persons exhibited symptoms of psychological disturbance, families made a great effort to keep such things hidden and simply did not deal effectively with this issue. Relatively minor problems which might have been alleviated by counseling services available through the local ethnic churches often became exaggerated as time went on. Thus, while the manifestation of Japanese culture in the United States can be broadly viewed as a very positive resource for the aged, particular facets of ethnicity can actually create more problems than they solve.

CONCLUSIONS

In this analysis, I am trying to be realistic about the capacity of informal support systems to deal with problems of the aged. My negative attitude may seem unusual based on my previously published work in the areas of gerontology and mental health (Sokolovsky et al. 1978; Cohen and Sokolovsky 1979; Sokolovsky and Cohen 1987). In these writings, I often sought to demonstrate the great benefits derived by inner-city elderly and released mental patients from the social networks in which their lives were enmeshed. Having recently completed the longitudinal and applied extensions of these studies, I am certainly more pessimistic than I was in the late 1970s, when some of my publications helped feed "informal support systems" euphoria.

By following the lives of the SRO elderly over time and in analyzing an experimental intervention program, the limits of informal supports are readily noted. In the case of black women whose social networks are comparatively interconnected and contained complex exchanges, these informal structures are adequate for handling many acute health and resource problems. But longer-term difficulties could not be handled well by these intense networks. Especially in the case of alcoholism, attempts to provide support by intertwined social network members have led to such levels of conflict that these tightly bound social matrices often disintegrate. An experimental project in one SRO to test the efficacy of interventions using informal support found that only about 20 percent of the attempts to use social networks to solve problems (such as obtaining food, getting to a hospital) were successful (Cohen, Adler, and Mintz 1983).

Admittedly, SRO environments are characterized by low levels of material resources, high personal alienation, and a lack of a sense of ethnic affiliation. One should expect greater levels of success when applying network intervention techniques in strong ethnic communities. Certainly this is indicated by the work of Valle and Mendoza (1978), who studied, in Southern California, the *servidor* (community service broker) system, In this program Hispanic-American community members informally function as catalysts for the utilization of services by Mexican-American elders.

Most studies indicate that it is those services that John Colen (1979) calls nonmechanism specific — services that can be provided in diverse settings (such as counseling, information, and referral) — that are most appropriately handled through the social organization of the ethnic community (Colen 1982). Informal coping mechanisms, which are proportionally more evident in ethnic communities, can and should be creatively used as structures in which the fulfillment of human needs in late life are realizable. These forms of ethnic compensation can be quite effective when coupled with nonfamilial systems of support such as respite and day care programs. Such formal systems of care in fact greatly enhance the capacity of families who seek to care for their elderly personally. But when generally dealing with such needs as long-term care, too much emphasis on the ethnic family would be a grave policy mistake. As was seen in the wake of the deinstitutionalization of mental health services, unrealistic or sentimental views of the strength of informal social resources can have the most unfortunate effects. The assumption that public benefits for the needy aged merely supplement or displace family help can and has been used by special interests whose primary concern is minimizing social welfare costs and cutting programs that constitute the basis for economic well-being and care for the aged (Crystal 1982:19). I urge gerontologists interested in the issue of ethnicity not to become unwitting contributors to this destructive trend.

NOTE

This chapter is adapted from my 1985 article, "Ethnicity, Culture and Aging: Do Differences Really Make a Difference?" *Journal of Applied Gerontology* 4(1):6–17, by permission of Sage Publications.

11 AGE OF WISDOM: ELDERLY BLACK WOMEN IN FAMILY AND CHURCH

Jane W. Peterson

Among all living organisms, the process of birth, growth, and death constitutes a familiar biologic cycle. For human beings this process is often divided into phases based on the development of the individual. Variations in importance of one phase versus another of this universal process occur as a result of the cultural context.

Age as measured in years is a fairly meaningless concept for the black American population with whom I worked. For them, age does not measure years on a fixed continuum but reflects those important life events which mature a person. This latter is believed to occur upon overcoming a struggle. One often hears this phenomenon referred to by the phrase, "You grew today." For this population the culturally significant phases of growth and development are: having a child, which is a sign of procreation; raising a child, a sign of maturity; and becoming a grandparent, a sign of having reached the "age of wisdom." This last stage refers to experience and knowledge gained while raising a child which can be imparted to the next generation.

"Old age" and "aging" are not part of the language of this community, although members understand these concepts as used by white Americans. However, when speaking among themselves these words are not heard. The words used are "maturity" and having reached the "age of wisdom." The old are commonly referred to as "the wise."

For black Americans, cultural meaning grows out of their African heritage, the experience of slavery, and their continued oppression within a largely white Anglo-Saxon Protestant American culture. Today, elderly women in the black community continue the oral tradition of passing on cultural meanings, such as the value of children and self-reliance, to succeeding generations.

It is therefore common for elderly women in the community to announce that "one more came along today" in reference to a birth. Children are highly valued. Because of their dependence on adults, they create the possibility of potential relationships between adults through kinship, biological or fictive. "Wise" women continually instruct others about the importance of human relationships. They admonish against becoming too attached to possessions, for these can be taken away easily. The reference used is "Remember slavery days." Therefore, one does not aspire to accumulate possessions but relies on one's self, an education which is "in your head," and relationships with others who can be "counted on." One way to build such relationships is through the care of children.

Two very strong beliefs, emphasized by virtually every elderly black woman to members of a younger generation, are the importance of family and the importance of religion. This chapter addresses these two issues.

Data are from fieldwork I conducted among a black urban population in the Pacific Northwest between 1979 and 1980, with continued intensive short periods of fieldwork since then. In this work, family matters were defined culturally as "women's area of concern." As a black woman, I was readily incorporated by "wise" women into discussions on family matters. Religion was quite different. My formal instruction came from a preacher, a "wise" man who sat me down with an indexed Bible and made me read passages that he, and only he, could interpret and analyze. When it became a matter of participating in church activities, I was assigned to the Nurses' Unit, a group of prestigious women who had the wisdom and the authority to monitor my behavior. Although I am a nurse, my nursing license was not the credential that allowed me to participate in this group. Rather, the preacher's perceptions of my interpersonal skills and my dedication to understanding the doctrines of the church were my credentials. These informants, the women who told me about families, the preacher, and the nurses, were respected elder members in their community, having reached the "age of wisdom."

OVERVIEW OF THE LITERATURE

A brief overview of selected references on the black family reveals that although the elderly are an integral part of the family they are not a major focus of black family literature. The exception is E. Franklin Frazier's classic study, *The Negro Family in the United States* (1939). The chapter devoted to "Granny" describes black grandmothers as wise, strong leaders. The 1960s literature focusing on women in the family is largely devoted to young black girls as unwed mothers (Moynihan 1965). Although this interest continues in subsequent literature, the focus shifts to issues of sex, marriage, and family (Staples 1973) as young girls reach womanhood (Ladner 1971; Dougherty 1978).

A study of older women by Jacquelyne J. Jackson (1972) finds similarities between married and single older black women in their instrumental and

Grandma and baby. Seattle University Publications Department.

affective relationships. The author suggests that relationships with oldest children and closest friends are most important. Faustine C. Jones (1973), writing about older women in families, describes the role of grandmother as highly respected and "lofty." They are a "source of love, strength, and stability for the black family. . . a steady, supporting influence, as well as a connecting link between branches of the extended family" (Jones 1973:19). Elmer P. Martin and Joanne M. Martin (1978) also explicitly address "the old" as members of extended families who impart "old-fashioned" values to "the young." More recently, Linda M. Burton and Vern L. Bengtson (1985) describe the timing of entry into grandparenthood for black women as critical in defining their role. Those women who enter this "elder" phase of life early (at ages twenty-five to thirty-eight) feel the pressure of role conflict and tension in the social support they receive. They perceive grandparenthood as a "tenuous" role. Those who enter grandparenthood "on time" (at ages forty-two to fifty-seven) have less conflict but can also feel the pressure of integrating family and occupational roles.

In this literature three salient points come through. First, marital status makes little difference to elderly black women in terms of role relationships. Second, grandmothers are highly respected individuals, and, third, early entry into grandmotherhood creates conflict in this role within the family.

Selected references from the literature on religion and blacks emphasize religion as an outlet for the oppressed. Religious beliefs, as Émile Durkheim (1915) suggests, are a collective representation that belongs to a whole group despite the fact that no one individual possesses total knowledge. Religion creates a social reality; this holds true for blacks and their religious outlook. Again, as with the literature on the family, there is no particular focus on the elderly in the literature on blacks and religion.

In one study on elderly blacks, Lena W. Myers (1978) describes religious participation as a way to help blacks cope with stress by offering material and emotional support. Elderly black women, specifically, believe that the church is important in this respect. Robert J. Taylor and Linda M. Chatters (1986) concur that church-based support is offered to black elderly especially during periods of illness. Similar to these findings, Gurdeep S. Khullar and Beverly Reynolds's (1985) study supports the thesis that females, blacks, and the elderly are the groups most likely to attend church services. However, contrary to these studies, their findings show blacks who score high on "religious participation" score lower than whites on "life satisfaction" indices. The reason for this finding is unclear. Economic security is the one intervening variable that markedly affects the association between "religious participation" and "life satisfaction." One can hypothesize that "life satisfaction" measures control over one's life, a feeling which many blacks do not share and the very reason they go to church. The church is perceived by these blacks as the one arena in which they have been able to maintain their cultural traditions in face of social ostracism, economic deprivation, and political marginality.

Peter Goldsmith (1985) also finds that religious participation is important among blacks in the Georgia Sea Islands. He suggests that ideological principles in church doctrine account for the differences between black Baptists and black Pentecostals. Baptists hold a belief of the accountability of the individual for life events, a view similar to the dominant white culture. They perceive a clear distinction between the scientific and religious spheres. On the other hand, Pentecostals embrace a holistic view of a "divinely directed social order" (Goldsmith 1985:94) in which it is impossible to separate healing from worship, mind from body, man from spirit, and natural being from social being. He then concludes that the use of healing in worship services can be seen as an index of nonacceptance of white culture by church members. This is noteworthy as, in the Pentecostal church discussed here, worship and religious matters are the concern of the preacher and the (male) elders only, whereas healing is also the concern of the wise women who are nurses.

Cheryl T. Gilkes (1985) explores the role of women in the Sanctified Church (of which the Church of God in Christ is the largest denomination) which emphasizes independence, education, economic status, and political autonomy. She finds that black women have been a well-organized force, self-reliant and economically independent since slavery. In the Pentecostal Church of God in Christ, where women are not allowed to preach from the pulpit, they have made a place as equal or interdependent with men. The powerful older women are leaders among church women (Gilkes 1986). The structure of the Pentecostal church is analyzed from a different perspective by Melvin D. Williams (1974). He describes a hierarchy of elite, core, supportive, and marginal members who range from socially close to socially distant to the pastor. The elite group includes powerful older women of the church.

The role of religion for older black women, as seen in this literature, is twofold. On the one hand, these women find within the church material and emotional support, especially in times of illness. On the other hand, the church offers them a place to gain power and exercise their leadership skills.

It is through the two themes of family and religion that the meaning of "maturing" and "age of wisdom" is elucidated in this chapter. The discussion on family centers around a wise woman, Lottie Waters (all names used are fictitious), who has "twice reached the age of wisdom." She is a great-grandmother and, like the wise women before her, keeps track of family relationships traced both through biological and nonbiological ties. The discussion on religion presents data on a group of respected wise church women known as "Mothers." In both instances, wise women are seen as organizers and leaders within their setting.

FAMILY

Here I want to introduce a woman who has reached the age of wisdom. She occupies a traditional family role, that "lofty" and respected position of

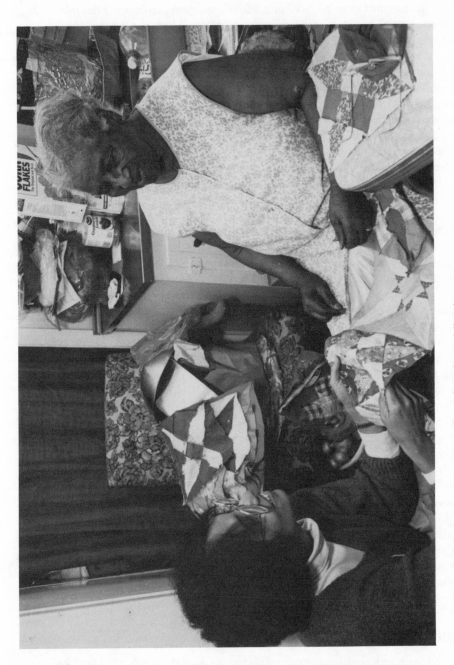

Great grandma and woman visitor. Seattle University Publications Department.

grandmother. She is also the nurturer and disciplinarian of children, the family historian, the hub of the family network in which decisions are made, and the convener of family events.

Mrs. Lottie Waters is a fifty-five-year-old great-grandmother who invited me to call her by her first name. She was born in a small rural town in southern Texas. When Lottie was born, her fifteen-year-old mother and her father lived with his older sister, Auntie Elsie, who became a midwife. Auntie Elsie and her mother, known to Lottie as Grandma Lucy, delivered Lottie. Lottie was "raised" by Grandma Lucy, who always retained parental rights and responsibilities over her, an uncle and his family, and Auntie Elsie.

Lottie, like her mother, delivered her first child when she was fifteen years old. Lottie says she did her best to "raise" her five children, giving them to Elsie to "keep" when she was unable to care for them. Elsie was by then a wise woman. When Lottie's second child, her oldest daughter, had her first child, Kermit, Lottie joined the ranks of wise women. She was thirty-two years old. When Kermit's first child was born, Lottie was fifty-two years old and her daughter thirty-five. Lottie celebrated being the mother of a wise woman as well as having "twice reached the age of wisdom." Lottie Waters's kinship (Figure 11.1) chart shows these relationships.

As a wise woman, Lottie was expected to care for children, her own and those of others. Often when she took her children to the park she "came upon childrun runnin' wild and unruly." She talked to them, teaching them right from wrong, and scolding them when necessary. It is not uncommon for the wise to admonish any youngster who is misbehaving. The wise do not need permission from biological parents to discipline children. It is their duty to teach any child should the opportunity present itself. It did not take long for these "unruly childrun" to call Lottie "Grandma," follow her home, eat with her, and a few even slept at her house. Two children stayed with her for over a year. As Lottie became mother to these children, their own relatives would visit, introduce themselves, and thank her for what she was doing for the children. Eventually, the adults would come to Lottie for advice in childraising or for themselves. Some would run errands for her; others would bring food or clothing. On one occasion she was given a car to "carry the children around."

Lottie's biological children considered all the children in the house brothers and sisters or sons and daughters, depending on their ages. When it came time to have a Waters family reunion, Lottie set the date and supervised its organization. She alone made up the invitation list. Those invited were all her grandchildren and those related to them. She was the anchor of a large family network held together by interactions involving children. All family members knew their obligation to her and honored the woman through whom they were all related. Lottie, the oldest, and her great-granddaughter, the youngest, were the center of attention on that day. Lottie says, "Had Grandma Lucy or Auntie Elsie been there they would have been honored with all manner of fine gifts."

Figure 11.1
Kinship Chart for Lottie Waters

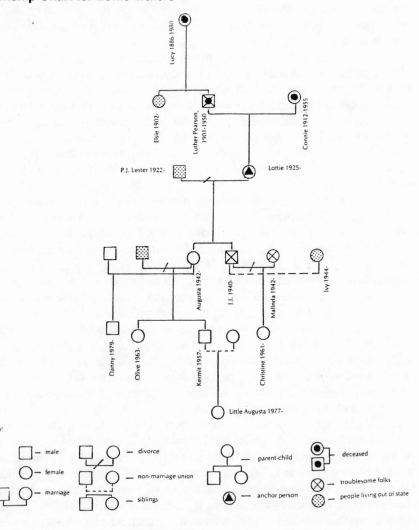

Key:

□ — male

○ — female

□○ — marriage

□―○ (with angled line) — divorce

□―○ (with dashed line) — non-marriage union

□---○ — siblings

○―□ — parent-child

▲ — anchor person

◉◉ / ◼ — deceased

⊗ — troublesome folks

⊙ — people living out of state

Mrs. Waters is considered a wise woman because she has "raised" two generations and is raising a third. She was fortunate also to have two living generations above her. Those in the younger generations know that only such a wise person can recite a family history. Such a request is honored only when the "wise one" is ready. The task of keeping track of family ties is no easy matter. Wise women, like the griots of West Africa, train and practice this oral skill until they have mastered it. Recounting and reckoning family is still part of an enduring tradition.

The "wisest of wise" were those, like Lottie's ninety-three-year-old grandmother Lucy, who seldom but with great ceremony correct a "wise" one or who are used to legitimize a recitation. No one would dare question Grandma Lucy's description of Lottie's birth. Grandma Lucy saw the caul over Lottie's face at her birth.[1] This unusual circumstance is believed to be a sign of an exceptional child. It is only by Grandma Lucy's account that Lottie's unusual birth is legitimately documented. When Lottie is challenged on incidents in her recitation of the family history, Grandma Lucy with a simple gesture could acknowledge Lottie as a wise woman not to be questioned and scold the questioner for daring to challenge a wise woman.

The position of wise women is also seen in childraising. As one reads even fragments of Lottie's life history one notes that she talks about "havin' children," "raisin' children," and "keepin' children." Her distinctions have to do with giving birth, being a parent with the rights and responsibilities that accompany this, and babysitting or temporarily taking care of children, which may be for extended periods of time. The relationship between children and adults or between adults is always clear to those involved. Thus, children can be biological or nonbiological. Because biological parents are not always mature enough to raise their own children, mature or "wise" women can parent or co-parent with biological parents. Thus a child can be "recruited" into a family (LaFargue 1981). This means a child might have several mothers and/or fathers. Terms of address and reference for all parents are the same. Lottie had five children; she "kept" many others, feeding and clothing them; and she raised her five plus the two who stayed for an extended period. Her experience with children means that as a grandmother she will be "wise." She will be sought for her wisdom and life experiences.

In analyzing Lottie Waters's account, the role of wise woman as nurturer and disciplinarian is seen. Wise women "keep" and "raise" children. They make a significant contribution to the family in this role both in teaching values to youngsters, as Martin and Martin (1978) suggest, and in freeing adults to concentrate on their occupational pursuits.

The wise are also the family historians, as Frazier (1939) found. Lottie fixes her place in the generations as Grandma Lucy's granddaughter and Kermit's grandmother. Her cultural identity as having reached the age of wisdom is secure. She is also the one to prove through the recitation of the family history that her daughter reached that stage with the birth of her son's child. However,

Lottie says her mother never reached the "age of wisdom." Her mother is literally in the same generation as her great-great-grandchild, as neither has raised any children. Lottie can verify that others have reached the age of wisdom or can cast doubt on their life circumstances and retard, if not prevent, entry into that stage of life. She can do this because all important family matters such as parent-child relationships are brought to her. Her decisions are final: only a wise person in a generation above her can reverse her decisions. Older people in this community are vulnerable if they have not raised a child. They have no markers to show they are maturing. They are treated like young persons, who have not yet learned to act responsibly and be accountable for their actions.

Lottie Waters became, at age thirty-two, what Burton and Bengtson (1985) call an "off-time" grandmother. But unlike the off-time grandmothers they discuss, she had a clear position in her family and clear functions to perform. Her fifty-five-year-old aunt and seventy-one-year-old grandmother mentored and prepared her for this role. Lottie's daughter expected her child's grandmother to be someone strong, independent, and one whom she could count on for sage advice. The extended family supported Lottie with services, goods, love, status, and information when she entered this phase of her life. Her family role was clear: she had achieved the status of wise woman. The only socially meaningful marker of time for Lottie is the passing of generations. She may become wiser with each generation, but it is never spoken of as "older." Grandma Lucy was grandmother to all generations except her children's. It was only when Grandma Lottie called Lucy "Grandma" that one had any inkling of Lottie's chronological age.

Children are highly valued by black families in general (Achenbrenner 1975; LaFargue 1981) and by the Waterses in particular. Not only do they demand cooperation from adults for their care and create the potential for increasing adult relationships, they also mark an adult's place in terms of which generation he or she belongs to. The family reunion stresses the relationship between generations. Lottie is the anchor of her family network. The relationship between child and grandparent forms the basic structure of the family. As Lottie says, "All those related to my grandbabies are my family, and they are welcome." The young parent generation knows that they depend on their children to establish their place in the family and on the wisdom of their parent to legitimize their place in the family. The greater the number of generations between the old and the young the more prestige the wise person is accorded.

RELIGION

The following data come from fieldwork with the Refuge Church of God in Christ. Members of this church refer to themselves as "Pentecostals, Holiness people, or Holy Rollers." The literature also refers to them as members of the Sanctified Church (Hurston 1983; Gilkes 1985). The Refuge Church is part of the larger Church of God in Christ, International. It is Pentecostal in nature because of the belief that the Holy Ghost resides in all believers. The outward sign of a believer is the ability to speak in tongues as occurred on the Day of Pentecost. The church has a formal structure with traditional gender-defined roles for its members, yet "it is well understood that men and women complement each other" (Curtis and Cyars, n.d.:1).

In the church there are age-grades which cross-cut specific gender roles. For females, these are best exemplified in some of the auxiliaries of the Women's Department. They are: the Cradle Roll for newborns to age four, the Sunshine Band for ages five through twelve, Purity Classes for ages twelve through nineteen, the Young Women's Christian Council (YWCC) for nineteen to "indefinite," and the Church Mother's Board, exclusively for wise women, with no specific age stated. The first three age-grades, for ages up to nineteen, are mixed girls and boys. The last two age-grades are sex-specific. The age range is not specified for the YWCC but includes the years of "college, marriage, and motherhood" (Curtis and Cyars, n.d.:32). The Mother's Board is composed of women who have raised their children and have also shown a commitment to the church both in their participation in activities and financially. They are able and willing to assume leadership positions within the church organization. They have reached the age of wisdom.

The church uses a reference from Scripture as the basis of its definition of a wise woman: "Let not a widow be taken into the number [of elders] under three-score years old, having been the wife of one man, well reported of for good works; if she have brought up children, if she have lodged strangers, if she have washed the saints' feet, if she have relieved the afflicted, if she have diligently followed every good work" (I Timothy 5:9–10). This passage serves to legitimize women over sixty as "wise." It names the activities a wise woman should have engaged in and reflects values held high by the church.

Within the men's age-grade, "elder" is used to designate those men who have reached the age of wisdom. However, the church precludes the use of the word "elder" for women (Range 1973:159–60). "Mother" is the term of reference and address used for such women. One refers to a Mother by saying, for example, "Mother Gibson will lead the prayer group on Friday." Addressing her as "Mrs. Gibson" is a sign of disrespect or the mark of an outsider. A woman who is a member of the YWCC and a biological mother is referred to as a new or young mother and addressed as "Sister."

Age brings status, respect, and prestige to women who have raised a child. Only Mothers teach and instruct and are "seasoned and well informed" (Curtis and Cyars, n.d.:18). They understand their obligations to others. Mothers are in leadership positions within the Women's Department of the Church and have the ability to informally cross gender role lines and influence the elders. Wise women in the Refuge Church of God in Christ are economically autonomous and are the main fundraisers and contributors of the church. It is a combination of these factors plus Mothers' special knowledge about birth, their experience with illness and death, and their strong faith that gives them their power. This is what makes them part of what Williams (1974) calls the elite group, a group in which gender lines are crossed. Among the Mothers, one is chosen to be the Mother of the Church. This Mother has the most experience, shows a deep commitment to the church, is of unquestionable faith, is well versed in the Bible, and has alliances with many groups in the church. She is recommended by the Mother's Board to the Pastor who appoints her Mother of the Church. This is a lifelong position and the highest one a woman can attain. Because of physical illness or inability to carry out her duties, the Mother of the Church may retire. However, she is still treated with utmost reverence.

The entire denomination stresses education. A Mother who is an educator with "book learning," experience, and oratory skills is highly regarded. The Church Mother is the only female sanctioned to teach from the pulpit. She takes the occasion to reinforce passages from the Bible, restate acceptable codes of behavior, and remind the congregation of what it means to be a Mother. She usually ends her teaching on an inspirational note. The fourth Sunday of every month is Mother's Day, and the collection taken up at that service goes to her. In turn she uses the money for her own "necessities" and distributes the rest to Mothers in key leadership positions for their work in the Department of Women.

One of the Refuge Church of God in Christ's most important units within the Department of Women is the Nurses' Unit. This unit is composed of women with certain characteristics. They are understanding people, have excellent communication skills, are experienced taking care of the ill, can work compassionately with alcohol- and drug-related problems (two areas the church has targeted), and have a strong religious faith. Most nurses are also Mothers. A license in nursing is needed by only one member to satisfy the legal requirement for giving medications.

Nurses "serve at meetings, on trips, in the home, funerals or whatever and whenever there is a need for their service" (Curtis and Cyars, n.d.:33). This ability to move in and out of settings is permitted of only a few groups within the church.

For nurses in the Refuge Church of God in Christ, treatment is holistic. The areas of spiritual, mental, and physical health spelled out in the *Official Manual with the Doctrines and Discipline of the Church of God in Christ* (Range 1973) overlap in actual practice. However, they are discrete conceptual categories that guide the nurse in her assessment and diagnosis of clients. The spiritual dimension is treated with prayer, scriptural reading, and interpretations of biblical passages. The mental health dimension is treated with counseling, teaching, and a recommitment to belief in God along with visible proof through practice. Giving up of "evil practices" (such as smoking and dancing) and being able to have a positive self-regard and high self-esteem are important. The physical aspect is treated with herbs, ointments, teas, and referral to professional medical help when necessary.

Among nurses there is a hierarchy. The younger nurses focus primarily on the physical aspects; then with experience and increased understanding of the

Bible, they work with the mental and the spiritual problems of others. This latter area is dominated by nurses who are strong in faith and have much experience in successfully healing others. These are nurses who are also Mothers. Only they can care for persons "between," those who are vulnerable to being possessed by spirits or of having their spirits leave their bodies "between worlds." This can occur when a person is unconscious, dying, or during a seizure. At such a time a nurse-mother is needed to protect the ill. This is most clearly seen during the dying process.

During the course of my fieldwork, Mrs. Ella Wilcox, a ninety-eight-year-old retired Mother of the Church, died. Just before her death, the Mother of the Church called the head of the Nurses's Unit, a renowned nurse-mother in her mid-seventies, and asked her to be present when Mother Wilcox died. The nurse-mother was to make sure that the death was peaceful and that Mother's body, soul, and spirit were one at the time of death.

In anticipation of her death no artificial orifices were to be made in her body. Mother Wilcox's body should be whole. The spirit is known to be able to leave a body of a sleeping or comatose person and wander around. At the time of death, to be whole means that the body, the soul, and the spirit are together. Because Mother Wilcox was comatose and becoming increasingly weaker, several nurse-mothers kept vigil at her bedside. At times they cried and made noise to call the spirit back to the body should it have wandered off. At other times they were quiet and subdued so as not to call the spirit out of the body should it be in the body.

In analyzing perceptions of the elderly in this Pentecostal church, it is necessary to understand the traditions that underlie the practices observable to the anthropologist. Such tradition is the belief in the wisdom of the ancestors and those who have lived experiences. There is also a belief in the need to keep separate the world of the spirits and the world of the living. Nurse-mothers carefully mediate between these two worlds.

The church reflects the community's values and its social structure. The Church Mother is the center of a redistribution system in which women pool resources and from which they receive material and social support. Such was the case when services were pooled during Mother Wilcox's death. Independent from men, women have built their own social structure within the church. Elders and Mothers have complementary roles in the church. They are like fathers and mothers in families. They preside over religious celebrations which affirm life. Who better to give meaning to life than those who have reached the age of wisdom? For they know of what they speak when they celebrate life.

Church members respect their Mothers. Mothers are looked to for advice. Their knowledge of history, their lived experience, and religious faith give them access to information others do not have. This is the source of their power. Although the Pentecostal church has a clear and strong patriarchal structure, women have created an alternative structure which provides them with power and authority. Mothers in this religious setting are foremost spiritual role models. They are the powerful, capable women who can provide or mobilize both material and emotional support for persons in need. They are the teachers who endorse power through education. They are the nurses who combine healing with worship. Nurse-mothers simultaneously protect the dying and the living while managing the spirit and everyday worlds. They are among the most powerful and feared women in the church, for they walk between the sacred and the profane.

CONCLUSION

The age of wisdom is a venerated life stage in the black community I studied. I have drawn from both the family and religion to shed light on the meaning of "maturing" and "the wise" for this particular group. The women I have focused on are actively engaged in work which is essential to the continuation of the family and the church. Their wisdom, gained through lived experience, is both sought and respected by others.

Comparing the literature on elderly black women in the family and Lottie Waters, one notes that indeed marital status makes little difference. It is hardly mentioned in the Waters family. However, tracing relationships through children and imparting values to the young are seen as essential roles of a wise woman. Unlike the literature cited, Lottie's status is conferred by both preceding generations who know of her parenting ability and subsequent generations who establish her position within the family structure. For Lottie, there was minimal conflict in terms of role, despite her "off-time" entry into grandmotherhood. This may be due to the generational pattern of early motherhood followed by early grandmotherhood with the expectation that older women (Aunt Elsie and Grandma Lucy) provided guidance. As a grandmother, regardless of chronological age, Lottie is highly respected.

Comparing the literature on religion and the ethnographic data from the Refuge Church of God in Christ, it is evident that older women can find material and emotional support in the church. However, the data do not emphasize this. What is described are the services wise women contribute to the church. Specific details of these activities are sparse in the literature. Notwithstanding, the ethnography concurs with the literature when describing wise women who can and do receive prestige and power based on experience, knowledge, and service separately from men in the Pentecostal Church.

Both in the family and in the church, experience, not chronological age, is considered the primary criterion for entry into the age of wisdom. For black women in the family this translates into raising a child who can make one's mother a grandmother. This value is also strong in the Refuge Church of God in Christ. However, there is the added dimension that wise women in the church must also possess profound religious faith and behave in the manner described in Scripture. Although this age is acknowledged to be sixty, it is not by accident that the Church of God in Christ does not give an age range for members of the

Mother's Board. Some women meet the criteria for entry into the Mother's Board before age sixty. Therefore, members of this board range in age from mid-forties up. Nurses' ages vary widely. A few nurses are young mothers, members of the YWCC who have the gift of healing, highly developed interpersonal skills, and show a commitment to study church doctrine. These women are permitted to join the Nurses's Unit before they have entered "the age of wisdom." Most nurses, however, are wise women who belong to the Mother's Board and also have the gift to heal.

Aging connotes lived experience. In the family, moving from one generation to the next and raising a child are the experiences women must have in order to reach the age of wisdom. In the church these experiences, as well as being spirit-filled, monitoring life transitions (mainly birth and death) and teaching, are the primary routes to gaining experience and hence becoming a "Mother."

Neither in the family nor in the church do people refer to the elderly as "old." Whether a woman is thirty-two or seventy-one, she can be described as single, a mother, a grandmother, healthy, disabled or ill—but not "old." Old age for black women is a matter of the functions they carry out. For wise women in families this is creating relationships, teaching values, and convening the family on certain occasions. In the church Mothers are religious role models; they establish a system of support for women and children, mediate between the secular and sacred worlds when necessary, and maintain independent but collaborative relationships with men in the church. Grandmothers in families and Mothers in churches are the women who have reached the age of wisdom.

NOTE

1. A child is said to be born with a caul or veil if the amnion or inner membrane of the sac which contains the fetus and amniotic fluid does not rupture and covers the infant's head at birth.

12 ETHNIC IDENTITY AND BEREAVEMENT IN LATER LIFE: THE CASE OF OLDER WIDOWERS

Mark R. Luborsky and Robert L. Rubinstein

Culture shapes people's beliefs and experiences, and these, in turn, shape culture. Anthropologists not only study the relationship of person to culture in small-scale societies, which may have a relatively uniform culture, they also examine the role of culture in complex societies, such as the United States.

Ethnic identity exists within complex societies and at the boundaries between all societies. An ethnic identity, with its values, beliefs, and behaviors, is often considered to be a subculture within a larger shared culture. A part of culture, it is a phenomenon that anthropologists have examined with increasing interest. But people and circumstances change over time. Elsewhere (Luborsky and Rubinstein 1987) we suggest that ethnic identity be thought of as something with both "solid" and "fluid" properties. By this we mean that there is something ideally unchanging or irreducible about ethnic identity which gives it an enduring flavor of tradition, yet the experience of ethnic identity may change from situation to situation. So we see that ethnic identity is something that people can have to differing degrees. It is not fixed at birth but is sensitive to historic events, as well as to social, personal, and life-span developmental events. We need to understand more about how individual and group conceptions of ethnic identity may change over time and how people use ethnicity to achieve a sense of continuity despite change.

There is often confusion about the relationship among ethnic identity, religion, and family life. In one view, the family is the focal point of ethnic identity, because it is within the family that ethnic values and behaviors are transmitted. We have found, in addition, ethnicity may serve as a language or metaphor for family relations and processes. Ethnic background and religion are not always the same. In some cases, such as Judaism, religious and ethnic identities usually correspond, while for others, such as Catholicism, it may not.

Our view is that family life and religion are separate, important aspects of ethnic identity. Catholicism may be equally important to Poles, Italians, and Irish, but each group has its own ways of observing the religious traditions, and, for members of each, participation in religious activities may be an important expression of their distinct ethnic identity as well as religious belief.

Social gerontologists and others who study old age and the elderly find that ethnic identity is an important aspect of how we age. One difficulty in studying this issue, however, is that ethnic identity is built up from interwoven conscious and unconscious behaviors and beliefs. For example, a person may willfully behave in an ethnic way (by attending an ethnic festival), or may unconsciously behave ethnically, as when reacting to the experience of pain (Zborowski 1969) or in craving certain foods. Or an individual may consciously reject his or her present-day ethnic group but unconsciously retain some traditional beliefs and attitudes. Despite these complexities, it is clear that ethnicity does account for significant differences in a wide variety of life experiences including: how people face physical pain (Zborowski 1969); their ideas about illness and death (Suchman 1964; Kalish and Reynolds 1976); types of family relationships (Cohler and Grunebaum 1981; Wylan and Mintz 1976); the context of life crises and ritual (Myerhoff 1978a, 1978b); alcohol consumption (Greeley et al. 1980); institutionalization (Markson 1979); and mental health and mental illness (Al-Issa 1982).

THE RESEARCH

The study described in this chapter concerns such questions about ethnic identity. We report on a project conducted at the Philadelphia Geriatric Center involving Irish, Jewish, and Italian men (N = 45), age sixty-five and older, widowed two to eight years after a long-term marriage. We questioned them about how they reorganized their lives after the initial bereavement period, the first two years, had passed. The focus is on how they reformulated their sense of identity, on changes in health and activity patterns, ethnic identity, and lingering attachment to the deceased spouse. One goal of the study is to discover how ethnic identity shapes or is shaped by the bereavement experience. The focus on men led us to examine this question without confounding gender differences.

Loss — especially the death of a loved one — is one of the most significant and difficult human experiences. Research has shown how those surviving the death of a significant other may pass through a number of experiential stages leading to some kind of acceptance and reorganization (Bowlby 1980). Often the key to the recovery from loss is a period in which many kinds of attachments to the deceased remain and are only gradually relinquished. Although a person may "recover" and return to an active life, ties to a deceased loved one are never fully let go.

As we get older, loss becomes more and more a part of the experience of life. The death of a spouse in late life can be especially difficult, not merely for the emotional distress of the loss itself, but also for the social and psychological challenges it brings to the survivor to shape a new, whole life. A good deal of research has been done on this topic. Areas which have received the most detailed investigation include the experience of widowhood for women (Lopata 1973, 1979), the first year or two of adjustment after the death of a spouse (Glick, Weiss, and Parkes 1974; Parkes and Weiss 1983), and the question of whether men and women differ in how they react to their grief (Arens 1982; Berardo 1970; Gallagher et al. 1983). The focus on these topics is not surprising, since women tend to outlive men, the first two years may be most difficult, and because of deeply embedded gender differences in American culture. The topics of the study we describe here, the experiences of men and ethnic differences in long term readjustment have received little study.

We selected the Irish, Italians, and Jews because of the lack of qualitative material on so-called white ethnics in later life and because of the large populations of these groups in metropolitan areas in the United States, including the Philadelphia area. Today, many elders from these backgrounds are first or second generation immigrants. The countries from which these immigrants' ancestors hailed maintained distinctive cultural and religious traditions. Influenced by a new society and the rapid changes of twentieth-century American life, many customary practices and beliefs have disappeared. Others have disappeared for a time, only to resurface in new ways, while still others, both conscious and unconscious, have been preserved or modified to fit with life as it is today.

Each of the three ethnic groups studied is distinctive. Some important features of Irish-American culture are the central role accorded to the Church, the importance of verbal talent and ability, a focus on propriety, a sense of suffering, emotional repression, the use of alcohol, and a focus on death as a central life passage (McGoldrick, Pearce, and Giordano 1982). Important features of Italian-American culture include a concern with keeping a tight-knit family life; an emphasis on sharing and eating food; the family as the unit that provides security, identity, and affection; a focus on the expression of emotions and feelings; strong parental roles; and an emphasis on marriage as a central life passage (Rotunno and McGoldrick 1982; Johnson 1985). Important features of Jewish-American culture include the centrality of the family; an ethos of enduring hardships; a high value on intellectual achievement, learning, and success; highlighting of verbal expressions of feelings; and a focus on life-cycle events such as *bris* (circumcision) and *Bar Mitzvah* (ritual passage to manhood) (Herz and Rosen 1982). While on the surface some characteristics, such as the central value of the family, may be equally important for all groups, there are deep differences in their cultural styles of conducting family relationships.

SOME CASE STUDIES

Here we discuss the role ethnic identity plays in overcoming a profound challenge to one's personal identity in later life, such as that occurring through loss. Our goal is to reveal the nature of ethnic identity and differences in later life and to show how they operate after a loss. Again, we need to note that adjustment to loss is complex, involving influences such as health, personality characteristics, opportunities, social support, the historical situation, in addition to ethnic style. We suggest, however, that ethnic identity, while often overlooked by researchers, can represent an individual's most central values and symbols and, as such, is especially worthy of examination in order to understand how people come to grips with change and maintain continuity of self despite change.

In order to encourage readers to put together their own views of how ethnicity intertwines with other factors, we prepared three studies of how widowers from each ethnic group reacted to widowerhood. We describe a widower's background, the events surrounding his wife's death and his reactions to it, and an account of ethnic identity as part of this. We hope to make clear differing patterns of experiencing the loss, of reactions to widowerhood, and the course of reorganizing a new life.

Morris Stern: Case One

Morris Stern is a quiet, youthful seventy-nine-year-old man who lives alone. Married forty-three years, he has been a widower for five years. He worked in his family's wholesale business after college until retiring eight years ago. His children, grandchildren, and siblings live near him.

Mr. Stern repeatedly described his life as "not over exciting, but enjoyable." To learn what he saw as stages in his life, we asked him, "If you wrote your autobiography, what would be the chapters?" (a task we asked of each subject); he enumerated four chapters. First was "early days," consisting of close friends and school life. Second was college and a new circle of friends. Married life was the largest chapter he reported. The last chapter consisted of the period of his retirement and his wife's death. They shared three years together after he retired. Mrs. Stern had developed heart trouble four years before dying. Because her health declined slowly, few restrictions were imposed on their life until her final year, when Mr. Stern took over all daily tasks. For some time he was able to care for her, and he felt that the time allowed him to prepare ahead for her death. Of his current life, he noted, "I enjoy myself without a hectic existence."

Mr. Stern, a Jew, said his parents emigrated from Poland to escape poverty and discrimination. Today, he belongs to a conservative temple and volunteers delivering kosher meals to homebound elderly. Most of his friends are Jewish, and being Jewish is important to him. Key to his life now, his wife is credited with making him more aware of being Jewish. Together they regularly attended religious services and kept Sabbath observances at home. Her family was, in his eyes, "part of the Great Jewish Tradition."

Traditional mourning customs which he followed scrupulously included daily prayers and breakfast at a synagogue. This provided a daily structure to his life and helped him recover during the period of grief after her death. "It did me good to go daily to the synagogue to say prayers and to honor her memory," at a time during which he reported feeling despondent and aggravated. He observed the tradition of *shiva* — a household gathering of family and friends for seven days after a death — in the home of his son and said prayers with them daily for a month. "It was a big help because I was retired and there was nothing else to stop me from just sitting and moping." One month is the traditional observance, but he attended both morning and evening services for eleven months. In addition, these practices let him meet other people who themselves were overcoming losses. It was also important to him to feel part of a community of fellow observers. Thus, just as each chapter of his life featured a new circle of friends, so too did the bereavement period.

The difficulties he encountered in adjusting to his wife's death included learning the daily tasks such as cooking, washing clothes, and housecleaning. These were "low on my totem pole when she was here." He felt these difficulties despite her teaching him some skills the year before she died. Many friends told him he would be remarried within one year, but he was not interested in dating. Another dimension of this period was a "great sense of uncertainty about what to expect next."

One year later, he said, he no longer lamented his fate and began to live again. "I surprised myself by taking it in the right light, taking things for what they are." He spoke of a transformation of his feelings about the loss. Formerly he was preoccupied with "lamenting what might have been," but later came to accept and enjoy those people and activities which are present. Part of this new perspective hinged on fully accepting that his wife was dead and would not be back.

Mr. Stern's Jewish identity provided him with key dimensions of continuity in the face of the loss he experienced, as well as a framework for daily life through customary mourning observances at the outset of widowerhood. One important resource for him, he reported, was his family. "I had their cooperation, but never told them the big things, they were good to me." That is, he felt he never burdened them with his feelings of loneliness, depression, and loss but relied for uplifts on their continued visits, talking, and sympathy. Perhaps, more subtly, the religious observances instilled by his wife allowed him to keep alive sentiments and her presence in his life in a positive fashion. That is, by attending the funeral services and mourning practices over the months after her death, he was not only honoring her memory but was thereby also performing roles that relived important experiences they shared when she was alive.

Horace McGraw: Case Two

Horace McGraw is a sixty-six-year-old Irish man, stout, and with a sharp brand of humor. He lives in a squalid room in a run-down area. Married for thirty years, but childless, he was bereaved six years ago.

Mr. McGraw left high school before graduating to begin a career of unskilled labor, mostly loading trucks. A heavy smoker and an alcoholic (not drinking now), he suffers health problems including emphysema, high blood pressure, and diabetes. Today his social network consists of only three "others" — a sister, a niece, and "TV, one of my best friends."

His parents came from Ireland, and he grew up in a mostly Irish neighborhood. His family shopped only in stores run by Irish, and he got into "good fights" with Irish kids in the next parish after baseball games. Reportedly, his family "keeps up the old-fashioned stuff, speaking in heavy brogues," and they continue traditions such as wakes. He mused, "Sometimes it is hard to believe we carried the casket after the drinking." Most of his family are Catholic; Protestant converts are outcast members. That may represent tension between upwardly mobile Irish who are taking positions once held by a WASP elite and the mostly urban, middle-class and lower-class Irish who retain positions traditionally held by Irish immigrants.

In discussing his life as an autobiography, he labeled the final chapter of his wife's death and the changes in his health and lifestyle as "my craziness." His wife died suddenly of a heart attack just after they returned home from shopping; she had been in good health. After her death he went unshaven and unwashed for many months, "lacking a purpose in life." To him, it was like "living in a dream," as it all seemed unreal. "It seemed like everything was closing in on me." He moved in with his sister right away, but after growing tensions with her husband he moved out. From the time of the funeral he developed an alcohol dependence so severe that he lost his job, sold his home at a tremendous loss for drinking money, and alienated all his friends. For a time, he feared having a nervous breakdown.

A typical day for him during this period included visiting his sister for two hours every morning. Then he went to a bar and stayed until closing time. After staggering home he was unable to sleep well and watched TV, he reported. He sold everything in order to have money for drinking. He lost weight and had "an appetite only for beer."

The bouts of drinking were certainly self-destructive behavior, but in addition were a mechanism for coping with pain and feelings of loss and, further, were perhaps a way to rekindle a sense of earlier family life and Irish traditions — "the old days" and the milieu in which he met his wife. In a sense, he also returned to some basic identity by drinking in the manner he believed people did in the past.

This bleak period ended with the help of a friend who, typical of Mr. McGraw's relationships, he later alienated. This person pulled him aside, got him treatment for alcoholism, and arranged for him to be reinstated at work and in his union. Mr. McGraw stayed sober, and after more than two years of intense grief, began to put his life in order. The friend helped give him "a reason to live again," taking him fishing after work and doing things with him. Now, however, he was living in poverty, with only a small veteran's disability pension and without the house he and his wife shared for twenty years.

He not only stopped drinking, he "got religion" again. One day he met the local priest and asked to be allowed back in the Church because, he said, he was "afraid of dying," and also "needed to do something socially." Since he had not been to Confession or Mass in many years, he first went to a church that saw many transients and was lenient concerning Confession. After going to Confession and Mass there, he returned to the mostly Irish parish where he lived (and in which he had grown up) and could tell the priest he had been to Confession and Mass recently. Church attendance, he believed, led him to "face the fact of her death and that nothing would bring her back." He came to believe that grieving "must be cut off, or like gangrene it will kill you."

"Getting religion" marked a period which he describes as one in which the grief is still with him but is not overwhelming. He is no longer self-destructive. He is still lonely and longs for his wife at times. He does not go often to the gravesite as he gets upset just thinking about her.

Vito Crazza: Case Three

Vito Crazza is a sixty-five-year-old Italian man whose wife died six years ago. He lives in a very Italian, tight-knit, poor neighborhood, in the same row house in which he was born. His father died when the oldest of nine children was fifteen; some of his siblings were put up for adoption. As a child he worked with his family harvesting crops to earn money to heat the house. He worked a variety of jobs until, suffering an incapacitating injury, he opened and ran a small corner grocery store (offered by a neighborhood *paesano* at a low price) until a heart attack forced retirement.

He suffers from multiple health problems yet is able to perform all the daily tasks for himself. Having suffered many losses of friends and family, he is often depressed. While his remaining friends, family, and acquaintances are very close at hand, he views himself today as isolated. He misses many lifelong ties and the Italian life of the past, recalled when he walks the neighborhood streets and sees many strangers and new stores. Being Italian is very important to him, and most of his friends are of Italian descent. He speaks what he calls "an Americanized Italian." However, after the death of his favorite sister, with whom he participated in religious events, he "gave up regular church and the Italian community stuff."

He pools his monthly cash with a sister and her husband, and he eats with them at their house, seldom cooking or eating in the house he shared with his wife. Yet despite, or perhaps because of, ambivalence toward his wife which he felt throughout their marriage, he now experiences a deep sense of longing for her.

The chapters of his life story concern "day and night" differences between the impoverished but happy and healthy childhood and today's sadder life with

TV, telephones, and adequate heat in winter. He often feels that the world is against him today, and all his old friends and family members are dead. About three years before his wife's death they had experienced marital strife, and he left to live with a sister two houses away. A severe heart problem led the family doctor to advise him to either move out or settle things with his wife. He reported that they had argued constantly, but later in life it had become especially acrimonious.

His wife underwent a double mastectomy and apparently recovered fully. Thereafter, he had "started coming back to her," but the meaning of this was unclear since he still lived with his sister. He intended it to mean that they had become closer again. Six months before her death his wife fell down the stairs and had surgery to repair a damaged vertebra, during which widespread cancer was discovered. She stayed in the hospital; he was not told of the cancer although other family members, he believes, knew of her serious condition. Two months before her death, their son finally told him. Still, the son, a player in their strife-ridden family arena, would not let his father visit her. Mr. Crazza had to stay away because it was felt that if he visited her, she would know her death was near. It was deemed more important to keep up the proper front of "business as usual," although this was produced by unresolved conflict, rather than resolving existing conflicts. He did talk daily with her by phone, however.

When his wife died, he experienced additional health problems which he related to "nerves" caused by the stress of her death. Not unexpectedly, arranging the funeral and burial plot led to bitter family arguments. She was buried in a Catholic cemetery with others from her family. He will not be buried with her, but rather with his oldest sister elsewhere. He reported being grief-stricken, depressed, and remorseful over her death. It took six months to "get over the worst part," including his concerns about having a nervous breakdown. He repeatedly emphasized how he tried to "make amends" before she died but never made things up to her satisfactorily.

Two months after her death, while passing by their house (vacant, because he felt he could not live there), he noted, "Finally I decided, it is my house," and his son and sister helped him move back. A typical day for him at this time consisted of spending time with his diabetic sister, eating his meals there, going for long walks, and passing the evenings at his own home. He confided that Italian mourning customs prohibit "amusements," including radio and television after a death, but to escape his grief he watched TV with tightly closed curtains so that no one could see the light.

Today, his feelings of grief and remorse continue unabated, he reported. The enduring sense of abandonment is exacerbated by his bad health and multiple losses of friends and family with whom, as with his wife, he had conflictual relationships. He still has dreams of his wife in which they are fighting, and, he reported, in the mornings he fears going downstairs just as he did when living with her. At other times he awakens, believing that she is talking downstairs, and calls to her. He concludes that he feels worse now than when she was alive.

Romanticizing about the past of a close Italian neighborhood, friendships, commensality, and the presence of his wife, he states, "When she was alive I was making a decent living with the store and buying her stuff. It was good then. As kids, we told my mother, 'Do we gotta eat this crap macaroni again?' Now, we miss it and go to restaurants for it. Same with missing my wife. Living at home, I couldn't stand it. She nagged about all the little things, and with my heart condition, as well. But now I think back and miss it."

ETHNIC DIMENSIONS OF WIDOWERS' LIFE REORGANIZATIONS

Morris Stern, Horace McGraw, and Vito Crazza each faced the same objective event, the loss of a spouse after many years of marriage. While there were similarities among their reactions, there also were contrasts in their experiences and behaviors when constructing new lives as widowers. The three cases summarize the experiences of men of their ethnic group and some of the areas in which ethnic identity enters into reorganization after a traumatic event such as a loss. These cases suggest that ethnicity is significant to bereavement life reorganizations in several ways.

As individuals, the men revealed some general features of widowerhood, despite the specifics of ethnic backgrounds. Most significant was that the wife's death left them with a sense of social isolation and loss of a singularly important intimate confidant. There was only some diminution in the sense of attachment to their wives over time. That was coupled with a need to come to understand who one now was in the world, the need to face later life alone, and a heightened concern for a meaningful family life.

These findings are interesting in light of theories about recovery from grief. Freud posited that recovery from grief was marked by the replacement of the lost one with another. Myerhoff (1978b), however, suggests that for the elderly recovery from grief involves integrating memories and values of the deceased into current life, not replacement.

The cases also show an increased involvement with activities of earlier family and locale which themselves may be infused with traditional ethnic sentiments and practices. Each man's distinctive heritage was a potential basis for involvement in a community of spirit — both religious and cultural — and in social ties. The men may re-form parts of their identities around central ethnic values and themes; some of these are discussed below. Yet while such involvement may foster a new life, there is also a sense of the possibility of reinvolvement with ways from earlier in life when each man was single and times were quite different. In a certain sense, it is the fact of being single again that helps to rekindle memories of how things used to be and forges unexpected continuities where a discontinuity existed while their wives were alive.

What elements of reorganization does ethnicity provide for in a concrete way? First, ethnic identity, itself, regardless of specific differences among the ethnic groups discussed here, provides dimensions of continuity for facing a major late life disjunction such as widowerhood. The raw material for continuity is provided both by conscious and by unconscious ethnic behaviors and feelings that may emerge in times of stress. From the array of raw material, each individual selects those behaviors or feelings that suit his psychological and social needs and creates new meanings, patterns of involvement, and activities. Ethnic identity thus provides a sense of continuity through both identification with and participation in (1) what are idealized as enduring traditional values, sentiments, and practices and (2) guides as to what to do in times of stress. Ethnic identity may be infused with early family values, sentiments, and actions. A refocusing on these can provide a desired sense of rootedness in a time of turmoil. Such continuity was clear for all three men described here. We thus see in the context of late life and bereavement that the widowers draw on different elements of their ethnicity to revivify their lives, including religion, the parish and synagogue, and family traditions.

Those findings accord with Gananath Obeyesekere's (1982) view that commitment to one's ethnic identity is enhanced, or revitalized, when commitments to other identities have weakened through social, local, and individual lifetime changes. But note that we also saw how revitalizing ethnic and family traditions also may awaken past difficulties or old feelings of loss or anxiety about one's family or cultural heritage. This was especially so for Mr. Crazza, for whom neighborhood change was utilized as a means of expressing his continuing sadness.

Among the three ethnic groups major contrasts also emerged in our study. Each, in a sense, conceived of different meanings for the loss, differences in the social contexts in which they remade significant relationships and experiences of the self, and notions of guidelines for bringing one's self back into some balance. We discuss this last point first.

Our study suggests that differences in ethnicity are associated with distinct styles of locating the disruption and differing notions of a proper state of "self." Widowers in each group described experiences of an "inner" and "outer" self in bereavement. They related that their inner, experiential, individual self was set off balance, but they appear to differ significantly in their notions of what dimensions went askew. Thus, the men share a concept of the desired emotional condition as one of "smoothness," or calm, and the less desired condition as one of "roughness," or turmoil. Yet the nuances of this self-appraisal appear to differ ethnically.

For example, Mr. McGraw reported bereavement created "craziness" inside him. He described acting out angry, wild inner emotions in a self-destructive way. He experienced a breakdown of his emotional balance and of his social life by becoming insensibly alcoholic and "irrationally" selling his home, losing his job, alienating friends and family, and ending up in a slum. He lived out these "wild" inner states for several months until his behavior led to intercession by a friend and a priest whom he needed to help calm his turmoil. Today, he feels, as do the other Irish informants, his inner and outer life are again the desired "okay." Mr. Crazza, too, described how his wife's death gave him "nerves," how he feared "losing my mind." But, unlike his Irish counterpart, he struggled to keep a calm, smooth exterior and to adhere properly to daily life. Today he still expects to feel disruption and some craziness inside and continues to work to maintain a smooth exterior as is reported by the Italian widowers. In contrast, Mr. Stern did not describe or seem to manifest "craziness" in his inner or outer sense of self. At his wife's death, he grieved over her loss and felt desolate at being alone, but did not label the feelings of suffering as a kind of "crazy" inner feelings. He describes endeavoring to accept his pain and to present a calm inner and outer self, neither "lamenting" inside nor being irresponsible to his family or community.

Our findings are consistent with Lola Romanucci-Ross's (1982) portrait of traditional Italian perceptions of the individual as beset by a hostile world and urged to display proper behavior, a "business-as-usual attitude," by means of coercive public social pressure and shame. That contrasts with the coercion by guilt typical of the Jewish tradition. Further, we found many of the Italian men fought to keep the dying wife from learning of her exact condition; this also fits the beliefs Romanucci-Ross describes. One wonders if these prescriptions might hinder the resolution of grief, especially if there are ambivalences remaining, as in Mr. Crazza's case.

At this point, the power and limits of in-depth, case approaches are apparent. We have discovered some key dimensions and processes of widowerhood experiences and life reorganizations. Our findings are general to the fifteen men from each ethnic group studied. But we are limited in generalizing from this data because of the scarcity of other data on widowers, as opposed to widows, and by our case study approach. Yet we have collected the kind of data, the subjective "emic" aspects of ethnicity, "dramatically needed" (DeVos 1982), since ethnicity cannot be defined by behavioral criteria alone.

It will be useful to speculate, at this point, about some of the other cultural differences that emerge from our study.

As a preliminary finding, it appears that the Jewish men tend to express their loss in terms of separation from a valued companion, while Italian men mourn the loss of a dutiful wife, housemaker, caretaker, and moral center of the family. In addition, it appears that Irish and Italian men, more than the Jewish men, may take up the wife's role in food and caregiving exchange networks. We speculate that this is a differential mechanism by which Irish and Italian, as opposed to Jewish men, endeavor to build for themselves the ties to community and family that formerly their wives provided for them. These findings concur with Cohler and Lieberman's (1980) study of elderly in Chicago in which they found high levels of life satisfaction and psychological functioning among Italian and Irish men who were enmeshed in ethnic relations. Thus the Italian men's ethnic heritage may predispose them to be more vulnerable than the Jewish men to the disruptions caused by the loss of a wife.

We speculate further that ethnic identity in general shapes the overt behaviors of these three men and the other widowers, in terms of expressions of grief, mourning practices, and more unconsciously in terms of the patterns they follow — for example, in family relationships and food. These men also exemplify the situational and life course fluidity of ethnicity in the recasting of female roles in the family to meet their needs.

We found, as did Cool (1981) in her study of elderly Corsicans in Paris, that ethnicity may be a key source of continuity. We suggest again that revitalizing ethnic dimensions may lead to a reemergence of family tensions associated with that identity as Ikels (1983) and Luborsky and Rubinstein (1987) find among Chinese émigrés in Boston.

These data indicate direct mental health implications for health professionals and informal supports. The findings suggest specific, culturally sensitive guidelines for use in making ethnically relevant professional evaluations of personal adjustment and recovery behaviors. The data also may aid informal supports by clarifying helpful and unhelpful support behaviors (Lehman et al. 1986) tailored to the socially expected outcomes of bereavement reorganization by each of these ethnic groups.

We have discussed some of the ways that ethnic identity may be viewed as a fixed identity and set of traditions and also a fluid set of vital new meanings which, according to each person's background, shape the experience of bereavement and the rebuilding of life afterwards.

NOTE

The data described in this chapter were collected in a research project entitled "Ethnicity and Life Reorganization by Elderly Widowers," supported by the National Institute on Aging (Robert Rubinstein, principal investigator). We wish here to express our gratitude to NIA for its continued support of our research.

PART V
COMMUNITY, ENVIRONMENT, AND AGING

This is truly the age of aging. With 75 to 80 percent of populations born in industrial countries now surviving to age sixty-five, huge masses of people are beginning to experience upward of two decades of postparental and post-employment existence. Throughout such nations, there are underway a multi-tude of attempts to provide some shape and culturally valid meaning to this last phase of active adulthood. These range from numerous social and political movements, such as the Gray Panthers, to a myriad of new residential schemes, and the creation in countries such as Sweden of constitutionally imbedded principles for maximizing the potential of the aged.

Two central questions, antecedent to comprehending the benefits of such attempts at innovation are: How does the nature of community shape the way aging is perceived? How does this relate to accomplishing a successful old age. Project AGE (Age, Generation, and Experience), the focus of chapter 13, represents the first sophisticated cross-cultural approach to answering these questions. When the entire project is completed in 1990, complex ethnographies of age and aging will have been completed in two American communities (Momence, Illinois, and Swarthmore, Pennsylvania) in Hong Kong, two Irish peasant villages, and among hunter-gatherers and herders in Botswana, Africa. Keith, Fry, and Ikels present some results of their research in the first three sites. Using the same qualitative methods in each community, they show how both "systemwide" community features (such as social inequality) and "internal mechanisms" (such as values) create distinct contexts for conceptualizing the life cycle, establishing age norms, and how a host of variables influence the perception of well-being in old age. It is particularly interesting to note that, despite the continuing ideals of filial concern and intergenerational coresidence, it is among the families in Hong Kong that old age has the lowest status (for another study in Hong Kong, see Kwan 1988; for elsewhere in East Asia, see Chow 1988).

One of the salient contributions of Project AGE is an emphasis on relating the variable nature of communities to well-being in old age (Vesperi 1985). This has increasingly loomed as a controversial topic because following World War II most industrial societies embarked on developing a spectrum of new types of noncustodial social environments for the elderly. In the early 1960s sociologists such as Arnold Rose (1962) were predicting the emergence of a distinct elderly subculture with a new status system predicated on health and activity levels. This was to be based on a growing age consciousness and a segregation of the elderly from younger persons. At the time, it was generally perceived that living in environments such as retirement homes, which enforced a separation of the generations on a daily basis, would result in a decreased quality of life compared to life in "natural" communities. Part of the aversion to such residential settings in the United States and Europe is the historical connection of public homes for the elderly to harsh dumping grounds of last resort for the economically dispossessed, the mentally ill, and the frail aged. Still, today, in many countries it is difficult for the populace to distinguish between age-homogeneous communities of the independent elderly and the variety of long-term care facilities for the very dependent aged.

Yet gerontological research in the 1960s began to show that extreme age density as a community feature did not automatically impose alienation and social oblivion. This was demonstrated by Irve Rosow's (1967) study of Cleveland city housing projects where the elderly lived in buildings with a wide range of age homogeneity. His findings showed that the elderly living in buildings with the highest levels of age-peers possessed the best morale, the largest number of friends, and the highest level of social integration. Particularly in terms of social interaction, anthropological studies of a wide variety of age-segregated environments in Great Britain, France, and the United States have generally corroborated Rosow's findings (Keith 1982; Lawton, Moss, and Moles 1984). It is in such public housing (Hochschild 1973; Ross 1977; Francis 1984; Smithers 1985), mobile home parks (Johnson 1971; Angrosino 1976), and private retirement communities (Byrne 1974; Jacobs 1974; Fry 1977; Perkinson 1980) that an ethnographic approach to aging has been most frequently used. These new environments in which aging takes place can also include clubs, day centers, and senior centers (Cuellar 1978; Jerrome 1988). Their importance in helping people construct a meaningful old age is just being recognized.

In the chapter by Haim Hazan, we see that such community settings as special residences and day centers can provide the social cornerstone for the construction of "personhood" as an aged individual. This renegotiation of the self is mandated not only by the potential loss of valued statuses in old age but also by the existential dilemma of coping with physical decline. Instead of using the life-history approach favored by Luborsky and Rubinstein (chapter 12), he employs a "situational-contextual" analysis to establish an understanding of the aged self. This ethnographic comparison of a residence for retired trade unionists in Israel and a day center for Jews in London demonstrate how divergent these norms of personhood can be.

AGING AND HOMELESSNESS

Despite the growing number of residential options available for the middle class elderly, it is difficult to stroll along the streets of urban America without seeing the devastating effects of recent government housing policy on the elderly poor. As the Coalition for the Homeless has demonstrated in its book, *Crowded Out: Homelessness and the Elderly Poor in New York City* (1984), the catastrophe of homelessness has a special meaning for the urban elderly. The combined effects of virtual abandonment of subsidized housing by the federal government and the actual destruction of much of low-cost housing stock has forced hundreds of thousands of older adults across the nation to be without a domicile.

The authors of the last chapter in this section, anthropologist Jay Sokolovsky and psychiatrist Carl Cohen, have been studying the inner city, poor elderly for over a decade. In 1975, when they began this research, in single-room-occupancy (SRO) hotels of Manhattan, there were over 50,000 rooms available (in all five boroughs), and about 20 percent were inhabited by older adults who typically had lived there at least a decade. While some of the SRO hotels they studied in the mid-1970s were dangerous, inadequate places to live, their research demonstrated that these environments for the most part provided affordable living quarters where most elderly were able to develop supportive, although small, social networks (Sokolovsky and Cohen 1981, 1987). Six years later almost two-thirds of the rooms had been gutted in a gentrification frenzy which was nearly matched nationwide where about one-half of such housing was lost (Hopper and Hamburg 1984).

The poor, including numerous aged, had been deprived of adequate shelter for the sake of subsidizing condominiums for the rich. It is little wonder that a 1984 HUD report indicated that 38 percent of people seeking public shelter had been evicted from their prior dwelling (U.S. Department of Housing and Urban Development).This destruction of housing has occurred at a time when the woefully inadequate shelters are already overflowing with younger, poor, alienated, and sometimes mentally ill homeless who cause the elderly to flee the shelter for their very lives. This has put a special stress on older, homeless women, who represent an extreme example of powerlessness and destitution (Roth 1982; Makiesky-Barrow and Lovell 1987).

The chapter by Sokolovsky and Cohen is based on a two year project funded by the National Institute of Mental Health.[1] Their study during the mid-1980s gathered 281 intensive interviews with males over fifty who were homeless or near homeless. This was combined with an ethnographic examination by Sokolovsky of the lifestyle of a smaller number of these men. In this selection the authors draw upon these qualitative data to let the lives of three older men speak for themselves—they show the reality of being old, poor, and homeless in America.

NOTE

1. This research was funded by the National Institute of Mental Health, Center for the Study of the Mental Disorders of the Aging, grant number RO1–MH37562, "Old Men on the Bowery in the 1980s."

13 COMMUNITY AS CONTEXT FOR SUCCESSFUL AGING

Jennie Keith, Christine L. Fry, and Charlotte Ikels

From Shangri-La to Sun City, many people have tried to invent or discover the ideal community in which to be old. The goal of the research described in this chapter is to approach this question in a scientific way, by asking what are the characteristics of communities around the world that influence the well-being of their older residents. Project AGE (Age, Generation, and Experience) is a team of anthropologists carrying out comparative community studies focused on age. In this chapter, we will highlight variability in what people in different communities define as successful aging and how those views affect their strategies for achieving what they see as desirable for the later years.

Reviewing the information available about aging in other societies reminded us of browsing through a fascinating but unsystematic museum of exhibits from many cultures. Preparing our research plan was a little like writing the catalogue for this museum, as we tried to discover connections among the varied reports of aging around the world. These connections would become the questions and hypotheses to guide our effort to collect systematic, first-hand, comparative data about community influences on old age.[1]

Two kinds of community characteristics appeared to be essential: broad system-level characteristics such as rate of social change or degree of social differentiation, and more specific internal mechanisms, such as cultural values, peer groups, or resource control, through which the global characteristics might affect the lives of individual old people. Guided by this model and by the availability of anthropologists experienced in the communities and fluent in the necessary languages, we chose the following sites for our research: four neighborhoods in Hong Kong, varying in socioeconomic status; Swarthmore, Pennsylvania, a suburb of Philadelphia; Momence, Illinois, located beyond the urban fringe of Chicago; Clifden, Ireland; Blessington, Ireland; the Herero herders and the !Kung foragers of Botswana.

CROSS-CULTURAL METHODOLOGY

The compelling need for cross-cultural research about aging poses extraordinary methodological challenges. Arguments for the necessity of cross-cultural research stress the importance of disentangling what is biological or "natural" about aging from what may be shaped by social and cultural context. Comparative analysis is the strategy anthropologists use to separate what is universally human from what is culturally diverse. However, the challenge is to collect information that is both valid within a particular cultural setting and usable for comparison with information from another cultural setting. Measures of key concepts cannot be standardized, or the cultural validity will be lost; but definitions cannot be completely "culture-centric" or the opportunity for comparison will be lost. In addition, our research grew from the assumption that since humans operate in community contexts, it is important to interpret information about human aging holistically.

Project AGE developed a research strategy that standardized key concepts and the strategies used to discover their measures, but left open as the goal of these discovery strategies the specific indicators of a concept in each community. Our research enterprise was a multilayered mapping endeavor, recording information about the significance of age in informal networks, in formal community structures, in the ways people perceived themselves, others, and the life course in general. Our research strategies included many classic anthropological techniques: participant-observation, life histories, use of "key respondents," genealogical interviewing, and sorting tasks. Researchers lived in each community for a year or more, participating in community activities such as holiday rituals, meetings of local political units, and family gatherings. A representative sample of 200 people in each community was interviewed formally, and life histories were collected from twelve individuals over 60 years old.[2]

An example of our attempt to balance comparison with cultural validity is the technique used to discover views of the life course. In each community, we wanted to know how people viewed or thought about the life course. What were the stages they saw people moving through as they aged: How many? What were they called? What were the personal attributes that defined people as in one life stage or another? At what chronological ages did people enter various life stages? How much agreement was there about these issues within a community? We obviously could not begin with questions based on our own definitions of life stages. As Peterson-LaFargue shows elsewhere in this book, to begin by asking, "At what age does a person become 'old'?" imposes the notion that there is a category called old *and* that it has a chronological basis.

In the "Age Game," we asked our respondents to sort written or sketched descriptions of imaginary people into piles representing stages of life. Then when they had defined and named the life stages they perceived, we asked them questions about the basis on which they defined them: the major issues they expected people in each stage to be concerned about; the good and hard things about each; markers of transitions from one stage to the next, and finally the approximate age range. We also inquired whether these answers were the same or different for men and women. This strategy was flexible enough to be adapted for our different research sites. In the two where preliminary efforts show that the "Age Game" is difficult to use — Clifden and !Kung — the difficulties themselves suggest important insights into ways people view age and the life course. In Clifden, respondents line up the card "people" by increasing age, but are reluctant to cluster them into groups or stages. In this small-scale community, there is little social categorization of any kind. In addition, the actual experiences of adults of different ages are not very differentiated except by loss of physical functionality. Two apparent reasons for this are the high level of unemployment and the high proportion of men who never marry. For the !Kung, making absolute social classifications is culturally unfamiliar. The spatial fluidity of their traditional foraging life promotes a focus on situational relationships. Age does appear to be salient, e.g. as a parameter for norms about behavior appropriate for age-mixed or age-similar circumstances. However, age is not used to define sharp boundaries of social categories or life transitions. The "Age Game" that has showed us variation in numbers and content of life stages in the more urban and industrial communities is revealing a deeper level of difference in the smaller scale communities where age is not used to define categories and lives are less staged on any basis.

Discovering the attributes of age used to describe the "people" to be sorted was a research challenge in itself, and the contrasts among the sets of attributes indicate important differences in these communities. We interviewed key respondents in each community about what they saw as attributes that indicated different ages or life stages. In Hong Kong, for example, in order to describe plausible persons who could be differentiated by age, we needed to provide information about marital status and parental status, household composition, and labor force participation. In the blue-collar American town, in addition to the domestic and occupational information, we needed to add whether or not the home mortgage had been paid off and in what kind of organizations the person participated. In the American suburb, the health status of an individual's parents was an important additional indicator of life stage. Preliminary work in Ireland suggests that in the rural town migration experience needs to be described; and in Botswana, Herero apparently want to know how many cattle an individual owns in order to make a judgment about his or her stage in life.

COMMUNITY CONTEXTS

Research has been completed in the first three sites: Momence, Illinois; Swarthmore, Pennsylvania, and the four neighborhoods in Hong Kong. These locales will be the focus of this chapter.

Momence is a small, rural community with a strong sense of distinctive identity as an "old border town." Nearly 4,000 people live in the town of

Momence and another 4,000 in the seventy square miles surrounding it. Seventeen percent of the total population is over sixty, and 30 percent of the adult population is over sixty. Social stratification has a narrow range, mostly within blue-collar classifications. Older people control important resources, in particular farm land, and are the most influential actors in community affairs. Momence is a highly stable community; 30 percent of the people in our sample had lived 90 percent of their lives in the town. During the time of study the effects of the early 1980s recession were very pronounced, with the local unemployment rate exceeding 17 percent. Momence has lost links to the outside economy as several industries have left. The community's response is an intensification of its distinctive identity through rituals such as a Sesquicentennial and the annual Gladiolus Festival.

An example of "successful aging" in Momence is Clara Walters. Clara moved to Momence when her three children were under five and still lived there over thirty years later when she was interviewed at the age of sixty-nine. Although she was widowed twenty years earlier, Clara is happy with her life for many reasons. She was able to fulfill her dream of becoming a teacher by going to back to school after her widowhood. She has three grandchildren; one lives across the street. Religion gives her strength, and she is very active in her church. She is surrounded by friends, themselves widows, whom she has known for many years. They travel often, to Europe, Hawaii, and the Orient.

In contrast to Clara is Eldon Dupont, a resident of Momence who is "less successful" in old age. He did hard physical labor all his life, and his greatest problem now is ill health. "They took me out of school and put me to work; I went to work on the hard road when I was fifteen years old. This is when my youth ended." When he was first married, Eldon picked ninety-eight bushels of large cucumbers in one day for one dollar. He later worked in a Pullman factory and in his fifties was getting up at 5:00 A.M. to stoke the furnace in another factory. His working days ended at the age of sixty-two with an industrial accident. "I'm a hot-headed Frenchman. I thought nothing could stop me. It wasn't the work that stopped me; it was the accidents." Now, the worst part of Eldon's life in old age is his poor health, the best his large family. "I'm not much good now. You don't want to know what's the matter with me. I have emphysema, and I have cancer. I have colitis. I have arthritis, and I get disability in both legs. I have had hard labor. That is all I can remember—just hard work. The most important thing about my life is that I have raised three kids. I have eight grandchildren and two great-grandchildren. Without a family, if you die tomorrow, you would have nothing to leave behind. I also own my own home."

Swarthmore is a suburb of Philadelphia, with a population of 5,950, of whom 25.5 percent (excluding the students at Swarthmore College) are over sixty. Our early interviews and observations showed that Swarthmore might be called a "suburb in spite of itself." There is a small-town core here that has been swept into a suburban flow of commuting and shopping malls, placing Swarthmore in an intermediate scale position between Hong Kong and Momence. The interdependence of Swarthmore with the outside world has increased in recent years, as the high school has merged into a larger school in the neighboring town, and several local businesses have become part of national or regional corporations. Concern about losing distinctiveness as a community is a theme that emerged from various kinds of observations and interviews. There is a wider range of occupations than in Momence, but the majority in Swarthmore are middle class, and the average educational level includes college.

Creating the card "people" in Swarthmore revealed the significance of the status of older parents as an indicator of life stage. This reflects the two categories of older people in Swarthmore, one including long-term residents, and the other new arrivals who have come to be near a child. The modal answer to number of years in Swarthmore is only five; the mean number of years is twenty; and 40 percent of the sample had lived less than one-fourth of their lives in town. Older people here are sometimes prominent in spite of their age, for example, as members of political bodies and local organizations, but age and seniority in themselves do not ensure prestige.

A "successful ager" in Swarthmore is Jim Block, who was interviewed at age sixty-nine. He attributes his own satisfaction with his life to his happy marriage, his love of his work, and his lack of financial worries. "When I go to bed tonight the only thing I think about is the solution to creative and aesthetic problems. We're laughing all the time!" He and his wife are already on the waiting list for a nearby Quaker continuing care community, where he expects to continue his graphic art work. He anticipates many social opportunities there and is relieved at the idea of never being dependent on his children.

A Swarthmore resident who is less content with her life is Martha Lucas, who was ninety when we interviewed her. She had had a highly successful professional career as a clinical psychologist and was liberal, even radical, all her life, advocating free love and trial marriage in 1910 and "living wills" today. She did not use her married name until she retired. Another marker of that life transition for her was that she began to read fiction instead of nonfiction. After being widowed at the age of eighty-five, she moved from her large home in Swarthmore to an apartment house occupied mainly by older women. She became a volunteer at the public library, and most of her social contacts at the time she was interviewed were with her coworkers there, other older women. She missed her husband very much and considered it a curse that she had continued to live for ninety years. She had difficulty walking and was worried that the cooperative grocery store half a block from her apartment might close, as she would then be unable to do her own shopping. "[Young people] have no concept, anymore than I had until about the last five years, of what it really is like to be *old*. They think a ninetieth birthday is something for which one should receive the conventional cards wishing one many more years. What one should be wished at that age is a quick and not a lingering death. Something with which too few of us old folks are blessed, in my opinion. Maybe I feel that way all the more because when I can no longer care for myself, which becomes more difficult each month, I shall have to give up the independence that has been, perhaps far too much, the chief character trait I developed."

In Hong Kong, we studied four neighborhoods of varying socioeconomic status. Hong Kong is highest in societal scale of our sites, with a population over 5 million, nearly total dependence on external markets, and very dense settlement. Old people are 16 percent of the adult population and 10 percent of the total population. Hong Kong has also experienced social change at a whirlwind rate, compared to the two American communities. Rapid changes in technology and in the availability of education have meant rapid turnover in types of occupations available to different cohorts as they enter the labor force. New opportunities are available to the young and educated, just as opportunities for the old and uneducated are declining. Residential stability is low in Hong Kong: 30 percent of the population and 31 percent of our adult sample had not been at the same address five years earlier. These rates vary a great deal across public and private housing, since public housing is a precious resource that people are reluctant to leave. Our sample neighborhoods included two public housing estates and two neighborhoods with private housing. Older people are not prominent actors in the Hong Kong political scene and cannot enjoy seniority in most organizations.

An example of "successful aging" in Hong Kong is sixty-three-year-old Mrs. Poon. She rated her health as poor, because she suffers from asthma and rheumatism and has considerable difficulty in getting around. However, she feels her life is good because of the quality of her relationship with her children: "My children support the family and do all the housework." The youngest three of the Poons' seven children are still unmarried and living at home. Their second son has also moved back in with his wife and two children, so that their two-room apartment now houses nine people in two households (the two nuclear families eat meals separately). Mrs. Poon loves to gamble and plays *mah jong* with her neighbors several times a week. She used to take the boat to Macao to gamble in the casinos, but now sees her traveling days as over and gave this as a reason that her life is less good now than five years ago. When Mrs. Poon was hospitalized for over three weeks, her sons insisted on transferring her from the public ward to the very expensive private ward. According to Mr. Poon, their sons are very filial and said, "Let's make the sacrifice, so that she can live more comfortably."

A Hong Kong resident whose aging is less successful is Mr. Luk. Born on the Chinese mainland in Guangdong in 1902, he was in his eighties at the time of our interview. He worked as a laborer on roads and docks until his leg was broken and he had to leave his job. He received no compensation of any sort and eventually took a series of odd jobs (guard at construction sites, miscellaneous worker in a factory) until he stopped working in his late seventies. His health is very bad, and he is nearly blind. Although some of his children helped him after a kidney operation, a great disappointment in his life is the younger son who is a ne'er do well. Mr. Luk maintains an apartment in a public housing project because he is convinced that eventually this son's gambling debts will prevent him from paying rent in the private sector, so that he and his young family will have to return to his father's apartment. Mr. Luk deeply regrets that he has been unable to raise this young man properly. Serving as a "moral guide" is a very important role for parents, according to Chinese tradition. He sighed to the interviewer, "I have no successful method to teach him no matter whether my tone is severe or not. Besides, he is too easily irritated and strong. I am not strong enough to fight with him."

COMMUNITY DIFFERENCES AND AGING

Our model predicts that characteristics of entire communities will have an impact on the well-being of older people: the greater the scale, the greater the specialization or social differentiation, the greater the rate of social change and the greater the residential mobility, the lower the levels of well-being in old age. The effects of all these community characteristics are neither simple nor direct, but work through intervening mechanisms in each community. Cultural values about independence and dependence, for instance, may exacerbate the effects of the system-level factors or offer buffers. Or the existence of peer groups may cushion the negative effects of residential mobility in communities which value independence. The research communities differ in all the system level characteristics described above. Hong Kong is a giant city, tightly linked into global politics and economy. Swarthmore is suburban and a part of the Philadelphia metropolitan area. Momence has the lowest scale position, more self-sufficient and more distinct from the Chicago urban area. The Hong Kong population is the least residentially stable, the Momence population the most. Hong Kong has experienced the most rapid social change. In addition, there are deep differences between Hong Kong Chinese and Americans in their bases for evaluation of persons in general, as well as of older people more specifically. Swarthmore is more affluent than Momence, and a greater proportion of residents in both American communities is financially comfortable than is true in Hong Kong. Hong Kong has the greatest social differentiation, with a vast array of occupations and organizational positions, Momence the least, and Swarthmore intermediate.

MEASUREMENT OF SUCCESSFUL AGING

Comparative research on successful aging exemplifies the challenges of cross-cultural research in general. The very notion of "success" has a Western ring to it, and measurement based on ethnocentric assumptions of what we think desirable is risky. One of our discoveries was that even such apparently universal goods as health have very different meanings in different communities. Strategies for discovering what people perceive as positive or as doing well, must be able to capture variation across communities. In addition, research about these ideas must encompass the diversity of lives within communities. To understand what people perceive as doing well in old age, it is also essential to know the context of what they think of as successful living at other times of life. In some communities, success for young people is different from success for older people, and an important aspect of aging well may be seen as changing goals. As individuals progress through their life course, they may "turn off" the salience of some domains and "switch on" others. In some communities, priority may be given to success most attainable at certain life stages, creating built-in problems for individuals at other stages.

It is also well known that whether questions are anchored in self, others, or a more generalized other, as well as in more or less concrete *vs.* hypothetical issues for any of these, shapes the responses. Those questions anchored in self and in a person known to the informant (although less so in the latter case) tend to elicit less normative responses. On the other hand, questions referencing a generalized other or category of persons tend to elicit the ideal and the normative, what people think they and others should be doing. Less concrete questions leave room for projection of wishes and fears. In our data collection, we followed two principles: (1) to obtain data from all three reference points (self, other, and generalized other) and about both concrete and hypothetical issues; and (2) to ask all questions both in the positive and in the negative. Guided by these principles, in 200 interviews in each community we asked people about the following topics to discover the meaning of aging well: (1)reasons for a person's own well-being; (2) definitions of the "best possible life" and "worst possible life," and (3) reasons why a specific older person is seen as doing well or poorly.

This chapter is focused on perceptions of successful aging tied to real individuals: the descriptions *by others* of older people seen as doing well or doing poorly and excerpts from life histories in which older people who evaluated their well-being more and less positively talk about their *own* lives.

When we asked people to evaluate their own well-being, each person was shown a picture which was a metaphor for levels or ranking of well-being. For the two United States sites a ladder with six rungs was used (for a discussion of this technique, see Cantril 1965). In Hong Kong people were more comfortable placing themselves on a set of stairs with six steps. The best possible life was on the top or sixth rung/stair and the worst possible life was at the first or bottom rung/stair. Each person we interviewed was asked to show us the rung or step that best represented how they felt about their present life. After deciding on the rank, each person was asked to explain why they placed themselves where they did and then to go on by telling us what it would be like to be at a 6, or the best possible, and to be at a 1, or the worst possible. Eldon, the person from Momence who was described as having a difficult old age, gave himself a score of 3; Clara, the widow who travels the world with her friends, gave herself a 6. Jim Block, who said, "We're laughing all the time," also placed himself on the sixth rung, while Martha Lucas, who feared losing her independence, gave herself a 4. Mrs. Poon, pleased with her filial children, gave herself a 5 in spite of her poor health.

As a part of the Age Game sorting task, each person interviewed had grouped the "people" into major divisions of the life course or life stages. For those age groups where the age ranges included the threshold of sixty years, we asked people to think of individuals in that group whom they knew and thought were doing well for that age and who they thought were doing poorly for that age. Once they brought that person to mind we asked for their age and gender and in what way they were doing well or poorly.

PATHWAYS TO WELL-BEING AND SUCCESSFUL AGING

According to our most general hypotheses about the effects of scale, social differentiation, change, and residential instability, the average level of well-being for older people should be lower in Hong Kong than in the United States. This is in fact what we found. The average evaluation of well-being by persons over sixty in Hong Kong is 3.5; for Momence 4.7, and for Swarthmore 5.1. However, for at least two reasons, this statement greatly oversimplifies patterns of successful aging in these three communities. First, the averages conceal variation *within* each community, and second, the high well-being level in the U.S. suburb indicates that other mechanisms are having important intervening effects on scale, social differentiation, and residential instability.

More complex patterns in the ways community context shapes what people want in old age and the strategies available to them for obtaining the old age they want appear in Tables 13.1 and 13.2. These show the descriptions people gave of individuals they saw as doing especially well or having problems in old age. Using these indicators of how people in the different communities perceive successful aging, it is possible to answer some of the questions about the influence both of system-level community characteristics and of mechanisms internal to each setting. How do cultural values about filial piety, Confucian moral guidance, or individualistic independence affect definitions of a good old age, and strategies for living it? How do pathways toward well-being differ between stable blue-collar and mobile middle-class communities in America?

Physical status — health and functionality — is an important reason that an older person is seen as doing well or poorly, whether in a Hong Kong housing estate, a suburban condominium in Pennsylvania, or a Victorian house in the midwest. Health was measured in this study by asking people a series of questions about their views of their own health, as well as their recent experiences of illness. Functionality refers to their evaluation of their own physical capacities, such as walking or seeing, and of their ability to do specific things, such as "get around" or "live alone," that were perceived as necessary for full adult participation in the different locations. However, as the tables show, the relative significance given to physical status by the people who talked to us is greater in both U.S. communities than in Hong Kong. This raises interesting questions both about what is seen as more important in

Table 13.1
Reasons for an Older Person Doing Well—Comparison of the Percentage of Responses Across Sites

	Momence	Swarthmore	Hong Kong	Total
Physical Status				
Health	23.94	13.12	8.33	16.20
Functionality	8.95	9.61	4.39	8.39
Marriage & Family				
Marriage	0.89	2.96	1.32	1.89
Bereavement	1.12	2.59	0.88	1.73
Children/Family	0.67	3.51	6.58	3.04
Adult Children	1.79	1.66	10.53	3.37
Work & Retirement				
Work	6.71	5.55	0.88	5.10
Retirement	3.58	2.59	1.32	2.71
Finances	18.34	7.58	13.60	12.66
Independence/ Dependence				
Independence	1.12	6.47	1.32	3.54
Dependence	2.01	0.74	10.96	3.13
Leisure/Social Life				
Leisure	4.92	8.87	4.39	6.58
Social Life	4.03	5.73	1.32	4.28
Personal Characteristics				
Personal Qualities	4.70	12.94	26.75	12.50
Active	10.74	7.39	0.00	7.24
Other	6.49	8.69	7.46	7.65
Total %	100.00	100.00	100.00	100.00
Total Responses	447	541	228	1216
Total Respondents	167	176	119	452

Test Statistic	Value	Df	Prob
Pearson Chi-square	320.736	30	.000
Likelihood Ratio Chi-square	319.842	30	.000

Table 13.2

Reasons for an Older Person Doing Poorly—Comparison of the Percentage of Responses Across Sites

	Momence	Swarthmore	Hong Kong	Total
Physical Status				
Health	41.76	21.04	8.67	26.28
Functionality	11.18	18.91	9.25	14.32
Marriage & Family				
Bereavement	2.65	7.09	2.89	4.70
Children/Family	2.35	1.42	17.34	4.70
Work & Retirement				
Work	2.06	1.89	6.36	2.78
Retirement	1.76	2.13	1.16	1.82
Finances	12.35	6.15	13.87	9.83
Dependence	6.47	7.80	13.29	8.33
Social	1.18	4.96	0.58	2.78
Personal				
Characteristics	8.82	13.71	8.67	11.00
Other	9.41	14.89	17.92	3.46
Total %	100.00	100.00	100.00	100.00
Total Responses	340	423	173	936
Total Respondents	159	167	92	418

Test Statistic	Value	Df	Prob
Pearson Chi-Square	203.386	20	.000
Likelihood Ratio Chi-square	185.723	20	.000

Hong Kong, and about why physical status is given such similar priority in an affluent suburb and a blue-collar town.

In Momence, as in Hong Kong, ill health is menacing in part because it threatens the ability to work. The blue collar occupations and lesser financial security of many people in these two settings are revealed also in the greater importance they give to financial issues as an explanation of well-being in old age. In the more affluent community of Swarthmore, the link between physical capability and well-being is not so direct as the ability to do physical labor. Why do people in this suburban setting emphasize physical status? They explained to us in response to many different questions that ill health was dreaded because it threatened, not livelihood, but independence. Table 13.1 shows the distinctiveness of this concern to the middle-class community. Only there does a substantial proportion of the sample name "independence" as a reason an older person is seen as doing well. The link between health and fears of dependence appeared in another way when people described for us their definition of a "worst possible life." Here again, the people in the suburb, whose health is, in fact, on average better than that of those in either Momence or Hong Kong, were more likely to talk about ill health as the cause of a "worst possible life." Since descriptions of an imagined terrible life are likely to say more about fears than about actual problems, these responses reveal the greater *fear* that the suburbanites have of ill health and concomitant dependence.

The position of independence as a core value for many Americans appeared in various kinds of information we collected – in the different layers on our map of the meaning of age. For instance, when we analyzed the many attributes people used to evaluate functionality, in the United States there was a cluster of abilities that we labeled "self-sufficiency." Central to this cluster was the ability to live alone. By contrast, in Hong Kong, people did not even see the sense of evaluating this ability: "Why would anyone want to live alone?" they asked their interviewers. In Hong Kong, people were far more likely to identify dependence, rather than independence, as a reason why an older person was doing well (Table 13.1). What they meant was that their dependency needs – financial, psychological and physical – were being met through the efforts of others, primarily members of their family.

Another example is what we began to call an "underground railway" from Swarthmore to nearby retirement communities. People consistently explain their decision to make this move in terms of their wish to remain independent. They perceive the quasi-institutional setting of a continuing care community as offering greater independence in the event of declining functionality than sharing a household with their children or receiving care from their children.

The fact that people in Momence are affected both by their blue-collar economic position and by core American values probably makes ill health a double threat to them. This would account for the extremely high proportion – well over half our sample – of people who identify poor physical status as a reason that an older person is doing poorly (Table 13.2).

What is it that residents of Hong Kong identify as more important than physical status when discussing reasons for doing well or poorly in old age? The category of explanation used by far most frequently to explain why an older person is doing well is "personal characteristics." The contrast with answers from the United States is not only in terms of quantity, but also of quality. A large proportion of the Chinese answers in this category refer to characteristics such as "tolerant," "easy-going," and "not a nag." These are qualities of an older person seen from the point of view of *how that older person's qualities affect the speaker*. The Americans who described successful agers for us spoke about qualities that influenced the way the *older person as an individual faced the world* – he or she is optimistic, courageous, motivated. This contrast in perspective appears most clearly in Table 13.1 in the category labeled "active." This word was used frequently by Americans in both communities to describe older people doing well. Although the description can be expressed in one word, it conveys complex meanings, involving visibility in the community and extensive social participation (this can be via telephone) as well as some physical vigor. Again, we see the American theme of independence, in sharp contrast to the Chinese focus on how the older person gets along with others.

Confucian tradition places great emphasis on the parent/child relationship, especially that between father and son. This relationship ideally should be characterized by "filial piety" from the son and "moral guidance" from the father. Probably the most stressful of the many differences in the ways old and young in Hong Kong view the world are those focused on the familial roles central to Confucianism. Most of the older Chinese we interviewed were living with relatives in multigenerational households, so that getting along with others meant getting along with younger relatives, and usually in very crowded circumstances. This living arrangement, combined with the estranging effects of educational and social differences between the generations, explains the emphasis placed by the Chinese on family relations as reasons old people were doing well or poorly. As shown in Table 13.1, relations with children and other descendants are used to explain the quality of an old person's life much more frequently in Hong Kong than in either United States community. The answers to why a person is doing poorly reveal a specific pattern in Chinese family life, as most of the responses in the category "children" are about difficult relations with a daughter-in-law. Traditional patterns gave an older woman great authority over her son's wife; great tension is caused by the decreasing willingness of young women to accept this role.

In the American communities, when family issues are discussed, they more often include marital relations than in Hong Kong, where the focus is on relations with descendants. We were surprised at the generally low frequency of responses about bereavement (Fry and Garvin 1987). The exception is in Swarthmore where, as in most middle-class communities, social relations focus on couples, so that widowhood causes greater disruption of social networks (Bott 1971).

VARIATION IN DEFINITIONS OF WELL-BEING AND SUCCESSFUL AGING

Within each community, individuals also vary in the ways they define satisfying lives in old age. We compared the views of men and women and also the views of individuals of different ages in each community. The clearest gender differences appear in terms of the relative importance of physical status. Physical status is discussed more frequently by men in Hong Kong, by women in the United States. Our interpretation of the concerns behind these responses is that they focus on the strenuous nature of work itself for men in Hong Kong, but on the fear of frailty and dependence for women in the United States. Support for this interpretation comes from the gender differences within the American responses referring to independence, being "active," and to functionality vs. health. In both American communities, women talk more frequently than men about independence and being "active"; in suburban Swarthmore, women also give replies more focused on functionality than on health. This issue of being able to remain independent is especially pressing for American women, who may spend many years as widows in a cultural context that does not favor shared households and acceptance of care from others. The problem is poignant for the widows who move *into* Swarthmore and must create new social identities as "active" members of the community or risk falling into the faceless category of "old lady."

In general, there is greater variation in views about successful aging between people of different ages in our research settings than between men and women. The substance of what people of a certain age said to us was not the same in the three settings, and in response to some questions, the extent to which older people answered *differently* from other age groups varied among our communities.

When people of different ages talked about why older people were doing well or poorly, there was *more* difference in answers given by people of different ages in Hong Kong and in Swarthmore than in Momence. The tidal wave of social changes in Hong Kong has separated from each other, in terms of experience and values, individuals of different generations who still must live their daily lives close together in crowded, multigeneration households. In Swarthmore, most local-born younger people are away in college. Those under thirty available to be interviewed were either students at Swarthmore College or members of young families who had recently moved to the town. Individuals in neither category were likely to have close ties with older individuals in the town, and older members of their own families often lived a considerable distance away. The greater social and residential stability of Momence leads to more consensus across the generations in perceptions of why people are doing well or having problems in old age.

When we focus on how the *older residents* of our three locations viewed older people doing well or poorly, there are further differences, highlighting the boundaries of class and culture. Values about marriage, independence, and filial relations, in particular, influenced the way older people talked about physical condition and about relations with children. Although physical health and functionality are spoken about by both American and Chinese older people, the emphasis differs considerably. There is relatively more emphasis on physical condition by the Americans over sixty, especially when they are talking about reasons some older people are not doing well. When the older Chinese are talking about another older person having problems, they frequently mention family, in particular children. In the United States family is less frequently described as a reason for problems in later life, and when it is, the problem most often talked about is loss of a spouse.

Class differences between the three contexts in which we listened to older people talk about successful aging influence the differing emphases they place on leisure, finances, and marital relations. In Momence and Hong Kong, where many people have incomes lower and less secure than those in Swarthmore, there is more focus on financial aspects of a good life in old age. In Swarthmore, we heard more about leisure, travel, and vacations as reasons some people were enjoying old age.

Patterns of age difference also appear within the three research locations. One is a pattern of "caretaker" concerns that occurs in the answers of younger and middle-aged people in Swarthmore and Hong Kong. The Chinese people under sixty, for example, talked more about family relations as reasons some old people were doing well in old age than older people themselves did. The younger people also gave more emphasis to the personal characteristics of older people doing well than the older people we interviewed did themselves. We interpret these patterns to reflect the concern of the younger people about how the care of older people may affect them. In Swarthmore, where older people often move into the community because a younger relative is located there, there may be a similar concern suggested by the frequency with which those between thirty and sixty discuss physical condition, especially functionality, as an important characteristic of the elderly individuals they describe as doing well.

CONCLUSION

"Well, where should I move to have a good old age?" is the question we are often asked about our study by people who are only half-joking. The gloomy reading of this preliminary view of "successful aging" in different communities might be that there is no Shangri-La. There are unhappy older people in all three places. However, our comparisons also show that even though there are threats to well-being, such as poverty and disease, with universal potential to blight lives, there is variation in the extent to which the elderly in different contexts are especially vulnerable to such threats or cushioned against them. The more complex—and more optimistic—reading of our preliminary findings is that the vision of a "successful" old age differs for residents of these communities, and that in each there are pathways, shaped by the social system and by many intervening factors, such as values, peer groups or residential stability, that lead some individuals to great satisfaction with their later years.

The system-level characteristics in terms of which our communities contrast most dramatically do have their effect on successful aging. The greater scale and social differentiation of the suburb compared to the small town, in combination with high residential mobility, confront older people with the challenge of dodging assignment to a faceless category of "old" by maintaining, or re-creating, their personhood. Peer groups are an important strategy in this effort and are more widely used in Swarthmore than in Momence, where social life crosses age lines more often.

The effects of rapid social change are seen most poignantly in Hong Kong, where we found old age given the *lowest* status of our three research locations. The great educational gap between young and old in Hong Kong combined with the multigenerational living arrangements offers high potential for conflict. In the context of great differences in values, such spatial closeness may promote emotional distance at best and intense conflict at worst. This paradox was illustrated in answers we heard to questions about the age groups in which individuals knew the most and fewest other people. According to these responses, social networks were *more* age-homogeneous in Hong Kong than in the United States. We had to remind ourselves that many of the people who gave these answers were in fact living in multigenerational homes! These issues are revealed in the painful focus by older Chinese on family problems (conflict with daughter-in-law, fear that children will not care for them) as a source of unhappiness and insecurity, and by younger Chinese on attributes that prevent the elderly from being a nuisance to *them*.

American values on individualism and independence contrast with the more communal Chinese issues of filial piety and the value of being a "moral guide" to others. These differences have important effects on attitudes about needing care. In the two American communities, the old are concerned that they *not* become dependent; the Chinese hope to raise proper children who *will* take care of them. Translating these concerns into strategies of successful aging, the suburban Americans often move into either formal or de facto retirement housing, with access to peers, and perhaps professionals, who can offer support that does not "count" as dependence. The Chinese are more likely to invest their effort in ensuring eventual support from children, through Confucian moral guidance — and perhaps now also by being "good" old people who do not nag or interfere.

Perhaps the best advice to American students wondering about good places to grow old is "stay home and do your homework." That is, a good investment in successful aging would be a clear understanding of the social and cultural factors affecting it in your own hometown. Although the effects of social and cultural influences on the aging experience become so familiar that they may be confused with biological necessity, they are *not* biology and not necessary. If such patterns as priority of the individual over the collective, independence over interdependence, or residential mobility over stability are judged to present obstacles to successful aging, they can be changed. As many observers of American culture have pointed out, there is an emphasis on the younger years. From the perspective of "successful aging," this emphasis appears in decisions made earlier in life, about education, occupation, residence, that take little account of consequences for later years. A more integrated view of the entire life course may eventually allow all of us to make decisions and consider goals of "successful living," that transcend the demands of any one life stage.

NOTES

This project is supported by grant #AG 03110 from the National Institute on Aging.

1. See Fry 1985, Keith 1980, and Keith 1985 for reviews of anthropological work on age and aging.
2. See Ikels et al. 1987 for details of project methodology; see Fry and Keith 1986 for anthropological methods of studying age more generally.

14 THE CONSTRUCTION OF PERSONHOOD AMONG THE AGED: A COMPARATIVE STUDY OF AGING IN ISRAEL AND ENGLAND

Haim Hazan

The problem faced by anthropologists in dealing with the aging self is how to identify the characteristics of that self within a social context which by nature does not inform such identification. Whether researchers are mindful of this difficulty or not, the practical solutions offered in the literature are socially telling and intellectually intriguing, for they reflect common attitudes toward the aged as well as mirror the analytic perplexity embedded in the whole subject of aging.

Two diametrically opposite models for handling the problem could be identified. One is based on the view that the life of elderly people is best understood in terms of their immediate environmental constraints and the exigencies of their functional, economic, and social conditions—all of which are unfolded in the form of "adjustment" problems. The other model recognizes the boundaries of the self as extending beyond the present and hence furnishing the conception of the self with content and meaning stemming from past identities and lifelong cumulative experience. In neither case is the process of continuous construction of self vis-à-vis existing interactional and symbolic contexts thrown into relief. Rather, in both approaches the self is viewed through its sociocultural resources rather than via the structure of relationships responsible for its constitution as a pragmatic response to an overall social arena.

This raises a host of important theoretical and methodological issues, some of which will be addressed at a later stage. For the purpose of this introduction, however, suffice it to state that unlike recent trends in sociocultural research, which put a premium on autobiographical narrative as a major source of ethnographic data about the self, the conception guiding this discussion draws mostly on situational-contextual analysis as a basis for establishing a perceived profile of the aged self. This is not to say that matters of life history and its interpretation are to be overlooked, but it does suggest that the independent set of variables for explaining the emergence of the construction of the aged self in question will hinge on the structural arguments rather than biographically slanted discourses.

The two case studies I will present — of a residential home and a day center — are interrelated primarily by virtue of the concept under study, the self. Even though the two groups studied have some limited cultural commonalities, the link between them is not to be sought in similarities of content or meaning, nor in shared cultural universals. It is my assumption that the discovery of the aging self in its manifestation within the context and structure of the varied realities under consideration provides the rationale for juxtaposing the two ethnographic descriptions in this chapter.

Having said that context and structure are at the core of our search for the concept of selfhood among the aged, it is necessary to stress that context and structure are not regarded as "given" or "taken-for-granted" arenas where action and interaction take place but are indeed viewed as the social product of behavioral patterns. In other words, by locating the idea of selfhood within a contextual-structural frame of reference, a host of cultural, interactional, and biographical factors would be reflected and identified.

This will be handled by addressing three sets of relevant units of information regarding images and construction of selfhood. The first consists of views and ideas concerning humanity, individuality, and the moral order associated with "proper" and desirable conduct. The second evinces emergent systems of categorization and corresponding social relationships delineating boundaries of the self, and the third describes some of the social strategies of exclusion and inclusion employed in maintaining these boundaries. This threefold account of the context wherein conceptions of selfhood are generated, constructed, and sustained constitutes the basis for the final section of this discussion, whose main objective is to arrive at some tentative propositions regarding the study of selfhood among the aged. In this analysis it is suggested that three major analytic categories should be considered as appropriate dimensions of the self. These are the mental — both emotive and intellectual aspects — the sociocultural, and the physiological. Evidently, all three are viewed merely as social constructs and not as objectively ascertained variables.

THE HOME

The first setting to be discussed is an old age home in Israel.[1] At the time of the research (1972/73) the institution catered to 400 able-bodied residents. It was established and run by the welfare agency of Israel's biggest trades union federation and admission was based on being a union member or a member's parent. However, the location of the home in the midst of one of the most desirable residential areas in Tel Aviv and the modern facilities with which it was equipped made demand for accommodation exceed supply. For an applicant to gain admittance he or she had to display not only mental alertness and functional independence but also to enjoy the backing of some influential figure in the political arena of the trade unions.

This last constraint contributed a great deal to molding the character and the composition of the population of residents. Those whose background and connections furnished them with a position of power and influence within the home usually upheld an uncompromising socialist ideology combined with strong nationalistic fervor. Having been deeply involved in the core of Israel's nation-building epoch and ethos, some of those residents became nationally famous living legends. This halo followed them to the home and was reflected in both their status among fellow residents and their own behavior.

Thus articulation and fluency in the use of Hebrew were highly esteemed as linguistic insignia of previous involvement in political and educational scenes. Simple but tidy outfits were regarded as signs of nonostentatious yet respectable appearance and avoidance of jewelry and other means of bodily adornment was almost universal among residents. The value of austere living in the service of national and socialist goals was cherished as the foundation and the justification for the existence of Israel as a state and for the continuity of the Zionist enterprise. Some of the residents whose past seemed to represent such personal sacrifice and patriotic legacy set the indisputable principles for social esteem and moral judgment in the home.

This came into being by establishing a body of residents whose explicit purpose was to debate various subjects of interest. These discussions evolved into an arena for discussing the affairs of other residents, the administration of the home, and the desirable code of practice of institutional life. Eventually, the discussion group used outside connections in an attempt to influence the manager and wrest from him the power to regulate the flow of residents into and out of the institution. It was proposed that an executive committee of residents – all of whom were members of the discussion group – would be authorized to determine criteria for admitting new residents and to set up a disciplinary court whose jurisdiction would include decisions concerning the removal of unwanted residents from the home.

This last issue of conditions for transferring residents to other institutions or back to their families was a crucial one for a number of reasons. To begin with, adequate alternative care facilities for the frail elderly at the time of the research were scarce and, in any case, not within the financial reach of most residents. The pressure of applicants – many of them backed by influential connections – on the home was enormous (3,000 on the waiting list); hence the increasing vulnerability of residents without outside support. In addition, cases of genuine inability to perform as independent elderly people were in constant jeopardy of having their secret malfunctioning exposed with all the impending consequences incurred by such disclosure. The result was that public display of personal competence and social vigor became not only the order of the day among those whose future residence was at stake but also an imperative which put a whole new, institutionally conditioned, complexion on the concept of a person. We shall see how the components of physical ability, mental agility, and social capacity interplayed to delineate boundaries and to shape relationships and behavior.

If the internal, though externally inspired, pyramid of stratification is to be sketched, the following ladder would emerge. At the top, occupying the revered position almost belonging to a mythical sphere, were those residents whose life histories and present associations made them into the epitome of some of the most commonly shared values in Israeli society—patriotism, self-sacrifice, and socialism. Immune to removal and assured of future provision, these people advocated the idea of "good functioning" more than those residents who had cause for concern regarding their capacity to maintain the image of competence.

Out of the three dimensions of selfhood—the mental, the sociocultural, and the physical—they gave priority to the latter, setting it as the final yardstick for an ascription of human qualities and thus for participation in the home. Evidently, their social capacity was beyond dispute. Having been the stalwarts of Israeli society at large and of particular institutions in it, and being organized into a hierarchically ordered, well-disciplined group within the home, each was dependent upon the collectivity.

Their mental alertness was also beyond doubt, since it was constantly displayed in the form of linguistic articulation, heightened awareness of current affairs, and considerable reading. It was all thrown into relief in the course of the discussions where great importance was attached to being fluent, clear, and well informed. The debate procedures were made to safeguard these qualities through rigid agenda, orderly discussion, and lucid presentation.

However, the somatic element of personhood put members of the group on an equal footing with other elderly people and thus endangered the other two dimensions of a seemingly immutable existence. Three social contexts bear on the significance and the extent of the physical image of personhood as embedded in the notion of being old, incapacitated, and unworthy.

THE DISCIPLINARY COURT

The first was the attempt to remove from the institution all disabled residents through the already-mentioned disciplinary court. Although this claim for power was aborted by due agreement among residents, goaded by fear of the proposed "court" abusing its authority in internal disputes, there was a broad consensus among members of the group about its main objective: removing physically unsuitable residents from the home.

This position was explicitly formulated in a series of discussions concerning the desirable mode of institutional care for the aged. Out of the various proposed structures of care facilities on the agenda, one was unequivocally and unanimously favored, that of a functionally homogeneous residential population. The arguments made in support of that view were numerous, the most prominent being the need to avoid any visible reminder of the impending deterioration incurred by old age.

In a group reputed for its extensive intellectual activities and whose social image was one of solidity and viability, it was unexpected to witness the prevalence of the physiological criterion expressed not only in assertions regarding other residents but also reflexively. The outside world—that of nationwide admiration and almost sanctification—was often described in terms of its negative reaction to the appearance and physical faculty of members of the group. Thus, a member whose educational stature was much revered in the country told tearfully how a teenaged youth maliciously and scornfully tripped him over, causing him to fall and calling him "an old man."

Consistency in the categorization of the old into the physically fit and the physically unfit was accomplished and affirmed by applying this dichotomy to members of the group. Thus, a woman member who confessed that she lost control of her bowels while suffering from a stomach complaint was scoffingly laughed at and was made to leave the group for good. Other members expressed their wish to avert such disgrace and indignity by urging their coresidents to make plans for their removal from the home in case of physical incapacitation, even against their own will. Furthermore, if such eventuality should arise, any form of loyalty or solidarity which could shield, albeit temporarily, the handicapped resident ought to be dissolved. This unmitigated position is rendered even more forceful in view of the fact that the privileged status of members of this group in the home was a secure safeguard against any possibility of administrative decision taken to their detriment.

Other residents, however, were vulnerable to measures affecting their living conditions in the home, ranging from transfer to another institution to the imposition of an unwanted roommate. Here physical adequacy was not sufficient to guarantee continued residence. Obvious evidence of social involvement and mental capabilities was expected to demonstrate to the management of the home that the resident in question was "functioning" to the extent of extending his or her sojourn.

This challenge was met variously by different residents. One noted mode of reaction was the formation of groups of residents whose joint resources created a basis for negotiating terms with the administrative authorities of the home. Those who engaged in such efforts relied on their collective presentation rather than on individual achievements. Thus interdependency centered around common interest or in pursuit of a set objective was not just a manifestation of sociability and communication but a means of survival and an invaluable resource in its own right. Furthermore, such social formations, by the structure of their members' interaction and through their activities, generated boundaries and images of personhood based on group distinctions.

HANDICRAFTS GROUP

Attesting to these generalized principles was, among other clusters of activities, the handicraft group. This group was the result of the initiative of a few women residents whose main objective in setting it up was to provide a stage for displaying good "functioning." The manager of the home, having realized the potentialities of this enterprise for advancing some of his projects—particularly in promoting the institution's public image—offered extensive resources in aid of the operation of the group. Thus, sewing machines, materials, and paid instructors were provided to enhance and intensify the activities. Other residents who were aware of the manager's interest in the group joined in the activities in pursuit of recognition as well-functioning participants.

Indeed, not only did the recruits perfect a front of accomplished residents, but they also gained a host of benefits and privileges bestowed by the management on those favored by it. Hence, belonging to the group became a self-perpetuating engagement reinforced by constant rewards. Within the sponsored cohesiveness of the group there emerged social markers to define the position of members vis-à-vis other residents.

Being occupied was, for a member of the group, more than a mere badge of acceptable functioning or even an active behavior defying the passive image attributed to old age. It was, in the main, a way of relating to the elite echelon of the home, whose reputed socialist doctrines and dedication to a public cause were deemed to be faintly emulated in the mode of operation evolved in the handicraft group. Work was regarded as an ultimate value, sharing and equality were cherished as ideal forms of interaction, mutual care was advocated as a prime objective of the relationships within the group, and acting in the service of a collective goal was set as the main target of the activities.

All these characteristics were embedded in the daily meetings of the group. Incessant sewing, knitting, embroidery, and weaving constituted the major areas of work activity. The products—baby clothes, soft toys, crochet, decorations, and light repairs—were prepared for sale in a grand bazaar annually held at the home to raise funds for the Soldiers' Welfare Association. The amount of proceeds was considered an indication of the group's success. Furthermore, the event was attended by officials and dignitaries whose presence at the bazaar signified social recognition and endorsed the group's endeavor as a contribution to the public.

Thus, the production activities combined with the distribution proceeding, embodied values of work, nonprofit, charity, and involvement in a national enterprise. The implication of this for the perceived internal stratification in the home was asserted by a founding member of the group: "We are all hardworking people who did not have the chance to prove our dedication to the country and its ideals before we entered the home. Now we have been given this opportunity, and for this we ought to be thankful to the discussion group and its members.

Naturally, we are far from the standards they set, but we try our hardest to follow their example."

Under the aegis of that sheltered arena, a number of handicapped residents found welcoming sanctuary. These were residents whose functioning capacity was in doubt due to physical or mental disability. Yet by virtue of their faithful participation in the group they enjoyed an identification with the most turbulent display ground for active functioning in the home. The other members, mindful of the real purpose behind this type of participation, treated these joiners as equals, especially during encounters with the management. Hence, group membership provided a protective social cover under which both the able and the disabled could secure continued care and immunize themselves against the consequences of pejorative personal change. Social participation was infused with equivocal meanings spanning the whole gamut of existence in the home — from the survival prospects in the institution through the internal status system to the broad cultural arena.

SYNAGOGUE

If physical personhood dominated the activities of the discussion group and social personhood prevailed over the operation of the handicraft group, the mental sphere pervaded the actions of some of the most vulnerable residents whose locus of assembly was the institution's synagogue.

Religious persuasion and practices were much disdained and almost unanimously maligned in the home. Rooted in an atheist socialist stance and anchored in the long-established political schism in Israel between religious and non-religious parties, veteran trade unionists expressed little sympathy for anything remotely associated with religiosity. In contrast, coming from a nonsocialist background, most residents who participated in the activities of the local synagogue did not enjoy the shield of previous connections. Unable to associate themselves with the institutional elite and snubbed at other group activities, the synagogue participants could only construct their conception of personhood on resources other than physical and social. They resorted to some of the religious practices in Judaism which most practically and ritually suggested a high degree of mental alertness.

These practices were the assiduous study of religious lore and mores. Since such activities are often performed collectively in specially designated, communal study forums, this tradition of learning was adopted to justify the formation of a multitude of study groups attended by most members and led by hired tutors. Close observation of members' behavior in the course of such gatherings revealed that, far from following the arduous and mind-boggling lessons, the students were preoccupied in a host of extracurricular activities such as humming, gazing at a fixed spot, chatting, and browsing through other chapters. Having no student feedback whatsoever, the instructors would proceed unabated, getting through an outstanding amount of Talmudic material.

Provisions were made by the members to disseminate knowledge of their activities in the home and particularly to make the management cognizant of their learning capacity. The manager was often invited to witness the study groups, and his help was sought to enhance the scope of the lessons. In conversations, members took great pride in their participation, never failing to stress the implications of this activity for certifying their mental abilities.

To bolster the image of mental agility and grasp of reality, the members developed an explicitly resentful attitude toward those residents whose be- havior suggested disorientation and mental incapacity. Thus during the High Holy Days—the New Year festival and the Day of Atonement—when the majority of residents attend synagogue, the seemingly confused among them were forcibly denied access to the synagogue. This was done by blocking the gangway or by pushing them back to the elevators from which they emerged. It is interesting to note that these residents, negligible minority though they were, featured prominently in the self-definition of the other two groups. They were labeled "exhibitionist" by members of the discussion group, no doubt in line with the physical criteria applied by them, and "vegetables" or "animals" by members of the handicraft group in accordance with their social yardstick. The former represented the ultimate in physical ossification and inertia, while the latter referred to imputed lack of human communication and relationships. In effect this category served as an appropriate barrier between being a person and a nonperson for all the other residents. Having forfeited their attributes as *homo physical*, *homo social*, and *homo mental* in the respective eyes of members of the discussion group, the handicraft group, and the congregants of the synagogue, that category was made into a symbolic vehicle through which the three differently based identities could be forged.

THE DAY CENTRE

While external and internal boundaries in the old age home were contingent on isolating physical, social, and mental properties to generate referential frames of a "person," the members of the Day Centre[2] in the following case study eliminated all these to allow for a nascent idea of self or, as will be explicated later, a "selfless" self to emerge.

The day care center catered to elderly Jewish residents of the London borough of Hackney. It was administered by the biggest Jewish charity in England, the Jewish Welfare Board, and registered a total of 400 participants with a daily attendance of 150. The services provided by the center's staff—a team of two qualified social workers and eight other workers in various capacities—included hot lunches, tea, occupational therapy, transport arran- gements, and some welfare care. Recruitment was on a broad ground of needs ranging from destitution and loneliness to a general "inability to cope." The population served covered a wide age spectrum from the late forties to early nineties. Daily routine was leniently regulated by staff, with ample scope for members' initiative. Indeed, most activities unconnected with the financial running of the center were taken up by participants. Thus cooking and serving meals, tea making, light entertainment, and recreational pastimes were all organized and conducted by members.

Most members shared a common background of similar life histories. As first- or second-generation Eastern European Jewish emigrants to Britain, they experienced childhoods of poverty, unemployment, heavy reliance on extended families, and welfare assistance from the Jewish Welfare Board. Adulthood was characterized by unskilled or semiskilled, low-income occupations and by bringing up children of their own who, due to their parents' massive investment in their education, became professionals of a much higher socioeconomic status. Old age was typified by insufficient means, poor housing, malnutrition, and increased dependency. Added to that was almost invariably a disengaged and reluctant family, alienated Jewish establishment, run-down neighborhood with a high crime rate, and a paucity of community institutions.

This common socioeconomic background with its shared cultural heritage and similar existential and living conditions made for a nondifferentiated environment where past could not be used as a valuable resource and future prospects held no hope in store. The social structure created in the Day Centre reflected this state of affairs but was also a reaction to some of the main scourges encountered by the participants. Its constitution reinforced egalitarian behavior and disassociation from previous affiliations, disregarded physical differences and functional disability, and put participants of different mental capacities on an equal footing. To understand how this was accomplished, it is necessary to describe the main principles upon which relationships in the Day Centre were based.

Participants, with outstanding unanimity and without any form of external guidance, expressed and practiced a set of values of which the core symbol and the main uniting theme was the idea of unbounded care and unconditional help. This was *not* an ideology advocating mutual concern and reciprocal assistance. Rather the notion of a noncumulative, nonmutual communal pool of available-to-all resources was the most representative feature of this system. Thus participants were expected to spare any resource at their disposal—be it material possession, a piece of advice, a comforting gesture, or some relevant information—to whomever was in need of it. Inversely, those in need were entitled to lean on such help regardless of past relationships, loyalties, and obligations. Even married couples attending the Day Centre were pressured to stay apart and act with as little mutual acknowledgment as possible.

This structure was unaffected by the high turnover of participants, nor was it modified by changes in staff or services. Furthermore, the nature of other activities held in the Centre seemed to support and furnish its competitive games, and contests were avoided by converting them into no-win "learning situations" or laughing them off as "unreal." Patterns and designs of craftwork were incessantly repeated, and renegade attempts at creativity and ingenuity were suppressed through joking, derision, criticism, and, in extreme cases, ostracism.

The combined effect of these properties on the social context of center life resulted in lack of both hierarchical order and recognizable power structure among members. Since care was regarded as an absolute measure by which everybody and everything ought to be valued, and as no limits were set on participants' potential capacity to give and to receive, members found themselves in the simultaneously two-pronged position of helper and helped. Those who experienced a disproportion between need and contribution would usually restore the balance by creating mock events when an objectively unfounded plea for assistance was manufactured by a participant. For example, a man who was fit enough to climb the stairs pretended to have difficulties, inducing a prompt reaction from a disabled member who rushed to his aid with alacrity.

The obliteration of differences and the demolition of boundaries took various forms, of which the most persistent was the erasure of the past. Occupational careers were a taboo subject among participants, and so were familial associations and community ties. Children were renounced as "traitors," and the lack of contact and financial support from offspring who lived affluently not far away from their parents was often adduced as evidence of disregard and disengagement on the part of the former. The latter, however, insisted that the breakdown in relationship was mutual and that their interest in their children equalled the children's concern with them. Contrary to common stereotypes, the past was not imbued with nostalgia. Inversely, the hardship of childhood, the injustices of adulthood, and the frustrations of aging were viewed grimly as consequences of lack of economic opportunity, social inequality, cultural deprivation, and "bad luck."

Nevertheless, the center offered open opportunities and socioeconomic equality where physical, mental, and social differences were abandoned; participants considered themselves as agents of care and "humanity" rather than project-oriented beings whose predetermined goals are contingent upon past resources and future plans.

I shall restrict the rest of the discussion to the three constituents of self — body, mind, and society — as handled and constructed by the center people.

Physically heterogenous as they were, the participants did not adopt somatic yardsticks to erect social divisions. This was particularly evident in those activities which apparently, by definition, invoke differences in bodily ability. Noteworthy among them was the most popular pastime in the center, dancing. Every afternoon participants would gather in the dining hall and engage in old-time dancing to the accompaniment of a record or a member singer. No one was excluded; dancers aided by sticks and crutches, rolling and roving wheelchairs, and stooped handicapped men and women — all dancing out of time and irrespective of any rhythmical discipline — were a common sight on such occasions.

Illnesses and disabilities, abundant though they were among participants, were ignored as irrelevant to the experience of "living the day" or dismissed as mere annoyances. Even terminal conditions were publicly treated as belonging to another sphere of existence. A man suffering from an incurable cancer of the throat described himself as "always cheerful, no matter what. My throat bothers me only as far as my speech is concerned. I want people to understand what I say." When faced directly and explicitly in discussion groups or interviews with the problem of terminal conditions and physical deterioration, participants insisted on their right to euthanasia or suicide. Some, having experienced periods of institutionalization in old-age homes, geriatric wards, or mental hospitals, depicted such a past as "another life," "a state of vegetation," or "not being human." Leaving the center, therefore, was conceived of as a departure to such alternative modes of existence, and deaths occurring shortly after were attributed to such leaves rather than to any other causes.

Although differences in physical ability were considered irrelevant to participation in center life, an unavoidable cleavage existed between the severely handicapped and the rest of the members. This was due to the absence of an elevator to facilitate mobility between the first and the second floors. In effect, the ground floor was occupied mostly by disabled members far removed from the bustling hub of activity above them. Yet this territorial division was not recognized by members as a valid one, since the example of a few handicapped participants who struggled valiantly and successfully to make their way upstairs was invoked to demonstrate both the extent of willpower and the effectiveness of the care system.

Although the notion of care was pervasive, deviant behavior of a mental nature posed an intractable problem for participants. Though accounts of center-induced "recoveries" from a stroke or getting out of depression were widespread among members, other cases seemed to defy the idea of care as a panacea. Display in public of offensive behavior, idiosyncratic characteristics, and unsolicited allusions to the past and to death were viewed not only as embarrassing and unpleasant, but also challenged the fundamentals of the care system. A number of participants whose presence in the center evoked strong reactions were compelled, sometimes forcibly, to leave. Others, particularly those who were themselves a product of the care system, called for handling within and by means of the care principles. One example of such treatment was Sid.

Sid was a manic-depressive who suffered a severe relapse following a car crash involving his son. He arrived at the center subdued, withdrawn, and completely unresponsive. Attended by his wife, who acted as a volunteer in the center, he retired to a corner and spent his days gazing blankly at the others. A sudden mood swing reversed the whole situation. Sid entered into a state of boundless elation and exhilaration, became extremely talkative, and offered to help far beyond his capabilities. This transformation was welcomed by participants as a response to their incessant efforts and to the influence of the center atmosphere. Sid was introduced to outsiders as the "great success" or "miraculous recovery." These descriptions invariably were echoed by Sid himself, who would reassure the listener that he felt fine and that his only concern was to look after people who might have been through similar emotional distress. In discussion groups and informal gatherings, Sid always brought up the subject of helping other participants and preached the teachings of the care system to whomever was ready to listen.

Petty bickering and brawls with participants, coupled with unfounded claims to power "officially" delegated to him by staff, provided the first indications that Sid was diverging from the expected path of participation and might even prove to be a menace, particularly to the care system. In fact, occasional bouts of depression and recurrent defiance made it virtually impossible to handle Sid within the care system rules. The reaction among participants was to convert Sid into the center jester—a figure to be ridiculed, not to be taken seriously, and yet to be integrated into the light-hearted, joking atmosphere of the place. Thus, everything Sid said, regardless of its logical merits and contextual relevance, aroused laughter. His mere presence seemed to provoke waves of gaiety, and his apparent cooperation in building up this image contributed to establish this status. Gradually Sid sank into a long spell of depression and withdrew completely from center activities. Only then was he recognized by his fellow participants as "mental," "sick," and "a psychiatric case."

This assumption of pseudo-psychiatric labels was apparently borrowed from the extensively used, psychologically laden terminology employed by social workers. Yet being a "case" enabled Sid to remain within the domain of the care system and rendered his ascribed mental faculties acceptable, manageable, and inherently reversible. Such incorporation was structurally contingent on total segregation of the center reality from the outside world and on phasing out internal divisions within it. It was the maintenance of external boundaries and the lack of inner differentiations which fostered the free flow of resources among participants and the obliteration of somatic and mental factors as regulators of social relationships.

The society of participants, therefore, developed mechanisms through which differentiation processes were averted and threats and challenges could be handled. An attempt by several participants to form a "committee" to represent members' interests was aborted by those who were supposed to benefit from its operation on the ground that the self-nominated candidates were "power-mad" and "status seekers." Disputes and conflicts between participants were confined to short-term altercations taking the form of brief outbursts after which relationship would go back to normal. Those whose unsettling presence could not be contained were ostracized or expelled. This was the fate, for example, of a participant who was exposed as a beggar, thus subjecting his fellow members to shame, questioning by his actions the validity and efficacy of the care system. In another instance, a woman who, despite incessant demands, dwelt on her glorified past which stood in direct contradiction to the others and in any event negated the present-bound egalitarian ethos of the center's reality, also was forced to leave the center for good.

DISCUSSION

At first glance any attempt to ascertain some common ground between these two examples might seem to be a futile exercise. The materials and methods employed in the construction of a concept of personhood appear almost diametrically opposite. The residents of the home drew heavily on past experiences and cultural continuity; the center people endeavored to disengage themselves from their memories and heritages. The home's residents interrelated the categories of body, mind, and society in a hierarchical fashion, whereas the center's members fused them into a unitary immutable collective entity. Internal boundaries were dimmed in the center, highlighted in the home. Conversely, the center presented itself as an impervious environment while the home was an extension of its outside milieu. However, a more careful scrutiny of the data would unveil a different comparative dimension. Beyond the unrelatedness of the commitment to function and the idea of care, beyond the highly stratified society of residents and the egalitarian near-commune of participants, and beyond the differences in background and the organizationally contrasting care facilities looms a core of seemingly similar properties.

The idea of a "person" was built in both institutions on key cultural concepts derived from a common past and infused with nascent context-bound content and proportions. Thus neither "functioning" nor "care" could be placed on an uninterrupted continuum anchored in previous values, nor could they be regarded as realization or fulfillment of lifelong experiences. Rather the unreservedly caring person of the center as well as the functioning actor at the home arena were engaged in adapting themselves to the exigencies of one existential dilemma.[3] This was the problem of uncontrollable deterioration and unarrested adverse change associated with the aging process.

Erecting rigid boundaries based on physiological, social, or mental categories in the home and blurring these very three categories in the center, although apparently contradictory practices, serve the same ultimate objective—facing up to the uncertainties embedded in the futureless, unpredictable world of the inhabitants of either establishment. It would seem that the very idea of continuity is defied by the lack of progress and the loss of social time in old age.[4] Hence the attempt to reconstruct a concept of a person is induced and shaped by selecting and organizing cognitive and social components in a manner amenable to encounter such fundamental problems.

If values and life experiences are to be treated as manipulable resources rather than deterministic impositions, the two cases could illustrate the emergence of a context-bound conception of personhood among the aged without the bind of cultural presuppositions and psychological bias.[5] The key assumption for such an approach, however, must be that control of meanings and identity is accomplished through addressing a major existential predicament rather than through perfunctory reference to one's life history.[6] The process of "deculturation",[7] while divesting the personhood of aged of some of its symbolic anchorage,[8] makes for a reconstitution of cultural classifications based on a newly acquired balance between the desirable and the attainable.[9] If, as Myerhoff (1978a) suggested in her analysis of another Jewish day center, the aged are engaged in fighting their social invisibility and in securing their symbolic survival, then notions of continuity of personhood and preservation of identity should be viewed through the prism of present context rather than life course development.

NOTES

1. For an overview of the home, see Hazan (1980a).

2. For a detailed ethnography of the center, see Hazan (1980b).

3. It would seem that the existentialist perspective of "life project" advocated by Sartre and applied to the study of history by Langness and Frank (1981) is not attested to by the case of the center people.

4. As Fontana (1976), McCulloch (1980), and many others observe, the idea of continuity does not withstand the scrutiny of extending into a dubious future. Some solution to this dilemma is offered by Myerhoff (1978a), who suggests the presence of a myth-like orientation among the people she studied.

5. Viewing personhood as generated by culture (Geertz 1979) is an approach adopted by many anthropologists to the study of aged self. See, for example, Plath (1980), Bateson (1950), Myerhoff (1978b), and Henry (1963:391–474).

6. A similar approach emphasizing interaction rather than culture is proposed by Gubrium (1975) and Gubrium and Buckholdt (1977).

7. This is a concept proposed by Anderson (1972), whose study with Clark on older Americans (Clark and Anderson 1967) points to the gap between culture and the aged self.

8. For an analysis of some social complications of the growing incongruity between symbolic messages and the self conception of the aged, see Teski (1979, 1987).

9. Some indication to this line of argument could be found in Tornstam (1982) and is reflected in the works of Rosenmayr (1981) and Thomas (1970).

15 UNCLE ED, SUPER RUNNER, AND THE FRY COOK: OLD MEN ON THE STREET IN THE 1980S

Jay Sokolovsky and Carl Cohen

> The Bow'ry, the Bow'ry.
>
> They say such things
>
> And they do strange things
>
> On the Bow'ry, the Bow'ry!
>
> I'll never go there any more!

These popular lyrics from the 1891 hit show, *A Trip to Chinatown*, once helped introduce New York's Bowery to the American public. They also epitomize the contemporary situation of this urban zone which remains our nation's most infamous skid row. In the mid-1980s a trip into the world of older men who make this area their home illuminates America's emerging human tragedy of this decade — the dramatic growth in poverty and homelessness. Ironically, as President Reagan was proclaiming, "America is back — standing tall, looking to the '80s with courage, confidence, and hope" (State of the Union Address, January 25, 1984), the economic policies of his "opportunity society" were forcing thousands of older adults to find their abode on the mean streets of cities like New York. This chapter will provide an interior view of the daily existence of three such men who are battling homelessness in old age.

In examining the lives of Uncle Ed, Miles (the fry cook), and Roland (the super runner) it will become apparent that for men who are old, poor, and live in or rely on the Bowery for survival, each day is likely to present a major crisis. The three men do not represent by any means the total variety of social types on the Bowery. However, the dilemmas they face daily, the paths that led them to the area, and their future prospects constitute key patterns that were repeated in the lives of the several hundred men we studied.

PROFILE: UNCLE ED, THE CLASSIC BOWERY MAN

It was one of those rare times that Ed showed real anger when he was not drunk. In a rage he shouted, "How could such a freakin' stupid thing happen to someone who is so needy. I need my foodstamps back, you stupid bitch." He almost lunged across the table at the thin black woman working the computer in room 301 of the Human Resources Administration. Instead, he slumped back in his chair, embarrassed at the loss of his usually pleasant demeanor and feeling the wall of bureaucracy pressing on his head. Without another word he left the office and headed back toward the Bowery. Although only fifty-six years old, Ed worked to fight off a dependent, idle old age, but such frustrating experiences produced feelings of hopelessness and cravings for a bottle.

Before returning to his tiny cubicle he rested on a park bench and contemplated the oppressive reality of most Bowery lives — profound poverty. From a monthly check of $277.85 Uncle Ed pays $132.18 for a five-by-nine space with thin wooden walls and a chicken wire ceiling. Despite free mission clothing and 25 cent breakfasts and lunches from the Bowery Residents' Committee, between five and six dollars are spent daily to pay for coffee, cigarettes, his dinner, and other incidentals. It is indeed a rare month when he does not need to borrow money at the typical usurious rates — borrow $10 and pay back $14.

Ed is a jovial caricature of the classic skid row alcoholic. Nicknamed by a nurse after he provided help to others while himself a patient at a sobering-up station, he tries to show a nonoffensive helpful face to all he meets. A clean-shaven, comely person when sober, he is usually dressed in secondhand mission clothes, which as often as not are ill fitted to his bulky frame and pot belly. As he walks the streets of the Bowery hardly five minutes will go by without someone shouting "Hiya, Uncle Ed." Every other block will find Ed passing some deli or secondhand clothes shop where he used to find casual work running errands. He has been on his own since the age of sixteen, working menial jobs in restaurants, hotels, and construction sites.

Seldom without a cigarette, he chain smokes Camels — lighting up for a few minutes, putting it out delicately with his fingers, clamping the butt securely behind his ear, only to resume smoking a short time later. To emphasize a point while we speak, he will crinkle his pug nose, roll his eyes up into the side of his head, and discuss in raspy, measured words his life on the streets. "I have had in the past a bout with alcoholism where I was one time four months sober and then at one time six months sober, but then I went off the deep end, starting to drink again, but this time I'm sober five months." His last major drinking spree began about eight months ago following a bitter argument with a woman he was living with in Queens for a short time. As he put it:

Roland delivering food to the homebound in a flophouse.

The widespread destruction of single room occupancy housing has dramatically increased the number of older homeless adults. This photograph shows one such hotel in the process of conversion into expensive condominium apartments.

During the night, I guess John Barleycorn [alcohol] talked to me, I just got up. . . .Well, fuck it, I'm going back to the bottle. I've already got it in my mind that the only place I can go is back to the bottle so I drank a bottle. Three-quarters of a fifth of gin, and then I went out to the bus stop and I got on a bus to Penn Station, bought some more gin and came back to the Bowery and this is where I am now. I come right to the Pacific Hotel around three in the morning. I saw the clerk which I know personally, Pete's his name. He said, "What do you want, Uncle Ed?" I said, "I want a room. I gotta sleep this shit off."

As Ed was white, old, and could pay the $3.50 for the night he was given a cubicle and began one of his cyclical trips to oblivion.

I'd wake up in the morning and I'd be so discouraged, depressed, knowing that I just had another goddamned day with a bottle where I never made no plans, everything just came as they came, you know. I'm an early riser, up by six, even when I'm drinking, I sleep two hours and I think I got a good night's sleep. I'd usually see if I've got the dollar and a quarter for the first pint of T-Bird [Thunderbird wine] and if I didn't, I'd go out panhandle at Lafayette and Houston streets. There's a good light there where I'd bum a card [panhandle]) and I'd usually walk down Grand Street going up to drivers and they'd give me a quarter, or wipe his windshield and hope he gives ya a quarter. Usually I go up and tell 'em, I don't want a dime for a cup of coffee, bullshit. I just go right up to them and I'd say, "Excuse me, sir, could you pardon me, I'm thirty-five cents short on a drink, could you probably help me out?" And usually I found out that they think more of you if you were man enough to ask them towards a drink instead of the old bullshit you need a quarter for a cup of coffee. That went out.
By eight o'clock [A.M.] I've made a bottle, made the price. I would never guzzle it. I'd take a couple of good shots to kind of settle my nerves, put it in my back pocket, and go out and make another one. Usually I make my second before I finish the first. This way, I had reinforcements for the next day. I usually like to drink by myself but sometimes I get despondent and I want someone to talk to so I go to this park on Spring Street, if I've got a bottle or if I haven't, I go there to see who's got a bottle. Without a doubt I would find myself an associate or two. Usually, one would say, "Well, we need a bottle, Uncle Ed," and I'd say, "Let's go make it."

Ed had left Queens with $300, but inside of a week, maybe ten days, it was gone. Even when he still had the money he was often too drunk to get back to the hotel and he would spend the night in a park or a darkened doorway, and for four nights he slept in Penn Station, crawling behind a partition or sitting in a phone booth until the police finally kicked him out. "I was relatively 'holding the banner' [living on the streets] with money in my pocket because I was drinking around the clock until I went broke and my legs went bad." For over two months he slept at night on the subway and sometimes went to the Holy Name Mission to clean himself up. Finally, in a state of exhaustion and with his feet so bloated he could not get his shoes on, he was talked into entering a detoxification unit near the Bowery.

While in the detoxification unit a case worker recertified Ed for SSI and when he was released nine days later, the Pacific Hotel became his abode once again. In early August 1985 he celebrated at an AA meeting his last five months of sobriety. Each day he struggles to avoid drinking. His daily circuit takes him from his hotel to a local center for older men, for long walks to Greenwich Village to have coffee and read the newspaper in a quiet park, and finally a visit to one of the several AA groups to which he belongs. He is careful to avoid the Spring Street park where his old "bottle gang" usually gathers. Ed talks proudly of the young alcoholic in his hotel whom he recently "twelve stepped," that is, convinced through personal testimony and persuasion to join his AA group.

Constantly poised between hope and despair, Ed occasionally looks for a quiet job, a night watchman or doorman would be ideal he says, but he has given up looking for the time being. On occasion, to get some money, he will "make a run" for the older men in his flop house who are too frail or too drunk to leave their drab quarters. Having had mild heart attacks in the last several years, he can no longer play the quick errand boy for local merchants. Ed realizes old age is upon him, and each day ends with him wondering if the next morning will find him splayed in the gutter on Spring Street reeking of cheap wine.

PROFILE: MILES, THE FRY COOK

"It's my own damn fault," Miles said repeatedly to himself as he searched in vain for a comfortable sleeping position on the hard wooden bench. As if it had happened minutes ago, he could still feel the ragged edge of a broken mirror held tautly at his throat as a man he knew only as Paco relieved him of his savings. He had met this forty-year-old man from Puerto Rico while spending the prior month upstate at Camp LaGuardia, along with 250 other homeless men. Paco was a friendly type with an easy way about him, and the two quickly became "associates." He had confided to Miles that he could help him get a cheap apartment in the Bronx. Paco claimed to know the super in the building, and Miles would have to put a deposit down right away. At the beginning of July, Miles returned to the city, cashed his Social Security check, paid off some loans, and went to meet this supposed "close associate." He was promptly mugged by this con artist and relieved of the $380 he had brought along. This was virtually all the money he had in the world.

It was now July 25, 1985, and Miles arose before daybreak from his park bench at East 23rd Street. Despite his tall lean frame and healthy looks, old age hung on this black man's shoulders like a leaden cloak. At first light he would begin what for him was a humiliating task, collecting returnable soda and beer cans. He had slept even less than usual during the night, as at 12:30 A.M. an old acquaintance, Jack McDonald, wandered into the small park. Jack spotted Miles and offered to share his pint of Wild Irish Rose. Miles politely turned this down, since the cheap liquor sometimes made him sick.

When Jack learned of Miles's plan for the coming day, he was almost indignant when he asked, "What are you doing picking up cans for a living?" Trying to hide the growing depression he felt, Miles replied, "Tomorrow's my birthday, I'll be sixty-three, and I want to buy myself something real good to drink, get some cigarettes, and maybe go take in a movie, uptown." Jack finally dozed off on a nearby bench, but Miles just sat and stared at all the other homeless. By 4:00 A.M. the prostitutes and the cadre of gay men looking for a quick tryst had left the park to the almost ninety people who made this urban glade their home on a warm summer night. Most slept on the benches, but a few were in small tents on the grass.

Over the next two hours Miles smoked a handful of the tobacco stubs garnered earlier during his daily trek across Manhattan. Every once in a while he muttered to himself, "I can take this 'carryin a stick' [living on the streets] every once in a while, but I can't take much more 'pickin shit wit the pigeons' [scavenging in the street]."

Miles's life had not always been this way. Just after World War II he started working as a cook's helper at a famous seafood restaurant in Brooklyn. Miles developed great skill at cooking fish, and within five years he became one of the main fry cooks at one of the city's better places to eat. He would work at this same place from 1946 until 1972, when the restaurant was closed. By the early 1950s he had a good apartment in the Bronx and was living with a woman who worked for the electric company.

It was two decades later that his life began to come apart. In 1972, at the age of fifty, he had the first of several minor heart attacks, and shortly after he was released from the hospital, the restaurant closed down. Without his old job, in poor health, he began a pattern of periodic drinking; eventually he had to give up his apartment. Miles lived in a series of run-down SRO hotels on the upper west side and later, mid-town Manhattan. Every couple of years he was forced to look for a new place to live as gentrification began to decimate the available housing stock for low-income inner-city dwellers.

Although this proud black man has only twice slept on the Bowery for very short periods, by the early 1980s he had begun an economic and residential lifestyle common to many of the older skid row men. For most of the spring and summer he would live in cheap hotel rooms and take short-term manual labor jobs around the city or in one of the many Catskill Mountain resorts. If his money ran low or if his hotel was converted into expensive condominiums, he would spend a week or two "carrying the stick" until he could afford another "livable" room. During the winter, when jobs were scarcer and he tended to drink more, he would live for several months in Upstate New York, staying at various retreats for homeless men. Miles would remain at one such state-run place called Camp LaGuardia for up to three months.

When speaking about the Bowery Miles literally spits out angry words expressing his feeling of humiliation in just walking through the area. "I told this social worker, I'm not trying to be funny or smart. I refuse to sleep on the Bowery. I don't consider myself Bowery material 'cause I can remember years ago when I used to come down to the Bowery just to have a ball, because they had nice bars and shows down here." He is also quite aware of the continuing de facto segregation which offers blacks rooms in only the very worst flophouses. This in an area where even the best accommodations are barely fit for human habitation.

More than anything, Miles is a victim of one of the worst housing crises New York City has ever faced. His last residence for any length of time (twenty-six months) was a run-down single room occupancy hotel (SRO), with the rent ($260) eating up over one-half his monthly Social Security check. When he complained about the horrendous conditions in the hotel he was harassed by the management; he was forced to leave after being robbed by thugs hired by the management. Fearing for his life, Miles left shortly after this, retreating to the "holy mountains" (a religious sanctuary).

Now, three years later, he was back in the "carrying the stick" segment of his annual cycle. With almost no money to his name, he spent July sleeping in a park in good weather or taking to the subway when it rained.

Following his recent robbery he was able to get just $21.50 from the Welfare Department and promptly went to see Tony, the "buy and sell" man, where he pawned his watch and ring for another $15. Although Miles had not had any contact with his relatives in Alabama since 1960, he still retained two close friends whom he has known for the last forty years. Both these black men were in their mid to late sixties, had their own tiny apartments but subsisted on very low incomes. One man, Charles, kept Miles's suitcase in his apartment when he lived on the streets. The other person, named Jim, worked as a cook's helper at the Bowery Residents' Committee and had talked Miles into going there for the almost free lunches. From these friends he was able to borrow about $30 following his robbery.

Miles could have gotten a ticket for a free room through the Municipal Shelter or even paid for a couple of weeks at one of the lesser flophouses. The first option was ruled out; during his last visit to the "Muni" he had been violently attacked by a young man strung out on drugs. Paying for a room was not considered, as Miles refused to panhandle and he wanted to husband his resources in hopes of next month finding a better place to live.

All the other times Miles had been homeless he stayed by himself, but this time it was different. He had recently witnessed many attacks on older men and himself been robbed. Each night he slept with a group of three other black men whom he had come to know only in the last month. Two of them, Walt and John, were about his age, while the other was in his mid-30s. He had met John one evening while waiting on a line for sandwiches at the St. Francis of Assisi church. Miles had offered the other man a cigarette, and, as they struck up a conversation, they not only came to like each other but also discovered that they had been sleeping at opposite ends of the same park. Back at the park Miles was introduced to the two other men who had been staying together for the last month, and it was decided they would all sleep together, two men to each long bench.

For now he would sleep in the small park that stretched two blocks long and one block wide in a neighborhood that was safer for old men than the Bowery. To homeless men who lived in this area, skid row had come to be called "Little Vietnam." In fact, Miles was constantly scared living anywhere out on the streets and attributed his drinking a pint of wine a day to this situation. Besides witnessing various brutal attacks on older men by young thugs, twice in the last year he had been robbed and beaten. Miles usually arises earliest in the morning and gently shakes his sleeping partner and informs him that he will be leaving soon. The four men spent most of their waking hours apart. When they congregated in the early evening they would swap the day's news and information about the menus at various soup kitchens, trade surplus food, and perhaps split a pint of wine. Walt and John had steady jobs while James did household repairs around the neighborhood and sold old soda cans almost every day and had introduced Miles to this practice.

The day before Miles's birthday started off badly. Although he had enlisted Jack to help with the collection of cans, they had only made a little more than $5. Some merchants simply refused to take dirty cans even though the mayor had declared this unnecessary due to the severe water shortage in the city. He began to have the same suicidal thoughts that almost ended his life in 1972. However, over the course of the day he would meet up with all three of his oldest friends who each remembered his birthday and had given him gifts of money totalling $14. Better still, one of these buddies related to Miles a rumor claiming that "his" old restaurant might be soon opening again.

That night at the park benches he celebrated by sharing several bottles of vodka with Jack and his newly formed sleeping group. The liquor and the thought of his Social Security check coming next week made him almost ebullient as he discussed two plans he had for the coming week. First he would buy a copy of the *Amsterdam News* and begin scouting for a cheap apartment. Next, he would take the D train to Brooklyn and see if anyone could use a real fine fry cook.

PROFILE: ROLAND, THE SUPER RUNNER

"Not even the cops will bother me here," Roland thought confidently as he closed the top of his room for the night, a cardboard carton which last housed a new refrigerator. As a final ritual to evoke momentary security he pulled his woolen cap over his gaunt, well-scrubbed cheeks and curled up into a ball.

Satisfied for the moment with his comfort, he was less certain of how he would fare in the icy rain predicted for this night. His flimsy shelter had some big rips that were difficult to repair with the newspaper he had collected during the day. For the past week he had been scouting out this secret flop in a tiny alley off Bleecker Street where a short landing of steps led down to a basement door which was nailed shut. By 1:00 A.M., having prepared the steps with cans to warn of intruders, Roland drifted off into a light sleep. His last conscious thoughts that night were "just six more months until my sixty-fifth birthday, then I dig up my money, start collecting my Social Security checks, and get away from here."

It was the week before Thanksgiving, a time of the year which forced the street-dwelling homeless of New York to make life-and-death decisions. Roland had recently taken to wearing several layers of clothing and using extra caution in choosing his flop for the night. Not only was he now leery of marauding young black skid row men, but the mayor had declared that all homeless persons would be removed from the streets when the temperature dipped below 32 degrees. Just last month he had been sleeping in a cardboard box set behind a big shrub on a tiny street at the edge of Greenwich Village. The police had stumbled upon his abode and asked him to come along with them, but Roland told himself, "They're not taking me to the hospital and givin me no electric shock treatment." Despite a strange new pain in his left leg he ran like a frightened rabbit. The two patrolmen just stood there and laughed, glad to have chased another bum out of their patch.

Yet Roland is no ordinary bum. He has the money and, more importantly, the connections to get a room in a cheap hotel. Many years ago when he was still drinking he slept with 400 other men in a dormitory-style flophouse, resting on cloth-covered planks of wood. Periodically he would lose most of his accumulated money by either going on month-long drunken binges or being robbed in his hotel. Now a decade later he will relate with a slight shudder how he left the flop, began living in an abandoned building uptown, and simply decided that life on the street as a drunk was too dangerous. He ceremoniously broke his remaining bottles of wine and just sat in his room for a week of hell until the tremors of withdrawal had gone away. Since this time the streets have been his home.

Although for the last ten years he has slept somewhere on the streets of New York, he remains meticulously clean, has through his own willpower completely stopped drinking, and works a steady forty-hour week at various jobs on the Bowery. He is in fact a super runner. A "runner" does errands for cash. Roland is a supper runner in that he has graduated from the "get a bottle and keep the change from the ten" level to working only for social workers, priests, and nuns. He is now an amazingly fit and energetic sixty-four year old.

Roland is a do-gooder who labors for the charity establishment rather than the tavern owners or hotel managers, because he has acquired the social work ethic. Each weekday at noon he becomes the delivery unit of the Bowery's main "Meals on Wheels" program. Up and down the steps of flophouses he can be seen effortlessly hefting a cart laden with prepared lunches from a local soup kitchen. Moving in a fluid half-run through each building he deposits a meal, shouts "How ya doin," and accepts the quarter tip he receives in each of the forty-odd rooms he will visit. He is constantly ferreting out hotelbound and homeless old men who need food and clothing and bringing them together with the Bowery's social service resources. He will not buy a bottle for you, but he will get your prescription filled.

Although Roland rapidly moves through the streets with a gait seemingly born from confidence, his active participation in life dangles on a thin thread. In the course of being a super runner he is asked to operate a machine or deal with key, often with disastrous results. Not because he is careless. He attacks any job with metronomic precision, but he will always try to avoid work that involves any technology whatsoever. New employers (the local mission's pastor or a new social worker in an agency he patronizes), however, will take advantage of his great energy and willingness to help and press him into locking up or running a dryer or a dishwasher. Roland is no worse at these things than anyone else, yet when the inevitable happens, when a fan belt breaks or a key is lost or a fuse goes, Roland becomes frantic. He knows he has broken whatever he was working. It must be his fault. Inevitably he flees and avoids the embarrassment of dealing with his screw-up. His life is cast in cycles of such stories, which are used to explain how he came to the Bowery and why he has not had any contact in years with his sister or other relatives in nearby Connecticut.

Roland's affect, motor, and speech patterns are quite unusual. He is constantly in motion or asleep; his appetite is prodigious. Not more than 140 pounds, with a wiry body that looks no more than forty years old, he eats perhaps five times what other older men do. Many of his jobs involve food as well as cash payments. He talks in bursts, as if to mimic verbally his mode of motion and work. A voracious newspaper reader, he readily offers opinions on both front page and obscure items. Obsessed with stories of gore and violence, especially those perpetrated on Bowery men, he is a walking local history of murders and bizarre accidental deaths. If you walk the streets with him, every few minutes another sordid story will unfold. Passing a boarded-up paper processing factory, he will tell of a drunk old bum who slipped in late one winter night to sleep warmly between layers of cardboard. Unfortunately, the man slept too long and was tragically crushed to death when the bailing machines were started up in the morning.

Despite his varied jobs in Bowery institutions he always sleeps alone in one of several places off the Bowery. One is under the Manhattan Bridge, and several others are dispersed on the edges of the Greenwich Village area. Where he flops on a given night depends on the weather and his judgment of its safety, based on a scouting of the area. After spending his day on the Bowery he will walk a winding two mile route to the West Village where he meets a close associate who attends an Alcoholics Anonymous meeting there. On route he constantly scans the streets for two things, money and muggers. As he passes a garbage can he will quickly examine the top layer of refuse hoping to repeat a recent windfall when he found five twenty-dollar bills neatly folded in an empty pack of cigarettes. After a meal at McDonalds with his associate and an hour or so of casual conversation, the two men will separate and Roland makes his way to one of his "homes," always arriving around midnight.

Roland had not slept indoors more than a handful of times over the last ten years, giving in only when the winter weather reached Arctic dimensions. Now on this night in late November while Roland dozed in his leaking cardboard shelter, the temperature hovered just over freezing, and a mixture of rain, sleet, and hail pelted the city. Virtually paranoid over the possibility that the police would again try to drag him off the street, he would use his secret sleeping place. The bottom of the landing where he lay in dreamless slumber was impossible to see even from a few feet away.

Roland was startled awake at 5:00 A.M. by stinging pain that ran up and down his left leg and almost made him cry out. Most of his body was soaked, and he felt colder than he had been all last winter. What frightened him the most was that his lithe frame could not be supported by his usually dependable legs. Although almost sixty-five, his physique and energy level would be the envy of most men half his age. Now it was a great effort to move let alone walk. A terrifying thought ran through his mind – "My god, have I got AIDS or somethin'."

Fueled by his mounting fear, Roland willed himself to half crawl, half hop to the Holy Name Mission, one of the several places he worked on the Bowery. After two agonizing hours he had negotiated the mile to his hoped-for sanctuary and lay on his side across the street from the mission doors. However, he could not move another inch. Fortunately, he did not have to wait long before he could hail a young homeless man seeking an early morning shower. Roland gave him a dollar and asked him to call Father Charles in the Holy Name. The priest came out with another man and carried Roland into the mission and a temporary warm bed.

Later that day a doctor examined Roland and decided that he suffered from a severe sciatic nerve inflammation and prescribed some medicine and several weeks of rest. For the next month, he slept at the Holy Name, and then, to the shock of everyone who knew him, Roland checked into the best flophouse on the Bowery. This was the first time in over ten years that he had slept for any length of time with something more substantial than cardboard covering his head.

THREE LIVES IN PERSPECTIVE

These three profiles illustrate the world of recurrent crises which confront older Bowery men. Each of these men face acute crises that include falling through holes in the welfare "safety net," rapid deterioration in health, physical assault, alcohol craving, and loss of shelter. These short-term episodes are embedded within the patterns of chronic crises of impoverishment, alcohol abuse, physical and psychological disability, sporadic work opportunities, a public policy of reducing entitlement programs and destroying the housing stock available for low-income people, and the stigma attached to life on the skids.

It is easy to react to the plight of such individuals through popular stereotypes of the poor skid row derelict who is homeless by choice, unwilling to work, constantly inebriated, possibly psychotic, reluctant to conform to norms of personal hygiene and dress, beyond redemption. In order to address the problem of homelessness it is necessary to avoid such standard characterizations and to examine the interweaving of the numerous elements that generate and sustain these individuals.

To many, Uncle Ed must seem like their typical image of a "Bowery bum." In his worst moments, he can be seen as a hopeless drunk, living for days in the same wine-soaked garments and panhandling quarters for his next bottle. Yet like so many of the older Bowery men he desperately seeks employment beyond the occasional "gofer" job, in a quest for dignity and enhanced economic stability. Ed is convivial, articulate, of great support to others, and maintains a wide range of social relationships including women friends and kin. Despite frequent bouts of severe depression, he still nourishes the hope of staying sober long enough to escape the vicious consequences of his addiction and poverty.

Roland is a man who, due to his bad experiences in flophouses, has opted for a homeless existence that many would consider insane. His unusual speech and affective patterns amplify this image of a "crazy" person. If Roland were captured by the mental health system, and he has been there at times, he might be labeled a chronic schizophrenic. But, in his element, on the streets, Roland is a successful entrepreneur who provides useful services to more needy Bowery men. He does not drink, use drugs, or panhandle. Roland represents a rare type, but he is hardly unique. He may be homeless, but he is not a bum.

Superficially, Miles would appear to be a shiftless old street alcoholic. His street living, however, originates in the housing policy which has greatly depleted the stock of affordable apartments and hotel rooms. In fact, a 1985 survey indicated that 55 percent of the elderly in New York City shelters had lived independently in their own apartments or in SRO hotels before entering the shelter system; a majority of them had been evicted because of inadequate funds (Human Resources Administration 1987). His drinking problem is nurtured and exacerbated by fear and anxiety brought on by street living. Due to his strong desire to secure an apartment he prefers to sleep on a park bench rather than pay even small amounts for the inhuman housing available for blacks on the Bowery. Miles's intelligence is reflected in his ability to maximize the meager resources available to men on the street.

NOTE

This chapter is adapted from chapter 1 of *Old Men of the Bowery: Strategies for Survival Among the Homeless*, Carl Cohen and Jay Sokolovsky (New York: Guilford, 1989), and reprinted by permission. Research for this chapter was supported by grant number RO1 MH37562 from the National Institute of Mental Health. The authors thank Eric Roth for his assistance.

PART VI
CULTURE, HEALTH, AND AGING

A recent visitor to an Abkhasian family was being entertained at a feast, and following local custom, raised a glass of wine to toast a man who looked no more than seventy. "May you live as long as Moses [one hundred twenty years]," the visitor said. The man was not pleased. He was one hundred nineteen.

— Sula Benet

THE QUEST FOR GERIATRIC UTOPIAS

During the 1960s and 1970s reports filtered into the gerontological literature and popular press about a small number of mountain peoples who supposedly possessed extraordinary longevity. Not only were their ages said to exceed that of the man being toasted in the quote above, but their health was like that of spry sixty-year olds. In the Caucasus region of the Soviet Union, gerontologists by the 1950s were said to be studying, among the Abkhasian people, a well-documented group of 500 *dolgozhiteli* (very long living people) ranging in age from 120 to almost 150. Similar assertions were made for a peasant village in Vilacabamba, Ecuador (Davies 1975; Halsell 1976), the Hunzakut of the Karakoram mountains in Pakistan (Leaf 1975), and the inhabitants of Paros Island, Greece (Beaubier 1976).

It is usually very disquieting for my students to learn that none of these claims for a modern fountain of youth appears to be true (Leaf 1982; Palmore 1984; Beall 1987). In the case of the Abkhasian super-centenarians, we are dealing with one of the great scientific frauds of the twentieth century (Medvedev 1974). For this population, the oldest documented age is actually only 114, and in

Vilacabamba none of the reputed centenarians was found to be older than 96 (Mazess and Foreman 1979).

Despite the false claims for breaching the normal limits of human life-span, we seem to be dealing at least in Abkhasia with an exceptionally healthy group of 90- and 100-year-olds. Interestingly, the details of their lifestyles, when compared with that of healthy centenarians in the United States and other countries, exhibit a number of common factors that promote long life. Such persons tend to have low-fat, low-calorie diets, refrain from much caffeine, tobacco, and alcohol, and have been physically active throughout their lives (Hadjihristev 1988).

Still, it is important to realize that all populations must cope in some way with the biomedical imperatives of aging (Moore 1987). In human populations, typically fewer than .005 percent at any given time are 100 years or older, and starting before age forty many human functional capacities begin a steady process of decline. Of course, the level of physical functioning at any age is influenced by many cultural factors such as diet and activity patterns over the life cycle. As I can attest from my research experience in Mexico, many a twenty-five-year-old North American anthropologist has been worked or walked into the ground trying to keep up with a seventy-year-old peasant.

AGE, AGING, AND THE "AT RISK" ELDERLY

Not only does culture influence the degree of physiological change associated with aging but it also defines when old age is thought to begin and how it relates to the rest of the life cycle. In the United States, with a bureaucratic, public designation of sixty-five as the beginning of old age, there is a common linkage of the aged with illness and severe decline in most areas of life. When those both under and over sixty-five are questioned, a majority believe that persons past age sixty-five are in poor health (Harris and Associates 1975). This stereotypical linking of illness and old age has a long history in Western thought, going back to Hippocrates, and is still embedded in the diagnostic schema of Western medicine (Sankar 1984).

While a small percent of non-Western societies also use chronological age as a marker for the onset of old age, the large majority of such societies use some type of functional definition, based either on a social change (birth of a grandchild), alteration in physiology (such as menopause), or capacity (inability to carry out a full range of economic activities). A holocultural study by Glascock and Feinman (1980) found that some form of social change is the single most prevalent way cultures have of marking the entrance to old age. Since in such societies it is typical to begin labeling persons as old between the ages of forty-five and fifty-five, people are less likely to link the general concept of old age with the types of physical decrements most associated with the sixth and seventh decades of human life. Instead, as seen with the !Kung, entering elderhood is often linked to positive forms of maturity and spiritual growth.

However, as Glascock shows in chapter 2, many of these same societies recognize more than one phase of old age and the later stages are almost always defined by the appearance of bodily and mental deterioration and minimal levels of function. Persons bearing these designations of "decrepit," "near dead," or "childlike" are the ones most likely to be mistreated by society. It is important to realize that the actual level of frailty is not the only factor involved. Maxwell and Maxwell (1980) found in a worldwide comparative study that, although physical decline is a major factor in predicting negative treatment of the aged, lack of family support looms as the most important variable. This notion is consonant with studies in the United States showing that, controlling for other factors, elderly with a weak kinship network are by far the most likely to enter institutional forms of long-term care. Once again, culture meets context.

The complex dimensions of this issue are often lost in statistical analyses employing the coded data from hundreds of societies in the HRAF files. It is necessary then to turn to holistic ethnographies such as that found in Judith Barker's contribution. Having worked as a medical anthropologist on the Polynesian island of Niue, she explores the paradox of how a society known for its beneficent treatment of the healthy aged could show apparently heartless disregard of the unfit elderly. Barker shows that understanding the neglect directed at "decrepit" older folks does not yield to simple mechanical explanations. Such disregard is neither part of a uniform way of treating all disabled persons or an ecological expedient dictated by low surplus production. Rather, it is crucial to view how the label of "decrepit" itself is negotiated (again linked to the level of kin support) and constructed within Niuean conceptions of the life cycle, death, and ancestral states.

Of all the demographic changes occurring in the world, the one that will be most related to the health needs of the aged is the rapid growth of the population over seventy-five years of age (Kirwin 1988). Commonly now called the "old-old," these are the aged who are most "at risk" of having their ability to function hampered by chronic diseases (Sankar 1987). For example, in England it is estimated that while only 12 percent of persons sixty-five to sixty-nine years of age need home services to remain in the community, this figure jumps to 80 percent for individuals eighty-five years or older (Little 1982). In most countries, especially in the developing world, this older, high-risk group is the fastest growing component of the elderly. In nations like China, Nigeria, and Yugoslavia, health service providers are now coming to realize that with regard to the aged a major shift is needed involving less intervention for acute care and more continuous care for chronic states (Heisel 1985; Manton, Dowd, and Woodbury 1986). In Yugoslavia, for example, the rising number of older citizens with hypertension has caused considerable strain on medical services just to perform basic tasks of blood pressure regulation, let alone to cope with the various forms of disability related to high blood pressure. One recent response has been to promote local self-help groups trained collectively by medical personnel to take their own pressures and maintain required diet and drug regimens (Sokolovsky, Sosic, and Pavlekovic, in press).[1]

An expanding international literature attests to the explosive growth of such self-help/mutual aid groups, especially in industrial societies (Caplan and Killilea 1976; Guzlow and Tracy 1976). There is a growing body of data indicating that such groups can emerge as a critical resource facilitating a "health-promoting" approach to illness or psychosocial crisis, as distinct from a traditional "sickness approach" (Borman 1983). The essence of all these associations is a collection of people who share a common problem and band together for mutual support and constructive action toward shared goals. Those types of social entities that touch on the lives of the elderly tend to be of three types: life-cycle/crisis transition groups (such as widow-to-widow); affliction groups (hypertension, alcohol); and support for carer groups (caregivers for Alzheimer's victims support).

This last type of group is the subject of Neil Henderson's chapter 17. Even though only about 5 percent of those over sixty-five suffer from Alzheimer's disease, it is the most common type of dementia and evokes perhaps the greatest fears among old and young alike when they think about possible problems of old age. While many ethnic elders wax rhapsodic about the strength of their family-support system, few things can test the veracity of such claims as caring for victims of dementia (Valle, in press). Henderson's research addresses this topic by combining a focus on the ethnic context of aging and the function of a new social formation to deal with this problem. It provides a virtually unique study of a support group for Hispanic-Americans established in Tampa, Florida. It illustrates the need to consider the positive impact of nonfamilial, formal institutions (gerontology centers) in providing an organizational and educational role for strengthening the ability of the "natural," informal parts of support systems to provide community based care for the elderly (Antonucci and Jackson 1987). An important lesson of this chapter is that informal and formal supports seem to function best when they act together to strengthen each other rather than to operate as totally separate components of a care system. The effective interaction of formal institutions and ethnic families is no simple matter of merely providing information and help. Henderson clearly demonstrates how an understanding of the cultural context can overcome ethnic-based problems stemming from over-reliance on females as caregivers, generational differences, and low "service user" patterns in the Hispanic community.

LONG-TERM CARE AND THE INSTITUTIONAL ENVIRONMENT

Although about 80 percent of the aged in the United States report that they can get around by themselves (Butler 1975:175), the rapidly growing numbers of the "old-old," those over seventy-five are creating great strains on our system of long-term care. In fact, fewer than 2 percent of the "young-old" reside in long-term care institutions, as compared to 7 percent of the seventy-five to eighty-five-year-olds and 16 percent of those over eighty-five (Tobin and Liebermann 1976:211). For at least the last fifty years most industrial nations have recognized the necessity to construct settings outside of the home to attend to the needs of the very frail and dependent elderly. Even Japan has, quite recently, embarked on a policy of rapidly increasing the number of such places (Campbell 1984; Brown 1988). Western European countries facing demographic pressures earlier than the United States have developed a broader range of options and stronger geriatric medicine programs to deal with the medical needs of the elderly (Kane and Kane 1978, 1982).[2] Despite movements in many countries to institute an "open care" system (Amann 1980; Little 1982) stressing both multiple-care options and the goal of maximizing the time elderly remain in their own home, the needs for some forms of nursing care in specialized medical settings persist.

Nursing homes have had an infamous place in the spectrum of care settings and environments predominantly built for the elderly. For good reason much of the literature on such institutions have focused on the high level of abuse, especially in those proprietary care units where profit has attained a much higher value than caring for residents (Vesperi 1987; Johnson 1987). However, as Renee Shield demonstrates in chapter 18, even in a well-run, nonprofit nursing home, there are issues other than the physical elements of care which can be just as crucial to the resident's quality of life (Powers 1988). She uses anthropological models of life cycle-focused ritual to show how placement in a nursing home begins the change of status from adulthood to death, but typically fails to complete the ritual cycle, thus leaving the initiate in an incomplete liminal stage and having to endure an endless transition to oblivion. Students can profitably compare such a cultural transformation of personhood with that found among the Kililui of Papua New Guinea where very frail elderhood can be associated with a predeath ritual signifying that the person is in the process of dying and is already socially dead (Counts and Counts 1985). Here, as in the nursing home context, some elderly resist this process and seek to declare, "I am not dead yet!"

NOTES

1. For a comparative discussion dealing with hypertension in different countries, see Sheppard, Robinson, and Cuervo (1988).

2. Important sources of information about international innovations dealing with the aged include; Teicher, Thursz, and Vigilante (1979); Little (1982); Nusberg, Gibson, and Peace (1984). Students should also see the newsletter of the International Federation on Ageing, *Ageing International*.

16 BETWEEN HUMANS AND GHOSTS: THE DECREPIT ELDERLY IN A POLYNESIAN SOCIETY

Judith C. Barker

The distinction between decrepit and intact elders is now recognized as being an important one in all societies (Foner 1985; Glascock 1982, and this volume). Frequently, frail elders are seen as burdens on society and even are subject to "death-hastening" behaviors, such as neglect or abandonment by the rest of the community. Certain aspects of Polynesian life, however, lead to an expectation that the senescent old will not be abandoned or neglected but rather will always remain a focus of attention and concern. Is this in fact the case?

Until recently (Counts and Counts 1985; Holmes 1972, 1974; R. Maxwell 1970; Nason 1981; Rhoads 1984), relatively few works dealt explicitly with the status of the aged in Pacific nations. By and large, the picture we have of old age in Polynesian societies, showing that elders are not forgotten or devalued but powerful and active family and community members, comes from ethnographic studies, such as those of Firth (1936), Hanson (1970), Mead (1928), and Shore (1982). Generally, these works fail to distinguish between the treatment accorded the intact, mature elder and that given the frail, senescent old. Where this distinction is mentioned, the impression is given that frail elders are treated much like their intact peers: "The infirm aged are cared for with matter-of-fact kindness within the family, mostly by women and older children" (R. Maxwell 1970:140). Any variation in treatment accorded the frail elderly Polynesian is assumed to be idiosyncratic, a mere aberration having no societal or cultural basis.

Fieldwork on a little-known western Polynesian island, Niue, reveals the existence of considerable differences in the treatment of very frail and of intact elders. Very frail, decrepit elders, whom I came across when doing other sociomedical research, were by Western standards neglected. My encounters with these old people were so vivid, so at odds with my expectations derived from the literature and from observation of the lives of intact elders, that they remain indelible. The impression I formed about the lives of decrepit elders is confirmed through investigation of medical records and archival documents and by accounts from others.

This chapter shows that variation in the treatment of the elderly on Niue is not only well established and systematic but also makes cultural sense. Discussion shows not just how decrepit old people are treated and who constitutes this group of elders but also considers several different reasons why they appear to be neglected by family and community alike. The individual threads of discussion eventually intertwine to produce a complex understanding of how those aspects of Polynesian culture that lead to respect for the aged give way, in the face of severe physical or mental infirmity, to other values.

Certain striking similarities are evident in all Polynesian societies, similarities, for example, of language, ecology, social organization, and myth and history (Keesing 1953; Oliver 1961; Ritchie and Ritchie 1979; Topping 1977). Nonetheless, each Polynesian society is unique, different from all others. The description given here of Niuean responses to the elderly is a case study; it is merely suggestive but not proof of the existence of similar social processes in other Polynesian societies.

THE ELDERLY IN POLYNESIAN SOCIETY

Said to be well past the giddiness and frenzy of youth and comfortably settled into the responsibilities of marriage and family, elders are stable and influential figures. These people are in the prime of life, full of vigor, with complex political and social, including family, roles and responsibilities. An elder in Polynesian society is not necessarily an old person but simply an adult of mature years with some social standing. Having acquired political and social influence by middle age, a competent person maintains that power into advanced old age. Because the role of elder is well established before a person reaches chronological old age and begins to experience significant decline in physical or mental abilities, elders suffer little disruption of roles as a result of mere chronological aging.

Throughout this chapter the term "elder" is used to refer to those who both currently or formerly held important sociopolitical positions and have reached chronological "old age," that is, are sixty-five or more. Continue to bear in mind that the role of elder was well established by the time these people reached numerical old age.

Competence at performing a task and the need for it to be completed are more important factors than age or sex in the assignment of domestic roles in Polynesian society (Macpherson 1978). Hence, in old age both men and women can engage in household tasks or childminding without compromising their social position. Elders guide the younger generations in political decisions and are respected for their experience of life and for their knowledge, for being repositories of ancient lore and ceremonial custom.

Youngsters who go abroad for education or work or who become caught up in the modernization/Westernization processes currently affecting Pacific nations sometimes claim that traditional roles for elders appear irrelevant, restrictive, or irksome (R. Maxwell 1970; Rhoads 1984). While the traditional roles allotted to the elderly might chafe modern youth, the elderly themselves are still highly regarded. In the face of sometimes sweeping socioeconomic changes, Polynesian elders sustain their high status (Holmes 1974; R. Maxwell 1970; Rhoads 1984).

Elders are respected not just because of family background or accomplishments but also because they are chronologically older. A focus of socialization throughout Polynesian life, especially during childhood, is the inculcation of respect for those who are older (Ritchie and Ritchie 1979, 1981; Shore 1982). Older people are to be obeyed, respected, served, and emulated. In return, elders will nuture, teach, love, and protect. This form of relationship continues throughout life, younger persons always being socially obligated to care for older ones.

Not only is attention to relative age linguistically symbolized but it is bolstered by the entire social, religious, economic, and political organization of Polynesian life. On Niue, for example, a man who wishes to establish a closer relationship, perhaps for political purposes, with an influential male would not only call him by the kinship term *taokete*, older brother, but would act accordingly, doing tasks for and publicly supporting his mentor's political stance. Toward a young man whom he wished to sponsor, the man would use *tehina*, younger brother, and would expect the youth to behave appropriately toward him, doing the things a younger brother ought. Political power, at both governmental and community levels, devolves to mature adults, to those with experience and wisdom, to elders.

From these values comes an expectation that even in advanced old age or physical infirmity the aged will be well looked after by children and grandchildren, because they are still important family members and because it would be shameful to neglect an elder. Most ethnographers of Polynesian societies argue that this expectation is fulfilled (Holmes 1972, 1974; Holmes and Rhoads 1987). My research, however, casts some doubts on this.

NIUE ENCAPSULATED

Relatively little is known about Niue. A fleeting first contact with Niuean society was made by Cook in 1774 (McLachlan 1982; Ryan 1984). Except for shipwrecked sailors, traveling missionaries, and itinerant traders, the island was little visited until after the 1850s when mission stations were first established and some trade contacts set up (Niue Government 1982). Because it was outside the regular trade routes, had little commercial potential, and was not strategically or militarily important, unlike many other Pacific islands Niue was not colonized until very late. After the Anglo-German Convention became void, in 1900, Britain annexed the island but promptly handed over control to New Zealand (Niue Government 1982).

In both preannexation and contemporary times, observers of Niuean life have been few in number and somewhat reticent about writing (Ryan 1984:xi). Two dated ethnographies exist (Smith 1983 [1902/1903] and Loeb 1926), both based on very short periods of fieldwork over fifty years ago. More recent works, a few based on extensive firsthand observation, comprise mainly hard-to-find articles on specific topics (e.g., Bedford, Mitchell, and Mitchell 1980) or unpublished theses (e.g., Barker 1985; Frankovich 1974; Mitchell 1977; Ryan 1977). Writings by Niuean scholars (Niue Government 1982; Chapman 1976) give valuable though far from comprehensive accounts of Niuean life.

An isolated single island of raised coral, Niue does not fit the popular image of a tropical isle. It has no fringing reef, no sandy beaches, no lagoon. Access is difficult via steep cliffs 25 m high which rise directly out of deep ocean. Located about 500 km east of Tonga, 600 km southeast of Samoa, and 2,500 km northeast of New Zealand, at 19°S and 169°55′ W, this large (16 km x 10 km) island is covered by relatively sparse vegetation growing in shallow pockets of soil between jutting upthrusts of sharp coral rock. There are no streams or ponds, no surface water on this drought-prone island.

Though shallow, the soil is fertile (Miller 1980). Slash-and-burn (shifting) agriculture, arduous and labor-intensive, supplies the populace with its basic subsistence needs and is supplemented by fishing, hunting, and gathering. In sharp contrast to most other Pacific nations, the economic base of the island has changed recently from being primarily agricultural to service provision (Connell 1983), so that now nearly 80 percent of employed adults on the island work for wages for the Niuean Government. This gives Niue a high standard of living compared to other Pacific nations. Money, from wages or supplemented by cash cropping of passion fruit, limes, or coconuts, is used to buy durable consumer goods such as motorbikes, outboard motors, and refrigerators.

Administered by New Zealand from 1900 to 1974, Niue is now an independent nation. New Zealand continues to provide Niueans with citizenship, with protection against foreign powers, and with considerable economic aid (Chapman 1976, 1982; Connell 1983; Fisk 1978; New Zealand Coalition 1982; Pollard 1979). The island inherited upon Independence an infrastructure of communications, roads, and health and social welfare services of a standard far in excess of her nearest neighbors.

Demographics

Thought to have been originally settled from 120 A.D. by successive waves of Tongan and Samoan voyagers, contemporary Niue has both a language and a social organization similar to but different from those western Polynesian societies (Loeb 1926; Pollock 1979; Ryan 1977; Smith 1983 [1902/1903]). Daily life and interaction on Niue is much like that on any other Polynesian island (see Hanson 1970; Holmes 1974; Levy 1973; Shore 1982).

Though large in area for a Pacific island, Niue has never supported a population greater than about 5,000, probably because of the arduous nature of agriculture on this difficult terrain (Bedford, Mitchell, and Mitchell 1980). Depopulation, not overpopulation, is Niue's greatest worry (Bedford, Mitchell, and Mitchell 1980; Niue Government 1985; Walsh and Trlin 1973). Out-migration started in the late nineteenth century when young men left temporarily to work on plantations on neighboring islands; recently emigration has taken a new and more serious turn. Now out-migration is permanent and consists mainly of unmarried youth and of mature adult couples and their school-age children, going mainly to New Zealand to settle. In each of three five-year intercensal periods between 1971 and 1986 Niue lost 23 percent of her population. Such migration has had a considerable effect on the island's population structure.

The total population of around 2,500 now left on the island contains an increasing proportion of elderly adults. A 1988 census revealed a total of 178 natives on the island who were aged sixty-five or more (Niue Government 1988). Elders thus comprise 8.1 percent of the total population on Niue. This is low compared to the United States, where in 1980 older people made up 11 percent of the population, but high compared to other less-developed regions of the world such as Africa, Latin America, or Asia, where the proportion of over-sixty-five-year-olds is estimated to be under 4 percent (Hoover and Siegel 1986; Soldo 1980).

Aged dependency (those sixty-five or more years per 100 people aged fifteen to sixty-four years) on Niue is high for an under developed nation. At 15.3, Niue's current aged dependency is nearly three times that generally encountered in less-developed nations (Hoover and Siegel 1986:15), but it is still less than aged dependency in highly developed countries such as the United States, which in 1980 had an age dependency of 18.4 (Soldo 1980:39).

Hence, elders form a visibly large demographic group on Niue. Moreover, with a life expectancy at birth approaching sixty-seven years and a decreasing mortality rate (Taylor, Nemaia, and Connell 1987), elders will continue to form a large part of Niue's population in the future.

Central Niuean Values

Though typically Polynesian in many respects, such as in childrearing and family organization, major political forms, and central religious values, Niue is also atypical. The most distinctive features are a rudimentary and very flexible social hierarchy, egalitarian ideals, an emphasis on individual achievement, and a strong work ethic (Frankovich 1974; Pollock 1979; Ryan 1977). The influence of these features of Niuean life on the status of elders is clearly exemplified during political processes.

Political power on Niue is reserved for those who demonstrate competence and knowledge, from the wider world or accumulated in the course of a long life. An unmarried young adult man has little political influence; only *patu*, married men, men who have demonstrated their commitment to raising a family and to accepting village responsibilities, have a voice in the village or other political meetings. Chronological old age eventually brings elder status to those very few men who do not marry or do not produce children.

More elderly women than men have never married, but again, these are few in number, and virtually all those women have had at least one child. Women are not excluded from political power on Niue (Rex, n.d.), especially if they come from influential families, but generally they, too, must be married and demonstrate leadership qualities in other spheres of life before being accepted as important political figures. Like men, women vote and take an active part in work-related union affairs or village events. So, any person in a position of political or social power on Niue has arrived there through a combination of personal and social attributes. Their position is maintained because they continue to demonstrate competence, an ability to control younger, ambitious persons and to measure up to the demands of that position. Whenever competence begins to diminish for any reason, however, other, usually younger, people step in and attempt to wrest power from them.

Despite considerable size differences, each of the thirteen villages on the island is represented in the Fale Fono (Niuean Assembly) by one person elected by the residents of that village. These representatives are generally older men with prestigious backgrounds: pastors, government officials, or successful planters. The Fono is completed by the addition of six representatives elected by all eligible voters. These Common Roll Members, as they are known, tend to be younger and have very different life experiences from the other representatives. Many, for example, have been educated outside Niue and have returned to work as teachers or doctors before becoming politicians.

Thus modern Niuean politics conforms to tradition by having elders represent individual villages at the same time as it deviates from convention by rewarding individual achievement, by allowing younger Assembly representatives considerable influence. A flexible social hierarchy, egalitarian ideals, and an emphasis on individual achievement work against elders maintaining their privileged position once their competence is in any way compromised.

THE ELDERLY ON NIUE

The ethnographic picture of the aged in Polynesian societies, presented briefly above, portrays well the intact elder on Niue. Those in good health, those with important social functions, are respected community figures, political leaders, and vital family members. Their life is well discussed in the general literature on Polynesian societies (such as Holmes and Rhoads 1987). The frail, infirm Niuean elder, however, presents a very different picture. Decrepit elders are frequently ignored, even neglected, by kin and community, left to fend for themselves without any longer having the physical or psychological means to succeed. Exactly how are impaired elders treated on Niue? What kind of treatment do they receive from their kin and community? How is this possible?

The Treatment of Impaired Elders

I met elders with urinary or fecal incontinence, with wheezing chests and running eyes, with infected sores, with bleeding gums, or with painful joints, none of whom had been seen recently by a doctor or nurse. One elder I saw lay semicomatose on the floor, evoking rueful smiles from visitors and kin and comments about "going out the hard way."

Too frail to summon a physician themselves, these elders relied on their caretakers, who seemed not to bother asking for medical help. It is not difficult to get a physician to visit. A doctor visits each village on the island four times a week. A red flag hanging by the roadside brings the doctor in his van right to the door. Public health nurses, too, can be fetched in the same way on their monthly round to assist in the care of patients. All medical services, including hospitalization, are free.

When cases such as these do come to the attention of the medical profession, they are quickly attended to. Elders comprised a yearly average of 8 percent (N = 276) of all admissions to hospital on Niue between the years 1977 and 1982. Fourteen elderly patients (5 percent), most of whom remained in the hospital for over a year, were admitted solely for nursing care (Barker 1988).

Several types of old people were generally left unattended or received minimal care. They were: those old folk who yelled constantly, swearing at neighbors and kin; those who fought all the time, hitting out at all and sundry; those who forgot people's names or forgot what they were doing; those who wandered away at all times of day and night; those who talked only of events in the remote past, who conversed with absent friends and long-dead relatives; those who stared vacantly about them, constantly drooled, or were incontinent. Little effort seemed to have been made to bathe these elders, who were generally clad in filthy rags, to clean their homes, or to provide them with any material comforts. Many of these elders complained of being constantly hungry.

Just as a pregnant woman is warned not to steal from others lest her unborn child be punished for the act by being born with a withered arm, so were explanations found for the causes of some degenerative processes which afflict the old. Facial tics, involuntary vocalizations, and limb palsies in old age are regarded as belated punishments for evil-doing. Elders with these problems were held up as examples for children: "Old Togia makes noises like a chicken all the time now. That's because when he was young he must have stolen chickens and never confessed to doing so. If you don't want to be like that when you get old, don't steal."

Those old folk who were bent over or walked oddly or tried ineffectually to fend for themselves were figures of fun. It amused everyone that an elderly man was concussed by a dry coconut falling on his head. The danger of a dry nut falling from a tree is constantly pointed out to young children, who quickly learn this lesson. An old person who fails to avoid a falling nut demonstrates the loss of critical skills inculcated early in life.

Similarly, people were amazed that extreme thirst late one afternoon would cause an eighty-five-year-old partially blind woman to go searching for water only to end up falling into a disused water tank, breaking her arm, and dislocating her shoulder. Her feeble cries for help were finally heard by schoolchildren on their way home from classes. The children did call for help – amid much hilarity about the old lady's plight and some teasing and swearing at her for creating such a situation.

Anyone who gets injured on Niue is likely to be greeted with gales of laughter and ribald comment. Mocking, teasing, and ridicule are common strategies of social control, of making abnormal situations appear normal. These strategies are used especially to get children to acquiesce to adult wishes or to accept painful medical treatments (Levy 1973:308–14). Giggling and laughing also hides nervousness, fear, or embarrassment at some unusual event. Hilarity not only covers an underlying concern for the injured but also reinforces the fatalistic, stoic acceptance of misfortune that is expected of victims.

The children's laughter over the old lady's fate was at a pitch and intensity that revealed that they were especially disturbed. Teasing her, ridiculing her, and making rude jokes about her and her fate were attempts to establish control over the phenomenon, to make it conform to Niuean expectations, to normalize the unusual. Events of the sort in which the elderly sustain injury are not unusual. Between 1977 and 1982, for example, accident or injury was a leading cause of death for Niueans over seventy years of age, accounting for 14 percent of all deaths of elders (Taylor, Nemaia, and Connell 1987). Old men were especially likely to die as a result of accident or injury. In comparison, in New Zealand, where motor vehicles play a more prominent role in death statistics, only 3 percent of deaths of old people are due to accident or injury (Barker 1984).

Late in 1982, a visitor from New Zealand, a nurse with many years of experience in caring for geriatric patients, made an informal inspection of elderly people on Niue. Her findings paralleled mine. She told of seeing clear differences between the intact and the decrepit elderly. In her opinion, all elders showed some evidence of poor nutrition but especially the frail ones. She also spoke about elders with large pressure sores, the results of lying for hours in urine or feces. The homes and clothes of elders commonly reeked with the odor of stale urine. Hospital care of elders, she felt, was of an excellent standard, but the provision of care at family and community level was poor.

From all this evidence, I concluded that some frail elders on Niue were not receiving the kind of care and attention I had expected they would. By Western standards, some elders were clearly being neglected.

The Concept of "Neglect"

Each society has its own standards for conduct toward other persons, for conduct that is honorable, respectful, acceptable, proper, indifferent, demeaning, brutal, abusive, or neglectful. The age, sex, and relative social ranking of the persons involved in the relationship, as well as individual characteristics of the protagonists and the history of their interactions, have a lot to do with the conduct of one to the other and how it is defined. What is deemed "neglect" by Western societies may be acceptable, expected, normal behavior elsewhere.

When I say decrepit elders on Niue were ignored or neglected by their kin or community I do not mean they never received any attention or care. They were not completely abandoned but rather received inadequate care or minimal attention. Old people would be visited by kin but not necessarily every day, and then often only by youngsters sent to check on their well-being. They would be given food but in scant amounts, really only enough for one meal and not an entire day, and they would no longer receive the choice morsels they formerly enjoyed. They would be clothed, but in rags that were rarely laundered. It is this type of treatment that I refer to as neglect.

When Glascock (1982, and this volume) describes a group's behavior toward the frail elderly as "death hastening" or "neglectful," he means the outcome of the acts of behavior do not enhance the well-being of the aged individual from *our* understanding of the physical and mental processes involved. From the perspective of the people concerned, however, the outcome might be seen as helpful, if not to the individual at least to the group.

In this chapter, behavior toward the elderly is first described using Western notions of "neglect," and then it is related to other aspects of Niuean society to show why this apparently "neglectful" behavior is in fact understandable, even correct. Such behaviors cannot be understood outside their proper cultural context.

Frail and Decrepit Elders

Most elders either retain their abilities and relatively good health well into advanced age or die from acute disorders or accidents before they reach a stage of decrepitude. A recent survey found that less than 20 percent of the Niuean population aged sixty five or over was extremely frail or had many impairments (Barker 1989). Only about half of these frail elders are decrepit, however. Of the approximately 200 elders on the island during fieldwork in 1982–1983, for example, I met eleven old people (about 5 percent) whom I considered decrepit, while another four or five were rapidly losing their ability to maintain an independent existence and appeared to be on the road from frailty to decrepitude. So, I have been concerned with understanding the behavior of Niueans toward a small but nonetheless interesting segment of their society. I explore the cultural conditions that make it possible for behavior radically at odds with the expected norms to become comprehensible.

As a group, the characteristics of decrepit elders contrast sharply with the general elderly population on the island. A survey of the latter was performed in 1985 using a 50 percent random sample of elders whose names appeared on the Niuean Government pension list. In general, being over seventy-five years of age, being male, having never married, and having few children left on the island to care for one are all associated with impairment (Barker 1989). All these factors are even more strongly associated with decrepitude. Table 16.1 documents the major differences between decrepit elders, those who experienced some degree of neglect, and other elders on Niue. Contributing little to their family, decrepit elders fail to maintain even minimal social roles in the general village community; in particular, the important social role of churchgoer ceases. Furthermore, decrepit elders experience more limitations in work activities, more confusion or mental deterioration, and more sensory problems (blindness, especially) than do other elders on Niue.

Table 16.1
Characteristics of Elders on Niue

	Elders in Survey (N = 63)	Decrepit Elders (N = 11)
Average age[1]	under 75 years	over 80 years
Sex	30% males	64% males
Married	40%	19%
Living on own	14%	54%
Regularly attend church	71%	0%
Limited in doing work/family activities	48%	100%
Severe mobility impairments	14%	100%
Partly or completely blind	29%	45%
Some memory problems or confusion	16%	45%

1. See Barker (1989) for an extended discussion of the health and functional status of the elderly on Niue. Interpreting attributed age for Niuean elderly is extremely difficult. There is a tendency for chronological age attributed to the very old or the very frail, especially men, to be inflated.

Niuean Explanations for Neglect

Niueans themselves expressed ideas about the care of "oldies," as they commonly call all elderly people. In general, Niueans espoused respect and admiration for old folk, vehemently contrasting what they perceived as Western indifference to elders (signaled by the placement of elders in nursing homes) with their own respectful concern and loving care for the aged. Niueans did recognize, however, that their treatment of decrepit elders was not the same as their caring for intact elders, and they gave several explanations for their treatment of decrepit elders.

Niueans said some degree of decrepitude was to be expected in advanced old age and should be accepted, not complained about. Combined with a degree of fatalism (McEwen 1974), Niueans have the general Polynesian tendency to display little empathy for others (Levy 1973: 312). As we have seen when the old woman fell into the disused water tank, even those experiencing severe pain or in very adverse circumstances receive little overt sympathy.

Another explanation is that in old age people receive their "just deserts." Those who had been excessively individualistic, materialistic, ill-tempered, or nasty at a younger age are simply reaping the harvest of unpleasant seeds they previously sowed. Further, people who cared for kin and displayed their love throughout life are not neglected. People who took no time to raise a family, to help siblings and other family members through life, to establish a bond of love between themselves and younger kin have no one to call on in old age, have no one who is obligated to assist. There is a striking parallel between this native explanation for neglect in old age and the demographic characteristics of the decrepit elderly. Males predominate in the decrepit sample, with a relatively large number of them never-married, childless, or recently returned from overseas.

Some Niueans said old people now have a tough time because out-migration has so severely depleted the resources available to any one extended family that there are no longer several adult women available in any one household to care for both children and old people. There is undoubtedly some merit to this explanation, as the domestic work loads of individual adults, especially of women, has increased recently. What this explanation reveals, of course, is that care of old people comes low on the list of domestic priorities, well after the care of other adults and children. Indeed, doubts can be cast about whether decrepit old folk ever received adequate care even before permanent out-migration and demographic changes disrupted family organization.

Glascock and Feinman (1981:27) note that supportive treatment of the intact aged and nonsupportive, even death-hastening, treatment of the decrepit elderly can coexist in one society without strain as these behaviors are aimed at different populations. Niueans even signal the difference between the intact and the decrepit elderly populations linguistically. The term *ulu motua*, gray-haired one, refers to socially active, powerful, respected, intact elders. In contrast, the terms *penupenu-fonua* or *mutumutu-fonua*, gray fish of the land, are graphic if rather morbid metaphors used to describe very elderly, incompetent, decrepit old men. Obviously, senescent old men are not in the same category as other old men.

Negotiation of the Label "Decrepit"

Elders do not become decrepit overnight. Decrepitude is a gradual degenerative process during which negotiation over the applicability of the label "decrepit" constantly occurs between the elder and the rest of the community. Becoming decrepit is a process of "fading out" (Maxwell 1986:77). It is a process in which elders begin to deploy their resources differently, often in a more self-centered fashion, while displays of deference by others toward them are correspondingly recast. When an old person is unable or unwilling to use his or her resources to maintain even a minimal social role, the community successfully applies the decrepit label; then the elder accepts it.

Decreases in competence are fought against, minimized in several ways. One strategy is for elders to cease doing strenuous "bush work" but to continue engaging in household chores. The very strong Niuean work ethic insists that every person—man, woman, and child—assist in supporting the household. From an early age, three to five years, children are assigned and expected to perform regularly important household tasks, including weeding gardens, feeding livestock, washing clothes and dishes, or childminding. An elder who can no longer perform any of these tasks places a greater burden on the family than does any other member except an infant. Unlike caring for a frail elder, however, caring for an infant carries the promise of future rewards: in a few years a child will be an able worker; in a few years the elder be no more able than at present.

A second way elders can minimize their impending decrepitude is to adopt new but valued social roles inappropriate in younger persons, roles such as "storyteller" or "clown" (Holmes 1974; Holmes and Rhoads 1987; Huntsman and Hooper 1975). In contrast to the behavior expected of younger folk, old people, especially women, can tell lewd tales, can mock high-status public figures, and can act generally as court jesters at important social events or ceremonies such as weddings. This joking and ribald behavior is tolerated, even valued, as a commentary by which elders delineate social norms and indirectly control younger persons.

An elder too frail to do any household tasks or to engage in public jesting has little to offer his or her family or community, except perhaps as a teller of tales, a repository of lore and ceremonial knowledge. Unlike other Polynesian peoples, however, Niueans have long been noted for their negligence in recording traditions and their relative lack of oral histories (Ryan 1977:33). Thus, even a role demanding little physical skill and involving memory tasks most often maintained by frail elders, that of tale-teller, of oral historian, is generally unavailable to the elderly on Niue.

One exception concerns the role of traditional healer, _taulaatua_, which is still important on Niue and essentially is reserved for elders (Barker 1985:148–53).

Some healers are specialists who treat cases of major disorder from all over the island; others deal only with more minor problems within their own village. An elder in each extended family usually knows and uses the recipes. Because of the secret nature of the herbal ingredients, of the proper preparation and use of the recipes, and of the incantations, curers who become so frail that they can no longer gather the required herbs themselves begin to lose even this role. Some elderly healers maintain power through the gradual revelation of their secret knowledge to a grandchild or other younger relative who shows aptitude.

A third major way to demonstrate competence is to continue to raise children (Kirkpatrick 1985a). As Counts and Counts put it, people "recruit a new dependent whose presence testifies to the continuing ability of an aging person to care for himself and others" (1985:5). Adoption of a child by an old person is both a demonstration of competence and an insurance against neglect in advanced old age or frailty, for adopted children are under great obligation to repay their parents by caring for them in later life.

Most adoptions on Niue, especially of girls, take place through the child's mother's kin (Barker 1985), and the driving force behind most adoptions are closely related women, not men. Elders without daughters or granddaughters will not only make fewer adoptions than others but will be more likely to adopt children who are male and who are related only through distant or putative biological ties. This is especially true for elderly men who never married or are widowed at the time of adoption. Adoptive boys who have no close biological bond to the adoptive parent frequently feel little obligation to carry out their filial duties when the parent becomes aged. So, once more, men are more likely than women to reach advanced old age without anyone, even an adopted child, to care for them; decrepit old men are more likely to be neglected.

IS "NEGLECT" OF RECENT ORIGIN?

Thus a picture of Niue emerges. Socioeconomic change on the island has been rampant, recent, and rapid. Demographic change, too, has been of monumental proportions. Niue has a high aged dependency ratio and an increasing proportion of elderly in the community, partly as a result of out-migration (Niue Government 1985) and partly through reductions in mortality and increases in life expectancy over the past thirty years (Taylor, Nemaia, and Connell 1987).

It is tempting to see these factors—modernization—as causes for the differences in treatment between the decrepit and intact elderly, a difference that would be recent in origin. But is the distinction between decrepit and intact elders a modern phenomenon on Niue? Documents located in several archives soon dispelled the notion that variation in the treatment of the elderly on Niue is of recent origin. Neglect of the elderly, even in the past to the extent of abandoning them in huts in the "bush" where they literally had to fend for themselves, is not new.

Historical Evidence

In a letter written in November 1885 the European missionary on the island, Frank Lawes, quoted a Niuean *toa*, warrior, thus: "It was better to have the skull broken to pieces in war, than to die in old age from neglect" (quoted in Ryan 1977:100). The first ethnographer on Niue, S. Percy Smith, had only this to say about the elderly: "In very old age, it was not infrequent that old people requested their younger relatives to strangle them to cause death" (1983 [1902–03]:60). The accuracy of this statement is unknown. In 1922, a short article about life on Niue by a visiting scholar noted that Niueans "were not thoughtful of their old folk" (Juniper 1922:612). Edwin Loeb (1926:86), the next ethnographer, writes that the elderly were abandoned in the bush.

Reports by the New Zealand Administration's staff support the views of these scholars. In 1923 the medical officer noted a "tendency for the natives to neglect their old."[1] A few years later he more bluntly reported: "At times one encounters marked cases of neglect, especially of the aged. 'Only an old person' is an expression one commonly hears. In several instances one feels that this callous indifference has been a potent factor in the cause of death."[2]

Reporting an outbreak of influenza on the island in 1932, the resident commissioner said: "The old people when sick have rather a poor chance as the younger ones are most indifferent, and do not worry about feeding them or attending to their comforts."[3] Again, in 1945, another resident commissioner reports: "Old folk are left in hovels and begrudgingly fed. . . . I am quite convinced that neither the Church nor the people even recognise that it is a problem. It is quite taken for granted and *faka Niue* [the Niuean way]."[4]

Throughout the 1950s and into the 1960s, medical officers continued to report neglect affecting about 10 percent of the elderly population then on the island.[5] To help stem this widespread custom, a tax was levied from 1958 on to provide old people with a small pension. Abandonment of old folk into "bush huts" had ceased by the mid-1960s, but other improvements were slow in coming about. One 1964 medical report noted that "the elderly [living alone] fare worse than those living with relatives. . . several appeared poorly clad and neglected. Nearly all had inadequate bed clothing and some none at all."[6]

Accounts by Niuean Migrants

The general tenor of these reports is corroborated by Niueans who migrated from the island decades ago and have become acculturated in new communities. These informants recounted the incomprehension they experienced when making return visits to Niue. Their tales of seeing how formerly influential, vital community members were neglected in old age reverberate with now-familiar themes: "hunger," "filth," "smells," and "neglect."

When decrepit elders died, families were genuinely distraught with grief and loudly mourned the loss of their cherished family member. My informants asked: How could this be? Why did the community allow these families to neglect the elderly and not punish them for so doing? How could a family neglect an old person in life yet so sincerely grieve their death?

CULTURAL VALUES AND "NEGLECTFULL" BEHAVIOR

By now enough evidence has been presented for it to be clear that Niuean neglect of decrepit elders is a well-established, systematic pattern of behavior and not mere idiosyncracy or aberration. Moreover, it clearly is not a new phenomenon, not a response to massive, recent socioeconomic and demographic change. The question remains, however – given strongly espoused values about the aged and a social system organized around elders, how is this variant of behavior possible?

Egalitarianism in a Fragile Ecology

Recall that Niue's agricultural system is fraught with difficulties. Periodic drought, a fragile ecosystem, a harsh terrain – all make food production uncertain, arduous, and time-consuming. Subsistence requires constant work from every able body, even young children, and there is little surplus available for nonproducers. A decrepit elder, too sick or frail to garden, to work around the house, or even to mind infants and toddlers, creates obligations that he or she is unable to repay. Decrepit elders can easily be begrudged whatever small surplus is produced, especially in times when food is scarce.

Combine this with cultural values that stress hard work and individual achievement – looking out for oneself – and a system that neglects decrepit elders, leaves them to their fate, makes them cope on their own as best they can, starts to become comprehensible. This "ecological" explanation appears rather callous, though, and very different from the sentiments accorded the healthy old. Such an explanation is also at odds with the treatment given other handicapped people.

Others with Disability

As in many Polynesian societies, babies born with physical and mental disabilities are not rejected but rather receive special attention, are lavished with affection. When older, these children are expected, to the best of their abilities, however minimal those might be, to aid the family in meeting its subsistence and communal obligations. A handicapped child might occasionally be mildly teased by his or her peers, but no more so than any other youngster. No child would be excluded from social gatherings or village activities just because of physical or mental "difference" (Kirkpatrick 1985b:230).

Similarly, those who sustain injuries that result in permanent disabilities are not excluded from family or social activities and responsibilities. Adults with handicaps are expected to work to the extent of their abilities and to occupy whatever positions in village life are appropriate to their skills and social standing. One thirty-year-old paraplegic, for example, though confined to a wheelchair, tends his passion fruit and lime gardens by day and regularly attends village dances and other social gatherings by night. People banded together to build him a specially designed house and to pound down into level paths the coral rocks around his garden plots so that he could tend his crops unaided.

So, physically or mentally impaired children or adults are not excluded from society, are not subject to treatment any different from that given others of their age and status. Why then do Niueans neglect their decrepit elders? It cannot just be because of their handicaps or because of their minimal contributions to household welfare. Other cultural values must be at work.

One clue is that despite this acceptance of disability, being of imposing stature, being well built and sturdy, is culturally valued in Polynesian societies. High rank and social importance are frequently associated with being tall or fat. Excessively thin individuals or those losing weight or physical robustness are suspected of illness, curse, or serious misdemeanor (Finau, Prior, and Evans 1982:1542). Both literally and figuratively, decrepit elders on Niue are shadows of their former selves. Those who when younger were muscular, strong, and sturdy are now shrunken, stooped, and scrawny. Those who formerly were vital, influential figures are now ineffectual, pathetic beings with little interest in social life.

Such dramatic and obvious changes clearly raise suspicions about their origin. Degenerative changes are fundamentally different from any birth defect or disability resulting from accident and are unlike acute illnesses of rapid onset and resolution. Decrepitude is insidious, slow, and cumulative, a gradual and irreversible destruction of vitality. Very traditional ideas about the origin of such misfortunes, about the nature of death, and about the proper treatment of the afflicted give us an understanding of why these degenerative processes are suspect. They explain the treatment of the decrepit elderly on Niue.

The Origin of Misfortune and the Nature of Death

In the Polynesian view there are two parallel worlds, this world of humans and the world of the supernatural. Inhabitants of the latter keep a close watch on this world and punish those who offend. A person courts punishment by acting indecorously, by blaspheming, by transgressing the rules of proper conduct or by breaking *tapu*, rules specifying how to behave in certain localities or on special occasions. Punishment usually takes the form of sickness, especially intractable or life-threatening sickness, and is often brought about by possession by *aitu*, ghosts, the spirits of the dead.

In taking possession of a person, an *aitu*, usually a close ancestral spirit, aims to kill eventually, to take the person to the supernatural world, perhaps to avenge its own death. Once an *aitu* takes over, it speaks through the living in trance, delirium, or confusion, revealing secrets to the family and community at large, making salacious suggestions, and commenting generally upon the morality and correctness of the conduct of all and sundry (Barker 1985:143-52; Goodman 1971; Shore 1978).

As is common in Polynesian languages, Niuean uses the same word, *mate*, to encompass several states that we distinguish as delirium, unconsciousness, and death. Thus, there are no clear distinctions, linguistic or conceptual, between being incoherent, being comatose, being dying, or being dead. A *mate* person is somewhere out of this world, on the way to the next.

Death in Niuean perspective is not an instantaneous, unequivocal event (Counts and Counts 1985:17). Rather, death is a process of transition, a gradual shucking of the competencies and responsibilities of this world and a simultaneous acquisition of characteristics of the new world. So death occurs over a period of time, months or even years perhaps. Death is not unexpected, as all natural living things die. Death is not absolute as there is no irrevocable boundary between parallel worlds, worlds occupied by humans and by supernatural beings, by ghosts.

Burial is merely a disposal of a body, a former container for the soul and animating forces. To encourage the new ghostly beings to stay in the hereafter with their supernatural kin and to not return to this world, Niueans bury their dead quickly, usually within twelve to twenty-four hours. Large stones or concrete slabs are placed atop the grave to discourage the new *aitu* from wanting to return to this world, from wanting to remain in the world of humans.

Relations between the Living and the Dying

Decrepit elders, then, especially those who no longer look or behave like competent adults, who rave incoherently, who speak of long-past events or converse with long-dead kin, are being actively courted by *aitu*, are *mate*, in transition. They are "the nearly dead." In touch with the spirit world, they are alarmingly near to becoming *aitu* themselves. Decrepit elders are in transition, inhabiting a twilight world of not-quite-human-but-not-quite-ancestor. As human beings, the decrepit elderly are obsolete, but, as inhabitants of another realm, they are incomplete.

Such near-*aitu* threaten to break the barriers between the worlds. In possession of alarming characteristics from both worlds but not fully competent in either, this human-in-transition, this ghost-in-the-making, threatens to contaminate this world with things from beyond. This threat ceases only when the dying are dead, fully dead, when they have completed the transition to the other world and are buried.

In traditional times, the intractably sick, those possessed by ghosts, by *aitu* "were removed into the bush and placed in a temporary hut where they were left until they might recover or die. Their relatives took food to them, but no one remained with them" (Murray 1863:367).

Such isolation of the sick conformed to the custom for dealing with ritually unclean objects. Imposition of a long *tapu* prevented *aitu* from spreading possession to others (Luomala 1978:147). Hence, we can see that abandoning or neglecting decrepit elders is not simply a rather brutal means of relieving younger people of an economic burden (though that probably plays some role) but is a ritual activity undertaken for sensible reasons. It prevents contamination by ghostly influences from beyond.

Moreover, neglect is appropriate precisely because in reducing the customary ties and emotions between humans it allows decrepit elders to complete an expected transition as smoothly as possible: "Too much concern causes difficult processes (usually social or supernatural ones) to become even more difficult and unpleasant. In regard to dying, if you are too concerned . . . the transformed spirit of the dead person may gain power over you. . . . Being casual, then, frees the dying person from you, and you from him or her" (Levy 1973:229).(See also Levy 1973:225–28, 291–302, 493–97)

Men not only have greater power in life but also in death. *Aitu* of socially powerful men, particularly of traditional healers who mediate between the parallel worlds, can be especially malevolent and hard to control. This is yet another reason why it is predominantly males who experience neglect in old age.

To abandon decrepit elders or at least to limit contact even to the point of neglect makes sense. They are not elders but some other category of being engaged in a normal, expected, and important but nonetheless difficult social process, that of dying. Casualness, "neglect," with respect to decrepit elders is a way of distancing oneself from such powerful and potentially dangerous transformations.

Once the transition between the realms is complete, the cessation of life here can be noted and be grieved over. Thus can a family who apparently neglected an elder at the end of life grieve sincerely for the person who was. They had "neglected" no one whom they knew, no one who belonged in this world. Rather, they had maintained a prudent distance from a near *aitu* during the difficult process of transition between worlds. And if their actions hastened that process along, surely that cannot be thought harmful or harsh or uncaring.

For Niueans to abandon or neglect their decrepit elderly, to engage in what Glascock (Glascock and Feinman 1981; Glascock 1982) calls nonsupportive or death-hastening behaviors thus makes sense. To laugh at decrepit elders, to deride their feeble endeavors at being competent humans, to ridicule them, to neglect them, to be wary of and distant during interactions with them is not to disrespect an elder but to guard against foreign intrusion. These behaviors are not behaviors involving elders but an entirely different category of being. These behaviors are attempts to deal with "matter out of place," as Mary Douglas (1966) would put it, to persuade a near *aitu* to go to the proper realm, to cease to be human, to leave the land of the living and become an ancestor, a ghost, who can, once again, be revered.

NOTES

Fieldwork on which this chapter is based was supported by a project grant from the South Pacific Medical Research Committee of the Medical Research Council of New Zealand. The author gratefully acknowledges this support and the unstinting assistance of the Niuean people. References in these notes can be found in the National Archives, Department of Internal Affairs, Wellington, New Zealand, and in the Archives, Fale Fono, Alofi, Niue.

1. Ministerial report in Section A–3 of the *Appendix to the Journal of the House of Representatives*, New Zealand, 1923.
2. Ministerial quotation from the medical officer, Dr. Boyd, in the Report in Section A–3 of the *Appendix to the Journal of the House of Representatives*, New Zealand, 1926.
3. Report by Resident Commissioner Captain Bell on outbreak of influenza, 29 April 1932, in reply to a telegraph inquiry by Department of Island Territories, New Zealand.
4. Copy of report from Resident Commissioner Larsen, 6 August 1945, sent to director general of health, New Zealand, by Department of Island Territories, New Zealand.
Memorandum by Resident Commissioner Larsen, 3 September 1945, on visit by the New Zealand prime minister and his reaction to the plight of old people on Niue, sent to Secretary, Department of Island Affairs, New Zealand.
5. Minutes of the Island Council Meeting, 2 October 1958 and 30 October 1958.
Memorandum from resident commissioner, 9 August 1946, to secretary, Department of Island Affairs, New Zealand.
Minutes of the Island Council Meeting, 31 July 1958.
Monthly reports by chief medical officer to resident commissioner, March and May 1967.
6. Monthly Report by chief medical officer to resident commissioner, May 1964.

17 ALZHEIMER'S DISEASE IN CULTURAL CONTEXT

J. Neil Henderson

The Estradas of West Tampa, Florida, live in a lower-middle-income neighborhood with several houses that have garages obviously converted into additional interior spaces. Numerous mailboxes lining the street have Spanish surnames on them, and an occasional car will be seen with a Puerto Rican license tag or a bumper sticker such as one advertising the National Hispanic Chamber of Commerce meeting for 1986. This area has many people, like the Estradas, who moved here from Cuba in the early 1960s. The Estrada family is distinguished from others in their neighborhood by the fact that Mr. Estrada, although trained as a chemist, is now severely impaired with Alzheimer's disease.

Other members of the Estrada family include his wife's eighty-five year-old mother (who lives in the house with them in order to help her daughter care for Mr. Estrada), his brother who lives next door, and his sister who lives four miles away. While Mrs. Estrada implies that she provides nearly all the care, her mother and her husband's sister in fact participate in direct care on a regular basis. In addition Mr. Estrada's brother provides limited assistance in the form of regular social visits.

The Estradas also have two sons, one of whom lives on the same block and another some six miles away. Mrs. Estrada reports the two sons are of little help. One is unable to tolerate taking care of his father for even a few hours because it makes him "nervous," a nonspecific condition mentioned by many of the Latino families as a very real and acceptable emotional category. The other son has offered to pay to bring in an extra caregiver. Mrs. Estrada rejects this for three reasons. One is that it would only create more difficulties with her husband because he is so irritable and argumentative. Second, Mrs. Estrada describes herself as a meticulous housekeeper very concerned with odors in the house, and she therefore would feel compelled to clean her home thoroughly each time before a respite caregiver could come. Finally, she feels she would not get any rest anyway because she would feel obligated to keep the person properly entertained as a guest in the home.

Mrs. Estrada says that at times she has trouble accepting "the disease" because it seems as though her husband's crazy demands are merely an extension of his very domineering personality from his intact and lucid days. For example, he demands "real food," meaning fully prepared meals, which typically include a large portion of meat and seasoned vegetables.

When Mrs. Estrada first attended the support group meetings she was often in tears when trying to tell of her caregiving activities. In fact, for a time she was clinically depressed and was medicated by a psychiatrist on an outpatient basis. Therapy was unsuccessful since she adjusted the medicine because the initial dosage made her "groggy," and she did not know that the sedative effect would wear off with continued use.

During the time that Mrs. Estrada was being treated for depression, she continued to attend the support group meetings, and interviews in the home continued to take place. During one such interview, Mrs. Estrada simply sat by and watched as her husband tried to sit in a chair in the living room in sort of a half-crouched position, but he was too far away from the edge of the chair. He then slowly inched his way backwards toward the chair in the crouched position while she gave him no help or instructions. This was clearly a departure from her earlier attentiveness. She also reported an instance when her husband refused medications and she could not get him to take them by any strategy. He began calling her "dirty names" (which she would never specify), after which she began screaming and pounding the walls with her fists and forearms until they were sore.

Mrs. Estrada says she has never been depressed before. Much of her stress comes from her belief that she is a failure because she is unable to maintain the household and caregiving activities unaided. She talks explicitly about holding a self-controlled "face" in front of her family and her children. She says her children had not seen her cry although she has hidden in the bathroom to cry privately so she can maintain that outwardly powerful image in front of her family. She also reports that since joining the Alzheimer's Latin Support Group she has become aware that other caregivers experience some of the same frustrations. She feels that has given her better understanding of the disease and that she is now better able to cope with the caregiving requirements.

As a Latina with strong Catholic background, Mrs. Estrada says that her religion told her that she got married "for better or for worse." She feels that she has already had the "for better" and now is getting the "for worse." She refers to Alzheimer's disease in a fatalistic sense, indicating that it is out of her control and that she must simply endure her lot in life, which seems in some way to be supernaturally ordained.

Mrs. Estrada vacillates between the need for nursing home placement and the feeling that this would indicate failure as a caregiver. During one interview

Mrs. Estrada said, "Latin people, we are very stupid," in regard to an unwillingness to put people in a nursing home as she sees Anglos do. She said, "I will bury him before he dies," in response to the question of what would happen if she went ahead with the nursing home placement. She reports that her husband is now being put on a tranquilizing agent which calms his behavior down so that she can cope with him. A little before she had a "fit" in which she broke all of the dishes in the house because she was angry with Mr. Estrada. After this episode, she called the support group leader to ask for the phone number of one of the other members with whom she felt she could talk.

Mr. Estrada's dementia continues to worsen. For example, at the end of a very elaborate meal prepared by Mrs. Estrada and her stepdaughter, Mr. Estrada very matter-of-factly said, "We eat only air and water in this house." In addition, he is now incontinent and must be bathed and dressed by Mrs. Estrada.

EPIDEMIOLOGY OF DEMENTIA

The fourth leading cause of death in this nation is dementia, a group of diseases which destroys brain cells. But, before death, the victim, family, and friends can expect two to twenty years of slow, progressive decline in the victim's ability to think, remember, and control bodily functions. In fact, these losses are feared more than death by most older people (Besdine 1982). Family members who care for such patients refer to Alzheimer's disease (AD) and related dementias as "the long goodbye."

Human existence involves repetitive experiences of sickness episodes or "life under altered conditions" (Virchow 1849). Since humans are a culture-bearing species, anthropologists examine the impact of culture not only on the epidemiology of diseases but on the sociocultural reaction to them.

Sickness episodes have been examined from a sociocultural perspective in two categories: (1) disease as a biologically objectifiable condition; and (2) illness, which is subject to sociocultural influence. For example, Alzheimer's disease can be described in terms of pathological changes in the brain and symptomatic changes over time. However, this does not address the sociocultural context such as that in the Estrada case. The "folk" definition of the disease, interpretation of the symptoms, beliefs about etiology, beliefs about appropriate therapies, and social values placed on given disease conditions are all parts of the illness experience. Such aspects are subject to organization and structuring in accordance with prevailing sociocultural systems (Gubrium 1986, 1987). For complete analysis, the examination of human sickness demands a biocultural perspective incorporating the disease/illness dimensions.

Understanding health beliefs and behaviors in old age has become both a humanitarian and an economic imperative. The increase in the world's elderly population is due less to "high-tech" advances in biomedicine such as organ transplants and artificial organs and more to general public health measures, antibiotics, and improved nutrition. Along with the growing number of older people, geriatric specialists have increased and developed a more sophisticated awareness of the unique health patterns of the typical older person. Compared to middle-aged adults, for example, many older people experience multiple sicknesses simultaneously, unusual symptoms for ordinary diseases, impaired equilibrium of body chemistry balances, too many medications, and a reluctance to seek medical care.

Two prominent risks for long-term mental health disability are present in old age. One of these is depression, which can often go unrecognized, untreated, or incorrectly managed. Second, there is an increased risk for dementing diseases which gradually deteriorate the brain's ability to control thought processes and, eventually, body functions such as bowel and bladder control.

Unfortunately, the increased risk of dementing diseases with concomitant intellectual loss is associated with advancing age. The older a person is, the greater the risk of dementia. This is one of two epidemiologic facts known about the most common type of dementia: Alzheimer's disease. The second known epidemiologic fact is that dementia has a worldwide distribution. No social, racial, or ethnic group appears to have immunity from dementing disease. However, some societies or ethnic groups may have significant variation in certain types of dementia. For example, multi-infarct dementia (MID) is caused by numerous cerebral strokes which can be provoked by hypertension. Populations noted for high incidence of hypertension, such as American blacks and Japanese, may be at higher risk of MID.

Given the worldwide increase in length of life and the geographic distribution of dementia, many intriguing questions arise regarding the sociocultural response to dementia as it occurs in cross-cultural perspective. To date, little is known about dementia. There is no known etiology, no cure, no accurate mapping of epidemiologic patterns, no ability to predict the length of the disease, and very little information about differential sociocultural responses to the symptoms of dementia. It is this last issue which will be examined here, using examples from an ethnic population in the southeastern United States who are derived from Spanish, Puerto Rican, and Cuban ancestors.

DEMENTING DISEASE

Dementia refers to the permanent loss of brain cells due to a disease process. The most generic term for this type of disease is "organic brain syndrome." Under this label come several types of organic brain syndromes such as acute confusional states, pseudodementias, and true dementias. Acute confusional states and pseudodementias are reversible, whereas true dementias cause a permanent decline in cognitive function. For example, being drunk is a type of acute confusional state known as delirium, which in most cases is a temporary phenomenon. Alzheimer's disease and multi-infarct dementia both produce progressive and irreversible declines in cognitive functioning. Alzheimer's disease is the most common term used because it is the most prevalent of the dementias, constituting about 60 percent of all cases. At any one time, almost two million older American adults are victims of Alzheimer's disease.

Alzheimer's disease produces changes in brain tissues which include brain cell death and the formation of foreign substances in the brain. All brains develop those pathologies over time. The Alzheimer's patient, however, has sufficient numbers of these lesions to seriously impair normal cognitive function.[1]

In a living person, the only absolute diagnosis is a brain biopsy, but because this is such an invasive procedure, a clinical diagnosis is made by ruling out every other possible medical cause of symptoms relating to memory loss and confusion. If the patient's history shows a slow and progressive onset of dysfunction and no other medical cause can be found, a diagnosis of dementia of the Alzheimer's type is made. At autopsy, confirmation can be obtained by examining brain tissue microscopically.[2]

Alzheimer's disease worsens and eventually erodes the person's ability to remember recent events, think reasonably, and manage his or her own ordinary affairs. This places a demand on caregivers to maintain the victim's health and safety. Caregivers tell nightmarish stories of the patient wandering away from the house for hours at a time and often retrieved by the police; stories of patients driving cars on the wrong side of the interstate or breaking mirrors in the home due to fear of the "stranger" they see reflected there; they have to install locks and fences, hide keys, cover air conditioner controls, put paper in the bathroom floor in case the patient has difficulty with toileting. Eventually, the caregivers must live (by proxy) life for their demented loved one. This includes complete responsibility for dressing, feeding, bathing, and toileting the person. Eventually, the dementia patient becomes so debilitated that walking is impossible and other automatic abilities such as organ system regulation begin to fail. The person is often unable to speak, unable to walk, and subject to dying from bronchopneumonia or cardiac arrest.

SOCIOCULTURAL ASPECTS OF DEMENTIA

The burdens of old age as a minority group member has been described as "double jeopardy." Double jeopardy is compounded enormously when a chronic disease is present, particularly one which obliterates reason and independence. These detriments to health and well-being are happening to an ever-increasing number of people as this nation ages. Yet it is precisely the sociocultural aspect of aging and ethnicity that has been neglected (Holzberg 1982).

Widespread American values such as independence, domination over the environment, and high status of youth all operate against the caregiver when dealing with an elderly dementia victim. Ours is an ageist society in which we exalt a youth orientation, the "Pepsi Generation," and generally devalue the elderly individual. More specifically, the Alzheimer's-type patient is not only old, therefore losing the status of youth, but also suffers multiple losses of function resulting in the inability to negotiate even the simplest aspects of life unaided. The loss of youth, intelligence, and independence produces a social stigma akin to those with severe psychiatric afflictions such as schizophrenia.

Other sociocultural correlates impinging on Alzheimer's disease and care of the patient and caregiver include the American kinship structure, migration patterns, and division of labor based on gender. Typical nuclear family organization, dispersed postmarital residence patterns, and geographic mobility in the pursuit of occupation and finances all act in concert to create a home caregiving environment in which burdens are placed on only one or two individuals. Enormous emotional and physical burdens devolve on an individual caregiver. A popular guide for the home caregiver is titled *The 36-Hour Day* (Mace and Rabins 1981), reflecting the caregiver's perception of his or her job.

SELF-HELP GROUPS AND SOCIAL NETWORKS

The special difficulties imposed by the sociocultural environment on those families coping with Alzheimer's disease has given rise to the spontaneous emergence of mutual aid societies specifically designed for Alzheimer's disease patients and family members. Such mutual aid societies typically go under the rubric of a "support group" and are a specialized part of one's wider social network. Alzheimer's disease support groups can be seen as a cultural product that emerged in response to the deficits of an acute care medical system unable to meet the salient needs of a population experiencing a chronic debilitating brain disease. In fact, the informally organized Alzheimer's support groups developed by Bobbie Glaze in the early 1970s have led to a nationally incorporated network: the Alzheimer's Association.

Alzheimer's disease support groups function socially as fictive kinship groups. They arise in a culture in which fragmented kinship networks are typical; thus they supplement the immediate, face-to-face interactions and assistance that could occur were it not for socioculturally induced kindred dispersion. Support groups also fill gaps created by the acute-care medical system in the long-term management of the disease. One of the discreet internal functions of support groups is to provide knowledge as well as the sharing of techniques for in-home management of the demented patient (Middleton 1984). The in-home caregiver can also look to guidebooks to better develop the role of caregiver (Aronson 1988; Mace 1989), while professionals begin to evaluate the impact of caregiving on the caregiver (Zarit, Orr, and Zarit 1985; Kosberg and Cairl 1986). Ultimately, Alzheimer's disease support groups are types of social networks which create a facsimile of a healing community in which the population is brought together by a common experience related to brain failure, in an effort to better cope with this drastic and unpredicted change in the latter years of their lives (Henderson 1987).

Social networks develop through contacts with relatives, friends, and neighbors, through which individuals maintain a social identity and receive emotional support, material aid, services, and information, and develop new social contacts (Walker, MacBride, and Vachon 1977; McKinley 1981). Social networks, including support groups, can serve as a helping technology for coping with sickness. For example, research on reactions to stress show that the stressed individual with a working social network will tolerate or adapt to the stressful condition better than someone in a similar situation without a support group (Cassel 1976; Cobb 1976; Lowenthal and Haven 1968; Berkman 1985). Thus social networks are "buffers" shielding one from the full impact of stressors and helping the stressed person to adapt to the stressors.

Wide-ranging and adaptive networks do exist in older populations and have unique patterns depending on the nature of the health problem and the community in which the network exists. Goodman (1984) has shown a variety of helping styles within a retirement high-rise complex. "High-helpers" were ready to receive assistance and to give on an equal basis, and "isolates" were less likely to interact with others to receive or give help. Morgan, Patrick, and Charlton (1984) have demonstrated in a London sample the complex network of social ties among physically challenged people who initially appeared to be isolated and having little capacity to develop helping networks. These subjects had functioning social networks of between four and nine people. Also, ethnic differences emerged; West Indians had significantly more locally based kin network supports than those born in the United Kingdom, of whom 61 percent had dispersed kin networks. Fursten-berg and Davis (1984) have shown that lay consultation for health conditions among old people is very common. Rather than late life losses causing disintegra-tion of social network support, these older subjects maintained an adaptive response to health problems. Their discussion of disease episodes or exacerbation of chronic disease led to emotional and knowledge support. Also, subjects refined their ideas of what was wrong with them and received support for action. Action was observed in network members' promotion of current health practices, actual intervention, or persuasion to seek professional care. Studies also show that elderly people in inner-city single room occupancy (SRO) hotels are capable of generating working networks (Sokolovsky and Cohen 1987). These networks vary by their distribution patterns, intimacy patterns, and variable activation of linkages. Even in nursing homes, frail elderly patients have identified and used the housekeeping staff as providers of psychosocial support, which is a therapeutic function not formally ascribed to housekeepers (Henderson 1987a).

In summary, elderly people fluidly interact with one another in their com-munities on matters related to health, disease, and well-being. Old people in residential communities, high-rise complexes, in SROs, and in nursing homes are all known to be active participants in social networks of health-seeking behavior.

ETHNIC-SPECIFIC ALZHEIMER'S SUPPORT GROUPS

The Suncoast Gerontology Center of the University of South Florida Medical Center developed a plan for the implementation of Alzheimer's disease support group intervention in ethnic communities that generally do not use existing support group services. An Alzheimer's disease support group in the Latino community of Tampa, Florida, was developed by taking into consideration ethnic-specific local history and patterns of illness experiences. Nationally, Hispanic elderly people are 6.4 percent of all elderly (Census Summary 1980). In Florida, the sixty-plus age group of Hispanics is 16.1 percent of all elderly. In the advanced age group of seventy-five-plus, the Hispanics in Florida are 5.2 percent of all elderly, but in Tampa are 15 percent of all elderly (Longino 1983).

The development of Alzheimer's disease support groups in ethnic populations is designed to strengthen the coping capacities of the elderly minority caregiver by extending state-of-the-art information and fostering peer support in light of the immensely difficult job of being a caregiver to an Alzheimer's victim. As Jay Sokolovsky shows in chapter 10, ethnicity-based informal supports may be attenuated to the point of dysfunction due to changing urban conditions and overburden due to the inherent difficulty of caring for an Alzheimer's disease patient. Therefore, extrafamilial help is needed.

The proliferation of Alzheimer's disease support groups nationwide is direct evidence of the vigor of the informal health care sector in coping with dementing disorders. However, the AD support group system on a national basis is used primarily by a specific and limited population: white, middle-class caregivers. This user pattern constitutes an undesirable and unnecessary bottleneck to ethnic caregivers in need of help. This is particularly true in view of epidemiologic research which indicates that dementing disorders are present in all racial and ethnic populations (Henderson 1987b).

In an informal survey, conducted by the author, of twenty-three sociobehavioral scientists in the United States professionally involved in aging and minority issues, only one was involved in extending Alzheimer's support group intervention into ethnic communities. Also, key people in the professional and volunteer aging networks were contacted in New York, San Francisco, Los Angeles, Memphis, San Antonio, Jacksonville, Miami, and Tampa where significant ethnic populations live and where AD support groups are in operation. No plan for incorporation or extension of services to minority caregivers existed, and there was nearly zero participation in the existing groups by ethnic populations. To strengthen the coping capacities of ethnic caregivers, however, intervention must not be hastily thrust into the existing helping network but must be incorporated in such a fashion that it is an asset and not a competitive liability (Foster and Anderson 1978; Polgar 1962).

A need for cultural specificity in Hispanic health interventions is well documented. For example, the importance of family image in health and disease, intrafamilial expectations of caregiving, changes in extended family networks, language differences, and intraethnic diversity must be understood for effective intervention (Valle 1981, in press; Garviria and Stern 1980; Canino and Canino 1982; Spector 1979; Delgado 1983).

Considering all this, the basic steps for ethnic AD support group development are: (1) reliance on members of the target communities to coach project staff in the development of community compatible support groups; (2) understanding of the network of personal, familial, and community resources already used in coping with AD relative to the formal and informal health care systems; (3) training of indigenous support group leaders; and (4) building AD support groups in the Hispanic community.

The Latin Alzheimer's disease support group was started through the Department of Aging Services of Hillsborough County (Tampa is the county seat). Contacts in this agency led to a senior day care center located in the historic Latin district of Tampa called Ybor City. A bilingual Latin day care center aide who had family experience with dementia was interested in serving as a support group leader. Her supervisor would allow her to have compensatory time for the hours that she would use in conducting a support group, estimated at four to five per month.

The decision was made to use classrooms for training the leader at conferences conducted by the Suncoast Gerontology Center on dementing disorders and to conduct a series of three small group discussions with her. In addition, it was decided that the support group meetings would be jointly led by the psychiatric social worker, who was experienced with groups, and to allow the indigenous support group leader to engage in role model training so that she could, on a gradual basis, exert more influence in group dynamics.

The meetings were scheduled monthly and led by two professionals from the Suncoast Gerontology Center as well as the indigenous support group leader. The location suggested by the indigenous group leader was a Hispanic hospital in Tampa, Centro Español Hospital. Announcements were run in Spanish-language newspapers and radio stations in the community. The leader's work at the day care center provided her several potential support group participants.

These activities led to the initiation of a support group meeting that was considered attractive to Latinos, due to the participation of a Hispanic support group leader and the use of Centro Español Hospital, a culturally potent symbol in their health care domain.

As David Jacobson states, "The meaning of 'social support' is intelligible within its cultural context" (1987:58). Therefore, one of the assumptions tested by this project was the appropriateness and utility of support group intervention as a proper intervention in "Hispanic culture." Some investigators suggest that group psychotherapy, which is akin to family support group intervention, is prone to failure among Hispanics due to members' concerns about privacy (del Valle and Usher 1982). One support group member refers to the reluctance to discuss Alzheimer's disease in public:

> You know what I think happens in a lot of Latin people who have family members with this disease, they feel like they don't want other people to know about it. It is not that they are ashamed of it but I think they like to

keep it to themselves. . . . A lot of them feel that way. A lot of Latin people keep their things to themselves. They don't let everybody know their problems, their medical problems. I don't know why but I have noticed that . . . maybe they don't want people to know they are suffering.

Del Valle and Usher (1982) do note that with proper empathy from group leaders such concerns can be overcome. Other specialists agree that there are positive benefits of Hispanic group meetings. Acosta (1982) reports that although group psychotherapy among Hispanic people is not currently common, it "can be a powerful modality in treating the Spanish speaking Hispanic patients." Becerra, Karno, and Escobar state even more positively that:

One type of treatment strategy that has proven very useful with the Spanish speaking Hispanic has been group psychotherapy. The group acts as a support system that facilitates the disclosure of private experiences that many Hispanics find difficult to communicate outside the family or community setting. The all Hispanic group serves to promote greater identity and cohesion among the group members. The similarity in culture and lifestyle provides an environment that is conducive to openness, understanding and change. (1982:11)

The experience of this pilot project is consistent with the predictions that the support group will represent a fictive kinship network unit in itself. Thus, the support group serves as an extended family with a problem focus of coping with Alzheimer's disease. According to Escobar and Randolph (1982), the extended kinship network is a primary social resource among Hispanics, and the strong reliance on the *concepto de la familia* is a key element in Hispanic culture. Since the start of the support group, members have developed car pooling schedules, phone calling to check on members during nonmeeting weeks, and a repeated pattern of conversation in Spanish at the beginning and end of meetings while members arrive and depart. One of the earliest examples of mutual ethnic identity came from members detailing historical events surrounding life in Ybor City, where most of them used to live. Also, they talk about acquaintances they have in common. The number of these acquaintances and the fact that many turn out to be distant relatives comes as no surprise to the group. As the support group meeting is started in earnest, conversations spontaneously develop which tap members for information on the current status of their patients.

The prominence of the Latin kinship and family-dynamic structure is very clear in issues related to burden bearing and responsibility. The foremost of these is the sex-biased pattern of familial transmission of responsibility for care of the demented patient. Members commonly report that women are expected to provide care for the demented person, whether it be the women's spouse, a parent, or a parent-in-law. When the family has both males and females "available" for bearing the major responsibility, it is still the female who is expected to provide that type of care. One respondent reported that during the life of the patient (her father), her mother and she would be expected to provide the bed and body care for the patient; when death occurred, her brothers would take charge of the father because it then entered a business dimension, namely, the cost of the funeral, and a matter of public display.

If the family does not have a close "blood-relative" female to provide bed and body care for the patient, these duties will typically be assigned to a nearby daughter-in-law. This provides a source for a variety of intrafamilial irritations. For example, many Hispanic parents are concerned that their adult children may disengage from family responsibilities with the parents. In fact, a daughter-in-law is often the target of great hostility. By marrying the son, she becomes the recipient of attention and help, thereby reducing the amount of assistance available to the other family members (del Valle and Usher 1982). Nonetheless, the daughter-in-law may be pressed into service to her in-laws. Although a new household has been established, the expectation of direct caregiving support is placed on women. Therefore, selection of a helper from the new couple is strongly biased toward the bride.

The following case incorporates dimensions of cultural influence in multi-infarct dementia in a Latino family.

Case 1: Multi-Infarct Dementia in a Tampa Latin Family

Sixty-eight-year-old Mr. Perez is hospitalized at Centro Español Hospital with a diagnosis of multi-infarct dementia. The prognosis is not favorable and includes complete bed care for the remainder of his life. Consideration of nursing home placement is unthinkable to Mrs. Perez, who elects to care for him at their home.

The Perez local family consists of Mrs. Perez's able-bodied eighty-eight-year-old mother who lives with Mrs. and Mr. Perez. The Perez adult children are a married son with two small children and a divorced daughter with three older children and one grandchild whom she is trying to care for.

Having learned of her husband's diagnosis and prognosis at his bedside, Mrs. Perez leads her daughter into the hallway of the hospital and tells her daughter that now it is up to them (meaning her daughter and her) to provide the ultimate in care for the husband and father at home. The adult daughter recoils and begins to list the nearby family members who could likewise lend direct support and assistance but on whom Mrs. Perez is not calling. Mrs. Perez is unable to understand her daughter's reaction, in that she is the expected helper of the primary caregiver.

When a support group for the caregivers of dementia patients is formed at Centro Español Hospital, the daughter is actively involved. However, Mrs. Perez attends only one meeting because of her sense of public humiliation if she has to confront the nature of her husband's disease, which produces behavioral aberrations in a public context. Nonetheless, the adult daughter, who gave occasional "hands-on" care, attends the meetings regularly and serves as a broker of information and support from the meeting to her mother. The mother responds by initiating use of community services and reevaluation of her role as caregiver.

The patient remains at home (with brief episodes of hospitalization) for three and a half years before dying at home.

The expectation of a female caregiver is brought out very clearly in the case of Mrs. Perez and her adult daughter. This type of expectation of caregiving by women has been observed in this project and reflected in the fact that out of thirty-six actual caregivers twenty-nine or eighty-one percent, are women.[3] Based on data of caregiving frequencies and types, the ranked preference of Latino caregivers by sex and kinship relation in this study is as follows: (1) wife, (2) sister or other adult female "blood relative," (3) female nonkin, (4) male "blood relatives," and (5) male in-laws. Note that even before switching to kin-related male caregivers, nonkin females are relied upon.

Many Latino caregivers are worried that the community will interpret the sometimes bizarre behavior of the dementia victim as evidence of "craziness in the family." The following case is such an example.

Case 2: The Garcia Family

Mr. Garcia has suffered from dementia for several years. He is cared for at home now with a minimum of fanfare or help from kinsmen and neighborhood friends. Mrs. Garcia discusses the early stages of her husband's dementia. As she begins to tell of specific circumstances, she begins to explain a Latin ethic. "I tell you one thing about the Spanish, they will get very upset about someone who is crazy or does crazy things." She hastens to add that this is due to lack of education and not that they happen to be of Spanish descent.

Even during a time when her husband was so confused that he was urinating on the living room floor, Mrs. Garcia tried to put up a front that everything was okay, to her neighbors certainly, but also even to her children. Mrs. Garcia says, "How could I tell my family not to bring a girlfriend or boyfriend in here because the house smells of urine?" Mrs. Garcia says that even now former friends avoid her because they "fear the disease" or just feel uncomfortable about being there. This bothers Mrs. Garcia to the point of wondering if she is being penalized for some past sin.

An event that prompted Mrs. Garcia to put deadbolts without keys on doors of the house involved her husband wandering away from the house at night. She awoke at 5:00 A.M. to find Mr. Garcia not in bed. She immediately checked the house to find him gone. Her first response was to get in the car and scout the neighborhood for him. Only after this proved futile did she return to the house to call neighbors for assistance. They first checked their backyard pool and then decided to drive in separate cars around the neighborhood while Mrs. Garcia waited at home. A neighbor found Mr. Garcia about two miles from home, "just in his briefs," with blisters on his bare feet. His safety as well as the public nature of his "crazy behavior" mortified Mrs. Garcia.

Alzheimer's disease presents symptoms that the general public interprets as characteristic of someone who is "crazy." The stigma attached to mental disorders is well known within this culture and many others. Escobar and Randolph (1982) report that, for many Hispanics, mental illness is still seen as a dreaded affliction akin to *mal de sangre* or "bad blood." The issue of a family member being "crazy" is a common one in the Latin Alzheimer's support group meetings. There is often a personal crusade launched to be sure that friends and family understand that Alzheimer's disease is an organic disease and, therefore, not under the control of the individual, thus relieving the patient and family of social liability.

The Latin support group members extend their concern about social stigma and mental disorders into financial arenas like insurance coverage. They complain, as do other families of Alzheimer's patients, that insurance categories place all psychiatric afflictions in mental health domains. Because mental health problems often are not covered by policies, families find themselves negotiating with physicians to enter the diagnosis as an organic brain disease.

The families in this sample strongly value the image of being strong, tightly knit, and reliant on family resources to succeed in life. However, over time, a "generation gap" has developed. Older Latins are less likely to use social services and community resources than their adult offspring. Attendance at a support group meeting communicates publicly that help is needed; self-reliance has failed. The following case shows the adaptation made to bridge the gap.

Case 3: The Lopez Family

Maria Lopez attends her first support group meeting on September 11, 1984, in the company of her oldest son. Her stepdaughter had been summoned to go with her, but her work schedules prevented her. During the two-and-one-half-hour meeting, Mrs. Lopez's son, Roberto, introduces her and provides some details of his father's condition. Mrs. Lopez sits quietly during this discourse, which includes commentary and questions from others in the support group, answered by her son. During the support group meeting Mrs. Lopez herself commented only about her love for Cuban coffee and, due to its strength, the "lift" that it produces from the caffeine.

One month later Mrs. Lopez was again accompanied by her son to the support group meeting because the stepdaughter was unable to arrange her job in order to bring the stepmother. This time, Roberto Lopez talked mainly about their former upbringing in the Latino quarters of Tampa known as Ybor City. As discussion turned more toward caregiver issues, his mother began to comment in response to her son's status report of the father's condition. Roberto reported that the father had been very hostile and aggressive for the past few days, to which Mrs. Lopez had responded flatly and quietly, "I'm tired of this. If you don't straighten up, I'm going out this door." Roberto followed this comment by saying that when his mother responds sharply to his father this "brings him back to reality."

Roberto and his mother now alternate commentary about the father's history of being very strict and domineering. Mrs. Lopez summarizes her marriage by saying, "Forty-four years is a hell of a long time." Eight weeks later Mrs. Lopez is accompanied by her stepdaughter Marcella. Marcella began by saying her stepmother's problem is "lack of sleep." Mrs. Lopez says, "I'm very nervous," and then demonstrates with her hands by shaking them and saying, "Just like this." Maria now becomes outspoken and discusses a history of being physically abused by her husband and occasions of running into the street to solicit help from other Latin neighbors. In reference to her husband's current condition, Mrs. Lopez is now so bold as to demonstrate his stooped gait and short steps while shuffling his feet. Her stepdaughter interjects that "It's the Haldol" (a tranquilizing medication). It is clear that Mrs. Lopez is willing now to express her anger through her raised voice, rapid speech, and physical mimicry of her husband's condition.

Mrs. Lopez refers to her state of "nerves," which is affirmed by Marcella. Mrs. Lopez says that she doesn't take any *medicatinos* for herself because she can't afford them. But she does take honey to ward off heart problems. Mrs. Lopez also says that she keeps her husband fully medicated in order to "keep him cool."

One month later Mrs. Lopez attends the meeting by herself, having been "car pooled" by other members of the group. As a result of encouragement from the group, an aide comes to the home to give Mr. Lopez a bath twice a week. It is now clear that Mrs. Lopez speaks openly and freely within the group setting, having phased herself into the support group family.

David Maldonado (1985) suggests that Hispanic populations variably respond by age cohorts to available helping services such as Alzheimer's family support groups. This age cohort effect has been very clearly observed in the Latin Alzheimer's support group. The most active members are adult daughters and sons of parents who are coping with Alzheimer's disease. The older-generation Hispanics, thus far, seldom attend the group except when specifically brought by their daughters or sons. Furthermore, when knowledge of additional community resources are made known to the parent generation, arrangements for such resources are negotiated through the adult daughters or sons in the group.

It is common to see the older generation Latin person attending the group with an adult daughter or son. The older person sits quietly and occasionally adds an affirmation in response to a monologue delivered by the adult offspring. Usually, however, within a few meetings the older person speaks up, and the role of the adult offspring becomes less important.

SUMMARY

The effectiveness of the Latin Alzheimer's disease support group is high, as judged by sustained participation of members, development of interpersonal linkages between members, recruitment of new members by longstanding members, and direct reports of the comfort received from participants in support group meetings. However, no instruments have been used to measure effectiveness in terms of improved mental health or caregiver functioning. Nonetheless, this support group of Latins shows that certain cultural patterns such as extreme reliance on female caregivers, generational effects, and "low service user" patterns can be overcome when culturally compatible approaches are used.

Certain unique characteristics of these support group members contribute to the configuration of this ethnographic profile. For example, most participants are middle class and high school educated. All are bilingual and are second-generation residents of Tampa. Still, elements of ethnic culture remain very strong in the minds and behaviors of people considered to be highly acculturated. This definitely applies to the members of the Latin support group. There are vast numbers of poor, monolingual Latinos in Tampa who apparently are not attracted to this type of intervention. Other local factors are revealed by examining the one other Latin-specific Alzheimer's disease support group operating in the country. Dr. Ramon Valle worked with such a group primarily composed of Mexican-Americans in Los Angeles. He has told me that meetings are characterized by multiple generations of participants, including young children. In Tampa, however, the young children of the adult caregivers in the sample are seldom present. Valle attributes the difference to intraethnic variation. The Los Angeles support group participants are Mexican-Americans who came to California thirty to forty years ago. They exhibit the "Mexican heritage interactional pattern." The interdependence of family members produces a "group" approach to resolving family problems (Ho 1987).

The Tampa project also has included an effort to develop Alzheimer's disease support groups in the black community. The effort is now underway to rely on black Protestant churches and existing helping networks emanating from organizations within those churches. The early efforts appear to be promising. However, cultural issues are present and must be considered in the operation of a support group. These include knowledge of the role in the black church in community health, mental health implications of racism, negative social experience and clinical intervention programs, indigenous health practices, and familial and friendship helping networks (Levin 1984; Spector 1979; Carter 1978, 1981; Chatters, Taylor, and Jackson 1986; Neighbors 1984).

Most older people do not get dementia. For those who do, the devastation and impact on a patient and family members is enormous. The overwhelming impact of this disease on families is being perceived by the American government in terms of programs specifically for dementia victims in adult day care, respite care, and nursing home care. However, policies made for the majority population can neglect specific needs of ethnic and minority groups. This appears to be the case on a national basis with lay-developed Alzheimer's disease support groups. Yet this project shows that, with proper community involvement and sensitivity to sociocultural issues, a helpful intervention can be put in place.

NOTES

1. Alzheimer's disease is characterized by specific changes in the brain, including brain cell death and the formation of paired helical protein filaments that form when the brain cells die and are believed to be made from brain cell synaptic structures. Senile plaques are also found. These are masses of amyloid protein, a common component of connective tissue. The senile plaque is a by-product of neuronal degeneration (Reisberg 1983).

2. Other kinds of dementia that are less common include multi-infarct dementia, Pick's disease, and other very rare types like Creutzfeld-Jakob's disease, kuru, Binswanger's disease, and Huntington's chorea. Multi-infarct dementia represents about 15 percent of all cases of dementia. About 12 percent of cases represent a mixed pathology of Alzheimer's disease and multi-infarct dementia in the same person. The exact prevalence of Pick's disease is currently unknown. The more rare types occur at a frequency of 2 percent or less (Mortimer 1983).

3. There are sixty-nine potential caregivers.

18 LIMINALITY IN AN AMERICAN NURSING HOME: THE ENDLESS TRANSITION

Renée Rose Shield

The nursing home environment provides an excellent setting in which to examine processes of community formation and the impact of institutionalization upon the residents living there. Numerous factors impinge upon the frail old person living in institutions: inevitable functional decline, increased occurrences of disease, and the cultural effects of nursing home life. The experience of residing in a nursing home varies according to the particular nursing home and numerous individual factors of the residents. Many nursing homes are for temporary stays in which the individual recovers from a specific procedure or ailment and is then discharged. Nursing homes vary according to size, according to how they are funded, whether they admit individuals with dementia, and so forth. Some nursing homes allow considerable resident autonomy, and others do not. All of these factors influence whether or not a sense of community is developed within the nursing home and the shape the particular community takes if it does develop.

This chapter seeks to explain the lack of community formation in one American long-term care facility, which was studied for a period of fourteen months between 1981 and 1983. The Franklin Nursing Home, located in the northeastern United States, is a nonprofit, long-term care facility for 250, primarily Jewish, elderly who are unable to live on their own in the community.[1] This nursing home is considered to be a good one, with higher staffing ratios, more recreational activities, and better facilities than most. One-half to two-thirds of the nursing home residents, whose average age is eighty-five, suffer from Alzheimer's disease or other dementing illnesses. They typically live in the nursing home for approximately four years. Most of the residents die there. Evidence of community was expected, because many of these old people knew each other before admission and are of similar ethnic background. Instead, they were found to be isolated and only superficially involved with each other.

Two factors in particular illuminate the study of communities of the aged. First, entering and living in a nursing home can be understood as a rite of passage: the individual leaves his or her old status behind (separation), enters a new world with like individuals (liminality), and eventually dies (reincorporation). Because there are no rites to accompany this particular passage, the individual undergoing the passage is solitary and unaided. The second issue is how individuals in the nursing home help each other or somehow contribute to the institution. This ability of people to give and take with each other, reciprocate with one another, is an important hallmark of community formation and needs to be considered here.

Here I argue that: (1) the residents are undergoing a rite of passage from adulthood in the community to death—their residence in the nursing home is part of an unresolved liminal phase; and (2) their inability to contribute to each other and to the institution exacerbates their dependency and leads to their being considered children by staff members. This liminality is the result of, and in turn causes, a lack of coherence among staff members. Though most of the residents are Jewish, their differences from each other and their frailties are pronounced. The separation between the nursing home and the Harrison community in which it is located reflects an ambivalence by the community toward its institutionalized elderly. This situation exists despite the fact that many of the residents have relatives in the vicinity. In the following pages, I describe the factors which comprise this unresolved rite of passage and show how reciprocity is constrained. The combination of all these processes exerts a powerful effect on nursing home residents which prevents the formation of community.

RITES OF PASSAGE AND RECIPROCITY

Rites of passage and reciprocity are universal cultural forms that take on unique expression in the nursing home. In 1908, Arnold van Gennep's seminal *Les Rites de Passages* showed how rites of passage throughout the world have three parts: separation from the old status, transition (usually called "liminality") between the old role and the new role, and reincorporation into the new role. The stages are made routine and less stressful by the rituals that surround them. The liminal part of rites of passage is considered the most dangerous of the three segments. Mary Douglas described the threat of liminality vividly:

> Danger lies in transitional states; simply because transition is neither one
> state nor the next, it is undefinable. The person who must pass from one
> to another is himself in danger and emanates danger to others. During the
> marginal period which separates ritual dying and ritual rebirth, the

novices in initiation are temporarily outcast. For the duration of the rite they have no place in society. Sometimes they actually go to live far away outside it. They are not to be blamed for misconduct any more than the foetus in the womb for its spite and greed. It seems that if a person has no place in the social system and is therefore a marginal being, all precaution against danger must come from others. He cannot help his abnormal situation. (1966:116-17)

Another hallmark of rites of passage centers on the receptivity of learning about the new role into which the initiate is about to be socialized. As if stripped of all past knowledge, the initiate must be taught the basics of the new position which awaits him or her. "Because rites of passage occur at moments of great anxiety, they are dramatic occasions, naturally or socially provided crises, when the person is most teachable. Tension is heightened by rites, and resolution is eagerly sought" (Myerhoff 1982:113).

The anthropologist Victor Turner (1969) develops the idea of liminality in his work, expanding the concept to refer to all kinds of people and situations defined as neither in one category of social identity nor in another. He stressed the positive aspects of liminality and used the term "communitas" to describe the togetherness that initiates in a rite of passage often share with each other.

The aged individuals residing in the Franklin Nursing Home occupy the borderline, threshold state which typifies the liminal phase. They have been separated from their statuses as viable adults in the community, and, not having died, they remain in the transition. However, their liminality is not marked by communitas. Instead of the nursing home enabling the resident to prepare for the next stage, death, as in other rites of passage, the entire subject of death is avoided. Social and emotional withdrawal from the other residents is coupled with vigorous physical interventions that maintain life. Like other liminal states in other rites of passage, there is dependency and separation, but unlike other kinds of liminality, the dependency is not accompanied by teaching. Preparation for the next stage is actively discouraged; religion and ritual are minimal; involvement by the community is meager; and isolation is prevalent. There is little camaraderie or ceremonial notice to accompany this transition. These conditions are further described in "Aspects of Liminality." Separation and loneliness, not community, result.

RECIPROCITY

To give and to receive are basic in human life. Reciprocal relations are crucial to power, choice, and control. Because receiving and giving are cyclical and mutually indebting, humans are bound together. This inherent mutuality is aborted when one side always receives and the other always gives and there is little or no opportunity for the receiver to repay the giver.

Theorists have shown how reciprocity is important among the elderly.[2] Cross-cultural evidence has shown that elderly persons are able to maintain a fairly high status when they have something considered valuable by others in their society to exchange, whether it be customs, skills, historical knowledge, economic resources, or inheritances (Vatuk 1980; Gutmann 1976; Cool 1980; Palmore 1975; Amoss 1981; Amoss and Harrell 1981; Keith 1982; Glascock and Feinman 1981; Foner 1984; among others).

Because the residents of the nursing home are in the liminal part of the passage from adulthood to death, they are already dependent and vulnerable. Another layer of dependency is added because the basic facts of life in the nursing home are that the residents receive care and the staff members dispense care. The lack of resources with which the residents can repay staff members reduces their control and increases their dependency.[3] Given this unequal power balance, staff-resident interactions take on particular forms.

DIVERGENT STAFF BELIEFS

Aged and frail individuals who are unable to function in their former place of residence in the Harrison community enter a nursing home which has conflicting divisions within it. This factor is important because in most rites of passage there is general consensus regarding the purposes and processes of the rite in question. However, staff groups at this nursing home (administrators, nurses, social workers, aides, and orderlies) have different perceptions about the nursing home, including: who the nursing home residents are, how the staff members should behave toward them, and what their goals for the residents are (Shield, 1988). In other words, there is no shared perception about the nature of this rite of passage. The lack of cohesion concerning these cultural constructions of nursing home life prevents the formation of community, encourages competition in staff, and promotes isolation among the residents. These three issues translate into contested bipolar assessments of "home versus hospital," "employees versus friends," "life versus quality of life," and "rehabilitation versus maintenance."

HOME OR HOSPITAL

Some staff members insist that the nursing home is a "home." "I was talking with the maintenance man about the air conditioners in the nursing home when I happened to refer to the place as an institution. Tom stiffened and said, 'This is not an institution. This is a home.'"[4] Opposed to the notion of the nursing home as home is the idea that the nursing home is a hospital; thus medical dictates take over: "Esther Marks is obese and has hypertension. On a recent shopping trip downtown she bought smoked meats, pickled herring, and other foods of which her doctors disapprove. When she returned to the nursing home, she bragged about her purchases and announced her intention of eating them.

The administrator of the home confiscated the foods." Staff members try to determine whether to allow behavior that is "bad" for the resident or insist on distasteful preventive measures which the residents hate. Does the resident have the right to behave as if she were in her own home, or must she conform to medically determined treatment as if she were in a hospital? Frequently, there is inconsistency and little consensus.

EMPLOYEES OR FRIENDS

The home-hospital dichotomy also influences the nature of staff-resident relationships. At times residents as well as staff members refer to themselves as a family or as friends.[5] However, the inequality of the relationships is paramount.

Max Sager is fond of the social worker, Fran Rubin. She is wary of his affection because she feels it violates the professional distance between them, and it also seems to unnerve her personally. Since he has had a lithium imbalance and a history of manic-depressive illness, she tends to utilize these concepts in order to maintain her distance. For example, she says that Mr. Sager is in his manic phase now, and that is why he is more attentive to her lately. Today, he has walked into her office with a bottle of wine. He is happy because today marks one year since his woman-friend had her stroke, and she has been recovering well. There will be a party at her house later on today, and Mrs. Rubin will be transporting Mr. Sager there. To celebrate, he would like the two of them to have a glass of wine now. Mrs. Rubin refuses. He urges her to join him, but she becomes irritated. Since he continues to urge her, she says that if he wants to have his wine, he may drink it in his room, but that she may not have a drink with him because she is working. With considerable irritation, she places the wine bottle directly back into his hand, hands him his cane, and tells him she will see him later. After this incident, Mr. Sager expressed his disappointment with her rigidity.

Since Mr. Sager lives in the nursing home, he may have his glass of wine, but since the social worker works there, she may not. This distinction put Mr. Sager abruptly in "his place." While many staff members act "friendlike" to the residents, residents are more frequently reminded that staff members are employees first. They are rushed and overworked. They have fingernails to clean and charts to complete. Talking or visiting with residents has low priority.

LIFE VERSUS QUALITY OF LIFE

Of the various opposing definitions current among the nursing home staff, the most important division occurs in the use of two slogans, which I call "life" and "quality of life." These two models of care embody the home-hospital dichotomy, operate simultaneously at the Franklin Nursing Home, and often conflict with each other. They stem from the medical model of preserving life and the social work model of advocacy. As seen in the following observation of a resident-care conference, nurses and doctors prescribe routines to preserve life at all costs, and social workers argue for more family and resident choice in life-preserving measures.

> The meeting is about to break up, but the doctor wants to talk about his decision to resuscitate Mrs. Kerman. Long before, she had specifically told him not to do anything extraordinary for her, "should anything happen." A social worker, Lisa, asks pointedly now, "And did you?" "Yes!" answers the doctor adamantly. Lisa scoffs, "I don't want you to be my doctor!" The doctor says that if someone told him explicitly right before a procedure that he or she didn't want extraordinary measures taken, then okay. He can live with that, with not doing anything. But in this case, there was a long time lag from when Mrs. Kerman first expressed her wish for no intervention until the crisis that called for intervention. What should he do when the patient cannot express her wishes then? The doctor says, deliberately using the double negative, that he didn't want to do nothing. Lisa says, "But you are deciding on her quality of life for her and that's not right." When Mrs. Kerman had told the doctor that she wanted nothing extraordinary done, she had also explained that she'd had a long and full life and that when the time came, she wanted to die. She is angry at the doctor now for what he has done, but the doctor is saying, "I don't think I did the wrong thing." The nurse, Bernice, says with disgust, "No one ever used to talk like this. In all my thirty years of nursing, there was never a question. Our job is to save lives!" She shakes her head at the social workers across the table and walks out. The meeting is over.

Social workers refer to the residents as residents; physicians and nurses, on the other hand, more often refer to residents as patients. While physicians and nurses are trained to preserve life whenever possible, social workers have a priority to improve the "quality of life" of the residents. The medical personnel regard life-saving decisions as automatic, but the social workers question them. For example: "The suitability of an operation to be conducted on a terminal cancer patient who is eighty-seven years old was not questioned by some of the nurses, but was considered undesirable by social workers. The nurses and the social workers could not understand the others' points-of-view in the matter, and they criticized each other accordingly." Nurses and social workers also disagree about the appropriateness of cardiopulmonary resuscitation (CPR) in this setting. At times the discrepant points of view are irreconcilable.

REHABILITATION VERSUS MAINTENANCE

As frailer people are admitted, rehabilitation seems to be an increasingly less relevant goal of the facility. This belief operates against the physical therapy program, whose explicit purposes are to improve the resident's ability to ambulate and to regain weakened or lost motor control.

A stroke patient who had no use of his legs upon admission attended physical therapy three times a week. After prodding by the physical therapy staff, the resident was walking with the aid of a walker. However, back on the fourth floor where his room was, the nursing staff did nothing to supplement the gains that had been made in the physical therapy sessions. While there are standing orders for aides and orderlies throughout the institution to do "range of motion" exercises with all the residents, they are rarely done.[6] The people-work of the institution takes a higher priority. Therefore, nails are cleaned, hair is brushed, and beds are made while residents remain sitting in chairs, watching passively. Staff members do their jobs; the residents wait.

The effort to rehabilitate residents competes with the opposing notion that maintenance of residents at their current level of functioning is adequate. The divisions among the staff goals that have been described in this section prevent the smooth fulfillment of a team plan for nursing home residents. Two additional factors, described next, further complicate the picture. Residents are very different from each other (but are treated as a group), and much of the Jewish population of the city in which the nursing home is located avoids the nursing home residents in important ways.

HETEROGENEITY OF RESIDENTS

The Franklin Nursing Home cares for residents with varying degrees of neediness.[7] I divide these individuals into three general groups. One group is comprised of those individuals who are extremely ill or debilitated. Many of them are unable to fulfill any of their physical needs, but they may be capable of understanding and communicating. The second and largest group in the nursing home is comprised of those residents who are considered demented and may or may not be physically capable of certain activities. The final group consists of those residents who are considered the most physically and mentally capable. Each group has significant variety within it.

While these groups are fairly distinct and have quite separate needs, they are contained within the same institution and are often treated alike. Problems abound when the competing staff goals, described above, are added to the three different resident groups in the nursing home.

AMBIVALENCE BY HARRISON TOWARD THE NURSING HOME

The fact that the Franklin Nursing Home is linked to and cut off from the Harrison community at the same time helps create liminality. Tension and cooperation alternate in the relationship between the neighboring hospital (where the Franklin Nursing Home residents are almost invariably hospitalized) and the Franklin Nursing Home. While the nursing and social work staffs of the two institutions are separate, there is little communication between them. The hospital nurses misunderstand the nursing done at the nursing home to be inferior, custodial care, for example.[8]

The Jewish community behaves ambivalently toward the nursing home, too; though supporting it financially, members of the community tend to avoid personal contact with residents.[9] There is no consensus on numerous decisions facing the future of the nursing home, and it has been difficult to secure a rabbi to come to the nursing home. The services and clinics provided in the nursing home decrease the need for the residents to secure those same services in the community, so that dependency on the institution is ensured, and separation from the community is increased.

ASPECTS OF LIMINALITY

Thus far, I have presented certain background conflicts and pressures that exist in the nursing home and in Harrison and that create the particular environment into which nursing home residents come to live their last years. They begin their last rite of passage, made more difficult than it might be because it is not aided by already-socialized nursing home residents, by staff members of the nursing home, or by individuals from Harrison. Thus, this rite of passage accentuates the lonely aspects of liminality, and resolution is secured only by the physical fact of death.

Entering the nursing home is accomplished by a series of leave-takings: a home is relinquished; a driver's license is given up; various memberships lapse. Separation from a past status and from the mainstream of a community is a hallmark of rite-of-passage ceremonies. A sense of timelessness coupled with various rigid staff routines create a unique institutional time. Other characteristics of nursing home liminality are dependency, the belief that old people are like children, the denial and avoidance of death, and the lack of religious support and ritual within the nursing home.

TIME

Time is often described as endless or strange in liminal states. In the nursing home time looms large. It seems unfillable and fraught with future perils. It needs to be broken up because days and weeks seem the same. Certain strategies allow residents to get through the days and the weeks, much like Jaber Gubrium (1975) describes "passing time" in his ethnography of Murray Manor.

Time is tracked by the secular calendar, by the Jewish calendar, by clock, and by nursing shifts. Knowledge of what day it is is necessary to predict visits, telephone calls, outside doctor visits, and events relevant to family members. Residents know staff time because it affects their lives directly. Many become anxious as they anticipate the change in shift.

> The charge nurse on the third floor is describing how the atmosphere of the floor changes at about 2:30 in the afternoon. Many of the aides, orderlies, and nurses are lolling around the nurses' station, some are already in their coats, and they're chatting with each other animatedly, appearing restless to go home. At the same time, the new shift is coming on, and there are greetings and personal catchings-up that go on between members of the two shifts. Various residents act more disturbed at this time; they appear restless; they repeat their questions with urgent frequency; they are less soothed by reassurances.

Much time is spent sleeping and watching television. Meals, activities, visits, telephone calls, and other events further structure the day. Sicker residents are, to varying degrees, the passive recipients of routines performed on them by different staff members. Their attempts to alter staff schedules in their care meet with little success:

> Mr. Allen came down the hall again, still in his bathrobe. "May I speak to a nurse, please?" he asked. No answer from the four personnel at the nurses' station. Two of them are charting; two others are in conversation with each other. After a few more tries, one of the nurses looks up and asks Mr. Allen what he wants. "May I please have my shower now?" he asks. The nurse explains that Ned, his orderly, is on his break now, and he will be having his shower later on in the afternoon. "You are not the only person Ned has to take care of, you know," she reminds the resident testily.

The management of time for these residents is more contingent on staff schedule, union-management negotiations, and staff whim than it is on the needs of the residents.

> "Will you take me to the bathroom, please?" asks Mrs. Behrenbaum. After she repeats this request quite loudly, an aide calls over to her, "I'm not your aide. Wait 'til Bertha comes back."

Contacts with family structure time, as well, particularly on weekends, when the time seems unbroken and long. Receiving or placing daily telephone calls is another way of marking time and filling it:

"Is it time to call my daughter now?" Mrs. Deutsch, a somewhat confused resident, anxiously asks Sarah Zeldin, her competent neighbor. "No, dear," answers Mrs. Zeldin patiently. "You always call her after lunch. We haven't had lunch yet. I'll remind you. Don't worry."

Awareness of death and finality provides a prominent counterpoint to the other times at the Frank Nursing Home, including the cyclical staff time of nursing shifts, the static time of every day being the same as every other, and secular and Jewish calendar time which helps create some anticipation of the future. Cognitively intact residents bluntly acknowledge their closeness to increasing disability and death. They say things such as: "Well, we're all here to die," or, "Obviously, this is the last stop," or, "I hope I'll have a chance to pick some of your grapes, if I'm around in the fall, that is." Many of the Franklin Nursing Home residents see their fate clearly in the other residents around them. Residents witness their neighbors become sick, go to the hospital, and either die there, come back well enough to retake possession of their old room, or come back at a lower level of functioning. It is a reality that most of the residents acknowledge readily. One resident said: "At least I can still walk and talk. But if I have another heart attack, I might end up like him." Such observations create a time perception of "future peril" with each passing day, the risk of experiencing more deficits and of requiring increased care is greater and is witnessed continually in others. This time of future peril is fought by staff denial and cyclical nursing home routines. This contradiction intensifies rather than resolves the ambiguity of the liminality.

DEPENDENCY

Dependency is another marker of liminality. The subjects of rites-of-passage events are often acted upon by other members of the society. Enduring the transition promotes dependency. In the nursing home, residents guard the independence and evidence of autonomy that they still have, knowing that it is a time-limited, precious commodity. Measures of independence constitute a ranking system among individuals (Shield 1988).

Initiates in rites-of-passage ceremonies are made dependent by the event, but this dependency seems to have the purpose of preparing the initiates for the next stage. There are tasks and teachings which may be facilitated by the dependency. In the Franklin Nursing Home, however, the dependency is enforced by rules, enhanced by expectations, and leads to more dependency.[10] The expectation that residents' abilities will worsen prevents staff members from teaching residents to do more for themselves. Aides and orderlies do "people-work" duties (Goffman 1961) as efficiently as possible, instead. Rather than take the extra time to help stroke victims put on shoes one by one or help residents walk, eat, or dress, aides and orderlies do these jobs for them. The rehabilitation that is attempted in physical therapy sessions loses ground to maintenance regimes on the residents' floors. In short, the dependency that occurs in the nursing home is not necessarily an inevitable accompaniment to residence there. By being expected, dependency is in part fostered by these staff attitudes.

OLD PEOPLE AS CHILDREN

People undergoing rites of passage are often likened to children because they are ignorant about the new role into which they will be socialized. In the nursing home the equation between old people and children is often made; staff members say the aged person is "like a child," "regressed," or "entering a second childhood." But though the residents seem to be childlike initiates in a rite of passage, they are not taught.

Residents at the Franklin Nursing Home are called by the diminutive versions of their names or by generic terms, such as "honey," "dearie," "sweetie," and so forth: "'Good morning, honey,' croons Aymara to the still-sleeping form in bed. 'It's time to get up now, darling. Okay, sweetie? It's Tuesday, honey; time to get up.' She turns to me and says, 'Sometimes you have to baby them, you know.'" Most employees resist the social workers' preference that residents be called by their surnames.

The activities and events that the aged in this nursing home are supposed to enjoy are ones that children love: birthday parties are held monthly; and special outings include excursions to the zoo and the amusement park. One resident commented succinctly: "Whenever they go to the zoo, I don't bother to go. We used to live near the zoo when my children were little. I took them to the zoo every single week. I've had enough of the zoo. "

Simple behaviors become evidence of dependencies, inabilities, and childishness when framed by the nursing home environment. A person's verbal expressions and actions are ignored, trivialized, or become emblematic of other meanings not intended by the person. A request for something is likely to be interpreted as a complaint. Requests for individualized treatment may be understood as expressions of self-centered childishness: "'Tomato juice is the best part of my meal,' Mrs. Zeldin says with satisfaction. When she tells the dietician that the kitchen has mistakenly sent the unsalted kind to her, the dietician denies the charge, implying that Mrs. Zeldin has made the mistake. They assume that she cannot tell the difference, and her complaint is not valid. She finds this occurrence frustrating."

Nonperson status is often reserved for use with children, and some of these behaviors are evident in the Franklin Nursing Home. For example, adults frequently talk to each other about their children as if they were not present. So, too, in the nursing home:

In the resident-care conference the staff members are talking about the resident who is present. The resident is unable to hear what is being said because she has some deafness. The resident interrupts the conversation and asks what is going on. Several staff members look surprised. In an exaggerated way, a staff member turns to face her, and speaks very slowly and loudly. After this statement, staff conversation returns to its previous quick-paced, low-decibel quality.

Sometimes the social worker refers to the resident as "mother" or "dad," when talking to the adult offspring, rather than as "your mother" or "your father." Like children, institutionalized elderly people are expected to enjoy being in each other's company automatically. Residents who do not get along with each other are regarded by many staff as childish.

Along with the perception that old people are like children is the denial of their sexuality. Sexual behavior such as masturbation or residents' appreciative comments about the opposite sex are often treated by staff as inappropriate, disgusting, or amusing. "Mr. Bernstein is somewhat senile, and several of the orderlies on his floor have discovered that he has a vivid interest in talking about the females whom he sees. They egg him on, asking him what he thinks about this one, and that one. He is specific in his appraisal of those attributes on the women he admires and those he does not, and the orderlies listen, and giggle, and ask, 'What about this one? How about her?'" Attempts to establish sexual relationships take on an adolescent quality as the couples scramble for privacy (in unlocked rooms) and as staff members and other residents view the relationships as illicit or ridiculous. Residents, too, seem to think that sexual behavior in people their age is inappropriate. For example, an unmarried couple told me that sex is an unappealing idea to them. "I don't find old women attractive," the man explains later.

In mundane and myriad ways the residents are supervised. Decision making by residents is hindered by the perception that the residents are like children. While there is a residents' council with elected officials, it minimally influences the way the nursing home operates. Residents witness changes in administration, in policy, and in staff, and their role as passive recipients in the institution remains basically the same. The care that is provided the residents comes at the expense of considerable independence.

DEATH DENIAL

Though death looms at the residents constantly and is a subject they themselves discuss, staff members avoid the subject and cover it up whenever possible. While residents talk and joke freely about it, staff members seem repulsed: "Mr. Wolf walked over to an aide in the dining room and said, 'When I die, I'd like to be buried in Israel.' The aide responded immediately, 'Now, Mr. Wolf. We don't talk about dying here. We talk about living.'"

In other liminal situations one would expect active preparation for the next stage, including talk, but such preparation does not go on here.

Max Abel has been quite confused and isolated for some time. The physician asks if anything has precipitated his state. One nurse thinks he is depressed because of the death of his son-in-law with whom he was quite close. Another nurse does not think so; she thinks he does not know about the death. No one can agree whether he knows or does not know. The nurse says to the social worker that they had been told that they weren't supposed to say anything to the resident about the death. The social worker replies that they wanted the resident to learn the news from another relative. The nurse says that she thinks no one ever told him, and her understanding was that it should be kept from him. The issue is unresolved, and no one knows, first of all, whether he has been told, and second, whether he has the capacity to know, understand, or remember being told.

Different beliefs about what the residents should know collide with discrepant information about the resident that the staff have. Another resident has been admitted to the nursing home from the hospital with cancer. He has been told about the diagnosis, and the staff thinks he is depressed about the news. The social worker wants the resident and the staff to "deal with" the issue of his cancer explicitly. The nurses are not sure.

When a resident is about to die, most staff members seem to withdraw. As social and emotional supports from staff dwindle, medical props and life-prolonging interventions are fortified.[11] People's work goes on uninterrupted in its repetitive cycle. Nurses, aides, and orderlies sometimes discuss the impending death in hushed tones that residents are not intended to hear. When the death finally occurs, the room is closed, the physician is called so the body may be "pronounced," the next of kin is notified, the personal effects are picked up, and the body is taken away to the funeral home. Not all staff members agree with this procedure.[12] A social worker told me: "I was uncomfortable each time I saw how death was managed. All the residents are taken into the dining area, and the doors are closed. Mysteriously, two men in black suits appear on the floor with a stretcher between them. They take away the body, and five minutes after the residents have been taken into the dining area, they are let out again. No one ever says what just happened." Residents sometimes attempt to fight the predominant staff attitudes about death. On one occasion a resident organized a memorial service for a friend who had just died. He put notices up around the nursing home and was satisfied that he had expended the effort on his friend. Scoffing about the typical handling of death, he said: "When someone dies, it is as if the person never even existed. They pretend nothing has happened."

The silence regarding death in the Jewish nursing home may be due to an Orthodox prohibition restricting talk about death.[13] It may also be due to death anxiety or to Pamela Amoss's (1981) provocative idea that the elderly are degraded because they are more associated with "nature" than they are with "culture," since they are close to death.[14] The overall behavior contrasts sharply with how the hospice movement explicitly deals with death. Preparation for and acknowledgment of death might foster the development of transition-easing rituals that might spur the development of group solidarity and communitas. In rejecting talk of death, however, preparation and rituals are prevented.

The nursing home symbolically embodies the dangerous transition from adulthood to death. It is cut off, clearly bounded, and separated from "normal" life on the "outside." The nursing home residents, tainted as they are by their nearness to death, cannot spread it to those in the community because of the separation. The separation provides artificial safety to the Harrison community. People in the Harrison community and staff members in the Franklin Nursing Home make the nursing home resident into a category distinguishable from them as "other." The separation is maintained, continuity is denied, and the apparent danger of contamination made remote.

RELIGION IN THE NURSING HOME

More separation occurs within the realm of religion in the nursing home. While Jewishness is obvious among the residents — consisting of Yiddish expressions, jokes, and folk wisdom; common historical experiences; a religious identity; values in education and skills of survival; a widely shared though often argued about commitment to Israel; and foods and other sensory customs that have provided continuity throughout their lives — there is little attempt to make Jewishness a vital part of daily life in the nursing home. A superficial kind of Jewishness penetrates instead.[15] The typical trademarks of the holidays are used to depict the holidays rather than the deeper meanings that inform the symbols. Emblems of Jewishness, like the Star of David, a Chanukah menorah, or a typically Jewish food, are displayed instead.

It is unclear whether the Jewish community has abandoned its Jewish aged or the nursing home residents do not care about religion anymore.[16] There seem to be elements of mutual discard by both segments.[17] Few of the very religious people in the nursing home attend the Orthodox services.[18] In order to achieve the proper quorum at the Orthodox early morning service held at the Franklin Nursing Home, several Orthodox men from the community join the half-dozen nursing home residents for the service each day.

Few of the nursing home's staff are Jewish, and ignorance of Jewish customs and beliefs is widespread. Virtually no one on the staff understands or can speak Yiddish except for an expression or two. When staff members know a few words of Yiddish, however, they often use the words for instant rapport.[19]

Another problem concerns rivalries among the residents. Certain individuals are said to monopolize ritually important tasks. When honors are more fairly divided, however, there are complaints that the rituals are not performed properly.

When Ida Kanter was admitted, she noticed that there were no Friday evening candle-lighting ceremonies. When she talked to the social worker about it, the social worker suggested that the resident organize it, and she did. Mrs. Kanter remembers to procure the candlesticks, to put on a white tablecloth, and have wine glasses and wine available for the occasion. However, the fact that she is "de facto" in charge of the Shabbos candle ritual has made her the target of other residents who resent her position of assumed authority.

In all, an active Jewishness is not promoted or encouraged. Occasionally, a flicker of information about Jewish history or culture is exploited as the explanation of some heretofore baffling resident behavior. The fact that Jews were in concentration camps during World War II "explains" any reluctance by residents to wear identification bracelets now. These shortcuts to cultural and personal understanding rarely penetrate beyond or dissuade staff members from their original preconceptions. Since residents are not asked "how things were" or what meaning something has, staff members' beliefs about the residents need not be challenged or revised. The fervent debate that Barbara Myerhoff (1979) described among the Jews in their senior center does not go on here. Thus, there is no soil from which newly meaningful forms of formerly meaningful ritual can spring. Instead, the "chicken soup" Judaism of the nursing home acts as a thinly reminiscent shell of the real thing and fails to provide viable answers or to heal.

THE UNANSWERABLE QUESTIONS

Many of the residents have endured difficult lives and have been unable to devise satisfactory answers to the plaguing question, "Why me?" The setting of the nursing home offers no solace, even though some of the residents are bound together by similar experiences. For example, some of the children of the residents have married non-Jewish people or have divorced. Their parents have no good explanation for these events. More disturbing is the fact that numerous residents have outlived their children. The death of a child is considered a particularly harsh tragedy. Many of the residents believe themselves too old to still be living; it seems a cruel joke that a son or daughter of theirs should die from cancer, a car accident, or a sudden heart attack. As Sally Falk Moore has written about the Chagga of Kilimanjaro, people expect an orderly timing about the succession of deaths: "Over the course of life, men see themselves moving place by place up the seniority ladder of the lineage. It is clear who is due to die next and who is to succeed him. When people die out of turn, that is something to be explained. It means that something has gone wrong in the order of things, and there may be witchcraft or curses to reckon with" (1978:33).

At the nursing home, people struggle for explanations to satisfy, but rarely succeed. Mr. Sager looks baffled as he describes how his perfectly healthy son "just died" one day at age fifty. It does not make sense to continue a strange, day-to-day life in a nursing home for month after month and year after year, when it seems to be far past an appropriate time to die. One resident said, "Every day, I am surprised to wake up. 'Why didn't you take me last night, God?' I always ask Him." Residents do not have a ritualized or formal opportunity to discuss these inexplicable tragedies with each other. They may not know that they are not the only ones who have experienced these losses. Ritual, religion, and the companionship of caring others would help.

THE LIMITS OF EXCHANGE: RESIDENTS AS RECIPIENTS

The final major factor which confronts the nursing home residents and inhibits the development of community in this setting is the constraint on reciprocity. Even though initiates in rites-of-passage ceremonies are the passive recipients of activities, behaviors, and expectations by other members of the society, they are active because they overcome the obstacles of the passage and proceed to the next stage. Residents at the Franklin Nursing Home, on the other hand, have their basic needs provided and have no tasks to fulfill. Payment to their caregivers is indirect, whether it is paid by the resident or by Medicaid/Medicare, because it happens in two stages: the nursing home is paid, and the nursing home pays its employees. Residents have few, if any, resources to repay or otherwise affect those who provide the care. Their behaviors toward staff members have few consequences; they receive care, food, shelter, and medical attention regardless of their actions. Residents who complain about the conditions trespass the moral rule of reciprocity: they should not complain since they have no alternatives. Passivity is encouraged, and community formation has no incentive to survive.

The anthropological literature on aging documents the extensive network and support systems that poor and disabled aged individuals construct for themselves to fulfill their needs and help each other to survive (e.g., Hochschild 1973; Becker 1980; Sokolovsky and Cohen 1978). When aged individuals have no institutional provision for care, horizontal networks between the individuals stretch among them and maintain themselves through reciprocity. But when care proceeds vertically from staff to residents in the nursing home, there is no incentive for horizontal networks to evolve. On the contrary: there is reason for the individual recipients of care to vie among each other for more services.[20] Wax (1962) has written:

> One who observes the residents of such a home may be surprised at the relative absence of friendships among people of similar status and years, isolated from family and friends. Yet, friendships, as other human relationships, are built upon reciprocity and those who lack possessions, strength and health have relatively little to exchange with each other. What little they have might still be negotiable, except that in a home where the administration is in control of such great benefits in the form of food,

shelter, social and medical services. What can be given or gained from one's neighbor is minuscule.

RECIPROCITY AND CONTROL

Jeanie Schmit Kayser-Jones (1981) compared a Scottish nursing home with an American nursing home and found that the residents in the Scottish nursing home had more valuable things to exchange than did the Americans, and thus they had some control over their lives in the nursing home.[21] Because national health insurance is a right for everyone in Great Britain, the elderly are not singled out for conspicuous consideration as they are in the United States.[22] Further, it seemed that because the Scottish staff enjoyed higher pay and status than did their American counterparts, there was less theft of residents' belongings than in the United States nursing home.[23]

Residents of the Franklin Nursing Home are penalized twice. On the one hand, their inability to exchange commodities deemed valuable by others leads to dependency on others for aid. Acceptance of their dependent position and their demand for better services make them seem like greedy children who deserve the fate of living their lives in a nursing home. Conversely, attempts at independence and the refusal of staff supports result in the resident being labeled "difficult." Staff members infantilize and resent the residents as a result.[24]

The actions of residents have few basic consequences. Their past actions minimally affect the future and help create the timeless atmosphere of the nursing home. For example, in the nursing home, occupational therapy fills time. Some items made during these sessions decorate the institution and are admired and some of the other items are sold in the gift shop at the home, but there is no direct connection between the needlework that the residents do and the funds that these items may procure. The contribution made by the residents seems symbolic at most: "Sarah Zeldin refuses to accept credit for her needlework because she did not design the piece she made; she merely filled in the spaces. She maintains that if the staff member who designed the work will put her name on the finished piece, then she will sign her name to it, as well. If the staff member does not sign it, then how can Sarah take all the credit? It seems like charity to her."[25]

Many resent being the object of charity, understanding the gratitude and inferiority that are due in return. For this reason, some of the residents attempt to limit the favors that others do for them. "A resident would like to go downtown and window shop. But she has put it out of her mind because she would have to ask one of her relatives or one of the staff members to drive her. How could she pay back her debt to the person in that case? If she hears of someone going downtown, maybe then she'll ask to go along."

The responsibility that staff members exhibit toward the residents is also reduced by the constraints on reciprocity. Because residents have little power and always receive, they must be grateful. The staff member's obligation is to his or her bureaucratic duties. Staff members can perform their duties superficially and impersonally; they can decide what behaviors are in a resident's best interests or not; they may allow a resident to wet himself or herself; they may not bother to peel the orange so that a resident can eat it; they may forget to take a resident for a walk outside. If a resident complains, those complaints underscore his or her childish inability to wait. Resentment caused by the care-giving exacerbates victimization of residents, entitlement by residents, and increases the wedge between givers and receivers.[26]

CONCLUSION: NO COMMUNITAS – A DIFFERENT LIMINALITY

As Victor Turner theorizes in his work, communitas is an important and positive feature of liminal states. But, though existence in the Franklin Nursing Home is liminal, there is more isolation than communitas there. New admissions to the Franklin Nursing Home are effectively separated from their past lives in the Harrison community. But instead of the explicitly harrowing transition found in most rites of passage, the transition in the nursing home rite of passage is seen by staff members to be protected and tame. This perception belies the experience of the nursing home residents, whose passage is harrowing but unshared. As if separated from the ongoing rigors of life and from the deteriorating course of the body, the residents wait. The staff members believe the residents to be protected, but the residents have doubts and fears which they cannot express. There is no cultural, ritual resolution to the passage; it is resolved only by the physical fact of death.

Instead of communitas, residents stay by themselves and try to be good patients. Instead of the exuberance found in communitas, residents often distrust each other, compete with each other, and denigrate each other. There are no difficult tasks to undergo, and there seems little reason for the residents to bond together. Acknowledging that they share a similar fate, knowing that they all suffer from not having alternatives available outside the nursing home, referring to common Jewish customs, histories, and holidays – the sharing is minimal, if present at all. The individuals' past lives are not considered relevant to the present by the residents. In this nursing home, references to the past are often interpreted as symptoms of incipient dementia and therefore frequently self-squelched.

The timelessness in the nursing home is very different from that described by Haim Hazan (1980, 1984). Hazan characterized the experience of the elderly in a Jewish day care center as "limbo" because of the paradoxical juxtaposition of two conflicting conceptions of time, a static time derived from the welfare system which gave benefits without repayment and a deteriorating time caused by the ailments experienced by the aged. Hazan shows how these elderly construct an "alternate reality" of time in which they care for each other and are shielded from the outside. Time in the Franklin Nursing Home, in contrast, betrays the certainty of how limited the time actually is for the residents. The time of future peril that intact residents perceive as their fate threatens the quality of resident relationships rather than enhances them. The residents interact superficially and guardedly. Communitas is unlikely to flourish where the present is benignly misrepresented as safe and timeless, the future is known to be uncertain and perilous, and residents serve as reminders of each person's present fragile security and future certain danger.

If, as in other rites of passage, there are rituals that explain and cushion the actors' situation to themselves, there will likely be more communitas and sharing among the residents. In this nursing home, however, staff members disagree about goals for the residents and avoid preparation for the next stage. Staff members splinter among themselves, and residents do likewise. Instead of adapting bits and pieces of old ritual to novel crises and conflicts as in the senior center Myerhoff described (1979), the lack of ritual and of communitas in the nursing home gives way to loneliness. Instead of the Jewish community joining together to forge a new integration of past values, present experiences, and common anticipations about the future with the residents, it gives custodial care. If nurses and social workers discussed their differences, they might be able to create innovative approaches to care giving. If staff members talked with residents about death when the subject came up, the residents might be aided in their preparations for death and might, in turn, help staff members alleviate their own fears about death.

Nursing homes are not all like this one. Depending upon the leadership of the nursing home, the training levels of the staff members, the values of the community members, and the particular needs of the residents who are being served, nursing homes respond to their clientele in varied ways. For example, Giselle Hendel-Sebestyen (1969, 1979) studied a sephardic Jewish nursing home in New York City that provides an interesting contrast to the Franklin Nursing Home. The residents there had control and decision-making abilities. They even ousted a rabbi whom they opposed. Solidarity among the residents was obviously a strong force.[27]

A neutral rather than positive response to the frail elderly at the Franklin Nursing Home reflects the paucity of vital services. The nursing home liminality contains no tasks that residents must fulfill. While learning and trials are the initiate's ticket to admission to the next phase in most rites of passage, nothing is expected of the nursing home residents in their passage here.

This nonreciprocity makes them ineligible for serious treatment as adult persons. Symbolic and concrete ways for the residents to contribute could be found for the nursing home population. Right now, however, residence at the Franklin Nursing Home is a liminal state without communitas because it is a timeless state which merely ends when it ends. Unlike other transitions in which individuals can look forward to a new status where certain behaviors, activities, and prestige will be expected of them, the residents in the nursing home receive forever. No requirement for reciprocity and little incentive for exchange join the death denial and conflict of staff members to comprise the lonely liminality experienced here. By equating the aged with children, the staff members transform the threat of death into the familiarity of nurturance. The overwhelming needs of these frail individuals can be more easily manipulated by parent figures than by health professionals attempting to assuage the complaints and ailments of adults who are like them, only older and physically more helpless. In this way, the nursing home residents are made both unthreateningly familiar, as children, and distantly "other," and staff members are relieved of identification with them. The danger inherent in the liminality is thus contained, and the transition for the residents is endless.

NOTES

I wish to thank Stanley Aronson, M.D., William O. Beeman, Ph.D., George L. Hicks, Ph.D., Lucile Newman, Ph.D., and Jay Sokolovsky, Ph.D., for their helpful comments in the preparation of this paper.

1. All names in this paper are pseudonyms.

2. For example, Dowd (1975) postulates that elderly persons in the United States are constrained to exchange compliance (in retirement, for example) for benefits related to pensions, old age assistance, and Social Security. Because their control over social and economic resources decreases, compliance becomes the only thing left to exchange for continued security in the social system. Estes (1979) and Hochschild (1973) also note how the status of the elderly is related directly to their ability or nonability to produce economically.

3. Notwithstanding these hindrances, the institutionalized elderly of the Franklin Nursing Home have innovative strategies which are more fully described elsewhere (Shield 1988).

4. Throughout the paper, anecdotes such as this one come from the author's fieldnotes.

5. This observation has been noted in "helping" agencies such as mental health clinics (see, for example, Gubrium 1982). In such constructions, the real versus fictive family often depends on who "really" cares for the patient.

6. These are simple exercises to stimulate muscles in arms and legs in order to improve strength and mobility of the limbs.

7. There are three Medicaid-mandated "levels of care," including (1) residents in need of minimal nursing supervision, (2) residents who require 24-hour nursing supervision, and (3) those who require skilled nursing care. These designations have to do with the specific nursing procedures required as part of care, such as intravenous feedings, the use of catheters, and the like.

8. This belief is different from the reality. Geriatric nursing requires extensive specialized knowledge and experience. Syndromes manifest themselves differently in aged patients from middle-aged ones; psychosocial issues are different; many procedures, such as finding veins to do bloodwork on aged patients, require an exactness not necessary for younger patients.

9. In 1985, when there was a strike at the Franklin Nursing Home, community volunteers were numerous and devoted, however. The crisis brought the nursing home and the Jewish community closer to each other.

10. For example, residents are not allowed to bathe themselves. Ambulatory residents are not allowed to push their neighbors' wheelchairs because of insurance and governmental regulations.

11. The social and emotional withdrawal exemplified by these behaviors could be subsumed under Glascock and Feinman's (1981) "death-hastening behaviors."

12. To a considerable degree, the social workers struggle against the conspiratorial silence that surrounds the residents regarding death. The nursing home has recently made some changes in the handling of death, such as notifying residents and holding memorial ceremonies.

13. Another Jewish nursing home does deal directly with death. A Jewish chaplain, trained in counseling, has been hired for this purpose. When a resident dies, a memorial service is held on the premises, for the benefit of the residents and staff members; it serves as an explicit mark that the resident lived in the nursing home and has died. In addition, this nursing home has started a bereavement program in which the survivors, including family members as well as residents and staff members who were attached to the deceased, are encouraged to seek group support (Kronenberg 1983).

14. Where elderly persons do possess skills considered valuable by others, they are perceived as closer to culture rather than to nature; they thereby avoid the association to death and retain prestige. See also Greene (1980); Fleming and Brown (1981, 1983); Gunter (1971); Spence et al. (1968); Gillis (1973); Townsend (1971).

15. There are some Jewish events that go on in the nursing home. There are special holiday dinners and Jewish films and discussion sessions, here and there. There is often faint response by the residents.

16. There are numerous biblical and rabbinical references regarding the care and treatment of the aged, including the warning against abandonment of the elderly by the younger generation (Smolar 1986).

17. In his study of the elderly London Jews, Hazan (1980) reports that most of the day care participants expressed antipathy to organized Judaism. Having become poor, they were unable to afford the membership. They felt that the rabbis did not care about them now that they were old. They considered the teachings about reverence for the elderly to be hypocritical because of their own experiences.

18. Residents in need of assistance may be prohibited from coming to services because of insufficient staff on the floors.

19. A program to teach Yiddish to staff members of another Jewish home for the aged met with an enthusiastic response by the participants involved (Berman, Weiner, and Fishman 1986). The authors believed that sensitivity to the residents was thereby increased.

20. Goodell (1985) distinguishes paternalism, patronage, and potlatch by their effects on the cohesion of the group. Her analysis of paternalism is similar to the argument offered here: autonomy and solidarity are undermined by the ideology inherent in the unreciprocated "gift."

21. Each resident of the Franklin Nursing Home who is supported by Medicaid receives $30 a month. Residents often spend this amount on small pleasures such as candy, as well as for birthday cards for friends, relatives, and occasionally staff.

22. Hazan (1980) does not make a similar claim in his work on elderly London Jews, however.

23. There are theft and vandalism in the Franklin Nursing Home. Theft by employees and theft by residents are supplemented by misplacement and honest mistakes, making it difficult to distinguish which is which.

24. Whereas Kayser-Jones (1981) has stated that staff resentment of their lowly status in American nursing homes encourages them to dehumanize and infantilize the residents, it seems to me that processes of infantilization and victimization in the nursing home have more to do with residents' liminality, compounded by their inability to reciprocate.

25. In another Jewish-sponsored nursing home in the United States, the residents are active in raising monies and suggesting improvements (Kronenberg, personal communication 1984). Another nursing home for Jewish aged in a major United States city does not accept public funds for its survival and thus has more autonomy (Wilson, personal communication 1983).

26. The constraint on reciprocity inhibits other basic interactions. As has been described elsewhere (Shield 1988), residents try to stay out of trouble, not complain, and generally inhibit their conversations to reduce the likelihood of argument. These strategies are adaptive responses to institutionalization that, however, interfere with community formation. Others have noted that residents use incontinence and starvation in order to gain power over staff members (Vesperi 1987). While incontinence is widespread and the refusal of food is not uncommon at the Franklin Nursing Home, it is difficult to gauge whether or not these are attention-getting devices for some individuals.

27. Hendel-Sebestyen (1979) notes, however, that as the nursing home population becomes more heterogeneous and sicker, she doubts that the same kind of community formation will continue.

BIBLIOGRAPHY

Achenbaum, W. Andrew. 1982. "Further Perspectives on Modernization and Aging." *Social Science History* 6(3):347–68.

———. 1978. *Old Age in the New Land*. Baltimore: Johns Hopkins University Press.

Acosta, F. X. 1982. "Group Psychotherapy with Spanish-Speaking Patients." In *Mental Health and Hispanic Americans*. R. Becerra, M. Karno, and J. Escobar, eds. New York: Grune & Stratton.

Aimei, Jia. 1988. "New Experiments with Elder Care in Rural China." *Journal of Cross-Cultural Gerontology* 3(2):139–48.

Akiyama, H. 1984. "Resource Exchanges in Dyadic Family Relations in the U.S. and Japan: Towards a Theory of Dependence and Independence of the Elderly." Ph.D diss. University of Illinois at Urbana-Champaign.

Al-Issa, I. 1982. *Culture and Psychopathology*. Baltimore: University Park Press.

Altergott, K. 1988. *Daily Life in Later Life: Personal Conditions in a Comparative Perspective*. Newbury Park, Calif.: Sage.

Amann, A., ed. 1980. *Open Care for the Elderly in Seven European Countries*. New York: Pergamon.

American Medical News. 1983. "U.S. Panel Backs 'Right to Die' Policies. " April 1:6–8.

Amin, S. 1976. *Unequal Development*. New York: Monthly Review Press.

Amoss, Pamela T. 1986. "Northwest Coast Grandmother Myths." Unpublished paper presented at the 84th Annual Meeting of the American Anthropological Association, Philadelphia.

———. 1981. "Cultural Centrality and Prestige for the Elderly: The Coast Salish Case." In *Dimensions: Aging, Culture and Health*. C. Fry, ed. Brooklyn, N.Y.: J. F. Bergin.

Amoss, Pamela T., and Stevan Harrell, eds. 1981. *Other Ways of Growing Old: Anthropological Perspectives*. Stanford: Stanford University Press.

An Zhiquo. 1982. "Reforming the Cadre System." *Beijing Review* 25 (9):3–4.

Anderson, B. 1972. "The Process of Deculturation—Its Dynamics among United States Aged." *Anthropological Quarterly* 45(4):209–16.

Andersson, I., and Weibull, J. 1973. *Swedish History in Brief*. Stockholm: Swedish Institute.

Andrews, Gary R., Adrian J. Esterman, Annette J. Braunack-Mayer, and Cam M. Rungie. 1986. *Aging in the Western Pacific*. Manila: World Health Organization.

Angrosino, M. 1976. "Anthropology and the Aged." *Gerontologist*. 162:174–80.

Anonymous. 1984a. "The Distribution of China's Population." *Beijing Review* 27 (3):20–22.

Anonymous. 1984b. "Nice Place for the Elderly." *Beijing Review* 27 (24):30–31.

Anonymous. 1984c. "The Sound of the Bell: Establishment of Ling Hai Older People's University." *Renmin Ribao*, Sept. 14.

Antonucci, Toni C. 1985. "Personal Characteristics, Social Networks and Social Behavior." In *The Handbook of Aging and the Social Sciences*. R. H. Binstock, and E. Shanas, eds. New York: Van Nostrand Reinhold.

Antonucci, Toni C., and H. Akiyama. 1987. "Social Networks in Adult Life and a Preliminary Examination of the Convoy Model." *The Journal of Gerontology* 42(5):519–27.

Antonucci, Toni C., and James S. Jackson. 1987. "Social Support, Interpersonal Efficacy, and Health: A Life Course Perspective." In *Handbook of Clinical Gerontology*. L. L. and B. A. Edelstein, eds. New York: Pergamon.

Antoun, Richard. 1968. "On the Modesty of Women in Arab Muslim Villages: A Study in the Accommodation of Traditions." *American Anthropologist* 70(4):671–97.

Arens, D. 1982. "Widowhood and Well-Being: An Examination of Sex Differences within a Causal Model." *Aging and Human Development* 15:27–40.

Arensberg, C., and C. T. Kimball. 1968 [1940]. *Family and Community in Ireland*. Cambridge, Mass.: Harvard University Press.

Aronson, Miriam. 1988. *Understanding Alzheimer's Disease*. N.Y.: Charles Scribner's Sons.

Arnoff, F. N., H. V. Leon, and I. Lorge. 1985. "Cross-Cultural Stereotypes Toward Aging." *The Journal of Social Psychology* 5:41–58.

Asahi News. 1983. "Government Plans for Model Nursing Homes." *Asahi Shimbun*, August 29.

Aschenbaum, W., and P. Sterns. 1978. "Old Age and Modernization." *The Gerontologist* 18:307–12.

Aschenbrenner, J. 1975. *Lifelines: Black Families in Chicago*. New York: Holt, Rinehart & Winston.

Baker, H. 1979. *Chinese Family and Kinship*. New York: Columbia University Press.

Banfield, Edward C. 1958. *The Moral Basis of a Backward Society*. Glencoe, Ill.: Free Press.

Barker, Judith C. 1989. "Health and Functional Status of the Elderly in a Polynesian Population." *Journal of Cross-Cultural Gerontology* 4.

———. 1988. "Admission of Geriatric Patients to Hospital on Niue Island, 1977–1982." *New Zealand Medical Journal* 101:638–40.

———. 1985a. "Social Organization and Health Services for Preschool Children on Niue Island, Western Polynesia." Ann Arbor, Mich.: University Microfilms.

———. 1985b. "Obsolescence in Paradise: Variation in the Treatment of the Elderly in a Polynesian Society." Paper presented at the 84th Annual Meeting of the American Anthropological Association, Washington, D.C..

———. 1984. *Niue's Health Services: A Personal View*. Technical Report for Dr. H. T. Nemaia, QSO, Director of Health, Niue. Medical Anthropology Program, University of California, San Francisco.

Barkow, Jerome. 1972. "Hausa Women and Islam." *Canadian Journal of African Studies* 6(2):317–28.

Barnett, Homer. 1955. *The Coast Salish of British Columbia*. Eugene, Oreg.: University of Oregon.

Bart, P. 1969. "Why Women's Status Changes in Middle Age: The Turn of the Social Ferris Wheel." *Sociological Symposium* 3:1–18.

Bass, D. M., and L. S. Noelker. 1987. "The Influence of Family Caregivers on Elder's Use of In-Home Services: An Expanded Conceptual Framework." *Journal of Health and Social Behavior* 28:184–96.

Bateson, Gregory. 1950. "Cultural Ideas About Aging." In *Proceedings of a Conference Held in August 7–10, 1950, at University of California, Berkeley*, H. E. Jones, ed. New York: Pacific Coast Committee on Old Age Research, Social Science Research Council.

Bauman, Richard, and Joel Sherzer, eds. 1974. *Explorations in the Ethnography of Speaking*. New York: Cambridge University Press.

Baxter, P. T., and U. Almagor, eds. 1978. *Age, Generation and Time*. London: Hurst.

Beall, Cynthia M. 1987. "Studies of Longevity." In *The Elderly as Modern Pioneers*. Philip Silverman, ed. Bloomington, Ind.: Indiana University Press.

Beall, Cynthia, ed. 1982. "Biological Perspectives on Aging." Special Issue of *Social Science and Medicine* 16(2).

Beall, Cynthia, and M. Goldstein. 1981. "Modernization and Aging: Views from the Rural, Pre-Industrial Hinterland in Nepal." *Journal of Cross-Cultural Gerontology* 40(1):48–55.

———. 1986. "Family Change, Caste and the Elderly in a Rural Locale in Nepal." *Journal of Cross-Cultural Gerontology* 1(3):305–316

Beaubier, J. 1976. *High Life Expectancy on the Island of Paros, Greece*. New York: Philosophical Library.

Becerra, Rosina, Marvin Karno, and Javier I. Escobar. 1982. *Mental Health and Hispanic Americans: Clinical Perspectives*. New York: Grune & Stratton.

Beck, Lois, and Nikki Keddie, eds. 1978. *Women in the Muslim World*. Cambridge, Mass.: Harvard University Press.

Becker, Gaylene. 1980. *Growing Old in Silence*. Berkeley: University of California Press.

Bedford, R. D., G. Mitchell, and M. Mitchell. 1980. "Population History." *1976 Census Of Population and Housing, Niue*. vol 2. *Analysis of Demographic Data*. Alofi, Niue: Department of Justice.

Befu, Harumi. 1962. "Corporate Emphasis and Patterns of Descent in the Japanese Family." In *Japanese Culture: Its Development and Characteristics*. Robert Smith and Richard Beardsley, eds. New York: Viking.

Befu, H. 1968. "Gift-Giving in Modern Japan." *Monumenta Nipponica* 23:445–56.

Bellah, Robert, Richard Madsen, William Sullivan, Ann Swidler, and Steven Tipton. 1985. *Habits of the Heart: Individualism and Commitment in American Life*. Berkeley: University of California Press.

Benedict, Ruth. 1946. *The Chrysanthemum and the Sword*. Boston: Houghton Mifflin.

———. 1934. *Patterns of Culture*. New York: Mentor Books.

Benet, S. 1974. *Abkhasians: The Long-Living People of the Caucasus*. New York: Holt, Rinehart & Winston.

Bengtson, Vern L. 1973. *The Social Psychology of Aging*. New York: Bobbs Merrill.

Bengtson, Vern L., J. Dowd, D. Smith, and A. Inkeles. 1975. "Modernization, Modernity, and Perceptions of Aging: A Cross-Cultural Study." *Journal of Gerontology* 30:688–95.

Bengtson, Vern L., Michael J. Furlong, and Robert S. Laufer. 1974. "Time, Aging, and the Continuity of Social Structure: Themes and Issues in Generational Analysis." *Journal of Social Issues* 30(2):1–30.

Bengtson, Vern L., and L. Morgan. 1987. "Ethnicity and Aging: A Comparison of Three Ethnic Groups." In *Growing Old in Different Societies: Cross-Cultural Perspectives*. J. Sokolovsky, ed. Acton, Mass.: Copley.

Berardo, F. 1970. "Survivorship and Social Isolation: The Case of the Aged Widower." *Family Co-Ordinator* 19:11–25.

Bergstrom, V., G. DeFaramond, M. Harrington, and A. Martin. 1982. "Sweden Seen from the Outside." In B. Ryden, and V. Bergstrom eds. *Sweden: Choices for Economic and Social Policy in the 1980's*. London: George Allen & Unwin.

Berkman, Lisa F. 1985. "The Relationship of Social Networks and Social Support to Morbidity and Mortality." In *Social Support and Health*. Sheldon Cohen and S. Leonard Syme, eds. New York: Academic.

Berman, Rochel U., Audrey S. Weiner, and Gella S. Fishman. 1986. "Yiddish: It's More Than a Language; In-Service Training for Staff of a Jewish Home for the Aged." *Journal of Jewish Communal Service* 62(4):328–34.

Besdine, Richard 1982. "Dementia." In *Health to Disease in Old Age*. John Rowe and Richard Besdine, eds. Boston: Little, Brown.

Besmer, Fremont E. 1983. *Horses, Musicians & Gods*. S. Hadley, Mass.: Bergin & Garvey.

Bever, Edward. 1982. "Old Age and Witchcraft in Early Modern Europe." In *Old Age in Preindustrial Societies*. Peter Stearns, ed. New York: Holmes & Meier.

Beyenne, Ywubdar. 1985 "The Elderly Child: Status of the Unmarried Mayan Woman." Paper presented at the American Anthropological Association Annual Meeting, Washington, D.C..

Bianco, Lucien. 1981. "Birth Control in China: Local Data and Their Reliability." *China Quarterly* 85:119–37.

Biesele, Megan. In press. *Women Like Meat*. Hamburg: Helmut Buske Verlag.

Biesele, Megan, and Nancy Howell. 1981. "The Old People Give You Life." In *Other Ways of Growing Old*. P. Amoss and S. Harrell, eds. Stanford, Calif.: Stanford University Press.

Binstock, R. H. 1986. "Drawing Cross-Cultural Implications for Policy: Some Caveats." *Journal of Cross-Cultural Gerontology* 1(4):331–37.

Bledsoe, Carolyn. 1980. *Women and Marriage in Kpelle Society*. Stanford, Calif.: Stanford University Press.

Boddy, Janice. 1985. "Bucking the Agnatic System: Status and Strategies in Rural Northern Sudan." In *In Her Prime*. Judith K. Brown and Virginia Kerns, eds. S. Hadley, Mass.: Bergin & Garvey.

Boehm, Christopher. 1984. *Blood Revenge: The Anthropology of Feuding in Montenegro and Other Societies*. Lawrence: University Press of Kansas.

Bohannan, Paul. 1963. *Social Anthropology*. New York: Holt, Rinehart & Winston.

Borman, L. 1983. "Self-Help Groups, Professionals, and the Redefinition of Pathological States." In *Clinical Anthropology: A New Approach to American Health Problems.* D. Shimkin and P. Golde, eds. Lanham, Md.: University Press of America.

Bott, Elizabeth. 1971. *Family and Social Network: Roles, Norms and External Relationships in Ordinary Urban Families.* 2d ed. London: Tavistock.

Bourdieu, Pierre. 1977. *Outline of a Theory of Practice.* London: Cambridge University Press.

Bowlby, J. 1980. *Attachment and Loss.* vol. 3. *Loss: Sadness and Depression.* New York: Basic.

Bowles, S., D. M. Gordon, and T. E. Weisskopf. 1984. *Beyond the Wasteland: A Democratic Alternative to Economic Decline.* Garden City, N.Y.: Anchor Press/Doubleday.

Boyd, Jean, and Murray Last. 1985. "The Role of Women as 'Agents Religieux' in Sokoto." *Canadian Journal of African Studies* 19(2):283–300.

Brody, E. M., P. T. Johnsen, M. C. Fulcomer, and A. M. Lang 1983. "Women's Changing Roles and Help to Elderly Parents: Attitudes of Three Generations of Women." *Journal of Gerontology* 38(5):597–607.

Brown, Judith K. 1982. "Cross-Cultural Perspectives on Middle-aged Women." *Current Anthropology* 23(2):143–48.

———. 1981. "Cross-Cultural Perspectives on the Female Life Cycle." In *Handbook of Cross-Cultural Human Development.* R. Munroe, R. Munroe, and B. Whiting, eds. New York: Garland STPM.

Brown, Judith, and Virginia Kerns, eds. 1985. *In Her Prime: A New View of Middle-Aged Women.* S. Hadley, Mass.: Bergin & Garvey.

Brown, T. 1988. "Long-Term Care for the Elderly in Kyoto, Japan." *Journal of Cross-Cultural Gerontology* 3(4):323–48.

Brubaker, Timothy H., and Carol M. Michael. 1987. "Amish Families in Later Life." In *Ethnic Dimensions of Aging.* Donald E. Gelfand and Charles M. Barresi, eds. New York: Springer.

Buric, Olivera. 1976. "The Zadruga and the Contemporary Family in Yugoslavia." In *Communal Families in the Balkans: The Zadruga.* Robert F. Byrnes, ed. Notre Dame, Ind.: University of Notre Dame Press.

Burton, Linda, and Vern Bengtson. 1985. "Black Grandmothers: Issues of Timing and Continuity in Roles." In *Grandparenthood.* Vern Bengtson and Joan Robinson, eds. Beverly Hills: Sage.

Butler, R. 1975. *Why Survive? Being Old in America.* New York: Harper & Row.

Byrne, S.W. 1974. "Arden, an Adult Community." In *Anthropologists in Cities.* G. Foster and R. Kemper, eds. Boston: Little, Brown.

Callaway, Barbara, and Enid Schildkrout. 1985. "Law, Education, and Social Change: Implications for Hausa Muslim Women in Nigeria." In *Women in the World.* Lynne B. Iglitzin and Ruth Ross, eds. Santa Barbara, Calif: Clio.

Campbell, J. K. 1964. *Honour, Family, and Patronage.* Oxford: Clarendon Press of Oxford University Press.

Campbell, Ruth. 1984. "Nursing Homes and Long-Term Care in Japan." *Pacific Affairs* 57:1:78–89.

Campbell, R., and E. Brody 1985. "Women's Changing Roles and Help to the Elderly: Attitudes of Women in the United States and Japan." *The Gerontologist* 25(6).

Canino, G., and I. Canino. 1982. "Culturally Syntonic Family Therapy for Migrant Puerto Ricans." *Hospital and Community Psychiatry* 33:299–303.

Cantor, M. 1979. "The Informal Support System of New York's Inner City Elderly: Is Ethnicity a Factor?" In *Ethnicity and Aging*. D. Gelfand and A. Kutzik, eds. New York: Springer.

Cantril, Hadley. 1965. *The Pattern of Human Concerns*. New Brunswick, N.J.: Rutgers University Press.

Caplan, G., and M. Killilea, eds. 1976. *Support Systems and Mutual Help: Multidisciplinary Explorations*. New York: Grune & Stratton.

Carter, J. H. 1981. "Treating Black Patients: The Risks of Ignoring Critical Social Issues." *Hospital and Community Psychiatry* 32:281–82.

———. 1978. "The Black Aged: A Strategy for Future Mental Health Services." *Journal of the American Geriatrics Society* 26:553–56.

Cassel, John. 1976. "The Contribution of the Social Environment to Host Resistance— The Fourth Wade Hampton Frost Lecture." *American Journal of Epidemiology* 2 (102):107–23.

Census Summary. 1980. "Hillsborough Population and Housing by Census Tract." Census Summary Tape 1 Count.

Chai, C., and W. Chai. 1969. *The Changing Society of China*. New York: Mentor.

Chapman, Terry M. 1982 "Modern Times [*Ko e magahala fakamui*]." In *Niue: A History of the Island*. Niue/Suva, Fiji: Niue Government/Institute for Pacific Studies, University of the South Pacific.

———. 1976. *The Decolonization of Niue*. Wellington: Victoria University Press.

Chase-Dunn, C., and R. Rubinson. 1977. "Towards a Structural Perspective on the World Systems." *Politics and Society* 7(4):453–76.

Chatters, L., R. Taylor, and J. Jackson. 1986. "Aged Blacks' Choices for an Informal Helper Network." *Journal of Gerontology* 41:94–100.

Chen, A. 1970. "Family Relations in Modern China Fiction." In *Family and Kinship in Chinese Society*. M. Freedman, ed. Palo Alto: Stanford University Press.

Chen, J. 1973. *A Year in Upper Felicity*. New York: Macmillan.

Chen Xiangming. 1985. "The One-Child Population Policy, Modernization, and the Extended Chinese Family." *Journal of Marriage and the Family* 47:193–202.

Cherry, R., and S. Magnuson-Martinson. 1981. "Modernization and the Status of the Aged in China: Decline or Equalization?" *Sociological Quarterly* 22:253–61.

Childs, Marquis. 1980. *Sweden: The Middle Way on Trial*. New Haven and London: Yale University Press.

Chow, Nelson W. S. 1988. *Caregiving in Developing East and Southeast Asian Countries*. Tampa, Fla.: International Exchange Center on Gerontology.

Clark, Margaret, and Barbara G. Anderson. 1967. *Culture and Aging: An Anthropological Study of Older Americans*. Springfield, Ill.: Charles C. Thomas.

Coalition for the Homeless. 1984. *Crowded Out: Homelessness and the Elderly Poor in New York City*. New York: Coalition for the Homeless.

Cobb, S. 1976. "Social Support as a Moderator of Life Stress." *Psychosomatic Medicine* 38:300–14.

Cohen, C., A. Alder, and J. Mintz. 1983. "Assessing Social Network Interventions— Results of an Experimental Service Program Conducted in a Single-Room Occupancy Hotel. In *Rediscovering Self-Help: Professionals and Informal Care*. P. Parker and D. Pancoast, eds. Beverly Hills: Sage.

Cohen, C., and J. Sokolovsky. 1979. "Clinical Use of Network Analysis for Psychiatric and Aged Populations." *Community Mental Health Journal* 15(3):203–13.

———. 1989. *Old Men of the Bowery: Strategies for Survival among the Homeless*. New York: Guilford.

Cohen, Ronald. 1971. *Dominance and Defiance: A Study of Marital Instability in an Islamic African Society*. Anthropological Studies No. 6. Washington, D.C.: American Anthropological Association.

Cohler, B. 1983. "Stress or Support: Relations Between Older Women from Three European Ethnic Groups and Their Relatives." In *Minority Aging: Sociological and Social Psychological Issues*. R. Manuel, ed. Westport: Greenwood.

Cohler, B., and H. Grunebaum. 1981. *Mothers, Grandmothers and Daughters: Personality and Child Care in Three-Generation Families*. New York: Wiley.

Cohler, B., and M. Lieberman. 1980. "Social Relations and Mental Health." *Research on Aging* 2(4):445–69.

Cohler, B., M. Lieberman, and L. Welch. 1977. *Social Relations and Interpersonal Resources Among Middle-Aged and Older Irish, Italian and Polish-American Men and Women*. Chicago: The University of Chicago, Committee on Human Development.

Coleman, J. S. 1961. *Adolescent Society*. Glencoe, Ill.: Free Press.

Colen, J. 1979. "Critical Issues in the Development of Environmental Support Systems for the Aged." *Allied Health and Behavioral Sciences* 2(1):74–90.

———. 1982. "Using Natural Helping Networks in Social Service Delivery Systems." In *Minority Aging*, R. Manuel, ed. Westport: Greenwood.

Coles, Catherine M. In press. "Hausa Women's Work in a Declining Urban Economy: Kaduna, Nigeria, 1980–1985." In *Hausa Women*. Catherine Coles and Beverly Mack, eds.

———. 1983a. *Urban Muslim Women and Social Change in Northern Nigeria*. Working Papers on Women in International Development 19. East Lansing, Mich.: Michigan State University.

———. 1983b. "Muslim Women in Town: Social Change Among the Hausa of Northern Nigeria." Ph.D. diss. University of Wisconsin.

Coles, Catherine, and Beverly Mack, eds. In press. *Hausa Women*.

Collier, Jane Fishburne. 1974. "Women in Politics." In *Woman, Culture and Society*. Michelle Zimbalist Rosaldo and Louise Lamphere, eds. Stanford, Calif.: Stanford University Press.

Connell, John. 1983. *Migration, Employment and Development In The South Pacific*. Country Report Number 11—Niue. Noumea, New Caledonia: South Pacific Commission.

Cool, Linda. 1987. "The Effects of Social Class and Ethnicity on the Aging Process. In *The Elderly as Modern Pioneers*. P. Silverman, ed. Bloomington: Indiana University Press.

———. 1981. "Ethnic Identity: A Source of Community Esteem for the Elderly." *Anthropological Quarterly* 54:179–89.

———. "Ethnicity and Aging: Continuity Through Change for Elderly Corsicans." In *Aging in Culture and Society: Comparative Viewpoints and Strategies*. Christine Fry et al. S. Hadley, Mass.: Bergin & Garvey.

Cool, Linda, and Justine McCabe. 1987. "The 'Scheming Hag' and the 'Dear Old Thing': The Anthropology of Aging Women." In *Growing Old in Different Societies: Cross-Cultural Perspectives*. Jay Sokolovsky, ed. Acton, Mass.: Copley.

Counts, Dorothy. In press. "Aging, Health and Women in West New Britain." *Journal of Cross-Cultural Gerontology.*

Counts, Dorothy A., and David R. Counts. 1985a. "Introduction: Linking Concepts of Aging and Gender, Aging and Death." In *Aging and Its Transformations*. Counts and Counts, eds. Boston: University Press of America.

Counts, Dorothy A., and David R. Counts. 1985b. "I'm Not Dead Yet! Aging and Death: Process and Experience in Kaliai." In *Aging and Its Transformations*. Counts and Counts, eds. Boston: University Press of America.

Counts, Dorothy Ayers, and David R. Counts, eds. 1985. *Aging and Its Transformations: Moving Toward Death in Pacific Societies*. Boston: University Press of America. (ASAO Monograph Number 10.)

Cowgill, Donald. 1975. "Aging and Modernization: A Revision of the Theory." In *Late Life: Communities and Environmental Policy*. J. Gubrium, ed. Springfield, Ill.: Charles Thomas.

Cowgill, D. 1986. *Aging Around the World*. Belmont, Calif.: Wadsworth.

———. 1974. "The Aging of Populations and Society." *Annals of the American Academy of Political and Social Sciences* 415:1–18.

———. 1972. "A Theory of Aging in Cross-Cultural Perspective." In *Aging and Modernization*. D. Cowgill and L. Holmes, eds. New York: Appleton-Century-Crofts.

Cowgill, Donald, and Lowell Holmes, eds. 1972. *Aging and Modernization*. New York: Appleton-Century-Crofts.

Crystal, Stephen. 1982. *America's Old Age Crisis: Public Policy and the Two Worlds of Aging*. New York: Basic.

Cuellar, José. 1978. "El Senior Citizens Club: The Older Mexican-American in the Voluntary Association." In *Life's Career—Aging: Cultural Variations on Growing Old*. Barbara G. Myerhoff and Andrei Simíc, eds. Beverly Hills, Calif.: Sage.

Cuellar, José, and J. Weeks. 1980. "Minority Elderly Americans: A Prototype for Area Agencies on Aging." *Executive Summary*. San Diego: Allied Health Association.

Curtis, F. S., and M. Cyars. n.d. *Handbook for the Department of Women*. Church of God in Christ [Memphis: Church of God in Christ Publishing House].

Cutright, Phillips. 1965. "Political Structure, Economic Development and National Social Security Programs." *American Journal of Sociology* 70:537–50.

Daatland, S. O. 1985. "Care of the Aged in the Nordic Countries: Trends and Policies the Last Two Decades." Paper presented at the XIII International Congress of Gerontology, New York.

Datan, N., et al. 1970. "Climacterium in Three Culture Contexts." *Tropical and Geographical Medicine* 22:77–86.

Davies, D. 1975. *The Centenarians of the Andes*. Garden City, N.Y.: Anchor.

Davis, Kingsley. 1940. "The Sociology of Parent-Youth Conflict." *American Sociological Review* 5:523–34.

Davis-Friedmann, Deborah. 1985. "Intergenerational Inequalities and the Chinese Revolution." *Modern China* 11: 177–201.

———. 1983a. *Long Lives*. Cambridge: Harvard University Press.

———. 1983. *Chinese Elderly and the Communist Revolution*. Cambridge: Harvard University.

————. 1981. "Retirement and Social Welfare Programs for Chinese Elderly: A Minimal Role for the State." In *The Situation of the Asian/Pacific Elderly*. C. Nusbert and M. Osako, eds. Washington, D.C.: International Federation on Aging.

Delgado, M. 1983. "Hispanic Natural Support Systems. Implications for Mental Health Services." *Journal of Psychosocial Nursing and Mental Health Services* 21:19–24.

del Valle, A. G., and M. Usher. 1982. "Group Therapy with Aged Latino Women: A Pilot Project and Study." *Clinical Gerontologist 1:51–58.*

Deng Xiaoping. 1983. "On the Reform of the System of Party and State Leadership." *Beijing Review* 25 (9):3–4.

DeVos, G. 1982. "Ethnic Pluralism: Conflict and Accommodation." In *Ethnic Identity: Cultural Continuities and Change*. G. DeVos and L. Romanucci-Ross, eds. Chicago: University of Chicago Press.

Ding Hua. 1984. "Glorious Retirement of 813,000 Veteran Cadres Throughout the Country." *Chinese Elderly* 11:9.

Dixon, J. 1981. *The Chinese Welfare System*. New York: Praeger.

Djilas, Milovan. 1958. *Land Without Justice*. New York: Harcourt, Brace.

Doi, T. 1971. *The Anatomy of Dependence*. Tokyo: Kodansha International.

Donner, William W. 1987. "Compassion, Kinship and Fosterage: Contexts for the Care of the Childless Elderly in a Polynesian Community." *Journal of Cross-Cultural Gerontology* 2(1): 43–60.

Doty, Pamela. 1986a. "Health Status and Health Services Use Among Older Women: An International Perspective." In *Aging in the Third World*. Kevin G. Kinsella, ed. Washington, D.C.: Center for International Research, U.S. Bureau of the Census.

————. 1986b. "Family Care of the Elderly: The Role of Public Policy." *Milbank Memorial Fund Quarterly* 64:34–75.

Dougherty, M. 1978. "An Anthropological Perspective on Aging and Women in the Middle Years." In *The Anthropology of Health*. E. Bauwens, ed. St. Louis: C.V. Mosby.

————. 1978. *Becoming a Woman in the Rural South*. New York: Holt, Rinehart & Winston.

Douglas, Mary. 1966. *Purity and Danger: An Analysis of Concepts of Pollution and Taboo*. London: Routledge & Kegan Paul.

Dowd, James P. 1975. "Aging as Exchange: A Preface to Theory." *Journal of Gerontology* 30:584–94.

Dowd, James J. 1984. "Beneficence and Aged." *Journal of Gerontology* 39(2):102–8.

————. 1980. *Stratification Among the Aged*. Monterey, Calif.: Brooks/Cole.

Draper, Patricia. 1976. "Social and Economic Constraints on Child Life among the !Kung." In *Kalahari Hunter-Gatherers: Studies of the !Kung San and Their Neighbours*. R. B. Lee and I. DeVore eds. Cambridge: Harvard University Press.

Driver, Harold. 1969. *Indians of North America*. Chicago: University of Chicago Press.

Durkheim, Émile. 1915. *The Elementary Forms of the Religious Life*. J.W. Swain, trans. New York: Free Press.

Eagleton, Terry. 1983. *Literary Theory: An Introduction*. Oxford: Basil Blackwell.

Eastwell, Harry D. 1982. "Voodoo Death and the Mechanism for Dispatch of the Dying in East Arnhem, Australia." *American Anthropologist* 84:5–18.

Eisenstadt, Schmuel Noah. 1971. *Social Differentiation and Stratification*. Glenview, Ill.: Scott, Foresman.

————. 1956. *From Generation to Generation*. New York: Free Press.

Elkind, David. 1986. "Families of the 1980s." *The Journal of Family and Culture* 2(2):31–50.

Ellickson, Jean. 1988. "Never the Twain Shall Meet: Aging Men and Women in Bangladesh." *Journal of Cross-Cultural Gerontology* 3(1):53–70.

Ellovich, Risa S. 1980. "Dioula Women in Town: A View of Intra-Ethnic Variation (Ivory Coast)." In *A World of Women*. Erika Bourguignon et al., eds. New York: Praeger.

Elmendorf, William W., and Alfred Kroeber. 1960. *The Structure of Twona Culture with Notes on Yurok Culture*. Pullman: Washington State University.

Erikson, Erik. 1963. *Childhood and Society*. New York: Norton.

Erlich, Vera Stein. 1972. *"Americki Zivotni Stil*. [The American Lifestyle]." *Sociologija* (Zagreb) 14:43–59.

Escobar, Javier, and Eugenia Randolph. 1982. "The Hispanic and Social Networks." In *Mental Health and Hispanic Americans*. R. Becerra, M. Karno, and J. Escobar, eds. New York: Grune & Stratton.

Estes, Carroll. 1980. *The Aging Enterprise: A Critical Examination of Social Policies and Services for the Aged*. San Francisco: Jossey-Bass.

Evers, H. 1981. "Care or Custody? The Experience of Women Patients in Long-Stay Geriatric Wards." In *Controlling Women: The Normal and the Deviant*. B. Hutter and G. Williams, eds. London: Croom Helm.

Fandetti, D., and D. Gelfand. 1976. "Care of the Aged: Attitudes of White Ethnic Families." *Gerontologist* 16(6):544–49.

Federal Council on Aging. 1981. *The Need for Long Term Care*. Washington, D.C.: U.S. Department of Health and Human Services.

———. 1979. *Policy Issues Concerning Elderly Minorities*. No. 80–20670. Washington, D.C.: U.S. Department of Health and Human Services.

Filipovic, Rudolf. 1966. *Englesko-Hrvatskosrpski Rjecnik [English-Croato-Serbian Dictionary]*. Zagreb: Zora.

Finau, Sitaleki A., Ian A. M. Prior, and J. Grimley Evans. 1982. "Aging in the South Pacific." *Social Science and Medicine* 16:1539–49.

Finch, Janet, and Dulcie Groves, eds. 1983. *A Labour of Love: Women, Work and Caring*. London: Routledge & Kegan Paul.

Finley, G. E. 1982. "Modernization and Aging." In *Review of Human Development*. M. Fields, A. Huston, H. C. Quay, L. Troll, and G. E. Finley, eds. New York: Wiley.

Firth, Raymond. 1936. *We, the Tikopia*. London: Allen & Unwin.

Fischer, David Hackett. 1978. *Growing Old in America*. New York: Oxford University Press.

Fisk, E. K. 1978. *The Island of Niue: Development or Dependence for a Very Small Nation*. Canberra: Australian National University. Development Studies Centre Occasional Paper 9.

Fitzgerald, F. 1979. *America Revisited*. Boston and Toronto: Little, Brown.

Fleming, Stephen, and Isabel Brown. 1983. "The Impact of a Death Education Program for Nurses in a Long-Term Care Hospital." *Gerontologist* 23:192–95.

———. 1981. "Nurses' Educational and Personal Preparation in Caring for the Dying." Unpublished manuscript.

Folta, Jeannette R., and Edith S. Deck. 1987. "Elderly Black Widows in Rural Zimbabwe." *Journal of Cross-Cultural Gerontology* 2(4):321–42.

Foner, Nancy. 1985. "Old and Frail and Everywhere Unequal." *The Hastings Center Report* 15(2):27–31.

————. 1984a. *Ages in Conflict: A Cross-Cultural Perspective on Inequality Between Old and Young.* New York: Columbia University Press.

————. 1984b. "Age and Social Change." In *Age and Anthropological Theory*, David Kertzer and Jennie Keith, eds. Ithaca: Cornell University Press.

Foner, Nancy, and David I. Kertzer. 1978. "Transitions Over the Life Course: Lessons From Age-Set Societies." *American Journal of Sociology* 83:1081–104.

Fontana, A. 1976. *The Last Frontier*. Beverly Hills, Calif.: Sage.

Foreman, Grant. 1934. *The Five Civilized Tribes*. Norman: University of Oklahoma Press.

Fortes, Meyer. 1984. "Age, Generation, and Social Structure." In *Age and Anthropological Theory*. David I. Kertzer and Jennie Keith, eds. Ithaca: Cornell University Press.

————. 1978. "An Anthropologist's Apprenticeship." *Annual Review of Anthropology* 7:1–30.

Foster, George M., and Barbara G. Anderson. 1978. *Medical Anthropology*. New York: John Wiley.

Fowler, David, Lois Fowler, and Lois Landin. 1982. "Themes of Old Age in Preindustrial Western literature." In *Old Age in Preindustrial Societies*. Peter Stearns, ed. New York: Holmes & Meier.

Francher, J. S. 1973. "It's the Pepsi Generation: Accelerated Aging and the Television Commercial." *International Journal of Aging and Human Development* 4(3):245–55.

Francis, D. 1984. *Will You Still Need Me, Will You Still Feed Me When I'm 84?* Bloomington: Indiana University Press.

Francis, D., D. Shenk and J. Sokolovsky. 1990. *Teaching About Aging: Interdisciplinary and Cross-Cultural Perspectives.* St. Cloud, Minn.: Association for Anthropology and Gerontology.

Frank, A. 1979. *Dependent Accumulation and Underdevelopment.* New York: Monthly Review Press.

Frankovich, Marija K. 1974. "Child-Rearing on Niue: An Ethnopsychological Analysis of Aspects Relevant to the Goals and Acquisition of a Contemporary Western Education." M. Soc. Sci. thesis. Psychology Department, University of Waikato, New Zealand.

Frazier, E. Franklin. 1939. *The Negro Family in the United States*. Chicago: University of Chicago Press.

Freedman, M. 1961. "The Family in China, Past and Present." *Pacific Affairs* 34:326–36.

Friedl, Ernestine. 1967. "The Position of Women: Appearance and Reality." *Anthropological Quarterly* 40(3):97–108.

————. 1962. *Vasilika: A Village in Modern Greece.* New York: Holt, Rinehart, & Winston.

Friedman, E. 1982. "The Myth of the *Shiksa*." In *Ethnicity and Family Therapy*. M. McGoldrick, J. Pearce, and J. Giordano eds. New York: Guilford.

Fry, Christine. 1988. "Comparative Research in Aging." In *Gerontology: Perspectives and Issues*. K. Ferraro, ed. New York: Springer.

————. 1985. "Culture, Behavior and Aging in the Comparative Perspective." In *Handbook of the Psychology of Aging*. J. Birren and K.W. Schaie, eds. New York: Van Nostrand Reinhold.

————. 1981. *Dimensions: Aging, Culture and Health.* Brooklyn: J. F. Bergin.

————. 1980a. *Aging in Culture and Society: Comparative Viewpoints and Strategies.* Brooklyn: J. F. Bergin.

————. 1980b. "Cultural Dimensions of Age." In *Aging, Culture and Society: Comparative Perspectives and Strategies.* C. Fry, ed. Brooklyn: J. F. Bergin.

————. 1977. "Community as Community: The Aged Graded Case." *Human Organization.* 36:115–23.

Fry, Christine, and Lauree Garvin. 1987. "American After-Lives: Widowhood in Community Context." In *Widows.* vol 2. *North America.* H. Z. Lopata, ed. Durham: Duke University Press.

Fry, Christine, and Jennie Keith. 1986. *New Methods for Old-Age Research: Anthropological Alternatives.* S. Hadley, Mass.: Bergin & Garvey.

————. 1982. "The Life Course as a Cultural Unit." In *Aging from Birth to Death.* vol. 2. M. Riley, ed.

Furstenberg, A., and L. Davis. 1984. "Lay Consultation of Older People." *Social Science and Medicine* 18:827–37.

Gallagher, D., J. Breckenridge, L. Thompson, and J. Peterson. 1983. "Effects of Bereavement on Indicators of Mental Health in Elderly Widows and Widowers." *Journal of Gerontology* 38:565–71.

Ganshaw, T. 1978. "The Aged in a Revolutionary Milieu: China." *In Aging and the Elderly: Humanistic Perspectives in Gerontology.* S. Spicker, K. Woodward, and D. Van Tasel, eds. Atlantic Highlands, N.J.: Humanities Press.

Garviria, M., and Gwen Stern. 1980. "Problems in Designing and Implementing Culturally Relevant Mental Health Services for Latinos in the U.S." *Social Science and Medicine* 14B:65–71.

Geertz, Clifford. 1979. "From the Native's Point of View: On the Nature of Anthropological Understanding." In *Interpretive Social Science: A Reader.* P. Rabinow and W. N. Sullivan, eds. Berkeley: University of California Press.

Gelfand, Donald E. 1982. *Aging: The Ethnic Factor.* Boston: Little, Brown.

Gelfand, Donald E., and Charles M. Barresi, eds. 1987. *Ethnic Dimensions of Aging.* New York: Springer.

Gelfand, Donald E., and D. Fandetti. 1980. "Suburban and Urban White Ethnics: Attitudes Towards Care of the Aged." *Gerontologist* 20:588–94.

Gibson, Mary Jo. 1985. *Older Women Around the World.* Washington, D.C.: International Federation on Aging.

————. 1984. "Family Support Patterns, Programs, and Policies." In *Innovative Aging Programs Abroad: Implications for the U.S.* Charlotte Nusberg, with M. J. Gibson and Sheila Peace. Westport: Greenwood.

Gibson, Rose C. 1987. "Defining Retirement for Black Americans." In *Ethnic Dimensions of Aging,* Donald E. Gelfand and Charles M. Barresi, eds. New York: Springer.

————. 1986. "Blacks in an Aging Society." *Daedalus* 115(1):349–71.

Giele, J. Z. 1982. "Family and Social Networks". In *International Perspectives on Aging: Population and Policy Challenges.* R. Binstock, W.-S. Chow, and J. Schultz, eds. New York: United Nations Fund for Population Activities.

Gilkes, C. T. 1986. "The Role of Church and Community Mothers: Ambivalent American Sexism or Fragmented African Familyhood?" *Journal of Feminist Studies in Religion* 2 (1):41–59.

————. 1985. "Together and In Harness: Women's Traditions in the Sanctified Church." *SIGNS* 10 (4): 678–99.

Gillis, Sr. Marion. 1973. "Attitudes of Nursing Personnel Toward the Aged." *Nursing Research* 22:517–20.

Glascock, Anthony P. 1983. "Death-Hastening Behavior: An Expansion of Eastwell's Thesis." *American Anthropologist* 85:417–21.

————. 1982. "Decrepitude and Death-Hastening: The Nature of Old Age in Third World Societies." *Studies in Third World Societies*, Publication 22:43–65.

Glascock, Anthony P., and Susan L. Feinman. 1981. "Social Asset or Social Burden: An Analysis of the Treatment of the Aged in Non-Industrial Societies." In *Dimensions: Aging, Culture and Health*. Christine Fry, ed. Brooklyn: J. F. Bergin.

————. 1980. "Holocultural Analysis of Old Age." *Comparative Social Research* 3:311–33.

Glick, I., R. Weiss, and C. Parkes. 1974. *The First Year of Bereavement*. New York: Wiley.

Goffman, Erving. 1961. *Asylums*. New York: Doubleday.

Goldsmith, P. 1985. "Healing and Denominationalism on the Georgia Coast." *Southern Quarterly* 23 (3) 83–102.

Goldstein, M., and C. Beall. 1981. "Modernization and Aging in the Third and Fourth World: Views from the Rural Hinterland in Nepal." *Human Organization* 40(1):48–55.

Goldstein, M., S. Schuler, and J. Ross. 1983. "Social and Economic Forces Affecting Intergenerational Relations in Extended Families in a Third World Country: A Cautionary Tale from South Asia." *Journal of Gerontology* 38(6):716–24.

Golin, Carol B. 1985. "Euthanasia Feared as 'Solution' to Rising Health Costs." *American Medical News*, May 17: 3, 22.

Goodale, Jane. 1971. *Tiwi Women*. Seattle: University of Washington Press.

Goodell, Grace E. 1985. "Paternalism, Patronage, and Potlatch: The Dynamics of Giving and Being Given To." *Current Anthropology* 26:247–66.

Goodman, C. 1984. "Natural Helping Among Older Adults." *Gerontologist* 24:138–43.

Goodman, Richard A. 1971. "Some *Aitu* Beliefs of Modern Samoans." *Journal of the Polynesian Society* 80:463–79.

Goody, Jack. 1976. "Aging in Nonindustrial Societies." In *Handbook of Aging and the Social Sciences*. Robert H. Binstock and Ethel Shanas, eds. New York: Van Nostrand Reinhold.

Gordon, D. M., R. Edwards, and M. Reich. 1982. *Segmented Work, Divided Workers: The Historical Transformation of Labor in the United States*. London and New York: Cambridge University Press.

Gouldner, A. W. 1960. "The Norm of Reciprocity." *American Sociological Review* 25(2):161–78.

Gozdziak, Elzbieta. 1988. *Older Refugees in the United States: From Dignity to Despair*. Washington, D.C.: Refugee Policy Group.

Gratton, Brian. 1987. "Familism Among the Black and Mexican-American Elderly: Myth or Reality." *Journal of Aging Studies* 1(1):19–32.

Greeley, A., et al. 1980. *Ethnic Drinking Subcultures*. Brooklyn: J. F. Bergin (Praeger).

Greene, Roberta Rubin. 1980. "Ageism and Death Anxiety as Related to Geriatric Social Work as a Career Choice." Ph.D. diss. University of Maryland School of Social Work.

Gubrium, Jaber. 1987a. "Structuring and Destructuring the Course of Illness: The Alzheimer's Disease Experience." *Sociology of Health and Illness* 9:1–24.

———. 1987b. "Organizational Embeddedness and Family Life." In *Aging, Health and Family: Long-Term Care.* T. Brubaker, ed. Newbury Park, N.J.: Sage.

———. 1986. *Oldtimers and Alzheimer's: The Descriptive Organization of Senility.* Greenwich, Conn.: JAI Press.

———. 1982. "Fictive Family: Everyday Usage, Analytic, and Human Service Considerations." *American Anthropologist* 84:878–85.

———. 1975. *Living and Dying at Murray Manor.* New York: St. Martin's.

Gubrium, Jaber F., ed. 1976. *Time, Roles and Self in Old Age.* New York: Human Sciences Press.

Gubrium, Jaber F., and D. R. Buckholdt. 1977. *Toward Maturity: The Social Processing of Human Development.* San Francisco: Jossey-Bass.

Guemple, D. Lee. 1969. "Human Resource Management: The Dilemma of the Aging Eskimo." *Sociological Symposium* 2:59–74.

Guillemard, A. M., ed. 1983. *Old Age and the Welfare State.* Beverly Hills: Sage.

Gunter, Laurie M. 1971. "Students' Attitudes Toward Geriatric Nursing." *Nursing Outlook* 19:466–69.

Gutmann, David. 1987. *Reclaimed Powers: Toward a New Psychology of Men and Women in Later Life.* New York: Basic.

———. 1980. "Observations on Culture and Mental Health in Late Life." In *Handbook of Mental Health and Aging.* James Birren and Robert Sloan, eds. Englewood Cliffs, N.J.: Prentice-Hall.

———. 1976. "Alternatives to Disengagement: The Old Man of the Highland Druze." In *Time, Roles, and Self in Old Age.* Jaber Gubrium, ed. New York: Human Sciences Press.

Guzlow, Z., and G. Tracy. 1976. "The Role of Self-Help Clubs in Adaptation to Chronic Illness and Disability." *Social Science and Medicine* 10:407–14.

Hadjihristev. A. K. 1988. *Life-Styles for Long Life: Longevity in Bulgaria.* Gari Lesnoff-Caravaglia, trans. Springfield, Ill.: Charles C. Thomas.

Hagestad, Gunhild O. 1985. "Continuity and Connectedness." In *Grandparenthood.* Vern L. Bengtson and Joan F. Robertson, eds. Beverly Hills: Sage.

Halperin, Rhoda. 1987. "Age in Cross-Cultural Perspective: An Evolutionary Approach." In *The Elderly as Modern Pioneers.* P. Silverman, ed. Bloomington: Indiana University Press.

———. 1984. "Age in Cultural Economics: An Evolutionary Approach." In *Age and Anthropological Theory.* David Kertzer and Jennie Keith, eds. Ithaca: Cornell University Press.

Halpern, Joel M. 1958. *A Serbian Village.* New York: Columbia University Press.

Halpern, Joel M., and Barbara Kerewsky-Halpern. 1986. *A Serbian Village in Historical Perspective.* Prospect Heights, Ill.: Waveland.

Halsell, G. 1976. *Los Viejos—Secrets of Long Life from the Sacred Valley.* Emmaus, Penn: Rodale.

Hammel, E. A. 1969. "Economic Change, Social Mobility, and Kinship in Serbia." *Southwestern Journal of Anthropology* 25:188–97.

———. 1968. *Alternate Social Structures and Ritual Relations in the Balkans.* Englewood Cliffs, N.J.: Prentice-Hall.

———. 1967. "The Jewish Mother in Serbia, or *Les Structures Alimentaires de la Parente.*" In *Essays in Balkan Ethnology.* William G. Lockwood, ed. Berkeley, Calif.: Kroeber Anthropological Society Special Publications, No. 1.

Hammel, E. A., and Charles Yarbrough. 1973. "Social Mobility and the Durability of Family Ties." *Journal of Anthropological Research* 29(3):145–63.

Hanson, Allan R. 1970. *Rapan Lifeways: Society and History on a Polynesian Island.* Boston: Little, Brown.

Harlan, W. H. 1968. "Social Status of the Aged in Three Indian Villages." In *Middle Age and Aging.* B. Neugarten, ed. Chicago: University of Chicago Press.

Harris, L., and Associates. 1975. *The Myth and Reality of Aging in America.* Washington, D. C.: National Council on the Aging.

Hart, C.W. 1970. "Fieldwork among the Tiwi, 1928–29." In *Being an Anthropologist: Fieldwork in Eleven Cultures.* G. Spindler, ed. New York: Holt, Rinehart & Winston.

Hart, C.W., and A.R. Pilling. 1961. *The Tiwi of North Australia.* New York: Holt, Rinehart & Winston.

Hazan, Haim. 1984. "Continuity and Transformation Among the Aged: A Study in the Anthropology of Time." *Current Anthropology* 25:567–78.

———. 1980a. "Adjustment and Control in an Old Age Home." In *A Composite Portrait of Israel.* E. Marx ed. London: Academic.

———. 1980b. *The Limbo People: A Study of the Constitution of the Time Universe Among the Aged.* London and Boston: Routledge & Kegan Paul.

Health Insurance Association of America. 1984. *Source Book of Health Insurance Data: 1982–1983.* Washington, D.C.: Health Insurance Association of America.

Hearn, Lafcadio. 1955 [1920]. *Japan, an Interpretation.* Rutland, Vt: Tuttle.

Heckscher, E. F. 1954. *An Economic History of Sweden.* Cambridge: Harvard University Press.

Heikkinen, E., W. E. Waters, and Z. J. Brzezinski. 1983. *The Elderly in Eleven Countries.* Copenhagen: World Health Organization, Regional Office for Europe.

Heisel, Marsel A. 1985. "Aging in the Context of Population Policies in Developing Countries." *Population Bulletin of the United Nations.*

Hendel-Sebestyen, Giselle. 1979. "Role Diversity: Toward the Development of Community in a Total Institutional Setting." In *The Ethnography of Old Age.* Jennie Keith, ed. Special Issue, *Anthropological Quarterly* 52:19–28.

———. 1969. "The Sephardic Home: Ethnic Homogeneity and Cultural Traditions in a Total Institution." Ph.D. diss. Columbia University.

Henderson, J. Neil. 1987a. "Nursing Home Housekeepers: Indigenous Agents of Psychosocial Support." In *Dominant Issues in Medical Sociology.* H. Schwartz, ed. New York: Random House.

———. 1987b. "Mental Disorders Among the Elderly: Dementia and Its Sociocultural Correlates." In *The Elderly as Modern Pioneers.* Philip Silverman, ed. Bloomington: Indiana University Press.

Hendricks, J., ed. 1981. *In the Country of the Old.* Farmingdale, N.Y.: Baywood.

Henry, Jules. 1963. *Culture Against Man.* New York: Random House.

Herz, F., and E. Rosen. 1982. "Jewish Families." In *Ethnicity and Family Therapy.* M. McGoldrick, J. Pearce, and J. Giordano, eds. New York: Guilford.

Hill, Polly. 1972. *Rural Hausa: A Village and a Setting.* Cambridge: Cambridge University Press.

Hillebrant, F. 1980. "Aging among the Advantaged: A New Look at the Stereotyping of the Elderly." *Gerontologist* 20.

Hirsh, Harold L. 1985. "Who May Eat and Who May Starve?" *Nursing Homes* (July/August):9–10.

Ho, Man Keung. 1987. *Family Therapy with Ethnic Minorities.* Newbury Park, Calif.: Sage.

Hochschild, Arlie Russell. 1973. *The Unexpected Community: Portrait of an Old Age Subculture.* Berkeley: University of California Press.

Holder, Angela R. 1984. "Writing DNR Orders that Won't Get You Sued." *Medical Economics,* September 17:82–87.

Holmberg, A. 1969. *Nomads of the Long Bow.* Garden City, N.Y.: Natural History Press.

Holmes, D., M. Holmes, and J. Terisi. 1983. "Differences Among Black, Hispanic, and White People in Knowledge About Long-Term Care Services." *Health Care Financing Review* 5(2): 51–66.

Holmes, Eleanor. 1986. "Aging in Modern and Traditional Societies." *The World and I,* No. 9. Baltimore: Washington Times.

Holmes, Lowell D. 1987. "Cultural Values and Cultural Change." *Journal of Cross-Cultural Gerontology* 2:195–200.

———. 1972. "The Role and Status of the Aged in a Changing Samoa." In Donald O. Cowgill and Lowell D. Holmes, eds. *Aging and Modernization.* New York: Appleton-Century-Crofts.

———. 1974. *Samoan Village.* New York: Holt, Rinehart & Winston.

Holmes, Lowell D., and Ellen Rhoads. 1987. "Aging and Change in Samoa." In *Growing Old in Different Societies: Cross-Cultural Perspectives.* Jay Sokolovsky, ed. Acton, Mass.: Copley.

Holzberg, C. 1982. "Ethnicity and Aging: Anthropological Perspectives on More Than Just the Minority Elderly." *Gerontologist* 22(3):249–57.

Hoover, Sally L., and Jacob S. Siegel. 1986. "International Demographic Trends and Perspectives on Aging." *Journal of Cross-Cultural Gerontology* 1:5–30.

Hopper, K., and J. Hamburg. 1984. *The Making of America's Homeless: From Skid Row to New Poor.* New York: Community Service Society.

Hostetler, J., and G. Huntington. 1971. *Children in Amish Society: Socialization.* New York: Holt, Rinehart & Winston.

Howe, Irving. 1987. "The Spirit of the Times: Greed, Nostalgia, Ideology and War Whoops." Reprint from *Dissent,* distributed in January *Dissent* mailing.

Howell, Nancy. 1979. *Demography of the Dobe Area !Kung.* New York: Academic.

Human Resource Administration. 1987. *Comprehensive Homeless Assistance Plan.* Washington, D. C.: Human Resource Administration.

Huntsman, Judith, and Anthony Hooper. 1975. "Male and Female in Tokelau Culture." *Journal of the Polynesian Society* 84(4):415–30.

Hurston, Zora Neale. 1983. *The Sanctified Church.* Berkeley: Turtle Island.

Huseby-Darvas, Eva V. 1987. "Elderly Women in a Hungarian Village: Childlessness, Generativity, and Social Control." *Journal of Cross-Cultural Gerontology* 2(1):15–42.

Huttmann, Barbara. 1983. "A Crime of Compassion." *Newsweek,* August 8:15.

Ikels, C. 1983. *Aging and Adaptation: Chinese in Hong Kong and the United States.* Hamden, Conn: Archon.

Ikels, Charlotte. 1988. "Becoming a Human Being in Theory and in Practice: Chinese Views of Human Development." In *Social Structure and Aging: Comparative Perspectives on Age Structuring in Modern Societies.* D. Kertzer, J. Meyer, and K.W. Schaie, eds. Hillsdale, N.J.: Erlbaum.

―――. 1986. "Older Immigrants and Natural Helpers." *Journal of Cross-Cultural Gerontology* 1(2) 209–22.

―――. 1975. "Old Age in Hong Kong." *Gerontologist* 15:230–35.

Ikels, Charlotte, Jennie Keith, and Christine Fry. 1988. "The Use of Qualitative Methodologies in Large-Scale Cross-Cultural Research." In *Qualitative Gerontology.* Shulamit Reinharz and Graham Rowles, eds. New York: Springer.

Inal-Ipa, S. D. 1982. "Changes in the Abkhazian Traditional Way of Life Since the Late Nineteenth Century." (unpublished paper.)

Interrante, Joseph. 1987. "To Have without Holding: Memories of Life with a Person with AIDS." *Radical America* 2(6):55–62.

Jackman, Robert. 1975. *Politics and Social Equality: Comparative Analysis.* New York: Wiley.

Jackson, J. J. 1985. "Race, National Origin, Ethnicity and Aging." In *Handbook of Aging and the Social Sciences.* R. Binstock and E. Shanas, eds. New York: Van Nostrand Reinhold.

―――. 1980. *Minorities and Aging.* Belmont, Calif.: Wadsworth.

―――. 1972. "Comparative Life Styles and Family and Friend Relationships Among Older Black Women." *The Family Coordinator* 21: 477–85.

Jackson, M., and Z. Harel. 1983. "Ethnic Differences in Social Support Networks." *Urban Health* 9:35–38.

Jacobson, David. 1987. "The Cultural Context of Social Support Networks." *Medical Anthropology Quarterly* 1:42–67.

Jerrome, Dorothy. 1988. "That's What It's All About: Old People's Organization as a Context for Aging. *Journal of Aging Studies* 2(1):71–82.

Jochelson, Vladimir. 1933. *The Yakut.* New York: American Museum of Natural History.

Johnson, C. 1985. *Growing Up and Growing Old in Italian-American Families.* New Brunswick, N.J.: Rutgers.

Johnson, Colleen Leahy. 1987. "The Institutional Segregation of the Aged." In *The Elderly as Modern Pioneers.* P. Silverman, ed. Bloomington: Indiana University Press.

Johnson, S. K. 1971. *Idle Haven: Community Building among the Working Class Retired.* Berkeley: University of California Press.

Jones, F. C. 1973. "The Lofty Role of the Black Grandmother." *Crisis* 80 (1): 19–21.

Jonsson Gardens Document. 1983. Linkoping.

Juniper, Annie B. 1922. "Native Dietry on Niue Island." *Journal of Home Economics* 14(11):612–14.

Kaduna Polytechnic. 1981. "Urban Renewal Study." Kaduna, Nigeria: Department of Town Planning.

Kahn, R., and T. C. Antonucci. 1981. "Convoys of Social Support: A Life-Course Approach." In *Aging: Social Change.* S. Kiesler, J. Morgan, and V. K. Oppenheimer, eds. New York: Academic.

Kahn, R. L., and T. C. Antonucci. 1984. "Convoys over the Life Course: Attachment, Roles and Social Support." In *Life-Span Development and Behavior.* P. B. Baltes and O. G. Brim, eds. . New York: Academic.

Kalish, R., and D. Reynolds. 1976. *Death and Ethnicity: A Psychocultural Study.* Los Angeles: Ethel Percy Andrus Gerontology Center, University of Southern California.

Kane, R., and R. A. Kane. 1982. *Values and Long-Term Care.* Lexington, Mass.: Lexington Books.

———. 1978. "Care of the Aged: Old Problems in Need of New Solutions." *Science* 200:913–19.

Kart, Cary S., and Charles F. Longino, Jr. 1987. "The Support Systems of Older People: A Test of the Exchange Paradigm." *Journal of Aging Studies* 1(3):253–64.

Katz, Richard. 1982. *Boiling Energy: Community Healing Among the Kalahari !Kung.* Cambridge: Harvard University Press.

Katz, Richard, and Megan Biesele. 1986. "!Kung Healing: The Symbolism of Sex Roles and Culture Change." In *The Past and Future of !Kung Ethnography: Critical Reflections and Symbolic Perspectives. Essays in Honour of Lorna Marshall.* Megan Biesele, with Robert Gordon and Richard Lee, eds. Hamburg: Helmut Buske Verlag.

Kayser-Jones, Jeanie Schmit. 1981a. *Old, Alone, and Neglected: Care of the Aged in Scotland and the United States.* Berkeley: University of California Press.

———. 1981b. "Quality of Care for the Institutionalized Aged: A Scottish-American Comparison." In *Dimensions: Aging, Culture and Health.* Christine Fry, ed. Brooklyn: J. F. Bergin.

Keesing, Felix M. 1953. *Social Anthropology in Polynesia.* London: Oxford University Press.

Keith, Jennie. 1985. "Age in Anthropological Research." In *Handbook of Aging and the Social Sciences.* Robert Binstock and Ethel Shanas, eds. New York: Van Nostrand Reinhold.

———. 1982. *Old People as People: Social and Cultural Influences on Aging and Old Age.* Boston: Little, Brown.

———. 1980. "The Best Is Yet To Be: Toward an Anthropology of Age." In *Annual Review of Anthropology.* B. J. Siegel, A. R. Beals, and S. A. Tyler, eds. Palo Alto. Calif.: Annual Reviews.

———. 1977. *Old People, New Lives: Community Creation in a Retirement Residence.* Chicago: University of Chicago Press.

Keith, Jennie, ed. 1979. "The Ethnography of Old Age." Special issue, *Anthropological Quarterly* 52(1).

Kendig, Hal, Akiko Hashimoto, and Larry Coppard, eds. In press. *Family Support to Elderly People: The International Experience.* Geneva: World Health Organization.

Kerns, Virginia. 1983. *Women and the Ancestors.* Urbana, Ill.: University of Illinois Press.

Kertzer, David. 1982. "Generation and Age in Cross-Cultural Perspective." In *Aging from Birth to Death* vol. 2. M. Riley, ed. Boulder: Westview.

Kertzer, David, and Jennie Keith, eds. 1984. *Age and Anthropological Theory.* Ithaca: Cornell University Press.

Kertzer, David, and O. B. B. Madison. 1981. "Women's Age-Set Systems in Africa: The Latuka of Southern Sudan." In *Dimensions: Aging, Culture and Health.* C. Fry, ed. Brooklyn: J.F. Bergin.

Khullar, G. S., and B. Reynolds. 1985. "Correlates of Religious Participation and Life Satisfaction." *Free Inquiry in Creative Sociology* 13 (1): 57–59.

Kiefer, Christie. 1987. "Care of the Aged in Japan." In *Health and Medicine in Japan.* Edward Norbeck and Margaret Lock, eds. Honolulu: University of Hawaii Press.

————. 1974. "Lessons from the Issei." In *Late Life: Communities and Environmental Policy*, J. Gubrium, ed. Springfield, Ill.: Charles Thomas.

————. 1971. "Notes on Anthropology and the Minority Elderly." *Gerontologist* 11:94–98.

Kinoshita, Yashuito. 1984. "Social Integration in a Japanese Retirement Community." Ph.D. diss. University of California, San Francisco.

Kinoy, S. 1979. "Services to the Aging in the People's Republic of China." In *Reaching the Aged, Social Services in Forty-Four Countries*. M. Teicher, D. Thursz, and J. Vigilante, eds. Beverly Hills: Sage.

Kinsella, Kevin G. 1988. *Aging in the Third World*. Washington, D.C.: Center for International Research, U.S. Bureau of the Census.

Kirkpatrick, John. 1985a. "*Ko'oua*: Aging in the Marquesas Islands." In *Aging and Its Transformations: Moving Toward Death in Pacific Societies*. Dorothy Ayers Counts and David R. Counts, eds. Lanham, Md.: University Press of America. (ASAO Monograph Number 10.)

————. 1985b. "How Personal Differences Can Make a Difference." In *The Social Construction of the Person*. Kenneth J. Gergen and Keith E. Davis, eds. New York: Springer-Verlag.

Kirwin, Patricia M. 1988. "The Challenge of Community Long-Term Care: The Dependent Aged." *Journal of Aging Studies* 2(3):255–66.

Koblik, S. ed., 1975. *Sweden's Development from Poverty to Affluence 1750–1970*. Minneapolis: University of Minnesota Press.

Kohli, M. 1986. "The World We Forgot: A Historical Review of the Life Course." In *Later Life: The Social Psychology of Aging*, V. W. Marshall, ed. Beverly Hills: Sage.

Korpi, W. 1978. *The Working Class in Welfare Capitalism: Work, Unions and Politics in Sweden*. London, Boston, and Henley: Routledge & Kegan Paul.

Korte, A. 1978. "Social Interaction and Morale of Spanish-Speaking Elderly." Ph.D. diss., School of Social Welfare, Denver University.

Kosberg, Jordan I., and Richard E. Cairl. 1986. "The Cost of Care Index: A Case Management Tool for Screening Informal Care Providers." *Gerontologist* 26:273–78.

Koyono, W., H. Shibata, H. Haga, and Y. Suyama. 1986. "Co-Residence with Married Children and Health of the Elderly." *Shakai Ronengaku* 24:28–35.

Krieger, Lisa. 1985. "Former Senator Pleads for Dignified Death." *American Medical News* 25 (October):13–14.

Kroeber, Alfred. 1960 [1951]. "Is Western Civilization Disintegrating or Reconstituting?" In *The Golden Age of American Anthropology*. Margaret Mead and Ruth Bunzel, eds. New York: Braziller.

————. 1939. *Cultural and Natural Areas of Native North America*. vol. 38. University of California Publications in American Archaeology and Ethnology.

Kronenberg, Irving. 1983. "Bereavement Research and Intervention in a Long-Term Care Setting." Paper presented at the Northeast Gerontological Society Meeting, Newport, Rhode Island.

Kwan, Alex Y. H. 1988. *Caregiving among Middle and Low Income Aged in Hong Kong*. Tampa, Fla.: International Exchange Center on Gerontology.

Ladner, J. A. 1971. *Tomorrow's Tomorrow*. New York: Doubleday.

LaFargue, Jane Peterson. 1981. "Those You Can Count On: A Social Network Study of Family Organization in an Urban Black Population." Ph.D. diss., University of Washington.

La Fontaine, J. S. 1978. "Introduction." In *Sex and Age as Principles of Social Differentiation.* J. S. La Fontaine, ed. New York: Academic.

Lamphere, Louise. 1975. "Women and Domestic Power: Political and Economic Strategies in Domestic Groups." In *Being Female.* Dana Raphael, ed. The Hague: Mouton.

Landberg, Pamela. 1986. "Widows and Divorced Women in Swahili Society." In *Widows in African Societies.* Betty Potash, ed. Stanford, Calif.: Stanford University Press.

Lang, O. 1946. *Chinese Family and Society.* New Haven: Yale University Press.

Langness, L. L., and G. Frank. 1981. *Lives: An Anthropological Approach to Biography.* Novato, Calif.: Chandler & Sharp.

Laslett, Peter. 1976. "Societal Development and Aging." In *A Handbook of Aging and the Social Sciences.* R. Binstock and E. Shanas, eds. New York: Van Nostrand Reinhold.

Lawton, M.P., M. Moss, and E. Moles. 1984. "The Supra-Personal Neighborhood Context of Older People: Age Heterogeneity and Well-Being." *Environment and Behavior* 16(1):89–109.

Lazure, D. 1962 "The Family and Youth in New China: Psychiatric Observations." *Canadian Medical Association Journal* 86:179–82.

Leaf, A. 1982. "Long-Lived Populations: Extreme Old Age." *Journal of the American Geriatrics Society* 38:485–87.

———. 1975. *Youth in Old Age.* New York: McGraw-Hill.

Lebeuf, Annie. 1963. "The Role of Women in the Political Organization of African Societies." In *Women of Tropical Africa.* Denise Paulme, ed. Berkeley, Calif.: University of California Press.

Lebra, T. 1976. *Japanese Patterns of Behavior.* Honolulu: University of Hawaii Press.

Lee, G. R. 1985. "Kinship and Social Support of the Elderly: The Case of the United States." *Aging and Society* 5(1):19–38.

Lee, Richard B. 1985. "Work, Sexuality and Aging among !Kung Women." In *In Her Prime: A New View of Middle-Aged Women.* J. K. Brown and V. Kerns, eds. S. Hadley, Mass.: Bergin & Garvey.

———. 1984. *The Dobe !Kung.* New York: Holt, Rinehart & Winston.

———. 1979. *The !Kung San: Men, Women and Work in a Foraging Society.* New York and Cambridge: Cambridge University Press.

———. 1969. "Eating Christmas in the Kalahari." *Natural History* (December):14–22, 60–63.

Lee, Richard B., and Irven DeVore, eds. 1976. *Kalahari Hunter-Gatherers: Studies of the !Kung San and Their Neighbors.* Cambridge: Harvard University Press.

Legesse, A. R. 1973. *Gada.* New York: Free Press.

Lehman, D., J. Ellard, and C. Wortman. 1986. "Social Support for the Bereaved: Recipients' and Providers Perspectives on What is Helpful." *Journal of Consulting and Clinical Psychology.* 54:438–46.

Leslie, G. 1979. *The Family in Social Context.* New York: Oxford University Press.

Lévi-Strauss, Claude. 1936. "Contributions à l'étude de l'organization sociale des Indiens Bororo" [Contributions to the Study of the Social Organization of the Bororo Indians]. *Societé des Americanistes de Paris* 28:269–304.

Levin, J. 1984. "The Role of the Black Church in Community Medicine." *Journal of the National Medical Association* 76:477–83.

Levine, Edward M. 1986. "Sociocultural Causes of Family Violence: A Theoretical Comment." *Journal of Family Violence* 1(1):3–12.

———. 1982. "The Role of Cultural Values in the Etiology of Psychopathologies: An Interdisciplinary Approach." *International Journal of Sociology of the Family* 12:189–200.

Levine, R. 1965. "Intergenerational Tensions and Extended Family Structures in Africa." In *Social Structure and the Family*. Ethel Shanas and Gordon Strieb, eds. Englewood Cliffs, N.J.: Prentice-Hall.

LeVine, Sarah, and Robert A. LeVine. 1985. "Age, Gender, and the Demographic Transition: The Life Course in Agrarian Societies." In *Gender and the Life Course*. Alice S. Rossi, ed. Hawthorne, N.Y.: Aldine.

Levy, M. 1949. *The Family Revolution in Modern China*. Cambridge: Harvard University Press.

Levy, Robert. 1973. *Tahitians: Mind and Experience in the Society Islands*. Chicago: University of Chicago Press.

Lewis, Oscar. 1952. "Urbanization without Breakdown: A Case Study." *The Scientific Monthly* 75:31–41.

Liang, Jersey. 1985. "Aging in the PRC." In *Chinese Perspectives on Aging in the People's Republic of China*. Jersey Liang, Chu Chuanyi, and Yuan Jihui, eds. Tampa, Fla.: International Exchange Center on Gerontology.

Lieberthal, Kenneth. 1983. "Communication from the Party Center: The Transmission Process for Central Committee Documents." In *China's New Social Fabric*. Godwin Chu and Francis Hsu, eds. London: Kegan Paul, International.

Linn, M., B. Linn, and R. Harris. 1981. "Stressful Life Events, Psychological Symptoms, and Psychosocial Adjustment in Anglo, Black, and Cuban Elderly." *Social Science and Medicine* 15E:283–87.

Lipton, Michael. 1977. *Why Poor People Stay Poor*. London: Temple Smith.

Little, V. C. 1983. "Introduction: Cross-National Reports on Elderly Care in Developing Countries." *Gerontologist* 23(6):573–75.

———. 1982. *Open Care for the Aging: Comparative International Approaches*. New York: Springer.

———. 1978. "Open Care for the Aged." *Social Work* 23(4):282–87.

Liu, Alan. 1986. *How China Is Ruled*. Englewood Cliffs, N.J.: Prentice Hall.

Liu, Junjie. 1983. "Welfare Services for Elderly Peasants and its Impact on Births in the Countryside." *She Hui [Society]* 6:20–22.

Liu, Lillian. 1982. "Mandatory Retirement and Other Reforms Pose New Challenges for China's Government." *Aging and Work* 5:119–33.

Loeb, Edwin M. 1926. *History and Traditions of Niue*. Honolulu: Bernice P. Bishop Museum. Bulletin Number 32. (New York: Kraus Reprints.)

Lofgren, O. 1980. "Historical Perspectives on Scandinavian Peasantries." *Annual Review of Anthropology* 9:187–215.

Logue, J. 1986. "Can Welfare States Survive in the Global Economy?" *Dissent* (Summer).

Longino, Charles F., Jr. 1983. *A Statistical Profile of Older Floridians*. Miami: Center for Social Research in Aging, University of Miami.

Lopata, H. 1979. *Women as Widows*. New York: Elsevier.

Lopata, H. 1973. *Widowhood in American City.* Cambridge, Mass.: Schenkman.

Lopata, Helena Zananiecka. 1972. "Role Changes in Widowhood: A World Perspective." In *Aging and Modernization.* D. Cowgill and L. Holmes, eds. New York: Appleton-Century-Crofts.

Lopata, Helena Zananiecka, ed. 1988. *Widows: Other Countries, Other Places.* Durham: Duke University Press.

————. 1987. *Widows.* vol. 1. *The Middle East, Asia and the Pacific.* Durham: Duke University Press.

Lowenthal, Marjorie F., and C. Haven. 1968. "Interaction and Adaptation: Intimacy as a Critical Variable. *American Sociological Review* 33:20–30.

Luborsky, M., and R. Rubinstein. 1987. "Ethnicity and Lifetimes: Self and Identity Among Elderly Widowers." In *Ethnicity and Aging.* D. Gelfand and C. Barresi, eds. New York: Springer.

Luomala, Katherine. 1978. "Symbolic Slaying in Niue: Post-European Changes in a Dramatic Ritual Complex." In *The Changing Pacific: Essays In Honour of H. E. Maude.* Niel Gunson, ed. Melbourne: Oxford University Press.

McArdle, J., and C. Yeracaris. 1981. "Respect for the Elderly in Preindustrial Societies as Related to Their Activity" *Behavior Science Research* 16(3 and 4):307–39.

Macciocchi, M. 1972. *Daily Life in Revolutionary China.* New York: Monthly Review Press.

McCulloch, A. W. 1980. "What Do We Mean by 'Development' in Old Age." *Aging and Society* 1:230–45.

Mace, Nancy. 1989. *Dementia Care: Patients, Family, and Community.* Baltimore, Md.: Johns Hopkins University Press.

Mace, Nancy, and Peter Rabins. 1981. *The 36-Hour Day.* Baltimore: Johns Hopkins University Press.

McEwen, J. M. 1974. "Understanding Polynesians." In *Polynesian and Pakeha in New Zealand Education.* vol. 2. *Ethnic Differences and the School.* Douglas H. Bray and Clement G. N. Hill, eds. Auckland: Heinemann Educational Books.

McGoldrick, M., J. Pearce, and J. Giordano. 1982. *Ethnicity and Family Therapy.* New York: Guilford.

Mack, Beverly. In press. "Royal Wives in Kano, Nigeria." In *Hausa Women.* Catherine Coles and Beverly Mack, eds.

McKinley, J. 1981. "Social Network Influences on Morbid Episodes and the Career of Help Seeking." In *The Relevance of Social Science for Medicine.* L. Eisenberg and A. Klisman, eds. Dordrecht, Holland: D. Reidel.

McLachlan, Sue. 1982. "Savage Island or Savage History? An Interpretation of Early European Contact with Niue." *Pacific Studies* 6:26–51.

McNeely, R., and Cohen, J. eds. 1983. *Aging in Minority Groups.* Beverly Hills: Sage.

Macpherson, Cluny. 1978. "The Polynesian Migrant Family: The Samoan Case." In *Families In New Zealand Society.* P. G. Koopman-Boyden, ed. Wellington: Methuen.

Maeda, Daisaku. 1983a. "Family Care in Japan." *Gerontologist* 23(6):579–83.

————. 1983b "Health Schemes for the Aged in Japan." *Scientific Session Papers.* 9th Joint Tokyo-New York Medical Congress, Tokyo.

Maeda, Daisaku, and Yutaka Shimazu. In press. "Japan." In *Family Support to Elderly People: The International Experience.* Hal Kendig, Akiko Hashimoto, and Larry Coppard, eds. Geneva: World Health Organization.

Maher, Vanessa. 1976. "Kin, Clients, and Accomplices: Relationships among Women in Morocco." In *Sexual Divisions and Society: Process and Change*. Diana Leonard Barker and Sheila Allen, eds. London: Tavistock.

Makiesky-Barrow, Susan, and Anne M. Lovell. 1987. "Homelessness and the Limited Options of Older Women." *Association for Anthropology and Gerontology Newsletter* 8(4):3–6.

Maldonado, D. 1985. "The Hispanic Elderly: A Socio-Historical Framework for Public Policy." *Journal of Applied Gerontology* 4:18–27.

———. 1975. "The Chicano Aged." *Social Work* 20:213–16.

Manton, Kenneth G., J. E. Dowd, and Max A. Woodbury. 1986. "Conceptual and Measurement Issues in Assessing Disability Cross-Nationally: Analysis of a WHO-Sponsored Survey of the Disablement Process in Indonesia." *Journal of Cross-Cultural Gerontology* 1 (4):339–62.

Manuel, R., ed. 1982. *Minority Aging: Sociological and Social Psychological Issues*. Westport, Conn.: Greenwood.

Mao Zedong. 1969. "The Dead Still Rule Today." In *The Political Thought of Mao Tse-Tung*. S. Schram, ed. New York: Praeger.

Markides, K. S., and S. Vernon. 1984. "Aging, Sex-Role Orientation and Adjustment: A Three-Generations Study of Mexican Americans." *Journal of Gerontology* 39(5):586–91.

Markson, E. W. 1979. "Ethnicity as a Factor in the Institutionalization of the Ethnic Elderly." In *Ethnicity and Aging: Theory, Research, and Policy*. D. Gelfand and A. Kutzik, eds. New York: Springer.

Marshall, Lorna. 1976. *The !Kung of Nyae Nyae*. Cambridge: Harvard University Press.

———. 1961. "Sharing, Talking and Giving: Relief of Social Tensions among the !Kung Bushmen." *Africa* 31:231–49.

Martin, E. P., and J. M. Martin. 1978. *The Black Extended Family*. Chicago: University of Chicago Press.

Marx, Karl. 1963. *The Eighteenth Brumaire of Louis Bonaparte*. New York: International.

Matthews, Sarah H. 1979. *The Social World of Old Women: Management of Self-Identity*. Beverly Hills: Sage.

Mauss, Marcel. 1967. [1925]. *The Gift: Forms and Functions of Exchange in Archaic Societies*. New York: Norton.

Maxwell, Eleanor Krassen. 1986. "Fading Out: Resource Control and Cross-cultural Patterns of Deference." *Journal of Cross-Cultural Gerontology* 1: 73–89.

Maxwell, Eleanor Krassen, and Robert J. Maxwell. 1980. "Contempt for the Elderly: A Cross-Cultural Analysis." *Current Anthropology* 24:569–70.

Maxwell, Robert J. 1970. "The Changing Status of Elders in a Polynesian Society." *Aging and Human Development* 1(2):137–46.

Maxwell, Robert J., and Philip Silverman. 1970. "Information and Esteem: Cultural Considerations in the Treatment of the Elderly." *Aging and Human Development* 1:361–92.

Maxwell, Robert J., Philip Silverman, and Eleanor K. Maxwell. 1982. "The Motive for Gerontocide." *Studies in Third World Societies* 22:67–84.

Mazess, R., and S. Forman. 1979. "Longevity and Age Exaggeration in Vilcabamba, Ecuador." *Journal of Gerontology* 34(1):94–98.

Mead, Margaret. 1967. "Ethnological Aspects of Aging." *Psychosomatics* 8(4):33–37.

———. 1951. "Cultural Contexts of Aging." In *No Time to Grow Old.* New York State Legislative Committee on Problems of Aging, Legislative Document No. 12.

———. 1928. *The Coming of Age in Samoa.* New York: William Morrow.

Medvedev, Zhores A. 1974 "Caucasus and Altay Longevity: A Biological or Social Problem?" *Gerontologist* 14:381-87.

Meenaghan, Thomas M. 1986. "Family Welfare: Exploring a Nexus between Conservative and Liberal Perspectives." *The Journal of Family and Culture* 2(2):1-17.

Mernissi, Fatima. 1975. *Beyond the Veil: Male-Female Dynamics in a Modern Muslim Society.* New York: Schenkman.

Middleton, L. 1984. *Alzheimer's Family Support Groups.* Tampa, Fla.: Suncoast Gerontology Center, University of South Florida Medical Center.

Migdale, J. 1974. *Peasants, Politics, and Revolution.* Princeton: Princeton University Press.

Miller, R. B., comp. 1980. *Niue: Soil and Land Use.* Wellington: Soil Bureau, Department of Scientific and Industrial Research.

Ministry of Health and Welfare of Japan. 1987. *Health and Welfare Statistics in Japan: 1987.* Tokyo: Health and Welfare Statistics Association.

Minkler, M., and C. L. Estes, eds., 1984. *Readings in the Political Economy of Aging.* Farmingdale, N.Y.: Baywood.

Mitchell, G. D. 1977. "Village Agriculture in Niue: An Examination of Factors Influencing Participation and Productivity." M.A. thesis. Geography Department, University of Canterbury, New Zealand.

Moore, Mary Jane. 1987. "The Human Life Span." In *The Elderly as Modern Pioneers.* Philip Silverman, ed. Bloomington: Indiana University Press.

Moore, Sally Falk. 1978. "Old Age in a Life-Term Social Arena." In *Life's Career—Aging: Cultural Variations on Growing Old.* B. Myerhoff and A. Simic, eds. Beverly Hills: Sage.

Morgan, John H., ed. 1985. *Aging in Developing Societies.* Scholastic Monograph Series. Bristol, Ind.: Wyndham Hall Press.

Morgan, M., D. Patrick, and J. Charlton. 1984. "Social Networks and Psychosocial Support Among Disabled People." *Social Science and Medicine* 19:489-97.

Mortimer, J. A. 1983. "Alzheimer's Disease and Senile Dementia: Prevalence and Incidence." In *Alzheimer's Disease.* Barry Reisberg, ed. New York: Free Press.

Moynihan, Daniel Patrick. 1965. *The Case for National Action: The Negro Family.* Washington, D.C.: U.S. Department of Labor.

Murdock, George Peter. 1967. "Ethnographic Atlas: A Summary." *Ethnology* 6(2).

Murray, A. W. 1863. *Missions in Western Polynesia.* London: J. Snow.

Myerhoff, Barbara G. 1982. "Rites of Passage: Process and Paradox." In *Celebration: Studies in Festivity and Ritual.* Victor Turner, ed. Washington, D.C.: Smithsonian Institution Press.

———. 1979. *Number Our Days.* New York: E. P. Dutton.

———. 1978a. "A Symbol Perfected in Death: Continuity and Ritual in the Life and Death of an Elderly Jew." In *Life's Career—Aging: Cultural Variations on Growing Old.* Barbara G. Myerhoff, and Andrei Simic, eds. Beverly Hills: Sage.

———. 1978b "Aging and the Aged in Other Cultures: An Anthropological Perspective." In *The Anthropology of Health.* E. Bauwers, ed. St. Louis: C. V. Mosby.

Myerhoff, Barbara, and Andrei Simic., eds. 1978. *Life's Career—Aging: Cultural Variations on Growing Old.* Beverly Hills: Sage.

Myers, G. 1982. "The Aging of Populations." In *International Perspectives on Aging: Population and Policy Challenges*. R. Binstock, W.-S. Chow, and J. Schulz, eds. New York: United Nations Fund for Population Activities.

Myers, L. W. 1978. "Elderly Black Women and Stress Resolution: An Exploratory Study." *The Black Sociologist* 8 (1–4): 29–37.

Myles, J. 1984. *Old Age in the Welfare State: The Political Economy of Public Pensions*. Boston: Little, Brown.

Nadel, S. F. 1952. "Witchcraft in Four African Societies." *American Antrhopologist* 54:18–29.

Nahemow, Nina. 1987. "Grandparenthood among the Baganda: Role Option in Old Age." In *Growing Old in Different Societies*. Jay Sokolovsky, ed. Belmont, Calif.: Wadsworth.

Nakane, Chie. 1972. *Japanese Society*. Berkeley: University of California Press.

Naoi, Michiko. 1987. "Work Career and Earnings of the Young Old." *Shakai Ronengaku* 25: 6–18.

Naroll, Raoul, Gary Michik, and Frada Naroll. 1976. *Worldwide Theory Testing*. New Haven: Human Relation Area Files Press.

Nason, James D. 1981. "Respected Elder or Old Person: Aging in a Micronesian Community." In *Other Ways of Growing Old*. Pamela T. Amoss and Stephen Harrell, eds. Stanford: Stanford University Press.

National Commission on Aging, The. 1982. *Just Another Age: A Swedish Report to the World Assembly on Aging*. Stockholm: Departementens Reprocentral.

Navarro, V. 1984. "The Political Economy of Government Cuts for the Elderly." In *Readings in the Political Economy of Aging*. M. Minkler and C. Estes, eds. Farmingdale, N.Y.: Baywood.

Nedeljkovic, Yves. 1970. *Ostareli u Jugoslaviji [Old People in Yugoslavia]*. Belgrade: Institut za Socijalnu Politiku.

Neighbors, H. 1984. "Professional Help Use among Black Americans: Implications for Unmet Need." *American Journal of Community Psychology* 12:551–66.

Nelson, Cynthia. 1974. "Public and Private Politics: Women in the Middle Eastern World." *American Ethnologist* 1(3):551–63.

New Zealand Coalition for Trade and Development. 1982. *The Ebbing Tide: The Impact of Migration on Pacific Island Societies*. Wellington: New Zealand Coalition for Trade and Development.

Niue Government. 1988. *Census of Population and Dwellings 1986*. Alofi, Niue: Statistics Unit, Administrative Department.

———. 1985 *Report of a 1984 Mini-Census of Population*. Niue: Department of Economic Development.

———. 1982. *Niue: A History of the Island*. Niue/Suva, Fiji: Niue Government/Institute for Pacific Studies, University of the South Pacific.

Noguchi, Paul H. 1983. "Shiranai Station: Not a Destination but a Journey." In *Work and Lifecourse in Japan* David W. Plath, ed. Albany: State University of New York Press.

Norbeck, Edward. 1953. "Age-Grading in Japan." *American Anthropologist* 55: 373–84.

Nusberg, C. 1982. "World Assembly Seeks to Alert Developing Countries About Their Aging Populations." *Ageing International* 9(2):7–9

Nusberg, C., with M. J. Gibson and S. Peace. 1984. *Innovative Aging Programs Abroad: Implication for the U.S.* Westport, Conn.: Greenwood.

Nydegger, C. 1983. "Family Ties of the Aged in Cross-Cultural Perspective." *Gerontologist* 23:26–32.

Nydegger, C., ed. 1984. "Anthropological Approaches to Aging Research." Special issue, *Research on Aging.*

Obeyesekere, G. 1982. "Sinhalese-Buddhist Identity in Ceylon." In *Ethnic Identity: Cultural Continuities and Change.* G. DeVos and L. Romanucci-Ross, eds. Chicago: University of Chicago Press.

Ogbu, J. U. 1973. "Seasonal Hunger in Tropical Africa as a Cultural Phenomenon." *Africa* 43:317–32.

Okamura, Kiyoko. 1987. "The Employment of Fixed-Year Retirees: The Unemployed Situation and Its Main Regulating Factors." *Shakai Ronengaku* 26: 3–17.

Okojie, F. 1988. "Aging in Sub-Saharan Africa: Toward a Redefinition of Needs Research and Policy Directions." *Journal of Cross-Cultural Gerontology* 3:1:3–20.

Oksenberg, Michael. 1982. "Economic Policy-Making in China: Summer 1981." *China Quarterly* 90:165–94.

Oliver, Douglas L. 1961. *The Pacific Islands.* Honolulu: University of Hawaii Press.

Olson, Philip. 1988. "Modernization in the People's Republic of China: The Politicization of the Elderly." *Sociological Quarterly* 29:241–62.

———. 1987. "A Model of Eldercare in the People's Republic of China." *International Journal of Aging and Human Development* 24:279–300.

Orloff, Ann, and Theda Skocpol. 1984. "Why Not Equal Protection? Explaining the Politics of Public Social Spending in Britain, 1900–1911, and the United States, 1880s–1920." *American Sociological Review* 49:726–50.

Osako, M. 1979. "Aging and Family among Japanese-Americans: The Role of the Ethnic Tradition in the Adjustment to Old Age." *Gerontologist* 5:448–55.

Ottenberg, Simon. 1971. *Leadership and Authority in an African Society.* American Ethnological Society Monograph 52. Seattle: University of Washington Press.

Palmore, Erdman. 1987. "Cross-Cultural Perspectives on Widowhood." *Journal of Cross-Cultural Gerontology* 2(1):93–106.

———. 1984. "Longevity in Abkhazia: A Reevaluation." *Gerontologist* 24:95–96.

———. 1975a. "The Status and Integration of the Aged in Japanese Society." *Journal of Gerontology* 30:199–208.

———. 1975. *The Honorable Elders: A Cross-Cultural Analysis of Aging in Japan.* Durham: Duke University Press.

Palmore, Erdman, and Daisaku Maeda. 1985. *The Honorable Elders Revisited: A Revised Cross-Cultural Analysis of Aging in Japan.* Durham: Duke University Press.

Palmore, Erdman, and K. Manton. 1974. "Modernization and the Status of the Aged: International Correlations." *Journal of Gerontology* 29:205–10.

Palmore, Erdman, and S. Whittington. 1971. "Trends in the Relative Status of the Aged." *Social Forces* 50:84–91.

Papanek, Hanna. 1973. "Purdah: Separate Worlds and Symbolic Shelter." *Comparative Studies in Society and History* 15:289–325.

Parish, W. 1975. "Socialism and the Chinese Peasant Family." *Journal of Asian Studies* 34:613–30.

Parkes, C., and R. Weiss. 1983. *Recovery from Bereavement.* New York: Basic.

Parsons, Talcott. 1964. "Evolutionary Universals in Society." *American Sociological Review* 29:339–57.

Pastner, Carroll McC. 1980. "The Status of Women and Property on a Baluchistan Oasis in Pakistan." In *Women in the Muslim World.* Lois Beck and Nikki Keddie, eds. Cambridge: Harvard University Press.

Peace, Sheila M. 1981. *An International Perspective on the Status of Older Women.* Washington, D.C.: International Federation on Aging.

Peil, Margaret. 1985. "Old Age in West Africa: Social Support and Quality of Life." In *Aging in Developing Societies.* vol. 2. John H. Morgan, ed. Bristol, Ind.: Wyndham Hall Press.

Pepper, Claude. 1986. "Elder Abuse: The Problem that Still Persists." *Aging Network News* (September):24–25.

Peristiany, J. G., ed. 1966. *Honor and Shame: The Values of Mediterranean Society.* Chicago: University of Chicago Press.

Perkinson, M. 1980. "Alternate Roles for the Elderly: An Example from a Midwestern Retirement Community." *Human Organization* 39:219–26.

Petri, P. 1982. "Income, Employment, and Retirement Policies." In *International Perspectives on Aging: Population and Policy Challenges.* R. Binstock, W.-S. Chow, and J. Schulz, eds. New York: United Nations Fund for Population Activities.

Pettitt, George A. 1946. *Primitive Education in North America.* University of California Publications in American Archaeology and Ethnology 43:1–182.

Pittin, Renee. 1983. "Houses of Women: A Focus on Alternative Life-styles in Katsina City." In *Female and Male in West Africa.* Christine Oppong, ed. London: Allen & Unwin.

———. 1979. "Marriage and Alternative Strategies: Career Patterns of Hausa Women in Katsina City." Ph.D. diss. University of London.

Piven, Frances Fox, and Richard A. Cloward. 1982. *The New Class War: Reagan's Attack on the Welfare State and Its Consequences.* New York: Pantheon.

Plath, David. 1987. "Ecstasy Years—Old Age in Japan." In *Growing Old in Different Societies: Cross-Cultural Perspectives* J. Sokolovsky, ed. Acton, Mass.: Copley.

———. 1980. *Long Engagements: Maturity in Modern Japan.* Stanford: Stanford University Press.

———. 1964. *The After Hours.* Berkeley: University of California Press.

Polgar, Steven. 1962. "Health and Human Behavior: Areas of Interest Common to the Social and Medical Sciences." *Current Anthropology* 3:159–205.

Pollard, Brian. 1979. "The Problem of Aid-Dependent Economy: The Case of Niue." In *South Pacific Dossier.* Gay Woods, ed. Canberra: Australian Council for Overseas Aid.

Pollock, Nancy J. 1979. "Work, Wages, and Shifting Cultivation on Niue." *Pacific Studies* 2:132–43.

Poston, Dudley, and Baochang Gu. 1984. "Socioeconomic Differentials and Fertility in the Provinces, Municipalities and Autonomous Regions of the People's Republic of China, Circa 1982." *Texas Population Research Center Papers.* Series 6: Paper No. 6.011.

Powell, Lenore, and Katie Courtice. 1983. *Alzheimer's Disease: A Guide for Families.* Reading, Mass.: Addison-Wesley.

Powers, Bethel Ann. 1988. "Self-Perceived Health of Elderly Institutionalized People." *Journal of Cross-Cultural Gerontology* 3(3):299–321.

Powers, William. 1977. *Oglala Religion.* Lincoln/London: University of Nebraska Press.

Press, I., and M. McKool. 1972. "Social Structure and Status of the Aged: Toward Some Valid Cross-Cultural Generalizations." *Aging and Human Development* 3:297–306.

Prime Minister's Office, Bureau of Aging. 1982. *Lives and Opinions of Old People: Report of a Cross-National Survey*. Tokyo: Ministry of Finance Printing Office.

———. 1980. *The Present State of the Problems of the Elderly [Koreisha Mondai no Genjo]*. Tokyo: Ministry of Finance Printing Office.

Quadagno, Jill. 1982. *Aging in Early Industrial Society*. New York: Academic.

Range, Elder C. F., Jr., ed. 1973. *Official Manual with the Doctrines and Discipline of the Church of God in Christ 1973*. Memphis: Church of God in Christ Publishing House.

Raphael, Dana. 1975. "Women and Power: Introductory Notes." In *Being Female*. Dana Raphael, ed. The Hague: Mouton.

Reisberg, Barry. 1983. "Clinical Presentation, Diagnosis, and Symptomatology of Age-Associated Cognitive Decline and Alzheimer's Disease." In *Alzheimer's Disease*. Barry Reisberg, ed. New York: Free Press.

Reischauer, E. 1977. *The Japanese*. Cambridge, Mass.: Harvard University Press.

Rempusheski, Veronica F. 1988. "Caring for Self and Others: Second Generation Polish-American Elders in an Ethnic Club." *Journal of Cross-Cultural Gerontology* 3(3):223–71.

Rex, Lofa. (c. 1980). "Women in Politics." Unpub. ms., Niue.

Rhoads, Ellen C. 1984. "The Impact of Modernization on the Aged in American Samoa." *Pacific Studies* 7(2):15–33.

Riesman, David. 1972. "Some Questions about the Study of American Character in the Twentieth Century." In *Life Styles: Diversity in American Society*. Saul D. Feldman and Gerald W. Thielbar, eds. Boston: Little, Brown.

Ritchie, James, and Jane Ritchie. 1981. "Child-Rearing and Child Abuse: The Polynesian Context." In *Child Abuse and Neglect: Cross-Cultural Perspectives*. Jill E. Korbin, ed. Berkeley: University of California Press.

———. 1979. *Growing Up in Polynesia*. Sydney: Allen & Unwin.

Rivers, W. H. R. 1926. *Psychology and Ethnology*. London: Kegan Paul.

Robertson, Claire C. 1984. *Sharing the Same Bowl*. Bloomington: Indiana University Press.

Roebuck, J. 1983. "Grandma as Revolutionary: Elderly Women and Some Modern Patterns of Social Change." *International Journal on Aging and Human Development* 17(4):249–66.

Rohner, Ronald P., Raoul Naroll, Herbert Barry III, William Divale, Edwin E. Erickson, James M. Schaefer, and Richard Sipes. 1978. "Guidelines for Holocultural Research." *Current Anthropology* 19:128–29.

Romanucci-Ross, L. 1982. "Italian Ethnic Identity and Its Transformations." In *Ethnic Identity: Cultural Continuities and Change*. G. DeVos and L. Romanucci-Ross, eds. Chicago: University of Chicago Press.

Rosaldo, Michelle Zimbalist. 1974. "A Theoretical Overview." In *Woman, Culture and Society*. Michelle Zimbalist Rosaldo and Louise Lamphere, eds. Stanford: Stanford University Press.

Rosaldo, Michelle Zimbalist, and Louise Lamphere. 1974. "Introduction." In *Woman, Culture and Society*. Michelle Zimbalist Rosaldo and Louise Lamphere, eds. Stanford: Stanford University Press.

Rose, Arnold M. 1962. "The Subculture of Aging: A Topic for Sociological Research." *Gerontologist* 2:123–27.

Rosen, Lawrence. 1978. "The Negotiation of Reality: Male-Female Relations in Sefrou, Morocco." In *Women in the Muslim World.* Lois Beck and Nikki Keddie, eds. Cambridge: Harvard University Press.

Rosenmayr, L. 1981. "Age, Lifespan and Biography." *Aging and Society* 1:29–49.

Rosow, I. 1974. *Socialization to Old Age.* Berkeley: University of California Press.

———. 1967. *Social Integration of the Aged.* New York: Free Press.

Ross, J. 1977. *Old People, New Lives.* Chicago: University of Chicago Press.

Rostow, W. W. 1960. *The Stages of Economic Growth.* Cambridge: Cambridge University Press.

Roth, J. 1982. *Shopping Bag Ladies of New York.* New York: Pilgrim Press.

Rotunno, M. and M. McGoldrick. 1982. "Italian Families." In *Ethnicity and Family Therapy.* M. McGoldrick, J. Pearce, and J. Giordano, eds. New York: Guilford.

Rubin, V., ed. 1983. *Proceedings of the First Joint US-USSR Symposium on Aging and Longevity.* New York: International Research and Exchange Board.

Rubinstein, Robert L. 1987. "Childless Elderly: Theoretical Perspectives and Practical Concerns." *Journal of Cross-Cultural Gerontology* 2(1):1–14.

Rubinstein, Robert L., and Pauline T. Johnsen. 1982. "Toward a Comparative Perspective on Filial Response to Aging Populations." In *Aging and the Aged in the Third World.* Part I. *Studies in Third World Societies* (No. 22). Jay Sokolovsky, ed. Williamsburg, Va.: College of William and Mary.

Ruggie, M. 1984. *The State and Working Women: A Comparative Study of Britain and Sweden.* Princeton: Princeton University Press.

Ryan, Thomas F. 1977. "Prehistoric Niue: An Egalitarian Polynesian Society." M.A. thesis. Anthropology Department, University of Auckland, New Zealand.

Ryan, Thomas F., comp. 1984. *Palagi Views of Niue: Historical Literature 1774–1889.* Auckland: Auckland University.

Sahlins, Marshall. 1972. *Stone Age Economics.* Chicago: Aldine.

———. 1965. "The Sociology of Primitive Exchange." In *The Relevance of Models in Social Anthropology.* M. Banton, ed. ASA Monographs, No. 1. London: Tavistock.

Saith, Ashwani. 1981. "Economic Incentives for the One-Child Family in Rural China." *China Quarterly* 87:492–500.

Salamone, Frank A. 1986. "Will She or Won't She? Choice and Dukawa Widows." In *Widows in African Societies.* Betty Potash, ed. Stanford: Stanford University Press.

Samuelsson, K. 1975. "The Philosophy of Swedish Welfare Policies." In *Sweden's Development from Poverty to Affluence 1750–1970.* S. Koblik, ed. Minneapolis: University of Minnesota Press.

Sangree, Walter H. 1988. "Age and Power: Life Course Trajectories and Age Structuring of Power Relations in East and West Africa." In *Social Structure and Aging: Comparative Perspectives in Age Structuring in Modern Societies.* David Kertzer, John Meyer, and K. Warner Schaie, eds. Hillsdale, N.J.: Erlbaum.

———. 1987. "The Childless Elderly in Tiriki, Kenya, and Irigwe, Nigeria: A Comparative Analysis of the Relationship Between Beliefs about Childlessness and the Social Status of the Childless Elderly." *Journal of Cross-Cultural Gerontology* 2(3):201–23.

———. 1986. "Role Flexibility and Status Continuity: Tiriki (Kenya) Age Groups Today." *Journal of Cross-Cultural Gerontology* 1(2):117–38.

Sankar, Andrea. 1987. "The Living Dead: Cultural Constructions of the Oldest Old." In *The Elderly as Modern Pioneers.* Philip Silverman, ed. Bloomington: Indiana University Press.

———. 1984. "'It's Just Old Age': Old Age as a Diagnosis in American and Chinese Medicine." In *Age and Anthropological Theory.* D. Kertzer and J. Keith, eds. Ithaca, N.Y.: Cornell University Press.

———. 1983. "Cultural Alternatives for the Vulnerable Elderly: The Case of China Past and Present." *Studies in Third World Societies* 23:27–56.

———. 1981. "The Conquest of Solitude: Singlehood and Old Age in Traditional Chinese Society." In *Dimensions: Aging, Culture, and Health.* C. Fry, ed. Brooklyn: J. F. Bergin.

Saunders, Margaret O. 1980. "Women's Role in a Muslim Hausa Town (Mirria, Republic of Niger)." In *A World of Women.* Erika Bourguignon et al. New York: Praeger.

Scheper-Hughes, Nancy. 1979. *Saints, Scholars and Schizophrenics: Mental Illness in Rural Ireland.* Berkeley: University of California Press.

———. 1987. "Deposed Kings: The Demise of the Rural Irish Gerontocracy." In *Growing Old in Different Societies: Cross-Cultural Perspectives.* Jay Sokolovsky, ed. Acton, Mass.: Copley.

Schildkrout, Enid. 1986. "Widows in Hausa Society: Ritual Phase or Social Status?" In *Widows in African Societies.* Betty Potash, ed. Stanford: Stanford University Press.

Schnitzer, M. 1970. *The Economy of Sweden: A Study of the Modern Welfare State.* New York and London: Praeger.

Schultz, James H., and Deborah Davis-Friedmann, eds. 1987. *Aging China: Family, Economics, and Government Policies in Transition.* Washington, D.C.: Gerontological Society of America.

Schweitzer, Marjorie M. 1987. "The Elders: Cultural Dimensions of Aging in Two American Indian Communities." In *Growing Old in Different Societies.* Jay Sokolovsky, ed. Acton, Mass.: Copley.

Seefeldt, C. 1984. "Children's Attitudes Toward the Elderly: A Cross-Cultural Comparison." *International Journal of Aging and Human Development* 19(4):321–30.

———. 1982. "Paraguay and the United States: A Cross-Cultural Study of Children's Attitudes Toward the Elderly." *International Journal of Comparative Sociology* 23: 235–42.

Selby, P., and M. Schechter. 1982. *Aging 2000.* Lancaster: MTP Press.

Sered, Susan Starr. 1987. "The Liberation of Widowhood." *Journal of Cross-Cultural Gerontology* 2(2):139–50.

Shanas, Ethel. 1979. "Social Myth as Hypothesis: The Case of the Family Relations of Old People." *Gerontologist* 19:3–9.

Shanas, Ethel, and George Maddox. 1976. "Aging, Health, and the Organization of Health Resources." In *Handbook of Aging and the Social Sciences.* Robert Binstock and Ethel Shanas, eds. New York: Van Nostrand Reinhold.

Shanas, Ethel, and Marvin Sussman. 1981. "The Family in Later Life: Social Structure and Social Policy." In *Aging: Social Change.* Sara Kiesler, James Morgan, and Valerie K. Oppenheimer, eds. New York: Academic.

Shanas, Ethel, P. Townsend, D. Weederburn, H. Friis, P. Milhojano, and J. Stehouwer. 1968. *Older People in Three Industrial Societies.* New York: Atherton.

Sharp, H. 1981. "Old Age Among the Chipewyan." In *Other Ways of Growing Old: Anthropological Perspectives*. Pamela T. Amoss and S. Harrell, eds. Stanford: Stanford University Press.

Sheehan, T. 1976. "Senior Esteem as a Factor of Societal Economic Complexity." *Gerontologist* 16:433–40.

Sheppard, Harold L., Bruce E. Robinson, and Colleen Cuervo, eds. 1988. *Geriatric Hypertension*. Tampa, Fla.: International Exchange Center on Gerontology.

Shield, Renée Rose. 1988. *Uneasy Endings: Daily Life in an American Nursing Home*. Ithaca, N.Y.: Cornell University Press.

Shore, Bradd. 1982 *Sala'ilua: A Samoan Mystery*. New York: Columbia University Press.

———. 1978. "Ghosts and Government: A Structural Analysis of Alternative Institutions for Conflict Management in Samoa." *Man* 13(2):175–99.

Shostak, Marjorie. 1981. *Nisa: The Life and Words of a !Kung Woman*. Cambridge: Harvard University Press.

Silverman, Philip. ed. 1987. *The Elderly as Modern Pioneers*. Bloomington: Indiana University Press.

Silverman, Philip, and Robert Maxwell. 1987. "The Significance of Information and Power in the Comparative Study of the Aged." In *Growing Old in Different Societies*. Jay Sokolovsky, ed. Acton, Mass.: Copley.

———. 1978. "How Do I Respect Thee? Let Me Count the Ways: Deference towards Elderly Men and Women." *Behavioral Science Research* 13:91–108.

Simic, Andrei. 1987. "Aging in the United States and Yugoslavia: Contrasting Models on Intergenerational Relationships." In *Growing Old in Different Societies*. Jay Sokolovsky, ed. Acton, Mass.: Copley.

———. 1983a. "Urbanization and Modernization in Yugoslavia: Adapative and Maladaptive Aspects of Traditional Culture." In *Urban Life in Mediterranean Europe: Anthropological Perspectives*. Michael Kenny and David Kertzer, eds. Urbana: University of Illinois Press.

———. 1983b. "Machismo and Cryptomatriarchy: Power, Affect, and Authority in the Contemporary Yugoslav Family." *Ethos* 11(1/2):66–85.

———. 1982. "Aging in the United States: Achieving New Understanding through Foreign Eyes." In *Aging*. Aliza Kolker and Paul I. Ahmed, eds. New York: Elsevier Biomedical.

———. 1978a. "Winners and Losers: Aging Yugoslavs in a Changing World." In *Life's Career—Aging: Cultural Variations on Growing Old*. Barbara Myerhoff and Andrei Simic, eds. Beverly Hills: Sage.

———. 1978b. "Introduction." In *Life's Career—Aging: Cultural Variations on Growing Old*. Barbara Myerhoff and Andrei Simic, eds. Beverly Hills: Sage.

———. 1975. *The Ethnology of Traditional and Complex Societies*. Washington, D.C.: American Association for the Advancement of Science.

———. 1974. "Urbanization and Cultural Process in Yugoslavia." *Anthropological Quarterly* 47:211–27.

———. 1973. *The Peasant Urbanites: A Study of Rural-Urban Mobility in Serbia*. New York: Seminar.

———. 1967. "The Blood Feud in Montenegro." In *Essays in Balkan Ethnology*. William Lockwood, ed. Berkeley: Kroeber Anthropological Society Special Publications No. 1.

Simic, Andrei, and Barbara G. Myerhoff. 1978. "Conclusion." In *Life's Career—Aging: Cultural Variations on Growing Old*. Andrei Simic and Barbara G. Myerhoff, eds. Beverly Hills: Sage.

Simmons, Leo W. 1960. "Aging in Primitive Societies: A Comparative Survey of Family Life and Relationships." In *Handbook of Social Gerontology: Societal Aspects of Aging*. C. Tibbetts, ed. Chicago: University of Chicago Press.

———. 1959. "Aging in Modern Society." In *Toward a Better Understanding of Aging*. New York: Council on Social Work Education.

———. 1952 "Social Participation of the Aged in Different Cultures." *Annals of the American Academy of Political and Social Science* 279:43–51.

———. 1946. "Attitudes Toward Aging and the Aged: Primitive Societies." *Journal of Gerontology* 1:72–95.

———. 1945. *The Role of the Aged in Primitive Society*. New Haven: Yale University Press.

Skocpol, Theda. 1985. "Bringing the State Back In: Strategies of Analysis in Current Research." In *Bringing the State Back In*. Peter Evans, Dietrich Rueschemeyer, and Theda Skocpol, eds. New York: Cambridge University Press.

Smith, Mary F. 1981. *Baba of Karo: A Woman of the Muslim Hausa*. New Haven: Yale University Press. [Orig. pub. 1954.]

Smith, Michael G. 1978. *The Affairs of Daura*. Berkeley: University of California Press.

———. 1960. *Government in Zazzau*. London: Oxford University Press.

———. 1959. "The Hausa System of Social Status." *Africa* 29(3):333–47.

———. 1971 [1955]. *The Economy of Hausa Communities of Zaria*. Colonial Research Studies No. 16. London: HMSO Rpt.

Smith, R. 1961a. "Cultural Differences in the Life Cycle and the Concept of Time." In *Aging and Leisure*. R. Kleemeier, ed. New York: Oxford University Press.

———. 1961b. "Japan: The Later Years of Life and the Concept of Time." In *Aging and Leisure*. R. Kleemeier, ed. New York: Oxford University Press.

Smith, S. Percy. 1983 [1902, 1903]. *Niue: The Island and Its People*. Suva, Fiji: Institute for Pacific Studies, University of the South Pacific.

Smolar, Leivy. 1985. "Context and Text: Realities and Jewish Perspectives on the Aged." *Journal of Jewish Communal Service* 62 (1):1–7.

Soda, N., and B. Miura. 1982. *Illustrated White Paper on Aging [Zuzetsu Rojin Hakusho]*. Tokyo: Sekibusha.

Sokolovsky, Jay. 1986. "Network Methodologies in the Study of Aging." In *New Methods for Old Age Research*. C. Fry and J. Keith, eds. S. Hadley, Mass.: Bergin & Garvey.

———. 1985. "Ethnicity, Culture and Aging: Do Differences Really Make a Difference?" *Journal of Applied Gerontology* 4:6–17.

Sokolovsky, Jay, ed. 1987. *Growing Old in Different Societies: Cross-Cultural Perspectives*. Acton, Mass.: Copley.

———. 1982a. *Teaching the Anthropology of Aging and the Aged: A Curriculum Guide and Topical Bibliography*. Chicago: Association for Anthropology and Gerontology.

———. 1982b. *Aging and the Aged in the Third World:*. Part I. *Studies in Third World Societies*. No. 22. Williamsburg, Va.: College of William and Mary.

Sokolovsky, Jay, and Carl Cohen. 1987. "Networks as Adaptation: The Cultural Meaning of Being a 'Loner' Among the Inner City Elderly." In *Growing Old in Different Societies*. Jay Sokolovsky, ed. Acton, Mass.: Copley.

———. 1981a. "Being Old in the Inner City: Support Systems for the SRO Aged." In *Dimensions: Aging, Culture and Health.* C. Fry, ed. Brooklyn: J. F. Bergin.

———. 1981b. "Measuring Social Interaction of the Urban Elderly: A Methodological Synthesis." *International Journal of Aging and Human Development* 13:233–44.

———. 1978. "The Cultural Meaning of Personal Networks for the Inner-City Elderly." *Urban Anthropology* 7:323–43.

Sokolovsky, Jay, Carl Cohen, D. Berger, and J. Geiger. 1978. "Personal Networks of Ex-Mental Patients in a Manhattan SRO Hotel." *Human Organization* 37(1):4–15.

Sokolovsky, Jay, and Joan Sokolovsky, eds. 1983a. *Aging and the Aged in the Third World.* Part II. *Studies in Third World Societies*, No. 23. Williamsburg, Va.: College of William and Mary.

———. 1983b. "Familial and Public Contexts for Aging: Growing Old in a Rapidly Changing Mexican Village." In *Aging and the Aged in the Third World.* Part II. *Studies in Third World Societies.* No. 23. Williamsburg, Va.: College of William and Mary.

Sokolovsky, Jay, Z. Sosic, and G. Pavlekovic. In press. "Self-Help Hypertensive Groups in Yugoslavia: How Effective Are They?" *Journal of Cross-Cultural Gerontology.*

Soldo, Beth J. 1980. "America's Elderly in the 1980's." *Population Bulletin* 35 (4).

Sparks, Douglas. 1975. "The Still Rebirth: Retirement and Role Discontinuity." *Journal of Asian & African Studies* 10 (1–2): 64–74.

Spector, R. 1979. "Health and Illness in the Hispanic-American Community." In *Cultural Diversity in Health and Illness.* R. Spector, ed. Norwalk, Conn.: Appleton-Century-Crofts.

Spence, Donald L., E. M. Feigenbaum, F. Fitzgerald, and J. Roth 1968. "Medical Student Attitudes Towards the Geriatric." *Journal of the American Geriatric Society* 16:976–83.

Spence, Jonathan. 1981. *The Gate of Heavenly Peace.* New York: Penguin.

Spencer, P. 1965. *The Samburu: A Study of Gerontocracy in a Nomadic Tribe.* Berkeley: University of California Press.

Springer, D., and T. Brubaker. 1984. *Family Caregivers and Dependent Elderly.* Beverly Hills: Sage.

Stack, Carol. 1974. *All Our Kin.* New York. Harper & Row.

Staples, R. 1973. *The Black Woman in America.* Chicago: Nelson Hall.

Stearns, Peter. 1982. "Introduction." In *Old Age in Preindustrial Societies.* Peter Stearns, ed. New York: Holmes & Meier.

Stewart, F. 1977. *Fundamentals of Age-Group Systems.* New York: Academic.

Strange, Heather, and Michele Teitelbaum. 1987. *Aging and Cultural Diversity.* S. Hadley, Mass.: Bergin & Garvey.

Streib, Gordon F., Anthony J. La Greca, and William E. Folts. 1986. "Retirement Communities: People, Planning, Prospects" In *Housing an Aging Society.* Robert J. Newcomer, M. Powell Lawton, and Thomas O. Byers, eds. New York: Van Nostrand Reinhold.

Strobel, Margaret. 1979. *Muslim Women in Mombasa: 1890–1975.* New Haven: Yale University Press.

Suchman, E. 1964. "Sociomedical Variations Among Ethnic Groups." *American Journal of Sociology* 70:328–29.

Sundstrom, G. 1986. "Intergenerational Mobility and the Relationship Between Adults and Their Aging Parents in Sweden." *Gerontologist* 26(4):367–71.

————. 1983. *Caring for the Aged in Welfare Society.* Stockholm Studies in Social Work 1. Stockholm: LiberForlag.

Sussman, M. 1976. "The Family Life of Old People." In *Handbook of Aging and the Social Sciences*. R. Binstock and E. Shanas, eds. New York: Van Nostrand Reinhold.

Sussman, M. B. 1965. "The Isolated Nuclear Family: Fact or Fiction?" *Social Problems* 6:333–40.

Svensson, T. 1984. "Gerontological Research in Sweden." *Gerontologist* 24(4):427–34.

Sverdrup, Harold. 1938. *Hos Tundra-folket [With the People of the Tundra]*. Oslo: Gyldendal Norsk.

Swedish Institute. 1986. "Old-Age Care in Sweden." Stockholm: Swedish Institute.

Tao Liqun. 1986. Personal interview. Staff assistant for China National Committee on Aging, Beijing.

Tate, N. 1983. "The Black Aging Experience." In *Aging in Minority Groups*. R. McNeely and J. Colen, eds. Beverly Hills: Sage.

Taylor, R. J., and L. M. Chatters. 1986. "Church-Based Informal Support among Elderly Blacks." *Gerontologist* 26 (6): 637–42.

Taylor, Richard, Harry T. Nemaia, and John Connell. 1987. "Mortality in Niue, 1978–1982." *New Zealand Medical Journal* 100: 477–81.

Tefft, Stanton K. 1968. "Intergenerational Value Differentials and Family Structure Among the Wind River Shoshone." *American Anthropologist* 70: 330–33.

Teicher, M., D. Thursz, and J. Vigilante. 1979. *Reaching the Aged: Social Services in Forty-Four Countries.* Beverly Hills: Sage.

Teitelbaum, Michele. 1987. "Old Age, Midwifery and Good Talk: Paths to Power in a West African Gerontocracy." In *Aging and Cultural Diversity: New Directions and Annotated Bibliography*. Heather Strange and Michele Teitelbaum, eds. South Hadley, Mass.: Bergin & Garvey.

Teski, Marea. 1987. "The Evolution of Aging, Ecology, and the Elderly in the Modern World." In *Growing Old in Different Societies*. Jay Sokolovsky, ed. Acton, Mass.: Copley. @BIBLIO = ————. 1979. *Living Together.* Washington, D. C.: University Press of America.

Teski, Marea, and K. Teski. 1982. "Aging, Life Satisfaction and Perceptions of Stress in a Kalmuk Community." Paper presented at the Annual Meeting of the Gerontological Society. November.

Thomas, H. 1970. "Theory of Aging and Cognitive Theory of Personality." *Human Development* 13:1–16.

Thompson, Laura. 1940. *Southern Lau, Fiji: An Ethnography.* Honolulu: Bernice P. Bishop Museum.

Tien, Y. 1977. "How China Treats Its Old People." *Asian Profile* 5:1–7.

Time. 1985. "Merciless Jury." May 27:66–67.

————. 1984. "Question: Who Will Play God?" April 9:68.

Tobin, S., and M. Lieberman. 1976. *Last Home for the Aged.* San Francisco: Jossey-Bass.

Tokarev, S. A., and I. S. Gurvich. 1964. "The Yakuts." In *The Peoples of Siberia*. M. G. Levin and L. P. Potapov, eds. Chicago: University of Chicago Press.

Topeka Capital-Journal. 1986. "U.S. Loses in Study of Nations." December 9:36.

Topping, Donald M. 1977. "The Pacific Islands: Part I, Polynesia." *American Universities Field Staff Reports.* South East Asia Series. vol. 25 (2).

Tornstam, L. 1982. "Gerontology in a Dynamic Society." In *Aging and Life Course Transitions: An Interdisciplinary Perspective.* " T. K. Hareven and K. J. Adams, eds. London: Tavistock Publications.

Torres-Gil, Fernando. 1987. "Aging in an Ethnic Society: Policy Issues for Aging Among Minority Groups." In *Ethnic Dimensions of Aging.* Donald E. Gelfand and Charles M. Barresi, eds. New York: Springer.

———. 1978. "Age, Health, and Culture: An Examination of Health Among Spanish Speaking Elderly." In *Hispanic Families.* M. Montiel, ed. Washington, D.C.: National Coalition of Spanish-Speaking Mental Health Organizations.

Townsend, Claire. 1971. *Old Age: The Last Segregation. Ralph Nader's Study Group Report on Nursing Homes.* New York: Grossman.

Treas, J. 1979. "Socialist Organization and Economic Development in China: Latent Consequences for the Aged." *Gerontologist* 19:34–42.

Trela, J., and J. Sokolovsky. 1979. "Culture, Ethnicity, and Policy for the Aged." In *Ethnicity and Aging.* D. Gelfand and D. Fandetti, eds. New York: Springer.

Tripp-Reimer, Toni, Bernard Sorofman, Geoffrey Lauer, Miriam Martin, and Larry Afifi. 1988. "To Be Different from the World: Patterns of Elder Care Among Iowa Old Order Amish." *Journal of Cross-Cultural Gerontology* 3(3):185–95.

Trusswell, A. Stewart, and John D. L. Hansen. 1976. "Medical Research among the !Kung." In *Kalahari Hunter-Gatherers.* R. B. Lee and I. DeVore eds. Cambridge: Harvard University Press.

Tsai, Wen-hui. 1987. "Life After Retirement: Elderly Welfare in China." *Asian Survey* 27: 566–76.

Turnbull, Colin. 1972. *The Mountain People.* New York: Simon & Schuster.

———. 1965. *Wayward Servants.* Garden City, N.Y.: Natural History Press.

Turner, Victor. 1969. *The Ritual Process.* Ithaca: Cornell University Press.

Turner, Victor, ed. 1982. *Celebration: Studies in Festivity and Ritual.* Washington, D.C.: Smithsonian Institution Press.

Uhlenberg, Peter, and David Eggebeen. 1986. "The Declining Well-Being of American Adolescents." *The Public Interest* (Winter):25–38.

United Nations. 1985. *The World Aging Situation: Strategies and Policies.* New York: United Nations Organization.

U. S. Commission on Civil Rights. 1982. *Minority Elderly Services: New Programs, Old Problems.* Part 1. Washington, D.C.: U.S. Government Printing Office.

U.S. Department of Health and Human Services. 1982. *Social Security Programs Throughout the World 1981.* Research Report No. 58. Washington, D.C.: U.S. Government Printing Office.

U.S. Department of Housing and Urban Development. 1984. *A Report to the Secretary on the Homeless and Emergency Shelters.* Washington, D.C.: U.S. Government Printing Office.

U.S. Select Committee on Aging. 1987. *Exploding the Myths: Caregiving in America.* Comm. Pub. No. 99–611. Washington, D.C.: U.S. Government Printing Office.

Valle, Ramon. In press. "Cultural and Ethnic Issues in Alzheimer's Disease Family Research." In *Alzheimer's Disease Treatment and Family Stress: Directions for Research.* Enid Light and Barry Lebowitz. eds. Bethesda, Md.: Aging Research Branch, NIMH.

———. 1981. "Natural Support Systems, Minority Groups, and the Late Life Dementias: Implications for Service Delivery, Research, and Policy." In *Clinical Aspects of*

Alzheimer's Disease and Senile Dementia. N. Miller and G. Cohen, eds. New York: Raven.

Valle, Ramon, and L. Mendoza. 1978. *The Elder Latino.* San Diego, Calif.: Campanile.

Van Gennep, Arnold. 1960 [1908] *The Rites of Passage.* Chicago: University of Chicago Press.

van Willigen, John. 1989. *Gettin' Some Age on Me: A Study of Social Organization of Older People in a Rural American Community.* Lexington: University Press of Kentucky.

Vasa Hills Document. 1976. Stockholm.

Vatuk, Sylvia. 1980. "Withdrawal and Disengagement as a Cultural Response to Aging in India." In *Aging in Culture and Society: Comparative Viewpoints and Strategies.* Christine Fry et al., eds. S. Hadley, Mass.: Bergin & Garvey.

Velez, Carlos G. 1978. "Youth and Aging in Central Mexico: One Day in the Life of Four Families of Migrants." In *Life's—Career Aging: Cultural Variations on Growing Old.* Barbara G. Myerhoff and Andrei Simic, eds. Beverly Hills: Sage.

Vellenga, Dorothy Dee. 1986. "The Widow among the Matrilineal Akan of Southern Ghana." In *Widows in African Societies.* Betty Potash, ed. Stanford: Stanford University Press.

Vesperi, Maria D. 1987. "The Reluctant Consumer: Nursing Home Residents in the Post-Bergman Era." In *Growing Old in Different Societies: Cross-Cultural Perspectives.* Jay Sokolovsky, ed. Acton, Mass.: Copley.

———. 1985. *City of Green Benches.* Ithaca: Cornell University Press.

Virchow, Rudolph. 1959 [1849]. *Disease, Life and Man: Selected Essays.* L. J. Rather, ed. Stanford: Stanford University Press.

Vivelo, Frank R. 1977. *The Herero of Western Botswana: Aspects of Change in a Group of Bantu-Speaking Cattle Herders.* St. Paul, Minn.: West.

Walker, N. K., A. MacBride, and M. L. S. Vachon. 1977. "Social Support Networks and the Crisis of Bereavement." *Social Science and Medicine* 11:35–41.

Wallerstein, Immanuel. 1979. *The Capitalist World-Economy.* Cambridge: Cambridge University Press.

Walsh, A. C., and A. D. Trlin. 1973. "Niuean Migration: Niuean Socio-Economic Background, Characteristics of Migrants, and Settlements in Auckland." *Journal of Polynesian Society* 82: 47–85.

Wang, James. 1985. *Contemporary Chinese Politics.* 2nd ed. Englewood Cliffs, N.J.: Prentice-Hall.

Wang, Wei. 1986. "Population Policy and Population Aging." *Liao Wang [Outlook Weekly]*, July:7–8.

Warner, L. 1937. *A Black Civilization.* New York: Harper.

Watson, Wilbur H. 1976. "The Aging Sick and the Near Dead: A Study of Some Distinguishing Characteristics and Social Effects." *Omega* 7:115–23.

Wax, M. 1962. "The Changing Role of the Home for the Aged." *Gerontologist* 2:128–33.

Weber, Max. 1930. *The Protestant Ethic and the Spirit of Capitalism.* London: George Allen & Unwin.

Weeks, J. 1984. *Aging: Concepts and Social Issues.* Belmont, Calif.: Wadsworth.

Weeks, J., and José Cuellar. 1981. "The Role of Family Members in the Helping Networks of Older People. *Gerontologist* 21:338–94.

Weibel, Joan. 1978. "Native Americans in Los Angeles: A Cross-Cultural Comparison of Assistance Patterns in an Urban Environment." *Anthropology UCLA* 2: 81–98. Los Angeles: University of California Press.

Weissner, P. 1977. "Hxaro: A Regional System of Reciprocity for Reducing Risk Among the !Kung San." Ph.D. diss. University of Michigan.

Wenger, G. Clare. 1986. "A Longitudinal Study of Changes and Adaptation in the Support Networks of Welsh Elderly over 75." *Journal of Cross-Cultural Gerontology* 1(3):277–304.

———. 1984. *The Supportive Network: Coping With Old Age.* London: Allen & Unwin.

Wentowski, G. 1982. "Reciprocity and the Coping Strategies of Older People: Cultural Dimensions of Network Building." *Gerontologist.* 21:600–9.

Wilensky, Harold. 1975. *The Welfare State and Equality: Structural and Ideological Roots of Public Expenditures.* Berkeley: University of California Press.

Williams, M. D. 1974. *Community in a Black Pentecostal Church: An Anthropological Study.* Prospect Heights, Ill.: Waveland.

Wilson, Monica. 1977. *For Men and Elders: Change in the Relations of Generations and of Men and Women among the Nyakyusa-Ngonde People, 1875–1971.* New York: Africana.

Woon, Y. 1981. "Growing Old in a Modernizing China." *Journal of Comparative Family Studies* 12:245–55.

World Almanac, The. 1987. New York: Pharos (Scripps Howard).

World Bank. 1980. *World Development Report.* New York: Oxford University Press.

Wu, Y. 1983. "How to Let the Old People Play a Role in Society." *Lao Ren [Old People]* 1:4–8.

Wylan, L., and N. Mintz. 1976. "Ethnic Differences in Families' Attitudes towards Psychotic Manifestations, with Implications for Treatment Programs." *International Journal of Social Psychiatry* 22(2):86–95.

Yeld, E. R. 1960. "Islam and Social Stratification in Northern Nigeria." *British Journal of Sociology* 11:112–28.

Yin, P., and K. Lai. 1983. "A Reconceptualization of Age Stratification in China." *Journal of Gerontology* 38:608–13.

Yuan, J. 1984. "Call on the Whole Society to be Concerned About the Aged." *Lao Ren [Old People]* 5:4–6.

Yue, Qing. 1986. "Family Changes and Trends in Lanzhou." *Xibei Renkou [Northwest Population]* 3:8–12.

Zarit, Steven, Nancy Orr, and Judy Zarit. 1985. *The Hidden Victims of Alzheimer's Disease: Families Under Stress.* New York: New York University Press.

Zborowski, M. 1969. *People in Pain.* San Francisco: Jossey-Bass.

Zhao Shanyang. 1987. "The Retirement of Veteran Cadres in China: Its Causes and Impact on Elderly Chinese." M.A. thesis. University of Missouri-Kansas City.

Zheng, G. 1983. "Let the Old Be Held in Respect and Provided for—A Strategic Measure for Population Control." *She Hui [Society]* 2 (April):26–9.

Zimmer, Laura J. 1987. "Who Will Bury Me? The Plight of Childless Elderly among the Gende." *Journal of Cross-Cultural Gerontology* 2(1):61–78.

INDEX

CONTRIBUTORS

HIROKO AKIYAMA, Ph.D., is an assistant research scientist at the School of Social Work, University of Michigan. Her work has focused on social relationships in a cross-cultural perspective. She and her colleagues have conducted national and regional surveys of older adults in the United States and Japan and explored the intra- and intergenerational family support exchange rules distinctive to the two cultures.

TONI ANTONUCCI, Ph.D., is an associate research scientist at the Institute for Social Research, with additional appointments in the Institute of Gerontology and the departments of family practice and psychology at the University of Michigan. A developmental psychologist by training, her research has focused on social relationships over a life-span. Dr. Antonucci is currently the recipient of a Research Career Development Award from the National Institute on Aging.

JUDITH C. BARKER, Ph.D., is a research anthropologist in the Medical Anthropology Program and an affiliate of the Institute for Health and Aging at the University of California-San Francisco. After fieldwork in the South Pacific investigating dependency in children, the elderly, and migrants, her research interests now include chronic illness in late life.

RUTH CAMPBELL, M.S.W., directs the social work department of Turner Geriatric Services, University of Michigan Medical Center. She is also a faculty associate of the University of Michigan's Institute of Gerontology. She has conducted research on outpatient programs for the elderly, innovative nursing home programs and cross-cultural and intergenerational studies of Japanese and American elderly.

CARL COHEN, M.D., is professor of psychiatry and director of geriatric psychiatry at the SUNY Health Science Center at Brooklyn. He has published widely in the areas of social psychiatry and social gerontology and is coauthor of *Old Men of the Bowery* (1989).

CATHERINE COLES, Ph.D., has taught at Ahmadu Bello University (Nigeria) and is assistant professor of anthropology at Dartmouth College. She has published *Nigerian Women and Development: A Research Bibliography* (with Barbara Entwisle) and is currently editing a volume on Hausa women.

CHRISTINE L. FRY, Ph.D., is a professor of anthropology at Loyola University of Chicago. She is co-director of Project AGE which has investigated age in seven communities around the world. Within this project she carried out an ethnographic study of age in Momence, Illinois. Dr. Fry has written extensively on the life course and on retirement communities.

ANTHONY P. GLASCOCK, Ph.D., is currently professor of anthropology and head of the psychology/sociology/anthropology department at Drexel University. He is author of *Death in the Life Cycle* and has written extensively on the treatment of the elderly in non-industrial societies.

HAIM HAZAN, Ph.D., is a British-trained Israeli social anthropologist with special interests in temporal conceptions of aging, community studies and total institutions. He is the author of *The Limbo People* and *A Paradoxical Community*.

J. NEIL HENDERSON, Ph.D., is a medical anthropologist at the University of South Florida Suncoast Gerontology Center. He is assistant professor of psychiatry at the University of South Florida Geriatric Education Center, and principal investigator of an Administration on Aging grant to develop Alzheimer's disease support groups in ethnic communities.

CHARLOTTE IKELS, Ph.D., is an anthropologist at Case Western Reserve University. She is a researcher affiliated with Project AGE and has conducted extensive research in Hong Kong and the People's Republic of China as well as among Chinese-Americans. She has written widely on aging in Hong Kong and support networks of the elderly.

JENNIE KEITH, Ph.D., is professor of anthropology and chair of the department of sociology and anthropology at Swarthmore College. She is co-director with Christine Fry, of Project AGE, a comparative community study of social and cultural influences on aging and old age in Africa, Ireland, Hong Kong and the United States. She has written many articles and a number of books about retirement communities, qualitative research methods and aging in social and cultural contexts.

CHRISTIE W. KIEFER, Ph.D., teaches anthropology at the University of California's health science campus in San Francisco. He is director of the Human Development and Aging Program there. He has studied aging in Japan and among Americans of East Asian ancestry. His current research interest in moral development is reflected in his 1988 book, *The Mantle of Maturity*, and his current research on the biographies of outstanding altruists.

MARK R. LUBORSKY, Ph.D., is senior research anthropologist in the Behavioral Research Department at the Philadelphia Geriatric Center. His interests in gerontology include ethnicity and bereavement, retirement, mental health and computer-aided qualitative analysis.

PHILIP OLSON, Ph.D., is professor of sociology and director of the Center on Rural Elderly at the University of Missouri. He has done extensive research in the People's Republic of China and is now completing a research monograph entitled, "The Elderly in the Post-Mao Era in the People's Republic of China."

JANE W. PETERSON, Ph.D., professor of nursing at Seattle University, received a Ph.D. in anthropology from the University of Washington, Seattle. Her publications include articles on the organization of Black families and health care.

HARRIET G. ROSENBERG, Ph.D., is an associate professor in the Division of Social Science at York University, Canada, where she is the director of the Health and Society Program. Her research interests focus on social reproduction and social change. She is the author of *A Negotiated World: Three Centuries of Change in a French Alpine Village* (1988) and *Surviving in the City: Urbanization in the Third World* (1980), and co-author of *Through the Kitchen Window: The Politics of Home and Family* (1990).

ROBERT L. RUBINSTEIN, Ph.D., is assistant director of research and senior research anthropologist at the Philadelphia Geriatric Center. He has done research on older people in the United States and has made two field trips to Malo, Vanuatu, in the South Pacific. He is author of *Singular Paths: Old Men Living Alone* and many professional articles.

RENÉE ROSE SHIELD, Ph.D. in anthropology, teaches in the Program of Liberal Medical Education at Brown and is the author of *Uneasy Endings: Daily Life in an American Nursing Home* (1988).

ANDREI SIMIC, Ph.D., teaches social anthropology at the University of Southern California. He has written extensively on rural-urban migration and modernization in Yugoslavia, Euro-American ethnic groups, and the cultural aspects of aging. Most recently, he produced a documentary film dealing with the preservation of traditional culture among Serbian-Americans.

JAY SOKOLOVSKY, Ph.D., is a professor of anthropology and director of the Center for International Policy Analysis and Research (CIPAR) at the University of Maryland Baltimore County. Dr. Sokolovsky specializes in cross-cultural, comparative gerontology and has edited several books and many articles. In his research he has studied the elderly in a Mexican peasant village, New York's inner city, the new town of Columbia, Maryland, and most recently in Yugoslavia and England. He is co-author of *Old Men of the Bowery* (1989).

JOAN WEIBEL-ORLANDO, Ph.D., is an assistant professor in the department of anthropology at the University of Southern California. She has worked with American Indians in both urban and rural communities since 1973 and has published widely in the areas of Indian alcohol use and abuse, aging and bi-cultural adaptation. Her book, *Indian Country, L.A.: Ethnic Community Maintenance in Complex Society* is scheduled for publication in 1990.

BRUCE M. ZELKOVITZ, Ph.D., is associate professor of sociology at Washburn University and is an advisor to the Swedish Program at the University of Stockholm.